Amphibians of Central and Southern Africa

COMSTOCK BOOKS IN HERPETOLOGY
Aaron M. Bauer, Consulting Editor

Amphibians of Central and Southern Africa

Alan Channing

Comstock Publishing Associates
a division of
CORNELL UNIVERSITY PRESS
ITHACA AND LONDON

Copyright © 2001 by Cornell University

All rights reserved. Except for brief quotations in a review, this book, or parts thereof, must not be reproduced in any form without permission in writing from the publisher. For information, address Cornell University Press, Sage House, 512 East State Street, Ithaca, New York 14850.

First published 2001 by Cornell University Press

Printed in the United States of America

Library of Congress Cataloging-in-Publication Data
Channing, A.
   Amphibians of Central and Southern Africa / Alan E. Channing.
     p. cm.
   Includes bibliographical references (p.).
   ISBN 0-8014-3865-9 (cloth)
   1. Amphibians—Africa, Southern. I. Title.
QL662.A356 C43 2001
597.8′0968—dc21
                                              2001037091

Cornell University Press strives to use environmentally responsible suppliers and materials to the fullest extent possible in the publishing of its books. Such materials include vegetable-based, low-VOC inks and acid-free papers that are recycled, totally chlorine-free, or partly composed of nonwood fibers. For further information, visit our website at www.cornellpress.cornell.edu.

Cloth printing   10 9 8 7 6 5 4 3 2 1

Contents

Preface   vii
Acknowledgments   ix
Introduction   1
Frogs and Man   17
Identification of Adults   29
Classification   36
Species Accounts   39

   ORDER ANURA
   Squeakers—Family Arthroleptidae   41
   Toads—Family Bufonidae   56
   Ghost Frogs—Family Heleophrynidae   108
   Snout-Burrowers—Family Hemisotidae   119
   Tree Frogs—Family Hyperoliidae   127
   Rain Frogs, Rubber Frogs—Family Microhylidae   209
   Platannas—Family Pipidae   237
   Common Frogs—Family Ranidae   250
   Foam Nest Frogs—Family Rhacophoridae   375

   ORDER GYMNOPHIONA
   Family Scolecomorphidae   382
   Family Caeciliidae   384

Fossil Frogs   386
Tadpoles   388
Bibliography   427
Systematic Index   457
Alphabetical Index   463

Color plates follow page 164

Preface

Frogs and their wormlike relatives the caecilians are the only representatives of Amphibia in the southern third of Africa. Although we understand something of their identification, distribution, and habitat preferences, they are relatively poorly known. Much of the scientific literature is not readily accessible, and as more species are recognized, some of the older reports need to be reevaluated. I hope that this field guide will serve as an easy introduction to the identification of frogs and caecilians for the nonspecialist and also as a source of information and literature useful to the professional biologist.

Although this book attempts to synthesize all the known natural history of this interesting group of animals, it also does quite the opposite: emphasizes all that is not known. This is not a shortcoming, however, as hopefully this book will serve as further stimulation for the discovery of new species, missing details of natural history, variations in life-history strategies, and relationships between species.

Acknowledgments

This book is the result of the efforts of all the people who have published their observations through the last century and a half. All the authors whose work I have made use of are listed in the bibliography.

I would like to thank D. E. (Eddie) van Dijk of Stellenbosch, who kindly placed his complete collection of African frog literature at my disposal. His library represents a lifetime of dedicated collecting, and writing this book would have taken much longer without it. Eddie spent his university career instilling the value of literature into his students, including me. I hope this book repays in some small way his interest and encouragement.

Many friends and colleagues made their slides available: J.-L. Amiet, P. Bishop, J. Bogart, R. C. Boycott, W. Branch, M. Burger, M. Gadd, W. Haacke, H.-J. Herrmann, A. de Villiers, R. C. Drewes, M. Largen, E. Nevo, A. Pauw, J.-L. Perret, A. Schiøtz, R. Smith, C. Tilbury, J. Visser, and J. Vindum. Their contributions have made it possible to illustrate 173 species of living amphibians and 1 fossil species of the 212 species covered.

Recordings of frog calls were made available by R. C. Boycott, W. Branch, M. Burger, V. C. Carruthers, M. Cunningham, A. de Villiers, R. C. Drewes, L. Minter, N. I. Passmore, A. Schiøtz, and M. Vences.

The following made available records of their museum holdings: C. W. Myers (American Museum of Natural History), W. E. Duellman and J. Simmons (Museum of Natural History, University of Kansas), R. W. McDiarmid (Division of Amphibians and Reptiles, National Museum of Natural History), C. J. McCoy (Carnegie Museum of Natural History), J. P. Rosado (Museum of Comparative Zoology, Harvard University), H.-W. Koepcke (Zoologisches Museum, Universität Hamburg), W. Böhme (Zoologisches Forschungsinstitut und Museum Alexander Koenig), A. Resetar

(Field Museum of Natural History), and G. Schneider (Museum of Zoology, The University of Michigan).

I would like to thank the following friends and associates who helped in so many ways: R. Boycott, M. Burger, M. Cherry, R. C. Drewes, L. du Preez, E. Gracie, M. Griffin, K. Howell, N. H. G. Jacobsen, A. Lambiris, D. MacDonald, M. and C. Paxton, L. Minter, J. C. Poynton, R. H. Taylor, A. van Wyk, and my colleagues at the University of the Western Cape, Bellville, South Africa.

Assistance with discovering the meanings of the specific names was kindly provided by K. Adler, D. E. van Dijk, J. C. Poynton, and M. M. Stewart.

The many hours of fieldwork and writing involved in this project were made more pleasant with the active assistance and forbearance of my wife Jenny and my daughters Alison and Catherine. Between them they found many interesting frogs, assisted in the photography, and allowed me to work at the computer with little distraction.

A number of reviewers made constructive suggestions and I am grateful for their assistance. I thank Aaron Bauer, Peter J. Prescott, and the staff at Cornell University Press. They have efficiently and expertly guided the production of this book.

Amphibians of Central and Southern Africa

Introduction

About 4000 species of amphibians are known worldwide. In this book I have synthesized all that is known about the natural history of the amphibians in the countries that form the southern third of Africa: Angola, Zambia, Malawi, Mozambique, Namibia, Botswana, Zimbabwe, South Africa, Lesotho, and Swaziland (Fig. 1). A little over 200 species have been described for this area, and more are discovered every year. I have reviewed all the published information from the last century and earlier and mapped all the collections from most of the major museums.

Why study frogs and tadpoles? This often-asked question is easily answered. Anurans are intrinsically interesting as they display a wide range of shapes, color patterns, and behaviors. Each lives in a particular habitat and has a unique strategy to survive. The males produce loud vocalizations during the breeding season, and as these are specific for each species, they can be recognized easily by listening after dark. These animals have fascinating lives, some living in trees, some on mountaintops, some in streams and pools, and others underground in deserts. Each species has a special place for egg laying. The eggs of most develop rapidly into free-living tadpoles. The tadpoles usually live in pools or streams and are distinguished from the adults by the food they eat. The tadpoles consume largely algae and other plant material, while the adults eat insects and small animals. Many species have eggs that develop directly into small frogs, without a free-swimming tadpole stage. These are termed *direct developers*.

The study of frogs (batrachology) is a very important part of science. Frogs consume large numbers of insects and are important in pest control. The tadpoles are natural monitors of water quality. Both adults and tadpoles are important links in the food web, being eaten by snakes, birds, mammals, and other frogs. Apart from their environmental value, frogs can be considered as walking pharma-

Fig. 1 The countries of central and southern Africa, with their major cities

ceutical factories. Their skins secrete a range of pharmacologically active substances, including antibiotics and painkillers. Frogs do not have to be killed to harvest the active compounds in the skin, and these substances can be made in the laboratory once they have been discovered.

The worldwide concern about declining frog populations is encouraging baseline population studies in Africa. At the moment no studies on population numbers are available for any anuran in the area covered in this text, and there is no evidence to suggest that amphibian numbers are declining. Frogs are regarded as very sensitive environmental monitors, and significant declines could indicate a deterioration in the quality of the environment. The chapter titled "Frogs and Man" provides more detail.

The most common question asked of anyone studying this group of animals concerns the meaning of the words *frog* and *toad*. These common names in English derive from Britain, where only two families (Ranidae and Bufonidae) are present. Frogs with rough skin in the family Bufonidae are called *toads*. However, a similar distinction is found in other northern European languages where more families are present. In Africa there are many families of *anurans* (a term used to include all families of frogs and toads). Sometimes members of the family Pipidae are called clawed frogs or clawed toads. To avoid confusion, I use the word *frog* to refer to all anurans. The word *amphibian* refers to anurans and caecilians in sub-Saharan Africa and includes salamanders in other parts of the world.

Introduction

Arrangement

I have arranged this book so that it will be useful to the professional biologist, as well as to anyone interested in the natural history of Africa. Just over 200 frog species and 2 caecilians are covered. Local names and names used in the literature are listed, and the meanings of the scientific names are explained. Each species is described briefly, and information on distribution, advertisement call, breeding biology, and tadpole is provided. A section of notes and a guide to key references for further reading complete each species account.

I have not covered the extensive literature on parasites, nor have I reviewed taxonomic changes. The scientific names given here are complete and accurate at the time of publication.

Presently the system of naming and classifying frogs is being reviewed internationally. New information, often from detailed studies of important molecules, is rapidly becoming available. These data are analyzed using specialized computer programs, and a complete overhaul of the classification and naming system may happen in the future.

Identification

Keys aid the identification of adults and tadpoles. These keys are a series of pairs of options concerning details of the animal to be identified. A choice of one of the options leads either to the name of the animal or to a further set of options. Practically all the adults can be identified using the keys. Not all of the tadpoles are known, however, so the tadpole keys only lead to identification at the level of the genus. As only a small number of species usually are present at each locality, the distribution maps will suggest the presence of species, which then can be checked using the descriptions of adults or tadpoles. See the preamble to the keys for more explanation.

Layout of Species Accounts

Each species is listed by its common and scientific name, followed by alternative common names where they are known.

COMMON NAMES

Most languages spoken in Africa make no distinction between various species of frogs, except where they have some importance to the speakers, for example, as food items. Unusual frogs like the bullfrog also may have specific common names. In parts of Angola, for example, frogs are known as *kazoli* whereas toads of the family Bufonidae are called *tchizunda*. All tadpoles are known as *mawuluwulu* in Shangaan. Few features would make frog species readily identifiable by a layperson, so it is not surprising that there are hardly any common names.

DESCRIPTION

I have selected features that should assist in the identification of the species, rather than give a complete wart-by-wart description. The references in the bibliography should enable interested readers to find the original literature and detailed descriptions. Length is measured from snout to vent.

DISTRIBUTION AND HABITAT

This brief statement describes the known distribution and the habitat where the species is found. A map showing the distribution is available for each species. Please read the section below on maps to appreciate the information presented and to understand the limitations of distribution maps.

ADVERTISEMENT CALL

Male frogs use the advertisement call to attract females. This is a sure way of identifying a species, as each species has a unique call. The calls that are known are described. Commercially available recordings of frog calls can enable comparisons of calls heard in the field. Many frog species are so similar in shape and color that only the different calls show they are separate species.

BREEDING

This section describes the eggs, where they are laid, and other associated information. It should not be regarded as definitive but rather as a starting point. If you can, check the details that are presented. Only in this way will you begin to understand the variation in natural populations.

Introduction

TADPOLES

Relatively few tadpoles are known, despite the fact that tadpoles are easy to catch and to identify by family and often genus. Tadpole behavior is presented where it is known. Hopefully the gaps here will encourage more work on the tadpoles of this part of Africa. Keys for the identification of tadpoles are presented in a later chapter.

NOTES

In this section I include information that has some bearing on the life history of the species. In a few cases it has been necessary to subdivide the information for ease of organization.

KEY REFERENCES

This section lists important sources of information that will serve as an introduction to the literature. Each source is listed by author and date of publication. For example, "McDiarmid & Altig 1999" can be looked up in the bibliography to give the complete citation: McDiarmid, R. W., and R. Altig (Eds.). 1999. *Tadpoles. The Biology of Anuran Larvae.* Chicago: University of Chicago Press.

Maps

The maps have been compiled from three sources: recent literature, the collections of many major museums, and my field notes. Each symbol on a map represents one or more specimens in an area 1-degree square. Map interpretation is open to abuse. It is important to realize that the maps only show *localities where the species is known to occur* and not *all the localities where the species does occur.*

A number of possible errors can occur when mapping distributions. These include misidentification of the specimen, confusion of the locality, and errors introduced when transferring the data from a catalogue to a map. These errors sometimes can be detected as points far removed from the others on the map. I have been particularly cautious and ignored doubtful records or presumed misidentifications. Unrecognized new species are always mapped incorrectly. Many knocking sand frogs *Tomopterna krugerensis* are confused on the map for the cryptic sand frog *Tomopterna cryptotis*, which is itself often mistaken for Tandy's sand frog *Tomopterna tandyi*. Where the species occur together, this may not be a problem. Many difficulties might have been avoided if all the museum specimens had been checked individually. This has not been possible, and some species, like the sand frogs referred to, cannot be identified easily unless they are alive and calling.

Gaps in distributions are real only if the species does not occur there. As mentioned, however, the gaps may be due to a lack of collection. Negative collections (not finding a particular species) are indicated rarely, as collectors are always hopeful that they will discover range extensions or new species in the future.

Undercollected species can be recognized by their pattern of distribution. The map symbols will be plotted in lines that coincide with the roads along which casual collecting has occurred. Casual roadside collection and road running (driving slowly at night to find animals on the road) is a useful technique, but further extensive collecting should follow. Unusual species often are collected repeatedly at the same locality, as the collector does not want to waste effort searching in new places.

Bibliography

The bibliography is a list of useful reports and publications concerning the amphibians from this part of Africa. I have adopted the standard citations for the sources of information used. Any library should be able to obtain the original publication.

Habitats of Central and Southern Africa

Here the broad geographical features of the countries covered are outlined, along with a few typical frogs that occur in each region (Fig. 2).

Angola has habitats varying from the western part of the Namib Desert to the rain forests on the edge of the Congo River drainage. The highlands around Huambo receive much rainfall and provide water to rivers draining southward, significantly the Kavango (Cubango) that fills the inland Okavango Delta in Botswana, finally draining away into the Kalahari sands. Typical frogs include Osorio's spiny reed frog, the striped spiny reed frog, the rough sand frog, Lemaire's toad, and Parker's frog.

Zambia has a central highland that serves as a link between the high plateaus of Angola in the west and Malawi in the east. The

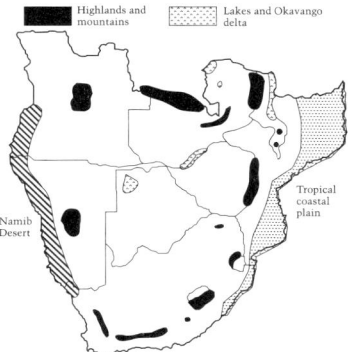

Fig. 2 Map showing important highlands, major water bodies, tropical coastal plain, and the Namib Desert

western highlands give rise to the Zambezi River, one of the best known but largely unnavigable waterways in Africa. Many large swamps and lakes provide habitat for frogs, including Lakes Mweru, Tanganyika, Bangweulu, and Kafue. Lake Kariba, created by the Kariba Dam, forms part of the southern border. On the highlands forming northwestern Zambia and northeastern Angola can be found Keiling's ridged frog, the Kachalola reed frog, Darling's frog, Power's rain frog, and the Kuvangu kassina. The highlands along the northeastern border of Zambia and the northern part of Malawi have Fülleborn's stream frog, the Nyika toad, the Taita toad, and the spotted reed frog.

Malawi is situated within a southern extension of the Great Rift Valley, where Lake Malawi is found. The granite massifs of Mounts Mulanje and Zomba in the south provide high-altitude refuges where many endemic frog species are found. This area, including the surrounding lowlands, is the home to the eastern puddle frog, the mongrel frog, Johnston's river frog, Lindner's toad, and the dwarf squeaker.

Mozambique consists mostly of a wide coastal plain that serves as a connection between the amphibian faunas of the northern tropics and the southern temperate areas. Savannas with isolated hills formed of granite domes, called *inselbergs*, are found inland. The coastal plain is typical habitat for the Schilluk ridged frog, Parker's reed frog, the gray tree frog, tinker reed frog, and the Galam frog.

Zimbabwe is a high woodland area, which is a continuation of the savanna found to the south and northwest. A chain of high-altitude mountains, known as the *afromontane highland*, occurs from Ethiopia southward to the Drakensberg Mountains of Lesotho. The afromontane highland extends along Zimbabwe's border with Mozambique, and in these eastern areas the Inyanga river frog, Chirinda toad, Chimanimani stream frog, long reed frog, and highland rain frog can be found. Many of these are localized endemics.

Botswana forms the dry central savanna in this region. Despite the mostly desert nature of the Kalahari sands, the Okavango Delta is a haven of swamps and waterways that fill and flood most years. In the Okavango Delta frogs like Lemaire's toad, Mababe puddle frog, Guinea snout-burrower, the spotted ridged frog, and the African bullfrog can be found.

West of the central savanna is Namibia, well known for the Namib Desert along its western edge, caused by the cold Benguela Current just offshore. Although the Caprivi Strip in the northeast is well wooded, the central highlands and southern plains are extremely arid. Despite this, a number of interesting amphibians including Hoesch's toad, the Dombe toad, Boettger's dainty frog, the marbled rubber frog, and the cryptic sand frog are found here.

Swaziland is a mountainous country at the southern end of the Mozambique plain. It is well watered and along with the northern areas of South Africa, is the home to frogs such as the golden spiny reed frog, the marbled reed frog, the marbled snout-burrower, the Mozambique tree frog, and the red toad.

Another very mountainous country is Lesotho. Although it is extremely cold in winter, many interesting frogs are found along the southern slopes of the Drakensberg Mountains and in Lesotho proper. These include the Drakensberg river frog, the large-mouthed frog, Hewitt's moss frog, the long-toed tree frog, and the Drakensberg stream frog.

South Africa, at the southern tip of Africa, has an arid interior, with a range of folded mountains along the southern and eastern margins that are a southern continuation of the afromontane system. The arid interior has the Cape river frog, Karoo toad, Power's toad, Pygmy toad, and the cryptic sand frog as typical examples. The southern mountains and southeastern areas have several frogs, many of which are endemic. Some of the frogs found here include Rattray's frog, Amatola toad, dwarf dainty frog, Weale's running frog, and Tandy's sand frog.

Brief History of Amphibian Studies in Central and Southern Africa

Carolus Linnaeus described the first African frog in 1758, based on a specimen of the giant rain frog *Breviceps gibbosus* from the environs of what is now Cape Town.

Up to the start of the First World War, collecting of amphibians was undertaken largely by colonial officers, visiting missionaries, and explorers. The German Wilhelm Peters was one of the first scientists to spend time in the field, mostly in Mozambique, during a 6-year stay in southern Africa. He described 12 species and provided details of biology not available before.

The Natural History Museum in London has had the most consistent influence on southern African frog studies. Every keeper of zoology or herpetologist at the museum has published works on the amphibians of southern Africa. These include J. Gray, A. Günther, G. A. Boulenger, H. W. Parker, A. G. C. Grandison, and B. T. Clarke, who continues to work on African amphibians as this book is being prepared. Boulenger's "Catalogues," a series of papers documenting the reptile and amphibian collections in the museum published between 1882 and 1896, set the baseline for future systematic works until well into the present century.

The most important worker in South Africa before the First World War was A. Smith. Smith was an army medical officer based in the Cape from 1821 until 1837. His medical duties allowed him to travel, and he was responsible for establishing the South African Museum in Cape Town.

The period between the two wars was characterized by a decline in publications from scientists based in Europe, particularly in Germany and Britain. The destruction of collections in Europe during the wars, the loss of colonies in Africa, and the loss of skilled workers slowed the scientific pace. In Brussels, G.-F. de Witte and R. Laurent actively reported on central African amphibians, while in the United States, A. Loveridge continued to publish. Based at Harvard, Loveridge had collected amphibians while serving in East Africa during the war.

In contrast to the declining contributions from European-based workers during this time, the output from South African scientists started to increase. J. Hewitt in Grahamstown made a valuable contribution by describing 24 genera or species in a series of papers from 1913 to 1937. Other southern African workers then included J. Power at the McGregor Museum in Kimberley, V. FitzSimons at the Transvaal Museum in Pretoria, and A. C. Hoffman at the National Museum in Bloemfontein. Although finances were difficult to obtain for fieldwork, the output from scientists in Africa exceeded that from America and Europe for the first time. Power funded the fieldwork for his research from his own pocket. The most prolific worker on southern African amphibians during this period was R. Laurent. He had worked in Belgium and various parts of Africa and is now based at Tucuman in Argentina. The importance of field data in systematics started to be recognized. G.-F. de Witte wrote a detailed report covering the amphibians of the National Albert Park in 1941, much of which is relevant to southern Africa. This publication was the result of 3 years of fieldwork. By the end of the second war, 178 genus or species names had been described, representing 75% of the currently valid taxa.

The next 26-year interval, up to 1971, led to the description of 27 genus and species names. It is characterized by contributions from scientists who were engaged in fieldwork. These included V. FitzSimons from the Transvaal Museum, A. Loveridge in East Africa, R. Laurent in Angola and the Congo, V. Wager in South Africa, J. C. Poynton based in Durban, D. Broadley in Zimbabwe, and A. Stevens in Malawi. J. C. Poynton, working at the University of Natal in Pietermaritzburg in association with the Natal Museum, produced the keystone monograph "The Amphibia of Southern Africa" in 1964. In a series of papers, Laurent continued to review the systematics of frogs from this area: the genus *Hyperolius*, the genus *Ptychadena*, and the family Hyperoliidae. Museum-based studies remained important, however, particularly those of R. Mertens at the Senckenberg Museum and Schmidt and Inger at the Field Museum in Chicago. R. Mertens produced a checklist of the amphibians and reptiles of what is now Namibia. Systematic publications up to 1971 are characterized by the work of authors who had been to Africa or who were based there. The trend toward including more than just adult morphology was encouraged with the publication of van Dijk's

Introduction

two papers reviewing southern African tadpoles in 1966 and 1971. It is interesting to note that many of the genera that had once been placed together were easily separated when tadpoles were considered, and that this approach has been supported by subsequent studies, some using nonmorphological and biochemical data.

From 1972 up to the end of the century, African amphibian studies were influenced by a rise in technology. Frog advertisement calls were known to be species-specific, and in this period sound recording and analytical tools became widely available. Although pictures of sound spectrograms of African frogs had been published in the 1960s, the systematics of southern African amphibians based on this technique started when M. Tandy and R. Keith employed this approach to group species of the genus *Bufo* in 1972. They made extensive use of the analyses of calls they had recorded over many years in Africa. Vocalization was also the key to recognizing the otherwise cryptic species *Tomopterna krugerensis* by Passmore and Carruthers in 1975. This period from 1972 to 2000 produced both systematic works of a traditional nature and many making use of the new technologies. Schiøtz reviewed the treefrogs of eastern Africa in 1975, also making use of vocalizations. His work was supported by field data for many species. Systematic reviews of many smaller taxa, utilizing field data, vocalizations, and biochemical data, such as that by Channing, Hendricks, and Dawood for the genus *Arthroleptella*, were published.

Not only did technology provide characters, but also improvements in computer speed and memory permitted the application of rigorous methodology to analyze the data and determine relationships. The rapid rise in phylogenetic systematics, or cladistics, is reflected in the use of this approach in frog systematic studies. Detailed anatomical work can provide many data suitable for cladistic analyses. B. T. Clarke used osteological characters for a generic-level phylogeny of African ranids in 1981. The systematic treatment of the family Hyperoliidae by Drewes in 1984 involved a cladistic analysis of data derived largely from a detailed study of osteology and muscle characters. Drewes was able to provide a genus-level phylogeny for the family. By the mid-1980s it was apparent that changing species concepts and new analytical tools would lead to large-scale revisions of taxa, both at the species level and in terms of systematic arrangements. The important systematic review of the amphibians of the world edited by Frost in 1985 satisfied a need for a starting point for this process.

One of the problems facing workers in southern Africa has been the confusion of repeated descriptions of the same species in different areas, often with the type specimens no longer available. An important series of papers by Poynton and Broadley from 1985 to 1991 on the amphibians in the Zambezi catchment has gone a long way toward sorting out the taxonomy and systematics of all the amphibians in the region. Other regional or smaller-scale systematic reviews included those of Lambiris on the frogs of KwaZulu-Natal in 1988 and Zimbabwe in 1989.

The use of simplified biochemical techniques recently has placed DNA sequencing within the reach of many laboratories. The application of this technique to phylogenetic studies of southern African amphibians is exemplified by C. Richards and W. Moore, who reported on the relationships of the tree frog family Hyperoliidae in 1996.

Special mention must be made of the work of Sanchiz, who reviewed the fossil frogs of the world in 1998. Many fossils are known from southern Africa, and this contribution surely will lead to a better understanding of the extant taxa. Apart from the systematic studies mentioned earlier, C. de Villiers and his students and colleagues at the University of Stellenbosch contributed greatly to the knowledge of the comparative anatomy of many amphibians, starting in the 1920s. Another center of research has been the University of the Witwatersrand, where N. Passmore and his students contributed detailed experimental studies on frog vocalizations and behavior, starting in the early 1970s.

Popular books have played an important role in synthesizing the information in technical publications and in bringing details of life history to a greater audience. The encyclopedic *Das Tierreich* has been an important source, especially the earlier editions by Nieden in 1923 and 1926. W. Rose was a dentist who inspired generations with his 1929 book *Veld and Vlei* and *The Reptiles and Amphibians of Southern Africa* in 1950. Although written for a regional market, Hewitt's 1937 guide to the vertebrate fauna of Eastern Cape Province has proved a useful source of information for much of southern Africa. R. Inger of the Field Museum in Chicago wrote the chapter on Amphibia for the series *South African Animal Life* in 1959. V. Wager was a well-known plant pathologist who produced a string of popular magazine articles on frogs and *The Frogs of South Africa* in 1965, with a second edition in 1986. Other regional guides include those by U. Pienaar on the frogs of the Kruger National Park in 1963, M. Stewart on the frogs of Malawi in 1967, R. Auerbach on the amphibians and reptiles of Botswana published in 1987, and L. Du Preez on the frogs and toads of the Free State in 1996. N. Passmore and V. Carruthers published *South African Frogs* in 1979, with a second edition in 1995 in which they presented illustrations of sonograms for most of the calls. A. Schiøtz published a book on the tree frogs of Africa in 1999 that brings together information on this interesting group. J. Poynton covered the distributions of sub-Saharan amphibians in 1999, in a book on the patterns of amphibians of the world, edited by W. E. Duellman. As this book is being prepared, many more species are in the process of being described, and many little-known areas are sure to yield other undescribed frogs. Local universities are starting to utilize approaches like DNA sequencing, and cladistic analyses are commonplace. The next few years are expected to produce a surge in amphibian systematic publications.

Adding to Our Knowledge of Amphibians

There are many gaps in our knowledge. Most of these can be filled in by careful observation and recording. People living in remote areas are in a unique position to assist, as they can be present at the start of the rains, when most frogs are active. Many societies cater to people interested in frogs, and provide newsletters for the presentation of casual observations, as well as scientific journals for the publication of detailed studies. The Herpetological Association of Africa offers membership to anyone interested in African frogs (and reptiles). The association produces a journal and a newsletter; any library or museum should be able to trace the current address of the association. Recently published books (listed in full in the bibliography) that will be useful for anyone interested in African frogs include those by Passmore and Carruthers (1995), Schiøtz (1999), and Duellman (1999) and the volume on *Xenopus* edited by Tinsley and Kobel (1996). Libraries may have copies of some of the other older books listed in the bibliography. A project to map the distributions of the frogs in South Africa, Lesotho, and Swaziland was completed recently. The resulting atlas is available from the Avian Demography Unit, University of Cape Town, Rondebosch 7700, South Africa.

Natural History Museums

Many natural history museums house collections of frogs and serve as a source of information about amphibian biodiversity. The collections include specimens along with important information about each. The specimens are preserved so as to be useful in the future, and may be the source of comparative material for purposes of identification, or as material for examining the diet of amphibians and their reproductive biology, among many other uses. The information associated with each specimen (e.g., the date and place where it was collected) is critical, as without this the material is all but worthless. Animals collected for a particular research purpose (e.g., a study of parasite transmission), are placed in the collection as voucher specimens. Voucher specimens serve as a reference so that other workers can confirm the identity and findings of the original investigation. New species and frogs from unusual places are particularly valuable as voucher specimens. Central and southern Africa has many unique amphibians, and the amateur herpetologist, as well as the general public, can play an important role in contributing toward the knowledge. Once the amphibians in an area are identified, their distributions and biology can be compared to what is reported in this book. New findings along with tape recordings of the advertisement call, a voucher specimen (properly labeled), and detailed observations can be conveyed to the institutions listed below.

At the time of writing, the museums listed here had amphibian collections and staff to look after them. Other museums may have collections, but unless they are being actively curated, it is better to ensure that the specimens be sent to one of the institutions listed. The telephone numbers are not given, as these can change, but it should be simple to find the current contact details. Zoology or biology departments at universities also will be able to offer advice.

MALAWI:
National Museum of Malawi, Blantyre.

Introduction

MOZAMBIQUE:
Museu de Historia Natural, Universidade Eduardo Mondlane, C.P. 257, Maputo, Mozambique.

NAMIBIA:
State Museum, P.O. Box 1203, Windhoek, Namibia.

SOUTH AFRICA:
Northern Flagship Institution (Transvaal Museum), P.O. Box 413, Pretoria 0001, South Africa.
South African Museum, P.O. Box 81, Cape Town 8000, South Africa.
National Museum, P.O. Box 266, Bloemfontein 9300, South Africa.
Bayworld (The Port Elizabeth Museum), P.O. Box 13147, Humewood 6013, South Africa.
Natal Museum, Loop Street, Pietermaritzburg 3200, South Africa.
McGregor Museum, P.O. Box 61, Kimberley 8300, South Africa.

ZAMBIA:
Livingstone Museum (National Museum of Zambia), Livingstone, P.O. Box 60498, Livingstone, Zambia.

ZIMBABWE:
National Museum of Zimbabwe, Bulawayo, Zimbabwe.

Collecting Amphibians and Information for Museums

Frogs usually are caught at night, with the collector using a strong light. The males can be located by their calls during the breeding season. It is important not to collect too many, or to collect species for no reason. Amateurs should collect frogs that will add to distribution records, or specimens that they cannot identify, as these may be new to science. Often tape recordings are adequate to identify a species. The specimens can be kept in plastic bags, one per bag. Keep the bags cool and add a little water to prevent the frog from desiccating. If possible, take the frog to the museum while it is alive, within a day or so of collection. If this is not possible, then the specimen can be killed using a little teething gel rubbed onto the top of the head. Alternatives include one of MS 222 (3-aminobenzoic acid ethyl ester), a little powder added to enough water to be 5 mm deep in the container, or 5% ethanol, or 1% formalin. In extreme cases the specimen can be placed in deep freeze for a few hours until frozen. After the specimen is killed, it must be fixed by laying it out, with the fingers and toes spread, and placing it between layers of cheesecloth or paper towel dampened with 5% formalin and then inside a closed plastic container. Fixation of large specimens, over 25 mm long, will require placement of a small incision in the side, to permit the fixing solution to get to the internal organs. After 24 hours the specimen can be placed in 70% ethanol for storage.

Each specimen must be labeled by attaching a piece of good-quality paper or plastic label with thread around the waist of the specimen, with the following details written in pencil or alcohol-proof ink: exact locality, given so others can find the place; date of collection; name of collector; identification; other useful information. Museum expeditions assign a collector's number to each specimen, and this is linked to detailed notes in a permanent catalogue.

Museum staff will be willing to advise on procedures and technical details like labeling paper. Be aware that a permit to collect amphibians may be needed.

Frogs and Man

There is currently much evidence to support the statement that frog populations are declining across the world, and human activities are implicated in most of the cases. There is, however, insufficient data to evaluate the past or present status of most species in Africa. This chapter reviews the present uses of frogs and their potential contribution to our well-being. What little is known of the ecology of African frogs is outlined. Frogs and tadpoles are useful biological indicators of a healthy environment and have been used in assays to determine the effect of water-borne pollutants. In Africa frogs are used as food and as laboratory animals, and they are known to play an important role in the food web. Frogs are threatened by habitat loss, changes in the ozone layer, and the spreading of infections, among other factors. They are important in Africa for the role they play in consuming vast numbers of insects, and research suggests that they may be very important in the future as a potential source of pharmacologically useful substances.

Frogs as Food

Frogs are not widely used as food. An exception is the African bullfrog *Pyxicephalus adspersus*, which today is eaten by people in many parts of the continent. Historically the early explorers like Livingstone also ate it. Bones of the African bullfrog and the platanna *Xenopus laevis* are found at various archaeological sites and are evidence that frogs have been a part of the human diet for a long time. Platannas are still collected from many African lakes, dried in the sun, and eaten.

Bushmen are recorded as being very partial to bullfrog meat. The early British explorers Lord and Baines (1876) reported that "the Bushmen grip them by the nape of the neck, strike them across the thighs and across the spine to disable them, and then, placing their lips to the vent blow till they force the stomach and all the entrails out at the mouth. The flesh of these frogs is exceedingly good, more like chicken than anything else, and we often found a good-sized one make us a very satisfying meal." The same method of cleaning is still used today. In Mozambique the African bullfrog is boiled whole, without skinning. The smaller edible bullfrog is skinned and cleaned and then roasted over a fire.

Although the African bullfrog is a substantial meal, only the smaller platanna has the potential for farming. It is not dependent on natural wetlands but can be reared easily in very large numbers in simple dams.

Laboratory Use

Although both toads and river frogs have been used in the laboratory, it is the platanna that has become a worldwide laboratory animal. The platanna became famous for its use in the *Xenopus* pregnancy test, in which a female platanna would produce eggs if injected with a little urine from a pregnant woman. This test was developed in 1933 and remained in use until the 1960s. So many frogs were required for laboratory tests worldwide that large numbers were exported from South Africa. Today the platanna is used as a model system for exploring important biochemical processes. Probably more detail is known of the cellular and subcellular workings of *Xenopus* than any other frog in the world.

Central and southern Africa could provide a number of other frogs that would be useful in laboratories. The various reed frogs are easy to keep and have a short generation time in the laboratory. These properties make them especially promising as a model system for studying inheritance and the mechanisms of gene expression.

Hormone Analogs

The toxins in the skins of frogs serve as a defense against predators, mostly mammals. The skin glands produce a range of substances that make the mammal predator very ill, without killing it. Mammals that have once tasted a frog will learn not to do so again! The young of many mammals learn from their parents how to hunt, and so the frog lesson can be passed on to new generations of predators. The skin toxins are often copies (analogs) of mammalian hormones. They are steroidal alkaloids, amines, peptides, and proteins. Few African frogs have been investigated thoroughly for skin toxins.

Four groups that have been investigated so far are the toads *Bufo*, platannas *Xenopus*, kassinas *Kassina*, and the ghost frogs *Heleophryne*. Characteristic substances have been found in the skin glands of each. *Heleophryne* species yielded a bradykinin that has been little studied, but the other genera have yielded toxins known as *xenopsin* and *kassinin*. Xenopsin causes contraction in the rat stomach, which implies that these frogs cause vomiting, a useful strategy to deter predators.

The skin of the red-legged kassina *Kassina maculata* contains some defensive chemicals, including a peptide related to physalemin. Physalemin is known from the skin of some Central and South American frogs. This peptide has a powerful hypotensive effect in dogs and stimulates the large intestine of the rabbit, suggesting that it lowers blood pressure and causes vomiting in the predator. The peptide known as leu^5-cerulein is also recorded from their skin. This agent has a potent spasmogenic action on the gallbladder and stimulates pancreatic juice, which is rich in enzymes but poor in bicarbonate. The effect of these peptides is to make any animal that comes into contact with the skin of a red-legged kassina violently ill, hopefully protecting the frog against any future attacks. These chemical defenses are very effective, as only a few nanograms (millionths of a gram) of secretion per kilogram of predator are required.

Tachykinins in the skin of many species are responsible for upsetting the heart rate of predators.

The guttural toad *Bufo gutturalis* is well protected by skin toxins. One of these is called *regularobufagin*. Cats, when injected with small amounts of the skin secretion, start vomiting and die. Epinephrine (adrenaline) is also found in the parotid secretion of toads.

Southern African anurans, like those of other parts of the world, have enormous potential pharmacological value. Some toxins occur across species, genus, and even family boundaries, while others seem to be species-specific. Every species is a potential contributor of useful chemicals. The value of frogs in this respect is little appreciated.

Antibiotics

The thin moist skin of frogs is an important potential avenue of entry for bacteria, fungi, and other invaders. Frogs avoid infections entering through the skin by producing many antibiotics, and these might be able to be synthesized for human use. Investigations have already yielded an antibiotic that is effective against *Staphylococcus aureus*, which often causes abscesses and boils, and against viruses that are rarely affected by antibiotics.

Magainins are another group of antimicrobial peptides discovered in the skin of *Xenopus laevis*. They inhibit the growth of numerous bacteria and fungi and are being exploited commercially. The bibliography lists a review of skin secretions by Clarke, published in 1997.

Conservation

Although conservation is always topical, especially in many first-world industrialized countries, this is not the case throughout much of Africa. Basic species lists are frequently not available, and the natural history of many species is not completely known. Before any decision can be made to determine if conservation action is necessary, the status of all the species should be evaluated. Official lists of threatened species published in Red Data Books or some equivalent should be available. South Africa is the only country of the 10 covered here that has a Red Data Book that lists threatened frogs.

Declining Frog Populations

There has been considerable publicity concerning apparent declining frog populations worldwide. Much of the decline has been attributed to habitat destruction, and this appears to be the case in central and southern Africa. Many African cities are experiencing rapid urbanization. Urbanization of the Cape Flats near Cape Town, for example, where once endemic frogs like the Cape dainty frog *Cacosternum capense*, the micro frog *Microbatrachella capensis*, and Gill's platanna *Xenopus gilli* were found, has destroyed the habitat in the space of a few years.

Many frog habitats have been lost owing to the draining of marshlands for agriculture or the expansion of human settlement. Fortunately the destruction of wetlands suitable for frogs is occurring in a relatively small area. Endemics are at risk, for example, Rose's ghost frog *Heleophryne rosei*, which occurs on the eastern slopes of Table Mountain, where pine plantations have dried up the streams. The most serious threat to frogs in this part of Africa is the extensive afforestation that has taken place on the moist mountain slopes in Zimbabwe, Malawi, Swaziland, and South Africa where many endemic species of frogs are found.

Prolonged drought may prevent frogs from breeding in temporary ponds in dry areas. This is a natural phenomenon, and the affected populations would be able to recover quickly during a wet cycle.

There is no evidence that any countrywide decline in frog populations is occurring in central and southern Africa, although the baseline studies are not available to contradict that view. The building of proposed dams on large rivers like the Zambezi, Kavango, Cunene, and Limpopo may seriously reduce water flow below the dams, with unpredictable effects on the habitat along the river edge, where annual flooding provides the stimulus and the conditions for many frogs to breed.

There has been concern that the Okavango Swamps in Botswana would be drained to facilitate mining. If the swamps were drained, a major frog habitat would be irretrievably damaged.

Why be concerned about frogs? We know that anurans consume vast numbers of insects and are in turn eaten by larger animals like birds, snakes, and small mammals. If frog populations were seriously depleted, there would be a potential increase in insects, including crop pests and those that carry disease. The transfer of energy to many larger animals in the form of a frog diet would be reduced, with unknown consequences on the ecosystem. Both terrestrial and aquatic amphibians play similar roles and need to be protected.

Habitat Requirements

Frogs are characterized by a soft permeable skin. Although they have a range of adaptations reducing water loss, in general amphibians are confined to damp places when they are active. The toads (*Bufo*, *Capensibufo*, and *Schismaderma*) possess thick glandular skins and can be found active in dry places, although they must return to moist shelters to rehydrate.

Fortunately not all frogs require clean water in which to breed. Frogs that permanently inhabit water bodies like the platanna *Xenopus*, the river frogs *Afrana*, and the ridged frogs *Ptychadena* are able to live in very-poor-quality (muddy) waters. Gray's stream frog *Strongylopus grayii* is a small animal often inhabiting ditches and rubbish tips and able to breed in turbid water with low oxygen tensions. The tadpoles of the tree frogs *Leptopelis* are found in water that is so dirty it might be described as thin mud. The tadpoles of many species come to the surface to breathe, enabling such frogs to make use of almost any water for breeding.

Population Densities

No studies of frog numbers and density have been published for the countries covered here. The crowned bullfrog *Hoplobatrachus occipitalis* is one of the few frog species in Africa for which detailed ecological information is available. Work done in West Africa showed that this species could reach a biomass of 30.5 to 44.4 kg/ha, at a density of 270 to 1000 individuals/ha. This is about half the density of Müller's platanna *Xenopus muelleri*, which was calculated to be between 400 and 1550 individuals/ha. The two species together produced peaks of 108,100 tadpoles/ha at a biomass of 324.3 kg/ha at Bangui. This significant biomass indicates that tadpoles in general must play an important part of the food web of temporary tropical ponds. The crowned bullfrog *Hoplobatrachus occipitalis* is ecologically similar to the southern African Cape river frog *Afrana fuscigula*, and the latter could be expected to produce similar population peaks. Explosive breeders like *Pyxicephalus adspersus*, the large African bullfrog, probably reach a very high biomass for a few weeks each season.

Ecological Early Warning

The eggs and embryos of frogs in wetlands are very sensitive indicators of any adverse changes in the water chemistry. The use of insecticides to control malaria is prevalent throughout much of the area covered here. Even DDT, banned in many countries, is still used in some African countries for spot treatment of mosquito sites.

Monitoring tadpoles and adults from year to year would offer early warning of a buildup of insecticides in the environment. Much of central and southern Africa is undeveloped, and the local people are not always aware of the problems of using insecticides. There have been reports of empty insecticide containers being cleaned in the local streams and ponds, to be used for domestic purposes. Clearly this has serious effects on both the environment and the unsuspecting users of such containers.

There is a very real danger of a profound effect of biocides on frogs. Because the adults have moist skins, which are poor barriers to chemicals, anurans are extremely sensitive to environmental degradation, and accordingly serve as very efficient early-warning systems.

Poisons dumped into city sewers have been known to cause large-scale die-off of resident platannas in the settling ponds. Poisons released in other wetlands would cause similar effects. The significance of anurans as an early-warning system means that they may be affected before other evidence of environmental degradation appears. Even quite low levels of chemicals such as fertilizers and herbicides may be dangerous to frogs, particularly the embryos and larvae.

Role in the Ecosystem

No study has been published concerning the role of frogs in African ecosystems. Amphibians are both primary consumers and predators. The eggs are generally free from predation, probably owing to toxins they contain. However, the eggs of Wager's stream frog *Strongylopus wageri* have been reported being eaten by the river crab *Potamon*. Apart from the direct developers, all African frogs have a larval stage that is essentially a primary consumer, feeding mainly on algae and plant material. In many wetlands tadpoles are probably the most important primary consumers. Older tadpoles are almost always predators, as are all adult frogs. The adults congregate in very large numbers during the breeding season and consume vast numbers of insects and other invertebrates. Tadpoles and adult frogs are variously preyed upon by dragonfly nymphs, fishes, waterbirds, snakes, monitor lizards and young crocodiles, and a few mammals, such as the clawless otter. Many batches of tadpoles do not reach metamorphosis due to the high level of predation.

Frogs occupy a range of trophic levels and are very important in the maintenance of wetlands.

Exotic Fish

The introduction of exotic fishes such as trout and bass into African streams and other wetlands deserves special mention. This practice may have had a serious impact on frogs, probably restricting some, such as the large-mouthed frog *Amietia vertebralis*, Johnston's river frog *Afrana johnstoni*, and ghost frogs *Heleophryne*, to only part of their former ranges.

Nature conservation departments have been responsible for the breeding and introduction of fish, like trout, in the past. These are the same authorities responsible for conservation! The concerned public should lobby for the conservation of all indigenous fauna.

Human Population and Pets

Africa has one of the highest rates of human population increase. The pressures on frogs and all other animals increase exponentially, as each new human needs a place to live, a place to work, and more land to grow food. The destruction of frog habitat is closely associated with the increase in human population.

The social and economic pressures in countries with rapid population growth result in less attention being paid to the welfare of animals like frogs. Not all the countries in central and southern Africa, for example, employ specialists concerned with frog conservation.

An important threat to frogs in Africa is indifference to them and to their fates. Indigenous frogs are virtually absent from zoological gardens and public aquaria in Africa, unlike the displays in Europe and North America. A good way of bringing the importance of frogs to the attention of the public is to promote common frogs as pets. In many parts of the geographic area covered, it is currently illegal to keep any wild animal, including frogs, without a permit. This policy does not enhance the chances of frog conservation, as the animals remain unknown to the public.

Captive Breeding and Reintroduction

Species that have restricted ranges and may be threatened by the destruction of habitats or invasion by other species could be bred in captivity. Attempts could be made to reestablish them in former habitats or in managed areas outside their former ranges. Animals like the reed frogs feature regularly in European vivarium journals, as they are easy to breed. Experienced breeders could be called upon to breed threatened species for reintroduction programs.

Fortunately many frog species are not in need of assistance, but species restricted to threatened natural forest are candidates for captive breeding. Throughout Africa much natural forest has been destroyed. Potential candidate species should be researched for captive breeding now, before their habitats are destroyed.

Research

An obvious priority in any conservation program is to know what species are present. This is a major research need as far as frogs are concerned. Frogs differ from members of the other vertebrate groups in that the populations and communities can be sampled safely, as tadpoles, with no significant impact on the numbers of adults. A reasonably good idea of what species are present can be obtained with little effort. Very little previous experience is required to collect tadpoles, and they are relatively easy to identify.

Recordings of calls also could be used to identify many species. Numbers can be estimated rapidly by sampling a road transect at night when the males are calling.

In South Africa, the South African Frog Atlassing Project is an attempt to determine the present distribution of as many species as possible.

Red Data Book Species

The World Conservation Union (IUCN) has defined Red List categories in version 3.1 that classify each species according to the perceived risk it faces, and the state of knowledge concerning that species. The relationships between these categories is explained below:

An initial distinction is made between the species that have not been evaluated according to the IUCN criteria and those that have. If they have been evaluated, a decision is made as to whether the data are sufficient or not. Species for which adequate data exist are assigned one of the following five categories: Extinct, Extinct in the Wild, Threatened, Near Threatened, or Least Concern. The species believed to be threatened are assigned one of the following categories: Critically Endangered, Endangered, or Vulnerable. Species in these three categories require immediate action by the appropriate authorities.

The IUCN has carefully defined the nine categories, but for the purposes of the proposed assignments here, the following explanations should be sufficient:

Extinct. This category applies when it is known that the last individual has died. No amphibian in this area is in this category.

Extinct in the Wild. This category applies to species that only exist in captivity. No amphibian in this area fits this category.

Critically Endangered. This category implies that the species is facing an extremely high risk of extinction.

Endangered. This category implies that the species is facing a very high risk of extinction but not quite as high as the previous category.

Vulnerable. This category implies that the species is facing a high risk of extinction but not quite as high as the previous two categories.

Near Threatened. This category is used for species that do not qualify for any of the three threatened categories now, but is likely to qualify in the future.

Least Concern. This category includes widespread species that are abundant.

Data Deficient. This category is used to show that more information is required before a proper evaluation can be made. Most of the amphibians in the area covered here would fall into this category.

Not Evaluated. Species that have not been measured against the criteria of the IUCN are placed in this category.

Below is a list of southern African species that were assigned IUCN categories during a workshop held in Cape Town in 2000, and my proposed assignments for species outside southern Africa believed to be in one of the threatened categories.

ARTHROLEPTIDAE
Schoutedenella troglodytes   Near Threatened
BUFONIDAE
Bufo amatolicus   Near Threatened
Bufo angusticeps   Least Concern
Bufo inyangae   Vulnerable
Bufo pantherinus   Endangered
Bufo pardalis   Least Concern
Bufo robinsoni   Data Deficient
Capensibufo rosei   Vulnerable
Stephopaedes anotis   Vulnerable
HELEOPHRYNIDAE
Heleophryne hewitti   Critically Endangered
Heleophryne rosei   Critically Endangered
HEMISOTIDAE
Hemisus guttatus   Near Threatened
HYPEROLIIDAE
Afrixalus aureus   Vulnerable
Afrixalus knysnae   Data Deficient
Hyperolius pickersgilli   Endangered
Leptopelis xenodactylus   Endangered
MICROHYLIDAE
Breviceps gibbosus   Near Threatened
Breviceps macrops   Near Threatened
Breviceps sylvestris   Near Threatened
Probreviceps rhodesianus   Vulnerable
PIPIDAE
Xenopus gilli   Endangered
RANIDAE
Afrana vandijki   Data Deficient
Amietia vertebralis   Vulnerable
Anhydrophryne rattrayi   Near Threatened
Arthroleptella drewesii   Near Threatened
Arthroleptella landdrosia   Near Threatened
Arthroleptella lightfooti   Near Threatened

Arthroleptella ngongoniensis   Critically endangered
Cacosternum capense   Vulnerable
Microbatrachella capensis   Critically Endangered
Natalobatrachus bonebergi   Endangered
Nothophryne broadleyi   Endangered
Poyntonia paludicola   Near Threatened
Ptychadena broadleyi   Vulnerable
Pyxicephalus adspersus   Near Threatened
Strongylopus springbokensis   Data Deficient
Strongylopus wageri   Least Concern

Identification of Adults

One of the aims of this book is to enable readers to identify frogs reliably. This is not always easy, however, as frogs have very few characters that are useful for this purpose. Generally, all frogs within a family or genus have similarly shaped bodies, with similar amounts of webbing, similar tubercles, and similar habits. Frogs do vary considerably in color pattern, but nearly all species are polymorphic in this respect, so that each species possesses a number of possible color patterns and there is often overlap in patterns between related species.

Characters Used for Identification

The surest way to identify frogs is by the male advertisement call. This vocalization is made by the male to attract a female of the same species. Female frogs have been shown experimentally to be very particular about their reaction to calls, so that only males and females of the same species are brought together for breeding. This system may break down occasionally, especially when the frogs are breeding in habitats disturbed by humans such that the specific cues that initially attract a particular species to the breeding site are confused. For example, damming a stream may bring together species that breed in rivers and those that breed in standing water. Fortunately this is not too common.

Readers are advised to follow five steps to identify an adult frog:

1. Follow the identification keys as far as possible.
2. Compare the photograph and brief description.
3. Compare the description of the advertisement call.
4. Check the known distribution of the candidate species.

5. Compare the description of the habits and behavior of the species.

Each species of frog will have a unique combination of the features included in these steps. Any one of the features can be equivocal, but using a combination should lead to a correct identification. Possible problems include unfamiliar terminology and the meaning of the phrases used in the keys, and the fact that like all other organisms, individual frogs vary within populations.

It has not been possible to provide keys to all the species. It also has not been possible to include photographs of all the possible color patterns, but I have tried to illustrate the common patterns rather than the most spectacular. Recordings of many frog calls are available, and the serious reader will no doubt wish to obtain these recordings. The distribution maps reflect only the known distribution, as opposed to the real distribution. It would not be unexpected to discover a species just outside the known area of distribution, but if a frog known to be confined to the Namib Desert is suddenly identified from the tropical east coast, then the identification must be in doubt. Each species occupies a particular range of habitats and normally can be characterized by certain behavior. Many squeakers *Arthroleptis* live in or near forests and conceal themselves under leaf litter. If one tentatively identifies an *Arthroleptis* frog that has been found in temporary puddles in the savanna, then a misidentification may be indicated. Perhaps there has been confusion with a superficially similar genus, like the puddle frogs *Phrynobatrachus*.

Finally, the destruction of the natural habitat of frogs, like wetlands, often for the purpose of building houses or planting exotic trees, has led to serious problems for many species of frogs. Many populations are now extinct, and others may be found in unnatural surroundings.

How to Use the Identification Keys

The terminology used in the keys is explained below.

The keys consist of a series of choices. Start at 1a/1b and select the phrase that best fits the frog you are identifying. Each choice will

Identification of Adults

lead you either to a new pair of phrases, to a group name with a new subset of keys, or to a species identification. For example, in the key to the species of *Arthroleptis* choice 1a will identify the specimen as *A. stenodactylus*, while choice 1b will lead to step 2, where you will be asked to choose between 2a and 2b, and so on.

The keys have been arranged so that the specimen is first identified to family. Within the family there is a key identifying the specimen to genus, and then another key to arrive at the species name.

Terminology Used in the Keys to the Adults

The thumbnail sketches alongside the relevant parts of the key will serve to illustrate the features discussed. Below are some brief definitions or explanations of the terminology used to describe adult amphibians. Some species key out in two places.

Claws on foot. Dark claws on three of the toes on each foot, as in the genus *Xenopus*.
Cusps on lower jaw. Sharp, toothlike projections at the front of the lower jaw, as in bullfrogs.
Digital discs. Flattened adhesive structures on the tips of the fingers and toes. These usually have distinct grooves around the edge.
Distal subarticular tubercle. See Tubercle.
Dorsal skin ridge. A very fine ridge along the midline of the back, characteristic of frogs in the family Arthroleptidae.
Dorsolateral stripe. A stripe along the back, between the side and the midline.
Dorsum. Back.
Fingers in opposing pairs. The four fingers of tree frogs *Chiromantis* are arranged in two pairs so that they can grasp branches with one pair on each side.
Foot length. The measurement from the tip of the longest (fourth) toe to include the metatarsal tubercle.
Fourth metatarsus. The foot bones extending back from the fourth toe.
Inner metatarsal tubercle. See Tubercle.

Inner toe. The first toe. The longest toe is the fourth, for orientation.
Internarial distance. The measurement between the nostrils.
Interocular bar. A marking, often dark, running from eye to eye over the head.
Interorbital distance. The measurement between the eyes, taken usually across the top of the head.
Last phalanx out of alignment. In tree frogs the last joint of the finger that has an extra piece of cartilage causing the tip to be offset below the rest of the finger.
Lumbar pattern. The pattern on the lower back.
Metatarsal. The base of the toe.
Metatarsal tubercle. See Tubercle.
Outer metatarsals. The metatarsal on the outside, or the side with the longest toe.
Outer metatarsal tubercle. See Tubercle.
Palate with transverse folds. The inside of the top of the mouth with ridges running from side to side.
Palmar tubercle. See Tubercle.
Paravertebral band. A longitudinal stripe next to the midline of the back.
Parotid. See Parotid gland.
Parotid gland. A large skin gland behind the eye in toads of the family Bufonidae.
Pectoral markings. Pattern, usually dark, on the chest near the arms.
Phalanges. Individual bony elements of the fingers and toes. See also Segments of toe free of web.
Posterior face of thigh. The back of the thigh.
Proximal subarticular tubercle. See Tubercle.
Pupil shape. The configuration of the pupil in live frogs, when closed in bright light. It may be a vertical slit, a horizontal slit, or rectangular.
Pupillary umbraculum. A small extension at the top of the pupil in high-altitude frogs that serves as a protection against sunlight.
Segments of toe free of web. The phalanges, counted from the tip, that are not webbed. See also Web reaching tubercle.
Snout hardened for digging. White and bony tip of the snout. This condition is found in *Anhydrophryne* species.
Snout-vent length. The body length measured as the distance between the tip of the snout and the end of the body.

Subarticular tubercle. See Tubercle.
Subocular tentacle. A small tentacle below the eye, found in *Xenopus.*
SVL. See Snout-vent length.
Tarsal fold. A longitudinal ridge running from the heel to the ankle, especially in some toads of the genus *Bufo.*
Tarsus. The lower leg between the ankle and the heel.
Teeth on upper jaw. Fine teeth along the edge of the upper jaw. These are best felt by running a fingernail softly along the jaw, as they are difficult to see.
Throat flap. A glandular flap of skin covering the throat in males of some frogs.
Throat gland. See Throat flap.
Tibia (plural tibiae). The lower leg between the knee and the ankle.
Tongue free behind. Tongue attached only in front, loose at the back.
Transverse skin groove. A groove or fold in the skin running across behind the eyes.
Tubercle. A raised hardened skin projection, often in the form of a flattened cone or ridge. Tubercles are frequently diagnostic and also serve as reference points to determine the amount of webbing. *Subarticular* tubercles are found ventral to the joints of the fingers and toes. Subarticular tubercles at the tip of the toe or finger are *distal,* while those at the base are *proximal. Metatarsal* tubercles are found at the back of the foot and can be *inner* or *outer.*
Tympanum. The eardrum, which is not always visible.
Urostyle. Part of the "hip" in frogs. This part is usually used as the most posterior bony element for measuring body length, as snout-urostyle length, in some species.
Ventral surface. The lower surface, including the chest and belly.
Vertebral band. A wide stripe running along the midline of the back.
Vertebral line. A thin line running along the midline of the back.
Vomerine teeth. Small toothlike projections on the roof of the mouth near the internal nostrils.
Web reaching (or passing) *tubercle.* A way of describing the amount of webbing. The web midway between two toes is measured against the subarticular tubercles. This is not the same as phalanges free of web (Segments of toe free of web).

KEY TO THE FAMILIES OF CENTRAL AND SOUTHERN AFRICAN ADULT FROGS

1a.	Tongue absent, 3 claws on each foot (Fig. 3)	Pipidae
1b.	Tongue present	2

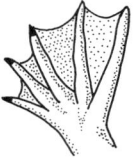

Fig. 3 Foot with three claws

2a.	Tongue not free behind	Heleophrynidae
2b.	Tongue free behind	3
3a.	Upper jaw toothless	4
3b.	Upper jaw with fine teeth (Fig. 4)	6

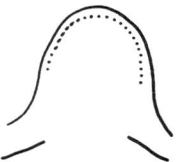

Fig. 4 Upper jaw with teeth

4a.	Snout pointed, hardened for digging; eyes small (Fig. 5)	Hemisotidae
4b.	Snout not hardened for digging	5

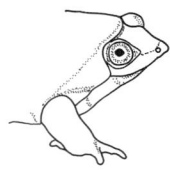

Fig. 5 Sharp snout and skin fold

5a.	Transverse folds on palate	Microhylidae
5b.	No transverse folds on palate	Bufonidae

Identification of Adults

6a. A fine dorsal skin ridge running along midline (Fig. 6)
   Arthroleptidae
6b. No fine dorsal skin ridge 7

Fig. 6   Middorsal skin ridge

7a. Last segment of finger out of linear alignment (tree frogs) (Fig. 7)
   8
7b. Last phalanx of fingers not out of alignment   Ranidae

Fig. 7   Finger tip out of line

8a. Fingers arranged in two opposing pairs (Fig. 8)   Rhacophoridae
8b. Fingers not arranged in two opposing pairs (Fig. 9)
   Hyperoliidae

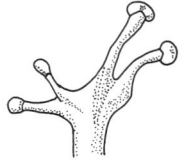   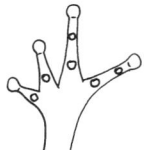

Fig. 8   Fingers in pairs   **Fig. 9**   Fingers not paired

Classification

Frogs, salamanders, and caecilians are placed together in the class Amphibia, one of the divisions of the vertebrate animals, or Vertebrata, which includes fishes, reptiles, birds, and mammals. All the members of this class are soft-skinned, most have lungs, and most have free-swimming larvae that develop into adults. The class Amphibia is divided into three orders.

Order Caudata includes the salamanders and their relatives, all of which have a long tail and two pairs of limbs. They are found in North and South America, Europe, Asia, and Africa north of the Sahara.

Order Gymnophiona includes the caecilians and their relatives. They are elongated, limbless animals that superficially resemble large earthworms. They occur worldwide in the tropics. Two examples are found in the area covered here:

Family Scolecomorphidae—Kirk's caecilian
Family Caeciliidae—Changamwe caecilian

Order Anura consists of the tailless amphibians and includes all the common frogs. They occur worldwide except in the Arctic and Antarctic. There are over 20 families of frogs, of which 9 occur in central and southern Africa:

Family Arthroleptidae—squeakers. These small forest floor frogs do not have free-swimming tadpoles.
Family Bufonidae—toads, Cape toads, red toads, forest toads. These small to large species of terrestrial frogs have thick glandular skin and small dark tadpoles.
Family Heleophrynidae—ghost frogs. This ancient group of frogs is restricted to mountains. The adults have discs on the fingers and toes, and the tadpoles are large and possess sucker-like mouthparts

with which they attach themselves to rocks in swift-flowing streams.

Family Hemisotidae—snout-burrowers. These smooth-skinned frogs have strong arms and a hard pointed snout. They burrow snout-first. Eggs are laid in burrows, and the tadpole has a large fin.

Family Hyperoliidae—kassinas, running frogs, tree frogs. These mostly arboreal frogs have large discs on the fingers and toes. Many are brightly colored. The tadpoles vary from large-finned pond types, to slender forms with a little fin.

Family Microhylidae—rain frogs, rubber frogs. These frogs have a narrow head and a small mouth. The rain frogs burrow backward and have eggs that develop directly into small frogs, without a free-swimming tadpole stage. The rubber frogs climb into crevices and have gregarious tadpoles.

Family Pipidae—platannas. These streamlined frogs spend their lives in water. The tadpole is transparent and gregarious.

Family Ranidae—These common frogs include a range of different body shapes and biology. Some have direct development, but most have typical tadpoles.

Family Rhacophoridae—gray tree frog. The only species in this area is large, camouflaged, and has big adhesive discs on the fingers and toes for climbing on trees. The eggs are laid in a foam nest, and the young tadpoles drop into the water to continue their development.

Species Accounts
ORDER ANURA

Squeakers—Family Arthroleptidae

The frogs within the family Arthroleptidae occur throughout sub-Saharan Africa, excluding the southwestern part of the continent. Much of Africa has been covered in forest at various times, and the remnants of this vegetation can still be found on mountain slopes and some lowlands. These forest patches are the habitat of the small leaf-litter frogs. The species in southern Africa have high-pitched calls, prompting the name "squeakers." Nine species are present in the area covered. All the frogs in this family are direct developers—the eggs hatch directly into small frogs, without a free-swimming tadpole stage.

KEY TO THE GENERA

1a. Proportion of first finger/distance between anterior borders of eyes = 80%–140% (Fig. 10)   *Arthroleptis*
1b. Proportion of first finger/distance between anterior borders of eyes = 38%–78%   *Schoutedenella*

Fig. 10 First finger and anterior borders of eyes

Squeakers—Genus *Arthroleptis*

KEY TO THE SPECIES

Arthroleptis carquejai is not included in this key, as it is not well enough known.

Fig. 11 Metatarsal tubercle

1a. Inner metatarsal tubercle as long as, or longer than, first toe (Fig. 11) *Arthroleptis stenodactylus*
1b. Inner metatarsal tubercle shorter than first toe 2

2a. Digital discs or swellings present 3
2b. No digital discs or swellings *Arthroleptis wahlbergii*

3a. Discs on fingers 2–4 dilated to more than width of subarticular tubercles of fingers (Fig. 12) *Arthroleptis reichei*
3b. Discs on fingers 2–4 not broader than width of subarticular tubercles of fingers *Arthroleptis francei*

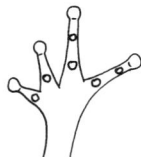

Fig. 12 Discs on fingers

Carqueja's squeaker
Arthroleptis carquejai Ferreira, 1906

This species was named for B. Carqueja, for his interest in the exploration of Angola.
Cambondo screeching frog.

DESCRIPTION: This is a small frog, known only from one 28-mm SVL specimen. The interorbital distance is greater than the eye diameter, and the tympanum is about half the size of the eye. The tongue is heart-shaped with an anterior papilla. Small discs are present on the fingers and toes. Webbing is absent. Tubercles below the fingers are distinct, with a single large flattened inner metatarsal tubercle. The

Fig. 13 *Arthroleptis carquejai*

skin is smooth. Coloration is uniform brown, darker on the back and the outer surface of the limbs. Darker spots are present on the snout and covering the eyelids. The throat and chest are black with whitish marbled markings. The lower lip possesses pale yellowish spots.

DISTRIBUTION AND HABITAT (FIG. 13): This frog is known only from Cambondo in Angola. It was found in an area with dense vegetation.

ADVERTISEMENT CALL: Unknown.

BREEDING: Unknown. It is presumably a direct developer.

NOTES: The description of this species is based on one specimen. Further fieldwork is required to confirm that this is a distinct taxon.

KEY REFERENCE: Ferreira 1906.

France's squeaker
Arthroleptis francei Loveridge, 1953
(Plate 1.1)

This species was named for F. H. France, forestry officer in charge of the depot at Chambe, who was swept over the Ruo Falls during an expedition with Lourens van der Post.
Ruo River screeching frog.

DESCRIPTION: This is a relatively large, heavy-bodied frog with long slender legs. An adult female may reach a maximum length of 49 mm SVL and a 32-mm male is known. The metatarsal tubercle is raised but not flange-like. The third finger in males is elongated, half to two-thirds the width of the head. The toe tips are slightly swollen but not broader than the tubercles below the fingers. The color pattern is very variable. Colors of the back include buff, green, russet, and gray. The abdomen is white, but the throat may be pigmented. Some specimens have a typical hourglass pattern. The forelimb has a small dark band, described appropriately as a "wristlet." The soles of the feet are very dark. The back and sides have lightly scattered pinpoint warts. The tympanum is distinct and small, about half the diameter of the eye. Webbing is absent.

DISTRIBUTION AND HABITAT (FIG. 14): This species is only known from Malawi, on Mount Mulanje. It occurs in leaf litter under bushes and small trees. This frog is common in lowland forests on Mulanje and in grasslands and cedar forest at higher altitudes. It has been suggested that it requires a very moist, cool environment, which is provided by the Ruo Basin on Mount Mulanje, with over 3000 mm of rain per year.

ADVERTISEMENT CALL: Unknown.

BREEDING: Unknown.

Fig. 14 *Arthroleptis francei*

Common Squeaker

Fig. 15 *Arthroleptis reichei*

NOTES: A specimen was found under bark 2 m above ground.

KEY REFERENCES: Stewart 1967, Stevens 1974.

Reiche's squeaker
Arthroleptis reichei Nieden, 1910
(Plate 1.2)

This species was named for Gustav Reiche, of the Koenigliches Zoologisches Museum in Berlin.
Large-toed squeaker, Poroto Mountains screeching frog.

DESCRIPTION: The female may reach 34 mm in length. This is a slender frog, with long hind limbs and expanded toe tips. The length of the third finger in the male is slightly more than half the head width. The metatarsal tubercle is very small, shorter than the first toe. The snout is sharp in profile, and the tympanum is distinct, nearly two-thirds the diameter of the eye. The tibia is about half the body length. Webbing is absent, and the second to fourth fingers and toes end in distinct discs. The discs on fingers 2–4 are wider than the subarticular tubercles. A typical hourglass pattern in browns is present on the back. There is a dark, thin ridge above the tympanum.

DISTRIBUTION AND HABITAT (FIG. 15): This frog is known from the mountains of northern Malawi and southern Tanzania. It has been found in moist evergreen mountain forests. It occurs at 2000 m at Misuku. Reiche's squeaker is not threatened directly, but the forest habitat is in danger from excessive logging.

ADVERTISEMENT CALL: Unknown.

BREEDING: Unknown.

KEY REFERENCE: Loveridge 1953a.

Common squeaker
Arthroleptis stenodactylus Pfeffer, 1893
(Plate 1.3)

The specific name *stenodactylus* refers to the long third finger of the male.
Dune squeaker, shovel-footed squeaker, shovel-footed bush squeaker, Kihengo screeching frog. *Mboru* in Chewa and Ngoni.

DESCRIPTION: The female may reach 45 mm SVL, while the smaller male may reach 33 mm in length. This is a heavily built species, with a relatively short leg. The tibia length is a third to less than half of the body length, and equal to the head width. The tibia length is less than the width of the head in a large specimen. The inner metatarsal tubercle is massive, flange-like, and as long as or longer than the first toe. Ventral markings vary from immaculate to very speckled. Dorsal markings consist of a pair of dark sacral spots, with various combinations of a three-lobed dorsal band, with or without a light vertebral line. A dark line is present from the tip of the snout to the shoulder. The soles of the feet are dark. The male has a dark throat, while the female has a white throat with some speckling in the pectoral region. The male also differs from the female by having minute spines on the back and limbs, and by its narrower head and elongated third finger. The elongated third finger grows rapidly after the male attains sexual maturity.

DISTRIBUTION AND HABITAT (FIG. 16): This frog is known from the northeastern areas, roughly northward of a line drawn from northeastern South Africa, through northern Botswana to eastern Angola. It is often associated with leaf litter. In Malawi it can be found at altitudes from 40 to 2000 m. This frog is very common and is able to live in gardens and natural vegetation.

Common Squeaker

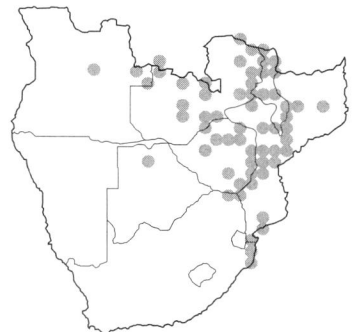

Fig. 16 *Arthroleptis stenodactylus*

ADVERTISEMENT CALL: The male calls from concealed sites in leaf litter and under vegetation, during the day and night after rain. The call is heard from December through February in northern Malawi, with a few calls heard until mid-June. The call is a short whistle, 0.05 s, high-pitched, 3.5 kHz, and repeated at half-second intervals. Males may call very rapidly in chorus. The call sounds somewhat similar to that of the marbled reed frog *Hyperolius marmoratus*.

BREEDING: Eggs are deposited in hollows or burrows in damp earth, often under bushes or around the roots of trees, or under loose-leaf mold. The 2-mm eggs are creamy white. Clutch size varies from 33 to 80. Breeding takes place between December and February. Metamorphosis occurs in the egg, so no free-swimming tadpole stage is present. Juveniles, 20–28 mm long, were present during March and April in Malawi.

NOTES: This frog appears to eat a wide range of insect and other arthropod prey, as well as earthworms, snails, and even other frogs. It is in turn preyed upon by many snakes, such as the olive marsh snake *Natriciteres olivacea*, the green water snake *Philothamnus hoplogaster*, the white-lipped snake *Crotaphopeltis tornieri*, the stripe-bellied sand snake *Psammophis subtaeniatus orientalis*, and the eastern vine snake *Thelotornis capensis mossambicanus*. This small frog is also a popular food of other frogs. A specimen was found hibernating in a hollow tree nearly a meter above ground level.

KEY REFERENCES: Loveridge 1953a, Stewart 1967.

Bush squeaker
Arthroleptis wahlbergii Smith, 1849
(Plate 1.4)

This frog was named for Johan August Wahlberg, a Swedish naturalist and member of the Swedish Academy who collected in southern Africa between 1839 and 1856.
Wahlberg's screeching frog.

DESCRIPTION: This is a small frog, with the female up to 25 mm SVL and the male 22 mm in length. The inner metatarsal tubercle is inconspicuous, rounded, and less than half the size of the inner toe. The tips of the fingers and toes do not possess discs, although they may be swollen. The color pattern is variable, with browns predominating. An hourglass pattern is common, and a pale vertebral stripe is found in some specimens.

DISTRIBUTION AND HABITAT (FIG. 17): This species is known from the tropical east coast of South Africa and in suitable habitats inland. It is found under leaf litter at the base of dense bushes or in forests and is common under lush hedges and shrubs in gardens. This frog is threatened by the large-scale replacement of natural vegetation by agricultural crops but is able to successfully coexist with humans in large cities like Durban.

Fig. 17 *Arthroleptis wahlbergii*

ADVERTISEMENT CALL: The call is a long, high-pitched "wheep" or "wheepee." The dominant frequency is around 4 kHz, with a duration of 200 ms. Calls are repeated each second. The males call while concealed, often under leaf litter at the base of dense vegetation.

BREEDING: The eggs are pale, about 2.5 mm within a capsule 5 mm in diameter. Clutches of 11–30 are known. Eggs are laid 20–30 mm below the surface of leaf litter, usually under cover of dense vegetation. The eggs are scattered over an area of 75 mm^2. The tadpole stage is passed in the egg. Development takes 4 weeks under laboratory conditions but may be shorter in the field.

NOTES: The call is popularly believed to herald rain. I recorded rainfall, temperature, relative humidity, and the presence of advertisement calls for a 6-week period in Pietermaritzburg during the breeding season. Analysis of the results showed that the male only calls after rain. In the wet areas where this species occurs, the rain that initiates calling is frequently followed within days by more precipitation, which leads to the belief that this frog foretells rain. It continues to call during the day and night, and the calls are very conspicuous.

KEY REFERENCE: Wager 1986.

Squeakers—Genus *Schoutedenella*

KEY TO THE SPECIES
1a. Adults small, not more than 25 mm long   2
1b. Adult length more than 25 mm   *Schoutedenella troglodytes*

2a. Stocky frogs, third finger in males up to 40% of body length (Fig. 18)   *Schoutedenella lameeri*
2b. Third finger in males less than 40% of body length   3

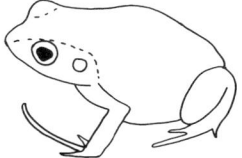

Fig. 18 Long third finger

3a. Metatarsal tubercles less than half the length of outer toe, not larger than subarticular tubercles of toes (Fig. 19)
Schoutedenella xenodactyloides
3b. Metatarsal tubercles longer than half the length of outer toe, about twice the size of the subarticular tubercles of the toes
Schoutedenella xenochirus

Fig. 19   Metatarsal tubercle–outer toe length comparison

Lameere's squeaker
Schoutedenella lameerei (Witte, 1921)

This species was named for Auguste Lameere.
Katanga screeching frog.

DESCRIPTION: This is a small, stockily built frog, with the male and female up to 23 mm SVL. The male has an extremely elongated third finger, reaching nearly 40% of the body length. The head is as broad as long. Tympanum size is more than half the eye diameter. The fingertips are swollen, and webbing is absent. Prominent tubercles are present beneath the toes, and the inner metatarsal tubercle is oval. The back is smooth, with isolated tubercles. Dorsal coloration is overall brown, sometimes with a darker double-hourglass pattern. The adult male has a single vocal sac, with densely pigmented throat skin.

DISTRIBUTION AND HABITAT (FIG. 20): This species has been collected from northern Angola where it is associated with leaf litter.

ADVERTISEMENT CALL: Unknown.

BREEDING: Breeding begins in November and continues until February or March. Details of the breeding biology are unknown.

NOTES: This otherwise cryptic frog is extremely common at certain times of the year.

Cave Squeaker

Fig. 20 *Schoutedenella lameerei*

KEY REFERENCE: de Witte 1921.

Cave squeaker
Schoutedenella troglodytes (Poynton, 1963)

The specific name *troglodytes* means "cave dwelling."
South Rhodesia screeching frog.

DESCRIPTION: The female may reach 27 mm in length, with the males smaller. The tibia is less than half the body length but longer than the width of the head. The metatarsal tubercle is very small, less than a third the length of the fifth toe. The third finger of the male is elongated, about equal to half of the head width. Discs are absent on the fingers and toes. The pattern of the back is very variable, usually dark patterns on a brown background, with the typical hourglass pattern frequently present.

DISTRIBUTION AND HABITAT (FIG. 21): This rare species is known from northeastern Zimbabwe. It has been found in caves and holes outside forest on the western Chimanimani Mountains above 1500 m.

ADVERTISEMENT CALL: Unknown.

BREEDING: Unknown. Presumably this species is a direct developer.

Fig. 21 *Schoutedenella troglodytes*

NOTES: This species has only been found once, in 1962, despite many subsequent searches. Climbers exploring the Chimanimani Mountains should be aware of this frog and attempt to discover more of its life history. Its conservation status is near threatened.

KEY REFERENCE: Poynton 1963.

Plain squeaker
Schoutedenella xenochirus (Boulenger, 1905)
(Plate 1.5)

The specific name *xenochirus* refers to the "strange hand" with the very elongate third finger in males.
Marimba screeching frog.

DESCRIPTION: This is a small frog, with the female less than 24 mm SVL. The tibia is between a third and a half of the body length, and equal to or slightly more than half of the head width. The metatarsal tubercle is very long and spurlike. It is usually more than half the length of the outer toe. There are no discs, although the tips of the fingers and toes may be slightly swollen. The third finger in the male is very long, four to five times the length of the second finger. The length of the third finger relative to the snout-vent length seems to increase with age. The inner edge of the third finger possesses a row of small spines. Adults tend to have a uniform back

Dwarf Squeaker

Fig. 22 *Schoutedenella xenochirus*

coloration, rose to brick red or tan to gray. The groin and forward areas of the thighs of adults are bright red, visible only when the frogs hop.

DISTRIBUTION AND HABITAT (FIG. 22): This frog is known from northern Malawi, across to northeastern Angola. It is associated with forest patches or streams in open grassland, between 1800 and 2500 m. The plain squeaker is not threatened.

ADVERTISEMENT CALL: The call is a high-pitched trill, consisting of about 7 notes, at a rate of 15/s. The emphasized frequency is 4.6 kHz.

BREEDING: Unknown. Gravid females have been collected in early November.

NOTES: They burrow beneath cover or into sedge tussocks when disturbed.

KEY REFERENCE: Stewart 1967 (as *Arthroleptis xenodactyloides nyikae*).

Dwarf squeaker
Schoutedenella xenodactyloides (Hewitt, 1933)
(Plate 1.6)

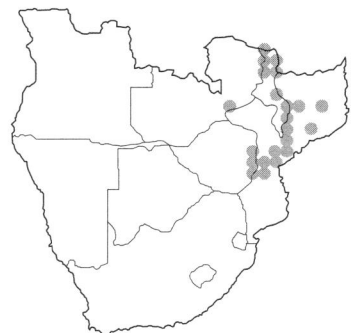

Fig. 23   *Schoutedenella xenodactyloides*

The specific name *xenodactyloides*, meaning "strange finger," refers to the long third finger of the males.
Hewitt's bush squeaker, Chirinda screeching frog.

DESCRIPTION: The adult is small, less than 22 mm SVL, slender, with the tibia between a third and a half of the body length. The metatarsal tubercle is very small, as are the weakly developed tubercles beneath the toes. The third finger in the male is less than two thirds of the width of the head. The digits possess distinct small discs. The hourglass pattern on the brown back is typical, but a pattern of two light dorsolateral stripes is also common. The insides of the thighs and the sides of the body can be reddish brown.

DISTRIBUTION AND HABITAT (FIG. 23): This species is recorded from Mozambique, Malawi, eastern Zimbabwe, eastern Zambia, and eastern Tanzania. This extremely common frog is not easily seen but can be traced from its cricket-like call. It has been found in grassland swamps at high altitudes and in forests at both high and low altitudes.

ADVERTISEMENT CALL: The call is a short cricket-like sound, consisting of about 3 brief clicks at 5.5 kHz. The call can be heard day and night from leaf litter.

BREEDING: The eggs are laid under leaf litter. I found a clutch 200 mm under litter against a wet granite face on the Zomba plateau. Clutch size is 20. Each white egg is 1.5 mm within a 4-mm capsule.

NOTES: It may climb 100 mm up shrubs above the leaf litter and is capable of 50-cm leaps, making it extremely difficult to catch, as it rapidly disappears from view under dead leaves. Frogs were found in the holes made by beetles in a fallen rotten tree trunk. The only recorded predator is the vine snake *Thelotornis capensis*.

KEY REFERENCE: Hewitt 1933.

Toads—Family Bufonidae

This cosmopolitan family includes some of the smallest to some of the largest frogs known. Many members of this family are known as toads, although the appellation is sometimes restricted to species of the genus *Bufo*.

Bufo males were used as substitutes for platannas *Xenopus* for human pregnancy testing in the early days of this technique. Today frogs are no longer used for this test.

Four genera are currently recognized from this area: *Bufo* (23 species), *Capensibufo* (2 species), *Schismaderma* (1 species), and *Stephopaedes* (1 species).

KEY TO THE GENERA
1a. Webbing present, although sometimes very little   2
1b. Webbing absent   *Capensibufo*

2a. Parotid glands present (Fig. 24)   3
2b. Parotid glands absent   *Schismaderma carens*

Fig. 24 Parotid glands

3a. Tarsal fold present (Fig. 25)   *Bufo* (part)
3b. Tarsal fold absent   4

Toads—Family Bufonidae

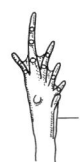

Fig. 25 Tarsal fold

4a. Throat not granular, parotid glands indistinct   *Bufo* (part)
4b. Throat very granular, parotid glands distinct
                                                 Stephopaedes anotis

Toads—Genus *Bufo*

The eye possesses a horizontal pupil, usually with a lower notch. The skin is thick and warty. The skin glands, especially the enlarged parotid glands behind the eyes, secrete an irritant that serves to deter predators. Despite their poisonous skin secretions, toads are caught in pit traps and eaten by the Mossi people from Upper Volta.

Large toads may be found far from water, and the smaller species are often found in mountainous areas. Toads frequently are found in disturbed habitats, and the larger toads are known to hybridize in such places. The construction of channels and dams seems to confuse the toads, permitting stream-breeding and pond-breeding species to be present in the same artificial habitat, and is known to lead to hybridization. Hybrids have been recognized by their advertisement call being intermediate between the calls of the parental species. Natural hybrids have been demonstrated from crosses of the guttural toad *B. gutturalis* and Ranger's toad *B. rangeri* in southern Africa. *Bufo* tadpoles produce a skin secretion when injured, which stimulates the "fright reaction" in other *Bufo* tadpoles, causing them to rapidly disperse. Toads are valuable agents of pest control and an important link in the food chain.

Some species of toads remain unknown; for example, Plate 2.1 illustrates a toad from northwestern Zambia that has not yet been formally named.

KEY TO THE SPECIES
1a. Tarsal fold present (see Fig. 25)   2
1b. Tarsal fold absent   15

2a. Skin smooth, parotids flattened and smooth   *Bufo robinsoni*
2a. Dorsal skin and parotids granular   3

3a. Throat not as granular as lower abdomen   4
3b. Throat as granular as lower abdomen   6

4a. Only two phalanges of third toe free of webbing (Fig. 26)   5
4b. At least two and a half phalanges of third toe free   14

Fig. 26   Two phalanges free of web

5a. Length of outer metatarsal tubercle about equal to half length of inner   *Bufo angusticeps*
5b. Length of outer metatarsal tubercle greater than half length of inner   *Bufo amatolicus*

6a. A prominent glandular ridge or series of tubercles on lower surface of forearm   7
6b. No such ridge or series of tubercles   10

7a. A light cross on head formed by light interocular bar and median line (Fig. 27)   8
7b. No light cross on top of head   12

Fig. 27   Cross marking

8a. Parotid glands prominent, not partly obscured by dark-tipped warts   9
8b. Parotid glands flattened and obscured by dark-tipped warts   *Bufo maculatus*

Toads—Family Bufonidae

9a. Parotid glands continue posteriorly as a pair of glandular ridges (Fig. 28) *Bufo lemairii*
9b. Parotid glands not continuing posteriorly 11

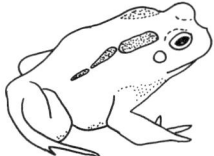

Fig. 28 Elongated parotids

10a. No spines around tympanum, yellow vertebral stripe 27
10b. Spines around tympanum, no yellow vertebral stripe
Bufo fuliginatus

11a. Tibia length less than 41% of body length (Fig. 29)
Bufo kisoloensis
11b. Tibia length more than 41% of body length *Bufo gutturalis*

Fig. 29 Tibia-body length comparison

12a. Dark interocular bar divided, with red markings on thigh 13
12b. No red marks on upper thigh, dark interocular bar absent or not divided if present *Bufo rangeri*

13a. Foot length less than 40% of body length (Fig. 30)
Bufo poweri
13b. Foot length more than 40% of body length *Bufo garmani*

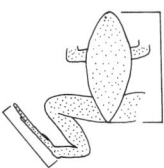

Fig. 30 Foot-body length comparison

14a. Length of outer metatarsal tubercle greater than half length of inner   *Bufo gariepensis*
14b. Length of outer metatarsal tubercle less than half length of inner
    Bufo inyangae

15a. A row of spinose tubercles along inside of tarsus
    Bufo funereus
15b. No trace of tarsal fold or row of tubercles   16

16a. Tympanum visible (Fig. 31)   17
16b. Tympanum not visible   24

Fig. 31   Tympanum

17a. Horizontal diameter of tympanum greater than internarial distance   *Bufo grandisonae*
17b. Tympanum size less than internarial distance (Fig. 32)   18

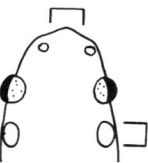

Fig. 32   Tympanum size–internarial distance comparison

18a. Outer margin of parotid glands distinct and straight   19
18b. Outer margin of parotids not distinct, or curved down   20

19a. A light vertebral line often present, no ventral markings
    Bufo kavangensis
19b. No light vertebral line, ventral markings present
    Bufo urunguensis

20a. Skin of snout and throat not, or only slightly, granular   22
20b. Skin of throat and snout granular   21

21a. No ventral markings   *Bufo fenoulheti*
21b. Dark ventral markings present   *Bufo beiranus*

22a. Ventral surface distinctly marked   *Bufo vertebralis*
22b. Ventral surface immaculate   23

23a. Toes with a distinct margin of webbing   *Bufo hoeschi*
23b. Toes without a distinct margin of webbing *Bufo dombensis*

24a. Pectoral markings in the form of a trident   *Bufo taitanus*
24b. Ventral markings not forming a trident pattern   25

25a. Outer margin of parotid markedly curving downward behind otic region   *Bufo lindneri*
25b. Outer margin of parotid more or less straight   26

26a. Very small, body length not more than 27 mm
                                            Bufo melanopleura
26b. Medium sized, reaching 44 mm long   *Bufo nyikae*

27a. Present in the Western Cape Province   *Bufo pantherinus*
27b. Present in the Eastern Cape and KwaZulu-Natal provinces
                                            Bufo pardalis

Amatola toad

Bufo amatolicus Hewitt, 1925
(Plate 1.7)

The specific epithet *amatolicus* refers to the Amatola Mountains, where this species was first collected.

DESCRIPTION: This is a small dark toad, with a maximum female length of 37 mm SVL. An umbraculum (a small outgrowth of the top of the pupil that protects the eye from sunlight) is present. The back is warty. The parotid glands are conspicuous, the front wider than the back. The inner metatarsal tubercle is well developed, and the outer metatarsal tubercle is at least half as long as the inner. The tarsal fold may be more or less distinct and is usually flattened. Two segments of the third toe are free of web. The toes are not fringed with webbing. The back is generally dark, yet a pattern is visible in many speci-

Fig. 33 *Bufo amatolicus*

mens, although it is not very distinct. A pale thin vertebral line is present in some animals.

DISTRIBUTION AND HABITAT (FIG. 33): This toad is known from the Amatola Mountains and adjacent ranges, with a similar but unidentified population on the Kamanassie Mountains. They are found in grasslands in the mist belt. This species is regarded as near threatened in terms of the IUCN Red List categories.

ADVERTISEMENT CALL: Males congregate in flooded grassland after rain and call concealed under grass. The advertisement calls can be heard during the daytime, reaching a peak after dark. The call is a brief nasal squawk, with a long interval between calls. The call has a dominant frequency range of 1.9–3.1 kHz, with a duration of 320 ms.

BREEDING: Breeding takes place after heavy spring rains from October to December. The eggs are laid in a single string. Each egg is 2 mm in diameter, within a 3.6-mm tube. The clutch size has been estimated as a few hundred. The eggs are laid in shallow water and may be very difficult to see in vegetation and against a muddy substrate.

TADPOLES: See the chapter on tadpoles.

NOTES: These frogs are common around pools in the Hogsback. During the breeding season they are very abundant, about $5/m^2$ at the breeding site.

KEY REFERENCE: Wager 1986.

Sand toad
Bufo angusticeps Smith, 1848
(Plate 1.8)

The specific name *angusticeps* means "narrow head."
Cape toad.

DESCRIPTION: This small frog resembles a half-grown common toad at first glance. Females may reach 58 mm in snout-vent length. The tarsal fold is distinct and ridged. The inner metatarsal tubercle is narrow and well developed, while the outer metatarsal tubercle is about half the length of the inner. An umbraculum is present. Fingers and toes possess a margin of web. Two segments of the third toe are free of web. The parotid glands are conspicuous but narrow. Rough warts cover the back, with a pattern consisting of a series of rectangular dark blotches on a brown background. A thin pale vertebral line is often present. The upper surfaces of the feet are yellow, with darker markings.

DISTRIBUTION AND HABITAT (FIG. 34): This species is known from the Cape Flats, and northward where soils are sandy.

ADVERTISEMENT CALL: Calls were recorded in flooded agricultural land on the Cape Flats in winter. The call is a high-pitched croak. It is pulsed, 0.3-s long, with the emphasized frequency at 1.5–1.7 kHz.

Fig. 34 *Bufo angusticeps*

The calling males are difficult to locate, as the calls are widely spaced, and the frogs become silent as one approaches.

BREEDING: Eggs are laid during June, July, and August in shallow temporary pools. The eggs are 1–2 mm in diameter, in strings 5–7 mm wide. Clutch size is 650–3000 eggs. Many clutches of eggs from the same female are often laid in the same pool. Sometimes a new clutch is laid in the same pool for three or four successive nights.

TADPOLES: See the chapter on tadpoles.

NOTES: Unusual food items recorded are snails.

KEY REFERENCE: Rose 1962.

Beira toad
Bufo beiranus Loveridge, 1932

The epithet *beiranus* refers to Beira in Mozambique, where this frog was first found.

DESCRIPTION: This is a small toad, with the female reaching 25 mm in length and the males being smaller. The tarsal fold is absent, and the tympanum is not visible. Parotid glands are present but not conspicuous. Two or more segments of the third toe are free of web. The dorsal pattern is dark, with a light vertebral line often present. Sometimes this line is absent, replaced by a light area in the shoulder region. A pale spot may be present on the back of the head. Gray flecking is usually present on the underside.

DISTRIBUTION AND HABITAT (FIG. 35): This small frog is known from the coastal plain around Beira, to southeastern Zambia. It is found in grassy areas that flood during the rains. More fieldwork is required to investigate its preferred habitat.

ADVERTISEMENT CALL: Unknown.

BREEDING: Unknown.

TADPOLES: Unknown.

Dombe Toad

Fig. 35 *Bufo beiranus*

NOTES: Until the advertisement call has been recorded, the status of this species and its relationships to other dwarf toads will remain uncertain. Some very useful fieldwork could be done by anyone with a tape recorder and a tadpole net during the rainy season when these frogs are breeding.

KEY REFERENCE: Loveridge 1932.

Dombe toad
Bufo dombensis Bocage, 1895
(Plate 2.2)

This species is named for Dombe in Angola, where it was first found.

DESCRIPTION: This is a small toad, with females reaching 40 mm and the male up to 36 mm in length. The tympanum is clearly visible and is equal in size to three-fourths of the distance between the nostrils. The parotid glands are flattened. A row of glands is present between the upper jaw and the arm insertion. The tubercles beneath the toes are usually double. Webbing is reduced, only reaching the base of the fourth toe. There are no spines on the top of the head and no belly markings. The pattern of the back is similar to that on other dwarf toads, with a light neck patch and various darker markings. A light vertebral line is sometimes present.

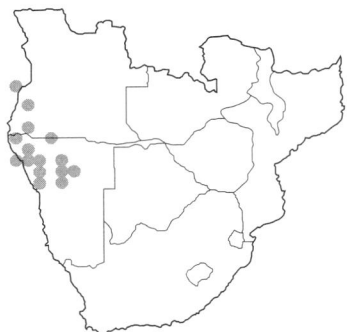

Fig. 36 *Bufo dombensis*

DISTRIBUTION AND HABITAT (FIG. 36): This frog is only known from the coastal lowlands of Angola and northwestern Namibia. It is found in grassland where there are rock outcrops.

ADVERTISEMENT CALL: The males commence calling around midnight. The call consists of a series of short 0.2-s bleats, at a rate of about 2 bleats/s. Each consists of a number of indistinct harmonics between 2 and 3.5 kHz, with emphasized frequencies at 2.9 kHz.

BREEDING: The eggs are laid in strings that soon collect as a cup-sized accumulation in small depressions and between river stones. One pair deposited a string of 900 uniformly black eggs measuring 1.6–1.8 mm in diameter.

TADPOLES: See the chapter on tadpoles.

KEY REFERENCES: Poynton & Haacke 1993, Channing & Vences 1999.

Fenoulhet's toad
Bufo fenoulheti Hewitt & Methuen, 1913
(Plate 2.3)

This frog is named for the collector, J. P. Fenoulhet.
Pygmy toad, Fenoulheti's pygmy toad, Newington toad.

Fenoulhet's Toad

DESCRIPTION: This is a small flat toad, with females reaching 43 mm in snout-vent length. The tarsal fold is absent and the snout is granular. Two and a half segments of the third toe are free of web. The pattern of the back is similar to that on many other small toads: gray overall, with a darker pattern of blotches, often with a pale blotch on the midline. The undersurface is white, but specimens with a few dark spots are known. The breeding male has a deep orange throat.

DISTRIBUTION AND HABITAT (FIG. 37): This species is known from northeastern South Africa, Zimbabwe, Mozambique, and eastern Botswana into the Caprivi Strip of Namibia. It is found in open bush and grassland and on granite inselbergs.

ADVERTISEMENT CALL: The male calls from the edge of small pools, often sitting near rocks, or even 150 mm above shallow water while clinging to grass. The call is a long, high-pitched creaking. Each call is about 0.5 s long, with a pulse rate of 70/s. Calls can be uttered in pairs, in rapid succession, at an emphasized frequency of 3.2 kHz. The release call is a series of clucks.

BREEDING: The eggs are 1.8 mm in diameter, black at one pole and gray at the other. They are laid in a pair of gelatinous egg strings 2.7 mm thick and 200 mm long. Size of one clutch was 245.

TADPOLES: See the chapter on tadpoles.

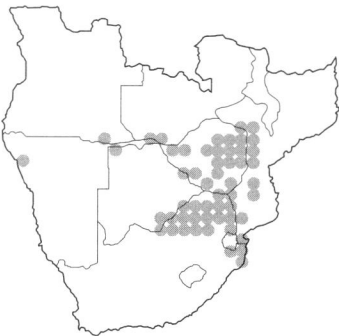

Fig. 37 *Bufo fenoulheti*

NOTES: Metamorphosis is rapid. Froglets leave the water only 18 days after the eggs are laid. Adults have been found on top of a small inselberg at Misika in Mozambique. They were sheltering under matted grass roots in a dry granite tank. Up to nine individuals have been found sheltering together during the day, often with scorpions and lizards.

KEY REFERENCES: Power 1927a, Wager 1986.

Sooty toad
Bufo fuliginatus Witte, 1932

The specific name *fuliginatus* means "sooty," referring to the uniform coloration.
Shaba Province toad.

DESCRIPTION: This is a medium-sized toad, with the male reaching 40 mm and the female 65 mm SVL. A serrated tarsal fold and tympanum are present. Two indistinct rows of tubercles mark the position of glands under the forearm. The parotid glands are prominent. Webbing is moderate, with two or less segments of the third and fifth toes free of web. The back is spiny. Males lack vocal sacs and are without darker throats. A dark eye-stripe extends from the eye onto the snout, but the back is nearly uniform brown, without strong contrasts, or a yellow vertebral stripe.

DISTRIBUTION AND HABITAT (FIG. 38): This little-known toad has been recorded from Zambia. It has been collected from forest edges.

ADVERTISEMENT CALL: Each call consists of a rapid series of pulses, with dominant energy at 1.9 kHz. The call duration is 0.25–0.6 s.

BREEDING: No details on the breeding biology are known for this species. Females exhibit a cyclic breeding pattern, with a peak in the rainy season. Frogs that live in forests can be expected to have very interesting breeding behavior and tadpoles. This species would be very rewarding to study.

TADPOLES: Unknown.

Somber Toad 69

Fig. 38 *Bufo fuliginatus*

KEY REFERENCE: Inger & Greenberg 1956.

Somber toad
Bufo funereus Bocage, 1866

The name *funereus* means "somber."
Angola toad.

DESCRIPTION: This is a medium-sized frog, with the male reaching 51 mm and the female 60 mm in snout-vent length. The tarsal fold is absent, replaced by a row of small spinous tubercles. The tympanum is smaller than the eye. The parotid gland is slightly more than twice as long as wide, oval, and distinctly marked. Limbs are short, and the back is a dark, overall brown. A distinct light band is found between the eyes. A pale vertebral stripe is sometimes present. The upper jaw is marked with contrasting light and dark bands.

DISTRIBUTION AND HABITAT (FIG. 39): This frog is known from Angola and the northern Democratic Republic of the Congo, extending northward to West Africa. It is found in rain forests and open forests.

ADVERTISEMENT CALL: Unknown. Males lack vocal sacs and this species may not produce an advertisement call.

BREEDING: This species breeds from August to January, although females have ripe ova for most of the year. Females and juve-

Fig. 39 *Bufo funereus*

niles possess spines on the back, but these are absent in breeding males.

TADPOLES: Unknown.

NOTES: This frog is common in limited areas. Recorded food items include earthworms, snails, arthropods, and the puddle frog *Phrynobatrachus anotis*.

KEY REFERENCES: Inger & Greenberg 1956, Perret 1966.

Karoo toad
Bufo gariepensis Smith, 1848
(Plate 2.4)

The specific name *gariepensis* refers to the Gariep River, from where this species was described.
Karoo-skurwepadda in Afrikaans.

DESCRIPTION: This is one of the larger toads, with the female reaching 95 mm SVL. The tarsal fold is well developed. The inner metatarsal tubercle is rounded and less than half the length of the outer. Two and a half segments of the third toe are free of web. The parotid glands are very large, about twice as long as the anterior width. The back is covered with rough warts, with a pattern consisting of dark brown or maroon rounded blotches on a background

Karoo Toad

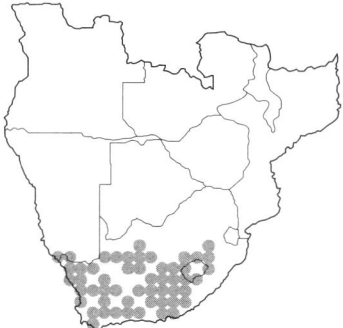

Fig. 40 *Bufo gariepensis*

of brown or olive brown. The underside is off-white. Juveniles and some adults have a few dark spots on a white belly.

DISTRIBUTION AND HABITAT (FIG. 40): This frog is known from the Karoo and inland areas of South Africa and Lesotho, drained by the Orange River, and from high on the Drakensberg Mountains. It is found in rocky areas and in dry thornbush.

ADVERTISEMENT CALL: The male utters a low squawk and is well separated from others while calling. The call has dominant harmonics between 1.5 and 2 kHz, with a duration of 380 ms. The call is repeated after an interval of about 600 ms.

BREEDING: This species breeds from September through February. The eggs are small, 1.5 mm in diameter, and dark and are laid in long, 7-mm-wide strings. These may be entwined among wet vegetation in waterlogged depressions. Animals breeding at high altitudes over 2000 m on the Drakensberg have fewer, larger eggs.

TADPOLES: See the chapter on tadpoles.

NOTES: These frogs tend to run rather than hop. Adults have been found in termite mounds.

KEY REFERENCE: Visser 1979.

Garman's toad
Bufo garmani Meek, 1897
(Plate 2.5)

This species is named for the ichthyologist S. W. Garman, of the Museum of Comparative Zoology at Harvard.
Light-nosed toad, olive toad. *Olyfskurwepadda* in Afrikaans.

DESCRIPTION: A large toad, with the female reaching 115 mm and the male 106 mm in length. The parotid glands are conspicuous. The species is similar to the guttural toad *B. gutturalis*, from which it is easily distinguished on the basis of color pattern. This species has long been confused with Power's toad *B. poweri*, in the west, but differs from that species by having a relatively longer foot more than 40% of SVL. The back is covered by warts, each with a dark tip. The tympanum is less than half the diameter of the eye. Three to four segments of the fourth toe are free of webbing. The back varies, being reddish brown in Malawi, to tan in Zimbabwe. The markings are edged with black. The top of the head is characteristically free of darker markings, and the bars behind the eyes do not fuse. Red patches are found on the backs of the thighs.

DISTRIBUTION AND HABITAT (FIG. 41): This species is known from the northeastern parts of South Africa, Zimbabwe, and northward. Fieldwork is required to determine the eastern boundaries of this species, the western boundaries of Power's toad *B. poweri*, and

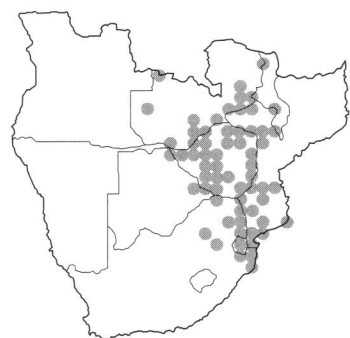

Fig. 41 *Bufo garmani*

the degree and kind of interaction between these two. This widely distributed frog can be described as a savanna inhabitant.

ADVERTISEMENT CALL: The call is a loud "kwaak," similar to Power's toad. It is, however, slower pulsed than a *B. poweri* call. Call duration varies from 0.2 to 0.9 s, with pulse rates of 50–105/s.

BREEDING: Black eggs measuring 1.2 mm are laid in two strings. Between 12,000 and 20,000 eggs are produced per clutch. At Bubi River a pair laid 1250 eggs one night, 25/100 mm of string. When laid, the eggs are 0.8 mm in diameter. Eggs are laid from September through January, although these toads may breed throughout the year when artificial ponds are available.

TADPOLES: See the chapter on tadpoles.

NOTES: During breeding, males attempt to grasp any female within reach. Females that are not ready to breed signal the male to release them by quivering and arching the back. Eggs are eaten by the terrapin *Pelusios sinuatus*, Müller's platanna *Xenopus muelleri*, and even Garman's toad *B. garmani* tadpoles. Young crocodiles eat the adult toads. Displaced toads are able to return to a specific pond from up to a kilometer.

KEY REFERENCES: Taylor 1982, Channing 1991.

Grandison's toad
Bufo grandisonae Poynton & Haacke, 1993

This species was named for Alice G. C. Grandison, who worked on dwarf African toads while based at the Natural History Museum, London.
Mossamedes toad.

DESCRIPTION: This species is only known from a few specimens collected in Angola. It is a small toad, with the largest female 38 mm and the only known male 33 mm SVL. This species is characterized by a very large, clearly defined tympanum, which has a horizontal diameter exceeding the distance between the nostrils. Parotid glands are not visible, but a glandular mass is present behind the tympanum,

Fig. 42 *Bufo grandisonae*

with two smaller masses below the tympanum. Tubercles beneath the fingers are usually single, except the outer tubercle of the third finger is double. Webbing is very reduced, with no margin of web on the toes. The markings consist of a light patch on the head and neck region, with a pair of light patches on the lower back. There are no belly markings.

DISTRIBUTION AND HABITAT (FIG. 42): This dwarf toad is only known only from the coastal region of Angola. The habitat is granite inselbergs on a sandy base.

ADVERTISEMENT CALL: Unknown.

BREEDING: Unknown.

TADPOLE: Unknown.

KEY REFERENCE: Poynton & Haacke 1993.

Guttural toad
Bufo gutturalis Power, 1927
(Plate 2.6)

The specific name *gutturalis* refers to the loud advertisement call. Leopard toad, square-marked toad, greater cross-marked toad, common toad, Lobatsi toad. *Gorrelskurwepadda* in Afrikaans; *Ixoxo*,

Guttural Toad

idemfu, *chimboto* in Angola; *rume* at Cap Delgado; *bota* in Chewa; *likelle* at Inhambane; *tchizunda* in Lwena; *napulo* or *numeu* on Mozambique Island; *makelle* at Maputo; *chula* at Misuku; *chimboto* in Muanha; *chule* in Yao and Nyanja; *chula tengu* in Nyungwe; *otchimbota* in Quimbundu; *ixoxo* or *isogode* in Xhosa.

DESCRIPTION: This is probably the most common toad in the area. It is large, with the female reaching 120 mm SVL. The glands under the forearm form a distinct row of pale tubercles that are never fused into a ridge. The parotid glands are large and without warts. The tibia is more than 41% of SVL. The back pattern provides the easiest means of identification, as the markings usually are arranged in pairs, outlined in a darker brown. A pale cross is present on the top of the head, with the transverse bar running between the eyes. Frequently a thin vertebral line is present. Red patches are present behind the thighs and in the groin, and are especially prominent in breeding animals. The ventral surface is white. Breeding males possess dark throats.

DISTRIBUTION AND HABITAT (FIG. 43): This widespread species is known from all the countries covered in this book, but is absent from southern South Africa and southern Namibia. It is found in thornbush and is common in towns around buildings.

ADVERTISEMENT CALL: The male calls from shallow water near the edge of a pool, and very large calling aggregations may be formed. The

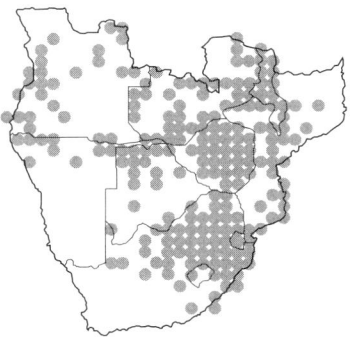

Fig. 43   *Bufo gutturalis*

call is loud and can be heard from some distance. It is a slow, pulsed snore. The individual pulses are usually clearly audible. The dominant frequency varies from 1.0 to 1.3 kHz. Each call consists of about 15–20 pulses, with a duration of 0.8–1.2 s. A characteristic of the voice of this species is that pairs of males call alternately. This behavior is referred to as *antiphony*. This leaves the impression of an "up-down, up-down" sound. A male guttural toad will also call antiphonally with a male of another species. The male possesses a single, pale vocal sac.

BREEDING: The female is approached by the male but only after she enters the breeding pool. The male apparently reacts to the stimulus of the female disturbing the water surface. A male will attempt to displace other males in amplexus, with the larger male usually winning. A pair will lay between 15,000 and 25,000 eggs in one clutch. The eggs are small, 1.4–1.5 mm in diameter, with one black pole. The eggs are produced in two gelatinous strings, each 5 mm thick, with about 6 eggs/cm along a newly laid string. The eggs are laid in shallow water at the edge of pools, often wound in and around vegetation. The species breeds throughout the year over much of its range but is seasonal in the south. For example, these toads breed throughout the year in Malawi, and females may lay two clutches per year in the north of South Africa, although the males are able to breed repeatedly.

TADPOLES: See the chapter on tadpoles.

SKIN SECRETIONS: If handled roughly, these toads secrete a white milky fluid from the parotid glands. This very sticky fluid will cause the death of other species of frogs that are placed in a bag together with the toad. Toads should not be placed together with other species of frogs for this reason. One of the compounds identified in the parotid secretion is epinephrine (adrenaline). Small mammals up to 5 kg will vomit and die if they absorb small amounts of the secretion.

NOTES: Toads become quite used to humans and will happily return to the lighted veranda of a house night after night to feed on moths and beetles. There are records of toads even spending the days under wardrobes or under floorboards in older houses.

Known food includes insects, earthworms, centipedes, spiders, scorpions, lizards, and other frogs like the common squeaker *Arthroleptis stenodactylus* and tree frogs *Leptopelis*. The tadpoles are eaten by dwarf bream *Pseudocrenilabrus philander*, platannas *Xenopus*, water insects, and birds. The cobra *Naja nigricollis*, the night adder *Causus rhombeatus*, and the green snake *Philothamnus angolensis* eat adults. Other known predators include the serrated terrapin *Pelusios sinuatus* and the African civet *Viverra civetta*. The toads are not defenseless, however, as the parotid secretion is a powerful poison.

Molting takes 1–2 hours, and they may molt every 3–5 days. Molting is more frequent with increasing light. Maximum longevity in captivity is recorded as 7 years. This species is hybridizing with Ranger's toad *Bufo rangeri* at Port St. Johns and in many other localities.

KEY REFERENCES: Low 1972, Wager 1986, Telford & van Sickle 1989.

Hoesch's toad
Bufo hoeschi Ahl, 1934
(Plate 2.7)

This species was named for the Namibian herpetologist and collector W. Hoesch.
Okahandja toad.

DESCRIPTION: This is a small toad, with the female up to 37 mm in length. The tympanum is not visible. The parotid glands are variable; sometimes they are distinct but they may be flattened. Toes with a distinct margin of webbing. The pattern of the back consists of lighter and darker markings with a prominent lighter neck patch. Pale projections from this spot may run to each upper eyelid, and a pale vertebral line or band may run backward to the sacrum.

DISTRIBUTION AND HABITAT (FIG. 44): This small toad is known from the central and western parts of Namibia. It occurs in very dry areas and is associated with rock outcrops.

ADVERTISEMENT CALL: The male calls from the edge of rock pools.

Fig. 44 *Bufo hoeschi*

The call is a short chirp, with each chirp consisting of about 17 pulses, uttered at a pulse rate of 170/s. The duration of each call is 0.1 s, and the calls are repeated rapidly, 3/s. Males only call after the first heavy rains, and then only for a few nights.

BREEDING: In the Namib Desert, oviposition occurs in shallow, sandy-bottomed pools. Eggs are laid in strings, with a clutch size of 400. Eggs develop into free-swimming tadpoles within 48 hours.

TADPOLES: See the chapter on tadpoles.

NOTES: Adults and subadults have been found actively foraging on bare rock in full sunlight during the heat of the day in the Namib. Even the tadpoles are able to withstand high temperatures. One pool containing tadpoles at Bluttkoppie in the Namib Desert Park reached 36°C during the day.

KEY REFERENCE: Channing 1976a.

Inyanga toad
Bufo inyangae Poynton, 1963
(Plate 2.8)

This species is named for the Inyanga area of eastern Zimbabwe, where it was first discovered.

Inyanga Toad

DESCRIPTION: This is a small toad, with the female reaching 47 mm in length. Head width is about one-third of body length. The tympanum is distinct, and the pupil possesses a small umbraculum, which serves as a sunshade. The tarsal fold is not well developed, being present only as a small glandular ridge. The inner metatarsal tubercle is elongated, nearly twice as long as the outer. Two and a half segments of the third toe are free of webbing. The parotid glands are distinct, their anterior width being about one-third their length. The back is warty, and the posterior warts have small black spines. The back pattern consists of dark brown markings on a lighter background. The belly pattern is very variable.

DISTRIBUTION AND HABITAT (FIG. 45): This frog is only known from the mountains forming the border between Zimbabwe and Mozambique, and adjacent isolated granite domes. They have been found under rocks and in cracks in the granite.

ADVERTISEMENT CALL: Unknown.

BREEDING: Details are unknown. Eggs have been found in rocky pools.

TADPOLES: The tadpoles have not been described, although they have been found in small pools or moving across wet granite faces.

KEY REFERENCE: Poynton 1963.

Fig. 45 *Bufo inyangae*

Kavango toad
Bufo kavangensis Poynton & Broadley, 1988

This species is named for the Kavango River.
Kavanga toad, Khwai river toad.

DESCRIPTION: This is a small toad, with the female up to 33 mm and the male reaching 30 mm SVL. The tubercles beneath the fingers are double, and the outer edge of the parotid gland is straight, with no bulge behind the tympanum. There is very little webbing, not extending beyond the first segment of the fourth toe, with a serrated margin along the toes. The vertical diameter of the tympanum is equal to the distance between the nostrils. The pattern of the back consists of a vertebral line, with various darker patches, including a band between the eyes and pairs of darker markings along the back. The lower surface is cream, with a yellow throat in males.

DISTRIBUTION AND HABITAT (FIG. 46): This species is known from the sandy areas of northern Namibia and southern Angola, northern Botswana, and western Zimbabwe, associated with temporary pools.

ADVERTISEMENT CALL: Males call from flooded grassland, while clinging to emergent grass stems about 100 mm above the water. The call consists of a series of short buzzes.

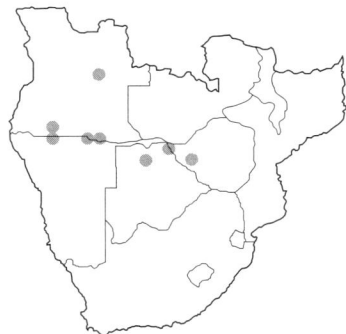

Fig. 46 *Bufo kavangensis*

BREEDING: Unknown.

TADPOLES: Unknown.

KEY REFERENCE: Poynton & Broadley 1988.

Kisolo toad
Bufo kisoloensis Loveridge, 1932
(Plate 3.1)

This species is named for the town of Kisolo in Uganda.

DESCRIPTION: This is a large toad, with the male up to 69 mm and the female 87 mm long. It is an aquatic species, with a pointed snout, slender tapering fingers, and extensive webbing that reaches or nearly reaches the tips of the toes, except the fourth one. The tympanum is distinct but smaller than the eye. The tibia is less than 41% of SVL. The parotid glands are two or three times wider than long. The male has a smooth back with flattened warts, while the female has a granular warty back. Coloration is a uniform olive, sometimes with darker markings. A light thin vertebral line is often present. The breeding male can be easily identified, as it is a bright yellow.

DISTRIBUTION AND HABITAT (FIG. 47): The Kisolo toad is known from the highland areas of northern Malawi and northeastern Zambia, northward to the Republic of the Congo, the Democratic

Fig. 47 *Bufo kisoloensis*

Republic of the Congo, Rwanda, Uganda, and Kenya. It is found in cool, moist montane forests.

ADVERTISEMENT CALL: The male calls from shallow streams, partly beneath vegetation. The call is a slow snore, about a second long, repeated rapidly. The emphasized frequency is around 600 Hz. The pulse rate is 66/s.

BREEDING: The male turns a bright yellow for the few hours while calling and during amplexus. Details of egg laying are unknown.

TADPOLES: See the chapter on tadpoles.

KEY REFERENCES: Curry-Lindahl 1956, Channing & Drewes 1997.

Lemaire's toad
Bufo lemairii Boulenger, 1901
(Plate 3.2)

This toad was named for the Lemaire expedition to the Democratic Republic of the Congo.
Lemair's toad, Pweto toad. *Tchizunda* in Lwena.

DESCRIPTION: The female reaches 70 mm and the male, 65 mm in length. This species is aquatic, resembling the common frogs in overall shape, including well-developed webbing. The tympanum is distinct and as large as the eye. The parotid glands continue backward to the sacral region as a glandular ridge. The feet are moderately webbed, with two or just more than two segments of the third toe free of web. The head is narrow, and the legs are long. Coloration is variable, usually greenish or reddish, often with a pale vertebral line. A light bar is found between the eyes, bordered by darker markings that do not meet at the midline. There is a red infusion on the inner surface of the thigh during the breeding season.

DISTRIBUTION AND HABITAT (FIG. 48): This species is known from northern Botswana, eastern Angola, and western Zambia to southern Democratic Republic of the Congo and has also been collected in the Caprivi Strip in Namibia. This toad always is found near permanent water, unlike many other species in this genus.

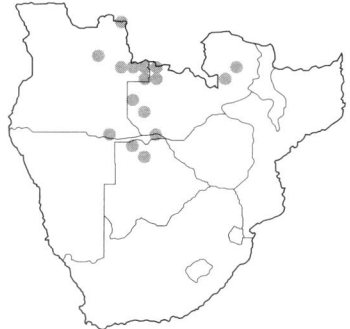

Fig. 48 *Bufo lemairii*

ADVERTISEMENT CALL: Males call from flooded grass. A call recorded in the Okavango Delta was a short creak of 0.06 s. It consists of 3 pulses with a broad band of energy between 2.5 and 4.1 kHz.

BREEDING: Unknown.

TADPOLES: Unknown.

KEY REFERENCE: Poynton & Broadley 1988.

Lindner's toad
Bufo lindneri Mertens, 1955

This frog was named for the collector Erwin Lindner, head of the Entomology Department at the State Museum of Natural History in Stuttgart.
Dar-es-Salaam toad.

DESCRIPTION: The female reaches 34 mm and the largest male, 21 mm in length. The skin is rough and spinose, except for the terminal phalanges that are smooth. The head is as wide as long. The nostrils are separated by a groove. The distance between the eyes is about equal to the width of the eyelid. The parotid glands are more than twice as long as wide and narrower posteriorly curving downward behind otic region. Finger and toe tips are somewhat pointed.

Fig. 49 *Bufo lindneri*

Two palmar tubercles are present. Only a little webbing is found between the toes. The throat is covered with small spines. Each spine in turn is surrounded by a ring of smaller white spines. The back is gray to brown, with orange to red tubercles. The color pattern is characteristic, with a vertebral stripe originating between the shoulders. Darker inclined markings are present on the snout and upper eyelid. Below, the back of the throat to the belly is marked with a series of gray flecks.

DISTRIBUTION AND HABITAT (FIG. 49): This frog has been collected from southern Tanzania, Malawi, and Mozambique. It is found in sandy areas with open bush.

ADVERTISEMENT CALL: Unknown.

BREEDING: Unknown.

TADPOLES: Unknown.

NOTES: This frog inhabits thicket in areas that were probably formerly forested. Specimens have also been collected from fallow fields.

KEY REFERENCE: Clarke 1989.

Flat-backed toad
Bufo maculatus Hallowell, 1854
(Plate 3.3)

Flat-Backed Toad

The specific name *maculatus* refers to the darker spots on the back. Lesser cross-marked toad, Hallowell's toad.

DESCRIPTION: This is a medium to large toad, with the female reaching 80 mm in length. A distinct row of white tubercles is present under the forearm. The back is warty, and each wart has a sharp dark tip. These warts are prominent in sexually active animals. The tympanum is less than one-half the eye diameter in males, although slightly larger in females. The parotid glands are large and obscured by smaller dark-tipped warts, but the edges are flattened and indistinct, giving the frog its common name—the flat-backed toad. A thin pale vertebral line is often present. A light cross is present on top of the head. The pattern of the back resembles that of the guttural toad *B. gutturalis*, with which it could be confused. However, the flat-backed toad does not possess the red marks on the thighs that the guttural toad has. The underside is off-white, often with darker speckles.

DISTRIBUTION AND HABITAT (FIG. 50): This frog is known from northeastern South Africa, northern Botswana, and Namibia, northward. It is associated with river banks, although it is found away from water in open savanna.

ADVERTISEMENT CALL: The male calls from the edge of pools and rivers, concealed under vegetation and well spaced. Each call has a duration of 0.5 s, with dominant harmonics between 1.8 and 2.1 kHz.

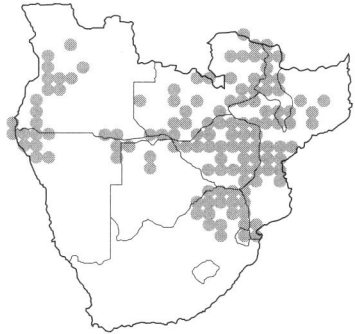

Fig. 50 *Bufo maculatus*

The male may call antiphonally. Calling starts at sundown along the Kavango River, peaking at intervals through the night, with a major peak as dawn breaks. During the day, calling may be initiated by mechanical noises, for example, an aircraft droning overhead. Choruses on one side of the Zambezi River are known to initiate calling by frogs across the river.

BREEDING: The female must make contact with the calling male before he will clasp her. Eggs are laid in a string 3 mm thick. Each egg is 1.2 mm in diameter.

TADPOLES: See the chapter on tadpoles.

NOTES: Sandflies are known to feed on this toad. Predators include the night adder *Causus rhombeatus*.

KEY REFERENCES: Stewart 1967, Wager 1986.

Dark-sided toad
Bufo melanopleura Schmidt & Inger, 1959

The specific epithet *melanopleura* refers to the darkly pigmented sides of the body.
Kankunde toad.

DESCRIPTION: This is a small toad, with the male up to 22 mm and the female reaching only 27 mm in length. This frog possesses no tympanum or internal ear. The parotids are flattened, with the outer edge of the gland straight. Webbing is reduced, with the broad web only just reaching the outer segment of the fourth toe. Conspicuous small pale spines are present on the back of both sexes. Patterning on the back may be absent or may consist of pairs of elongated markings. The sides of the body are darker than the top. The underside is marked with a dark patch in the belly region that narrows to the front. Some individuals have darker markings under the arm that may join with the belly patch.

DISTRIBUTION AND HABITAT (FIG. 51): This frog has been collected from southern Democratic Republic of the Congo, with one

Nyika Dwarf Toad

Fig. 51 *Bufo melanopleura*

specimen collected from south of Ndola in Zambia. This toad is found in forest.

ADVERTISEMENT CALL: This toad does not have an advertisement call.

BREEDING: Unknown. Up to 35 eggs are present in the female, each up to 2 mm in diameter.

TADPOLES: Unknown.

KEY REFERENCE: Poynton & Broadley 1988.

Nyika dwarf toad
Bufo nyikae Loveridge, 1953
(Plate 3.4)

This toad was named for the Nyika plateau in northern Malawi.

DESCRIPTION: The female may reach 44 mm in length. The male is smaller, up to 37 mm. The tarsal fold is not visible. The tympanum is lacking, and there is no vocal sac in the male. The skin is fairly smooth, although covered by very small warts. A few larger warts are scattered on the back and legs. The parotid glands are elevated, narrow, and long, up to three times longer than wide. The first finger is shorter than the second. The snout is rounded in profile. Webbing is reduced, almost absent. Color is either brownish yellow or brown with darker markings. Characteristic markings are a light vertical

Fig. 52 *Bufo nyikae*

stripe extending from the flank, behind the arm, to the parotid gland. There is also a dark streak between the nostril and the eye and a dark longitudinal band along the lower half of the parotid. A yellow vertebral line is present. The underside of the body and legs possesses small yellow pustulations and gray flecks. Males are bright greenish yellow in the breeding season.

DISTRIBUTION AND HABITAT (FIG. 52): This small toad is known from the highlands forming the border between Malawi and Zambia. It is found in open grassland.

ADVERTISEMENT CALL: This species does not possess an advertisement call, although males do make a release call. The tympanum and vocal sac, structures that are concerned with hearing, are absent.

BREEDING: This species breeds in early to late summer in the southern part of the range, and probably throughout the year farther north. Spawning has been observed during the day on the Nyika plateau. Eggs are laid in a string, in small shallow pools. The string is 5.5 mm in diameter. Each egg is 2.5 mm in diameter and is largely black, except for a small pale area at the vegetal pole. Clutch size is 125.

TADPOLES: Tadpoles develop rapidly, reaching metamorphosis after 3 weeks.

NOTES: This toad is slow-moving, walking on its toes. They do not always swim but can walk on the bottom of the pond under water. Known predators include the grey bellied grass snake *Psammophylax variabilis* and the rat *Lophuromys flavopunctatus*.

KEY REFERENCES: Stewart 1967 (as *Bufo taitanus nyikae*), Poynton 1997.

Western leopard toad
Bufo pantherinus Smith, 1828
(Plate 3.5)

The specific name refers to the leopard-like markings on the back.

DESCRIPTION: This is a large toad, with the female up to 122 mm long. The glands under the forearm are indistinct. Likewise the glands behind the angle of the jaw are small and not joined into a ridge. The parotid glands are large and very distinct, with a straight lateral edge. The back pattern is very bold, with red-brown markings edged in black on a bright yellow background. The top of the snout is free of dark markings. The dark markings between the eyes are not fused. The back is reddish or red-brown. A pale thin vertebral line is present. The underside is immaculate.

DISTRIBUTION AND HABITAT (FIG. 53): This species is known from the southwestern tip of Africa. It inhabits shallow temporary

Fig. 53 *Bufo pantherinus*

ponds filled by the winter rains. Much of its habitat is now covered with housing developments.

ADVERTISEMENT CALL: The call is a slow snore, uttered from vegetation at the edge of water or while floating in deep water. The pulse rate is 25/s at 2.5 kHz.

BREEDING: The eggs are laid in shallow marshy areas. Depending on the rains, eggs are laid during late August through October, with metamorphosis in mid-December. One clutch from the Cape peninsula consisted of 24,476 eggs.

The breeding system in this species is described as explosive, as all breeding activity takes place during four or five nights each spring. The male does not compete by attempting to displace other males in amplexus, as would be expected in a species such as this that breeds for only a few days each season.

TADPOLES: See the chapter on tadpoles.

NOTES: This species has been assigned endangered status.

KEY REFERENCE: Poynton & Lambiris 1998.

Leopard toad
Bufo pardalis Hewitt, 1935
(Plate 3.6)

The specific name *pardalis* means "leopard" and refers to the pattern of square markings on the back.
Gleniffer toad. *Igogode* in Xhosa.

DESCRIPTION: This is a large toad, with the female up to 147 mm long. The glands behind the angle of the jaw are small and not joined into a ridge. The parotid glands are large and very distinct. The markings are paired. The top of the snout is free of dark markings. The dark markings between the eyes are not fused. The back is reddish or red-brown. The underside is immaculate. The backs of the thighs do not have any red markings.

Power's Toad

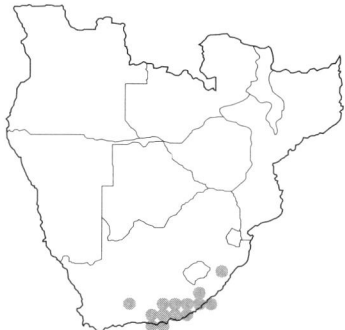

Fig. 54 *Bufo pardalis*

DISTRIBUTION AND HABITAT (FIG. 54): This species is known from Eastern Cape and KwaZulu-Natal Provinces of South Africa. It occurs in open scrub.

ADVERTISEMENT CALL: The male calls while floating or while sitting in shallow water. The call is a long snore, with a duration of up to 1.6 s, with dominant harmonics between 0.7 and 1.3 kHz. The pulse rate is 24–35/s.

BREEDING: The eggs are laid in shallow marshy areas. Depending on the rains, eggs are laid during late November through January, with metamorphosis in mid-March.

TADPOLES: See the chapter on tadpoles.

NOTES: In captivity they are known to eat lizards. Although most mammalian predators avoid toads, the water mongoose *Atilax paludinosus* is able to effectively deal with them. The mongoose flips the toad over and eats it from the ventral surface, avoiding much of the dorsal skin containing the skin glands.

KEY REFERENCE: Passmore 1977b.

Power's toad
Bufo poweri Hewitt, 1935
(Plate 3.7)

This species was named for the herpetologist J. H. Power, director of the McGregor Museum in Kimberley, 1947–1958.

Olive toad, Kimberley toad. *Power se skurwepadda* in Afrikaans, *Pantherkröte* in German, *Tchizunda* in Lwena, *Ohuimbota* in Muanha and Quimbundu.

DESCRIPTION: The female of this large-toad species reaches 100 mm long. In both sexes the parotid glands are conspicuous. It differs from Garman's toad in call and relative leg length. Foot length in Power's toad is 35%–40% of the body length but in Garman's toad is 41%–44% of body length. The back is covered by warts, each with a dark tip, and the tympanum is less than half the diameter of the eye. Three to four segments of the fourth toe are free of webbing. The species is similar to the guttural toad but is easily distinguished on the basis of color pattern. The color of the back varies, being greenish in Namibia. The pattern is variable, from perfectly symmetrical paired markings to an almost random pattern of blobs. The markings may be darkly edged. The top of the head is characteristically free of darker markings, and the bars behind the eyes do not fuse. Red patches occur on the backs of the thighs.

DISTRIBUTION AND HABITAT (FIG. 55): This toad is known from Angola southward to the central regions of South Africa and may occur eastward to Mozambique and Zimbabwe. It is found in thornbush and open savanna.

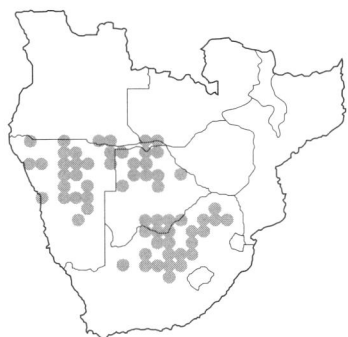

Fig. 55 *Bufo poweri*

ADVERTISEMENT CALL: The male is often found under vegetation at the edges of water bodies. It may call during the day after good rains, especially early in the breeding season. The call is loud, consisting of a rapidly pulsed "kwaak" with a duration of 0.3–1.0 s, and dominant harmonics between 1.0 and 1.5 kHz.

BREEDING: The first rains initiate breeding. Males were heard calling September 26 in Windhoek, coinciding with the first rains for that season. Eggs are laid in double strings, attached to submerged and floating vegetation. The eggs are black above and whitish below, and clutch size is about 23,000.

TADPOLES: See the chapter on tadpoles.

NOTES: Maximum recorded longevity is 4 years 8 months. Juveniles have been recorded sheltering in termitaria. Their appetite can be voracious; one large toad ate 147 beetles in four nights.

KEY REFERENCES: Channing 1972b, Power 1927a, Power 1931.

Ranger's toad
Bufo rangeri Hewitt, 1935
(Plate 3.8)

This frog was named for G. A. Ranger, a farmer near Kei Road. Raucous toad, Kei Road toad. *Lawaaipadda* in Afrikaans.

DESCRIPTION: This is a large toad, with the female reaching 115 mm in length. The legs are long, and the parotid glands are large and distinct. The glands under the forearm are flattened, forming a pale ridge. A broken ridge of glands runs from the angle of the jaw to above the arm. The toes have a well-developed margin of webbing. Back markings are usually outlined with a darker margin. A dark bar is sometimes present between the eyes and is rarely separated along the midline. The front of the snout is not heavily marked, although small blotches do occur. Red markings are never found on the backs of the thighs. A thin vertebral line running backward from the shoulders may be present.

DISTRIBUTION AND HABITAT (FIG. 56): This species has been found in Swaziland and throughout South Africa, excluding the

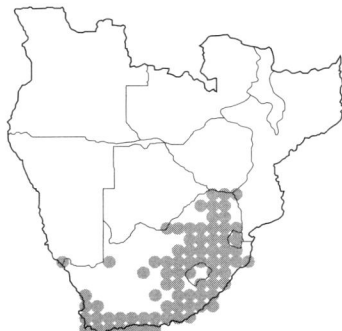

Fig. 56 *Bufo rangeri*

central Karoo region. This very common frog is able to exist in a variety of habitats.

ADVERTISEMENT CALL: The male calls from the edge of pools or streams and does not attempt to hide while calling. The call is very ducklike, each call being about 0.2 s long, with dominant harmonics between 1.8 and 2.1 kHz. With the onset of spring in September the male may call day and night.

BREEDING: These toads breed in the summer months in the Western Cape Province. Males call from the edge of water bodies, like dams or slow-flowing streams. The female approaches and nudges the male to initiate amplexus. This species prefers vegetation in deeper water for egg laying. The eggs are 1.3 mm in diameter, laid in double strings, each 5 mm thick. A pair deposited eggs in the Berg River in the southwestern Cape in January, allowing the eggs to drift downstream without entangling them in vegetation.

TADPOLES: See the chapter on tadpoles.

NOTES: The males may congregate in large numbers during the breeding season, when they compete vocally, and may fight to maintain their calling space. Blood protein and DNA studies show that this species is hybridizing with the guttural toad at Port St. Johns and at other sites. Adults have been found sheltering in termite mounds.

Paradise Toad

KEY REFERENCES: Guttman 1967, Tandy & Keith 1972, Visser 1979, Wager 1986.

Paradise toad
Bufo robinsoni Branch & Braack, 1996
(Plate 4.1)

This toad was named for G. A. Robinson, chief executive director of the National Parks Board of South Africa. The common name derives from the type locality, Paradise Kloof.

DESCRIPTION: The female is up to 57 mm, with flattened and smooth parotid glands. The tarsal fold is weakly developed and the tympanum is small. The upper and lower skin is smooth. The eye is large, 10%–13% of total length. The coloration is distinctive, with green markings on a tan to orange background. Breeding males are especially brightly colored. The ventral surface is speckled in juveniles but often immaculate in adults.

DISTRIBUTION AND HABITAT (FIG. 57): This species is restricted to springs draining the Vanderster Mountains in the Richtersveld, in arid Namaqualand, and the lower Gariep River. It is associated with rock outcrops.

ADVERTISEMENT CALL: The male calls from the edge of pools. The call is a quiet sigh, with a duration of 0.4 s, repeated at a rate of 3/min. Emphasized frequencies are at 2.0, 3.0, and 5.4 kHz.

Fig. 57 *Bufo robinsoni*

BREEDING: Unknown.

TADPOLES: See the chapters on tadpoles.

NOTES: The adults shelter in rock cracks.

KEY REFERENCE: Branch & Braack 1996.

Taita toad
Bufo taitanus Peters, 1878
(Plate 4.2)

The specific name *taitanus* refers to the Taita hills in Kenya. Black-chested dwarf toad, Taita dwarf toad.

DESCRIPTION: The female reaches 31 mm, while the male is smaller, up to 27 mm long. It is slender with spindly limbs. Small warts cover the back. The parotid glands are flattened but distinct, extending from behind the eye, continuous with the upper eyelid, to the level of the shoulder. Each parotid is up to four times as long as wide. One phalanx on the fifth toe is free of webbing. The underside is granular. The dorsal color pattern varies; males are light gray or tan with three pairs of darker markings, while females have a uniform light brown back with darker sides. The underside is pale with a distinct dark pattern with three anterior points. The limbs are also mottled with black marks. Males are smaller and thinner than females, with markedly more slender legs.

DISTRIBUTION AND HABITAT (FIG. 58): This species is known from Kenya to northern Zambia, Malawi, and adjacent Mozambique. It is found in sandy habitats in grasslands and open savannas.

ADVERTISEMENT CALL: This toad does not have an advertisement call. The sound production and hearing apparatus—tympanum, middle ear, and vocal sac—are absent.

BREEDING: Breeding takes place in early to mid summer. The 2-mm eggs are pale with a dark pole and are laid in strings in small pools. Clutch size is 125.

Fig. 58 *Bufo taitanus*

TADPOLES: Unknown.

NOTES: The Taita toad is found at high elevations. It occurs widely even in disturbed habitats. Unlike most other toads, it walks on toe tips. Recorded predators include the harsh-furred mouse *Lophuromys aquilus* and the skaapsteker *Psammophylax*.

KEY REFERENCES: Stewart & Wilson 1966, Stewart 1967.

Urungu toad
Bufo urunguensis Loveridge, 1932

This species is named for the Urungu region of southern Tanzania.

DESCRIPTION: This is a small frog, with the female up to 29 mm long. The tubercles under the fingers are double, and the tarsal fold is absent. The parotid glands have a straight outer edge, which does not project below the level of the pupil, although the edges may not always be clear. The tympanum is rounded, with the vertical diameter about equal to the distance between the nostrils. Broad web may just reach the base of the inner segment of the fourth toe. The back pattern consists of paler areas on the snout, neck, and lower back, while the underside is irregularly marked in black. The soles of the hands and feet are dark.

DISTRIBUTION AND HABITAT (FIG. 59): This is a forest species, known from Tanzania and Zambia.

Fig. 59 *Bufo urunguensis*

ADVERTISEMENT CALL: Unknown.

BREEDING: Unknown.

TADPOLES: Unknown.

NOTES: Fieldwork is required to investigate the breeding biology of this small toad.

KEY REFERENCE: Loveridge 1932.

Pygmy toad
Bufo vertebralis Smith, 1848
(Plate 4.3)

The specific name *vertebralis* refers to the pale vertebral stripe. Dwarf toad, African dwarf toad. *Dwergskurwepadda* in Afrikaans.

DESCRIPTION: The female reaches 36mm in length. The tarsal fold is absent. The parotid glands are present but not always clearly visible. Two segments of the third toe are free of web. The back markings consist of many small dark blotches intermingled with paler areas. Orange to reddish markings may be present. The ventral pattern consists of dark markings on a pale background. The throat of males may be yellowish.

Pygmy Toad

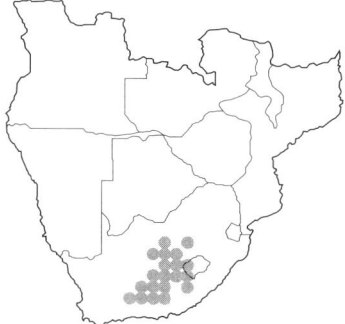

Fig. 60 *Bufo vertebralis*

DISTRIBUTION AND HABITAT (FIG. 60): This small toad occurs in the dry central regions of South Africa. It is found under rocks.

ADVERTISEMENT CALL: The call consists of castanet-like notes that can be heard at a great distance. Each note is short (0.05 s), consisting of 3 or 4 pulses, with emphasized frequencies between 2.5 and 2.7 kHz. The calls are repeated rapidly, at intervals of 0.05 s, and may continue for 10 s or longer.

BREEDING: Breeding occurs after midsummer, when the rains have filled the temporary pools in which this species breeds. The eggs are small, about 1 mm in diameter. They are laid in double strings, each 2.5 mm thick. The strings are laid in shallow water, amidst vegetation.

TADPOLES: See the chapter on tadpoles.

NOTES: Adults have been found in termite mounds.

KEY REFERENCES: Hewitt 1937, Power 1927b, Wager 1986.

Cape Toads—Genus *Capensibufo*

There are two small toads from the mountains of the southern parts of the Western Cape Province in this genus.

KEY TO THE SPECIES
1a. Tympanum present, parotids wider posteriorly (Fig. 61)
   Capensibufo tradouwi
1b. Tympanum absent, parotids wider anteriorly
   Capensibufo rosei

Fig. 61   Tympanum and parotids

Rose's toad
Capensibufo rosei (Hewitt, 1926)
(Plate 4.4)

Named for Walter Rose, who contributed much to our knowledge of frog natural history.
Striped Mountain toad, Cape mountain toad, Muizenberg Cape toad.

DESCRIPTION: This is a small toad with smooth soft skin and scattered blister-like ridges and warts on the back and flanks. The female may reach 39 mm in length, while the male is smaller, at 28 mm. The parotid glands are distinct and shaped like an inverted pear. The vent opens downward in sexually mature males but backward in females. The toes are not webbed, and the distal tubercles below the fingers and toes tend to divide. A tarsal fold is absent. Nuptial pads are found on the first and second fingers of breeding males. The back is black or dark brown, with three paler stripes and numerous red or orange tinges.

DISTRIBUTION AND HABITAT (FIG. 62): This small toad is only found on the mountains of the Cape peninsula and surrounding ranges. It is associated with the indigenous Cape vegetation known as fynbos. This species is listed as vulnerable in the South African Red Data Book.

ADVERTISEMENT CALL: This small toad does not have an advertisement call. A tympanum and the associated middle-ear elements

Rose's Toad

Fig. 62 *Capensibufo rosei*

involved in hearing are absent. The way in which females are attracted to males is unknown.

BREEDING: Breeding occurs at the beginning of spring from August to September on the top of Table Mountain, even though water is available throughout the year. During the breeding season both sexes possess bright pink corrugated oval belly patches. These patches may be involved in chemical attraction. Eggs are laid in single strings in shallow pools with dark mossy substrates. Clutch size is less than 100 eggs. These toads form large breeding aggregations, and thousands of eggs result from spawning by many females in the same pond. The eggs are dark at one pole and 2.6 mm in diameter. They are laid in a tough tube, where they resemble beads. The eggs may be separated up to 12 mm along the string. The jelly capsule reaches nearly 5 mm around each egg, thinning between eggs.

TADPOLES: See the chapter on tadpoles.

NOTES: Hundreds of adults, mostly males, have been found packed like sardines under decayed vegetation at the edges of breeding pools on top of Table Mountain. The relationships between populations on the Cape peninsula and the surrounding ranges need to be investigated, as considerable time has elapsed since these mountains were continuous, and genetic differentiation of these frogs would be expected.

KEY REFERENCES: Power & Rose 1929, Tandy & Keith 1972, Grandison 1980, Boycott 1988e.

Tradouw's toad
Capensibufo tradouwi (Hewitt, 1926)
(Plate 4.5)

The specific epithet is derived from Tradouw's Pass, where the species was first collected.
Cape mountain toad, Swellendam Cape toad.

DESCRIPTION: This toad has smooth soft skin and scattered blister-like ridges and warts on the back and flanks. The male is up to 37 mm long, larger than the female. The parotid glands are pear-shaped, and the tympanum is present. The toes are not webbed, and the outer tubercles below the fingers and toes tend to divide. A tarsal fold is absent. The vent opens backward in both males and females. Small spines occur in a patch under the arm of breeding males.

DISTRIBUTION AND HABITAT (FIG. 63): This small toad is known from the mountains north and east of the southwestern Cape. It is found in rocky areas at higher altitudes.

ADVERTISEMENT CALL: The male calls from concealed positions at the edge of seeps and slow streams. The call is a creaking sound,

Fig. 63 *Capensibufo tradouwi*

Red Toad

with a duration of 0.2 s. The dominant harmonics are between 1.9 and 2.1 kHz. The calls can be produced in rapid succession, about 2 calls/s.

BREEDING: Breeding takes place during the cold winter months. The eggs are laid singly in small pools of slow-moving water in seepage zones. Clutch size is about 60. Eggs are small (2 mm in diameter) and black at one pole. The eggs are not laid in strings, which is quite unusual for an African toad. Eggs have been collected in a small pool 300 × 200 × 50 mm deep in a seepage area.

TADPOLES: See the chapter on tadpoles.

NOTES: The male is active during the day in the breeding season and may be found walking about.

KEY REFERENCE: Hewitt 1926b.

Red Toad—Genus *Schismaderma*

The red toad differs from the other toads by its skin structure and by the schooling behavior of the tadpoles. Recent biochemical evidence suggests that the red toad has been separated from the other toads for 55 million years. There is only one species in the genus.

Red toad
Schismaderma carens (Smith, 1848)
(Plate 4.6)

The specific epithet *carens* refers to the lack of parotid glands.
Red-backed toad, African split-skin toad. *Kazoli* in Lwena and Manganja, *conga* in Sena, *naliwonde* in Yao, *zonde* in Cewa, *rooiskurwepadda* in Afrikaans.

DESCRIPTION: The size of this toad is moderate to large, with the male up to 88 mm and the female reaching 92 mm SVL. The tarsal fold is present. The back is less warty than the back of many similar-sized toads, and there is a distinct glandular ridge running from above the tympanum to the hind leg. The tympanum is large and round, about the same diameter as the eye. The eye-nostril distance is equal to the tympanum diameter. The breeding male has a vocal sac, and the first three fingers have nuptial pads. Parotids are not visible. The back pattern is characteristic of this species: a pair of small dark brown marks on the lower back, with a pair of shoulder markings. The ground color is pale brown, often pinkish. The outer part of the ridge has a darker lower edge. The flanks are pale or very dark, contrasting strongly with the reddish back. The underside is speckled with gray.

DISTRIBUTION AND HABITAT (FIG. 64): This toad is widely distributed from northeastern South Africa, northward through Botswana, Zimbabwe, Zambia, Malawi, and Mozambique. This toad is found in many different habitats and is even successful around human settlements.

ADVERTISEMENT CALL: The male calls while floating in shallow water. The call is a very loud, long whoop. Each call has a duration of 0.9–1.2 s. The dominant harmonics are between 0.1 and 0.8 kHz. Calls may be heard during the day.

BREEDING: Breeding starts from October after heavy rains in the northcentral areas of South Africa. They breed by day in muddy water. The males gather among emerging vegetation in deep water, separated by as little as 300 mm from each other. Calling males actively attempt to mate with other frogs, resulting in a lot of splashing as the groups of calling males chase each other. Females enter the

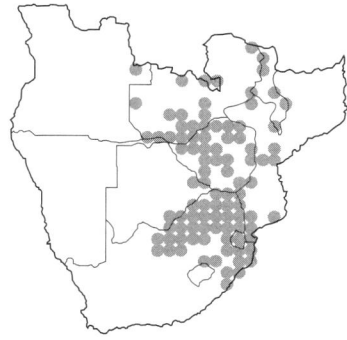

Fig. 64 *Schismaderma carens*

area of the calling males and leave after they have laid their eggs. The eggs are deposited in a double string, each egg being 1.6–2.5 mm in diameter, while the pair moves slowly along in the water. The pair may move back and forth, producing a number of rows of eggs attached to vegetation. Clutch size is 2500, but as large numbers of toads breed in the same place, tens of thousands of eggs may be deposited in the same part of the pond. Development from egg to toadlet may take 37–52 days.

TADPOLES: See the chapter on tadpoles.

NOTES: Calling is restricted to midsummer, unlike most other toads that call early in the rainy season. Dragonfly nymphs, hammerkops *Scopus umbretta*, and water tortoises, presumably *Pelomedusa subrufa*, may prey upon the mass of tadpoles. Young toads are eaten by the vine snake *Thelotornis*. Adults are known to be eaten by red-lipped snakes *Crotaphopeltis hotamboeia* and the giant eagle owl *Bubo lacteus*. The adult molts at about 4-day intervals.

KEY REFERENCES: Stewart 1967, Balinsky 1969, Maxson 1981, Wager 1986.

Forest Toads—Genus *Stephopaedes*

This genus has a tadpole that possesses a "crown", a ring of tissue around the eyes and nostrils, and lacks a mental gap in the papillae surrounding the mouth. Four species have been described in remnants of old forest along the eastern edge of Africa. Only one species occurs in the area.

Chirinda toad
Stephopaedes anotis (Boulenger, 1907)
(Plate 4.7)

The specific name *anotis* means "without ear" and refers to the tympanum, which is usually absent.
Boulenger's earless toad, Mashonaland toad.

DESCRIPTION: The female reaches 46 mm in length. The tarsal fold is absent. The tympanum is usually not visible. The parotid

Fig. 65 *Stephopaedes anotis*

glands are large and wide, and the back and top of the snout are granular. One segment of the third toe is free of web. The back is brown, with a lighter shoulder patch extending onto the head. Beneath is pale with a yellow belly and the yellow extending onto the legs. Adults are perfectly camouflaged against a background of dead leaves.

DISTRIBUTION AND HABITAT (FIG. 65): It is known from the Chirinda forest in eastern Zimbabwe and adjacent forests in Mozambique. It may be restricted to forests where particular tree species form small water traps in which these frogs can breed.

ADVERTISEMENT CALL: FitzSimons described the call as "a peculiarly plaintive medium-pitched chirrup quite unlike anything noted in our South African Bufos." This species possesses no tympanum or hearing apparatus and so would be expected to have no advertisement call. The dwarf squeaker *Schoutedenella xenodactyloides* from the same forest has a call that could be described as a "chirrup." This is a minor mystery that will be solved by fieldwork during the breeding season.

BREEDING: Eggs are laid in small pools between the buttress roots of large trees. In Chirinda it breeds in holes in the trunks and roots of *Chrysophyllum gorungasanum*. Clutch sizes vary from 57 to 105. The eggs are 2.5 mm and laid in strings that soon disintegrate. Each egg mass is about 50 mm across. I found eggs laid in very small pools,

Chirinda Toad

the smallest with a surface area of 50 × 30 mm and the largest, 60 × 160 mm.

TADPOLES: See the chapter on tadpoles.

NOTES: Breeding occurs in summer, and tadpoles were found on New Year's Day. Adults were discovered in holes in rotting logs—five were found together in one such waterlogged cavity. Diet includes a range of forest-floor arthropods, mostly ants. This species has been assigned vulnerable status.

KEY REFERENCES: Taylor 1973b, Channing 1978a, Channing 1993a.

Ghost Frogs—Family Heleophrynidae

The common name is derived from Skeleton Gorge on Table Mountain, where Rose's ghost frog *Heleophryne rosei* occurs.

These medium to large frogs have vertical pupils, a mottled color pattern, and large triangular discs on the fingers and toes. The male is smaller than the female, with more extensive webbing and an anal flap. The vent is directed backward in the female and downward in the male. A complex courtship behavior has been reported for Purcell's ghost frog.

The tadpole is large, with a streamlined wide body. It is found in fast-flowing mountain streams, although it is able to survive dry periods with minimal stream flow. It possesses a large oral disc, with which the tadpole is able to cling onto rocks and climb wet vertical rock faces. The presence of sheets of rock, or rocks of any size, appears to be an essential feature of the habitat for the tadpole. The tadpoles of the various species are remarkably similar, with populations from each locality displaying only small differences from others. The horny tadpole beaks are absent in all the species except the Natal ghost frog, which has only the lower beak. Fanglike teeth are present in the young tadpole and drop out as the regular teeth are formed. The tadpole appears to remain in the streams at least 12 months before metamorphosis.

These frogs are confined to areas of steep slope and high amounts of rainfall, 500–3000 mm/y. They favor fast-flowing wooded streams. The family is found only in South Africa from the mountains of Mpumalanga Province, southward along the escarpment to KwaZulu-Natal and the Western Cape Province. These are extremely difficult frogs to collect, and it will require much hard work to compile complete distribution maps.

There are six species in this family, although a better understanding of the ghost frogs may lead to more species being described.

KEY TO THE SPECIES
Museum specimens of *H. purcelli* and *H. regis* cannot be reliably distinguished, although in the field the advertisement calls of the males are different. No sympatry has yet been recorded, so the following guide to identification includes distributional clues.

1a. Snout-vent length of males is 35 mm or less, found east of Montagu along the Langeberg Mountains to the Gouritz River.
Heleophryne orientalis
1b. Snout-vent length of males more than 35 mm, found elsewhere   2

2a. Inner metatarsal tubercle oval   3
2b. Inner metatarsal tubercle compressed   4

3a. Width of disc of outer finger subequal to internarial distance, found on Table Mountain   *Heleophryne rosei*
3b. Width of disc of outer finger less than half the internarial distance, found in KwaZulu-Natal and Mpumalanga Provinces
Heleophryne natalensis

4a. Dorsal pattern a series of darker spots on a light brown background, found on the Elandsberg Mountains   *Heleophryne hewitti*
4b. Dorsal pattern a series of contrasting patches usually with a thin border   5

5a. Recorded from Robinson Pass in the west, to the Kareedouw Mountains in the east   *Heleophryne regis*
5b. Recorded from the Cedarberg, southward and eastward to Garcia's Pass   *Heleophryne purcelli*

Hewitt's ghost frog
Heleophryne hewitti Boycott, 1988
(Plate 4.8)

The specific epithet *hewitti* refers to the herpetologist J. Hewitt, director of the Albany Museum from 1910 to 1958.
Hewitt's African ghost frog.

DESCRIPTION: This moderately sized frog is slightly larger than the

Royal ghost frog that occurs to the west of its distribution. The female may reach 50 mm in length, while the male is smaller, at 47 mm. The frog has long legs with distinct discs on the fingers and toes. The color pattern consists of darker spots with a pale margin on a light brown background. All specimens collected so far have similar patterns.

DISTRIBUTION AND HABITAT (FIG. 66): This species is restricted to four rivers in the Elandsberg range, the Geelhoutboom River, Martins River, Klein River, and Diepkloof River. This species is found near clear, swiftly flowing permanent mountain streams. Unfortunately, the habitat where this frog is found has been planted with exotic pine trees. The danger that this poses to the populations, due to reduction in stream flow, cannot be overemphasized. This species also is threatened by the introduction of exotic fish into streams next to its limited range. The species is listed as critically endangered in the South African Red Data Book.

ADVERTISEMENT CALL: The call consists of 8 or 9 notes, where each note is a soft whistle. An initial longer whistle may precede the call. The initial note may have a duration of 250 ms, while the other notes are shorter, only 60–110 ms. The emphasized frequency range is 1.7–2.2 kHz.

BREEDING: Eggs are laid in clutches of 93–150, under rocks in quiet backwaters. One batch was found attached to the underside of a rock in a shallow fast-flowing stream.

TADPOLES: See the chapter on tadpoles.

Fig. 66   *Heleophryne hewitti*

NOTES: The brown water snake *Lycodonomorphus rufulus* preys on both tadpoles and adults.

KEY REFERENCES: Boycott 1988b, Boycott & Branch 1988.

Natal ghost frog
Heleophryne natalensis Hewitt, 1913
(Plate 5.1)

The specific name *natalensis* refers to the province of KwaZulu-Natal, the locality where this species was first collected.
Natalse spookpadda in Afrikaans.

DESCRIPTION: The female reaches 65 mm in length. The body is flattened, and the eyes are large and protruding. The back is brown to black with green or yellowish markings. The throat is marbled. During the breeding season the male develops rough spines on the upper surfaces of the first three fingers and around the shoulder. They have triangular discs that are only slightly wider than the fingers and toes with the outer finger disc less than half the internarial distance.

DISTRIBUTION AND HABITAT (FIG. 67): This species is known from Rode, through the KwaZulu-Natal midlands escarpment, and along the Drakensberg Mountains and western Swaziland to north-eastern South Africa. The adult can be found up to a kilometer from streams, in holes in banks and cliffs. They are found where the streams are fast flowing.

Fig. 67 *Heleophryne natalensis*

ADVERTISEMENT CALL: The male calls from vegetation near streams, or from a rock ledge or under a large boulder within the spray zone of small waterfalls. The call consists of a short, high note, repeated every second or less, for long periods. A typical call is 140 ms long, with an emphasized frequency of 1.5 kHz. The call is similar to the vocalization of the Egyptian fruit bat *Rousettus aegyptiacus*. Around Pietermaritzburg the males are particularly vociferous during misty nights. The call has been heard from March to May in various parts of the range.

BREEDING: Eggs are laid during March and April in the Durban and Pietermaritzburg areas.

TADPOLES: See the chapter on tadpoles.

NOTES: The Natal ghost frog is widely distributed, but further study may reveal that it consists of a number of unrecognized species. Detailed fieldwork and the appropriate laboratory studies will be needed to determine the status of populations from different mountains.

The skin secretions of this species contain a component that is also found as part of the poison molecule of the wasp *Vespa mandarina*. The skin secretions of many frogs contain substances that imitate the action of mammalian control proteins. These may affect the nervous system or the digestive system. Any mammal that eats one of these frogs would feel very ill indeed, and would probably not attempt to eat another frog.

KEY REFERENCES: Nakajima et al. 1979, Wager 1986.

Eastern ghost frog
Heleophryne orientalis FitzSimons, 1946
(Plate 5.2)

The specific name *orientalis* refers to the east.

DESCRIPTION: This is a small species, with the male up to 35 mm and female up to 46 mm long. The male usually has a pattern of large spots, while the female is variable, showing patterns of small or large spots, or sometimes blotches. A bar between the eyes is usually present.

Eastern Ghost Frog

Fig. 68 *Heleophryne orientalis*

DISTRIBUTION AND HABITAT (FIG. 68): This species is found east of Montagu along the Langeberg Mountains to the Gouritz River valley. It is found on slopes with indigenous vegetation and rocky outcrops.

ADVERTISEMENT CALL: The call is a short whistle, 50 ms long, with a dominant harmonic at 2.4 kHz.

BREEDING: The male is sexually active at 30 mm. Clutch size is between 114 and 191, and the eggs are laid under stones or boulders where surface flow is very slow or absent. The eggs are yellow and white. This species lays the smallest eggs, compared to those laid by Purcell's and the Royal ghost frog. The eggs are laid during November when the rains have stopped. The eggs may be placed between moss-covered boulders, where seepage is the source of moisture.

TADPOLES: The tadpoles are similar to the other species. See chapter on tadpoles.

KEY REFERENCE: Visser 1990.

Purcell's ghost frog
Heleophryne purcelli Sclater, 1898
(Plate 5.3)

The specific name refers to the collector R. F. Purcell, who found the species in November 1896.
Cape ghost frog, Purcell's African ghost frog.

DESCRIPTION: The adult female length reaches 56 mm, with the male a little smaller at 47 mm. The male has a fleshy anal flap. The discs are large, twice the width of the fingers and toes. The back color is yellowish brown to bright green with reddish brown markings. The male usually has a pattern of small spots, while the female commonly has a blotched pattern or a pattern of large spots. The feet are webbed, with webbing reaching the last segment of the fifth toe.

DISTRIBUTION AND HABITAT (FIG. 69): This species is known from the mountains of the southern, southwestern, and western Cape, excluding Table Mountain, in the winter rainfall region. The northern limit is Algeria forestry station in the Cedarberg Mountains, and the eastern limit is Montagu in the western Langeberg Mountains. They are found on rocky slopes. Adults have been found under "watergrass" growing on wet vertical rock surfaces.

ADVERTISEMENT CALL: The call is a high-pitched ringing note. The dominant energy in the call is concentrated between 2 and 2.5 kHz. Each note is short, between 30 and 70 ms, repeated at a rate of about 1/s. A faster, higher-pitched call is used by the male to guide the

Fig. 69 *Heleophryne purcelli*

receptive female to him, after which he leads her to the egg-laying site. Calling is most intense in the late afternoon and at dusk, becoming sporadic after dark.

BREEDING: The male is sexually mature at 36 mm. During the breeding season (spring to midsummer—October to January) the males develop swollen forearms and small black spines along the edge of the lower jaw, on the inside of the forearms, and on the chest. These spines occur on the surfaces that are in contact with a female during amplexus. During the breeding season the body skin becomes loose, forming large slimy folds, with the toes becoming fringed with web. Males move into the streams as sexual activity heightens, and remain aquatic until the breeding season ends.

This species, and probably other ghost frogs, exhibit a complex courtship display. The male attracts the female with a special call. A period of mutual touching of forearms and heads follows, with the female submerged. Eggs are laid in quiet backwaters. Eggs also may be laid out of water in seepage zones, singly in slow-flowing areas and small pools. They do not adhere and are scattered by the water flow. Clutch sizes between 50 and 146 are recorded, with larger clutches found in the eastern part of the range. Eggs are smaller in the east (2.5 mm) than the rest of the range (4.1 mm).

TADPOLES: See the chapter on tadpoles.

NOTES: The diet is known to include beetles, spiders, bugs, ants, cockroaches, crickets, earwigs, flies, grasshoppers, mites, moths, snails, and woodlice. In captivity, specimens took moss frogs.

The skin secretions contain the same component as the Natal ghost frog, a protein called Hyp^3-bradykinin. See the discussion on the effects and functions of these secretions in the Natal ghost frog species account. Adults are fairly resistant to desiccation when compared to most other frogs.

KEY REFERENCES: Boycott 1982a, Passmore 1985, Visser 1990.

Royal ghost frog
Heleophryne regis Hewitt, 1909
(Plate 5.4)

The specific name *regis* means "royal" and refers to George Rex, an early timber merchant of Knysna.

DESCRIPTION: The adult female length reaches 49 mm, while the male is smaller, only reaching 43 mm. This species is distinguishable from Purcell's ghost frog only by the male advertisement call. Both sexes have a pattern of small spots, although the bar between the eyes is absent but replaced by spots of various sizes. The male has a fleshy anal flap. The discs are about twice as wide as the fingers and toes.

DISTRIBUTION AND HABITAT (FIG. 70): This species is found in areas that receive rainfall throughout the year, with peaks in spring and autumn. This frog is known from the mountains east of the Gouritz River valley, from the Huis River in the west.

ADVERTISEMENT CALL: The call of this species is a harsh, low-pitched, creaking call. The dominant frequency occurs at 1.8 kHz. Each call is pulsed, producing the creaking sound, with a duration between 80 and 110 ms. There are about 13 pulses/call. The notes are repeated at roughly 1-s intervals and are only audible from a few meters.

BREEDING: The males become sexually mature at 35 mm. During the breeding season from October to February, the webbing of the feet increases in both sexes. The male forearms swell, and numerous

Fig. 70 *Heleophryne regis*

small, black spines develop on the surfaces that are in contact with the female during amplexus. This includes the chest, jaw, and inside surfaces of the forearms.

Breeding takes place during a period of minimum river flow, apparently protecting the eggs and young larvae from being washed away. Clutch size is recorded as 114–197, with a mean of 152. The mean egg size is 3.6 mm. At Deepwalls a partial clutch of 25 developing embryos was found attached under a rock in the river.

TADPOLES: See the chapter on tadpoles.

NOTES: The adult diet is known to include beetles, spiders, bugs, ants, cockroaches, crickets, flies, grasshoppers, moths, and woodlice.

KEY REFERENCES: Boycott 1982b, Passmore 1985, Visser 1990.

Rose's ghost frog
Heleophryne rosei Hewitt, 1925
(Plate 5.5)

The specific epithet *rosei* refers to the collector W. Rose.
Thumbed ghost frog, Table Mountain ghost frog, Skeleton Gorge ghost frog.

DESCRIPTION: This is a moderately sized frog, with the female up to 60 mm long and the male shorter, up to 50 mm. The coloration of adults is striking: a pale green background with purple to brown blotches. The eye lacks a transverse dark band. The fingers and toes have large triangular terminal discs. The disc on the outer finger is subequal to the internarial distance. The outer metatarsal tubercle is slightly elongated. A rudimentary "thumb" is present as a distinct inner metacarpal tubercle. The feet are half webbed, with one segment of the fifth toe free of web.

DISTRIBUTION AND HABITAT (FIG. 71): This species is known only from perennial streams on the eastern side of Table Mountain. Typical habitat includes moist, forested gorges, with vertical rock faces covered with moss. This species is listed as critically endangered in the South African Red Data Book. The population is small, geographically restricted, and threatened by the plantations of pines

Fig. 71 *Heleophryne rosei*

on the mountain that cause the streams to dry up. They do not keep well in captivity and should not be collected.

ADVERTISEMENT CALL: The call is a brief click, 30 ms long, with an emphasized frequency of 1.8 kHz. Males have been recorded calling in December.

BREEDING: The male secondary sexual characters include a number of small black spines on the outside surfaces of the forearms, on the back, and on the top of the back legs. It appears that they breed from November to February. Details on eggs are unknown.

TADPOLES: See the chapter on tadpoles.

NOTES: Adults have been found in caves on Table Mountain, although most have been collected under stones in running water. It seems, however, that perennial river flow is not essential for this species to complete the life cycle. This frog has been called a "trogloxene", which is defined as an occasional cave visitor that enters caves for various reasons but does not accomplish its full life cycle within a cave.

KEY REFERENCES: Boycott & de Villiers 1986, Boycott 1988c, Baard 1989.

Snout-Burrowers—Family Hemisotidae

Shovel-nosed frogs, sharp-nosed burrowing frogs

The medium to small frogs in this family use their hard snouts for burrowing. The snout moves soil out of the way while the strong hind legs propel the frog below the surface. The only recognized genus may contain up to eight species, of which four occur in the area covered here.

Snout-Burrowers—-Genus *Hemisus*

These heavily built frogs have particularly robust skeletons associated with their burrowing habits. They burrow forward into the soil; most other burrowing frogs burrow backward. The shoulder girdle along with the muscles is modified to permit this action. The forelimb muscles are three times as large as those in similarly sized non-forward burrowers. The advantage of burrowing forward is speed of entry into the soil—more than twice as fast as backward burrowers. Eggs are deposited in a burrow. The tadpoles are released when the nest floods. The tadpoles have been observed swarming on to the back of the female. Further field observation of the breeding biology of these frogs is required. The genus is found from Ethiopia southward to KwaZulu-Natal, South Africa.

KEY TO THE SPECIES
1a. Dorsal pattern of yellow dots on a dark background, inner metatarsal tubercle shorter than second toe   *Hemisus guttatus*
1b. Dorsal pattern of blotches, inner metatarsal tubercle longer than second toe   2

2a. Back rough, with a pale vertebral band   *Hemisus wittei*
2b. Back smooth, a pale stripe sometimes present   3

3a. Inner metatarsal tubercle shorter than eye-nostril distance (Fig. 72) 4
3b. Inner metatarsal tubercle longer than eye-nostril distance
Hemisus guineensis

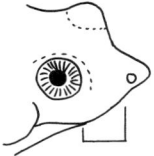

Fig. 72 Eye-nostril distance

4a. Eye small, upper eyelid less than eye-nostril distance
Hemisus sp.
4b. Eye larger, upper eyelid longer than eye-nostril distance
Hemisus marmoratus

Barotse snout-burrower
Hemisus sp. Channing & Broadley, in press
(Plate 5.6)

The specific name refers to the Barotse floodplain along the Zambezi River in western Zambia.

DESCRIPTION: The male length is known to reach 30 mm while the female may grow to 37 mm. The back and sides have silver-yellow markings on black, with a bright yellow vertebral line. Small yellow spots are irregularly spaced on the back. Breeding males have a nuptial pad in the form of a black transverse ridge on the wrist. The fifth toe may be equal to the length of the inner metatarsal tubercle, while the distance between the nostrils is always less than the distance between the eye and nostril. The upper eyelid is less than eye-nostril distance.

DISTRIBUTION AND HABITAT (FIG. 73): This new species is known from western Zambia to the Kafue Flats, and further fieldwork is required to determine its range.

ADVERTISEMENT CALL: The male calls from ground level near vegetation at the edge of standing water. The call consists of a long trill

Fig. 73 *Hemisus* sp.

at around 3.0 kHz. The call is different from that by the other species in this genus in that it consists of pulses arranged in groups of four. The pulse rate is around 28/s.

BREEDING: Unknown. Males call after rain and continue to call as the river floods.

TADPOLES: Unknown.

NOTES: Field recordings of the distinctive advertisement call would be an easy way to determine the range of this species.

Guinea snout-burrower
Hemisus guineensis Cope, 1865

The specific name refers to Guinea on the West Coast of Africa. Western sharp-nosed frog, Guinea shovelsnout frog. *Tchimbotwe* in Lwena.

DESCRIPTION: This is a medium-sized frog, with the female length up to 53 mm and the male length up to 37 mm. The snout is sharp and the eye is small. A fold of skin runs behind the eyes. The inner metatarsal tubercle is larger than the first toe and longer than the eye-nostril distance. The frogs are black above with small yellow or orange dots. The male has a black throat and glandular areas on the upper surface of the hand.

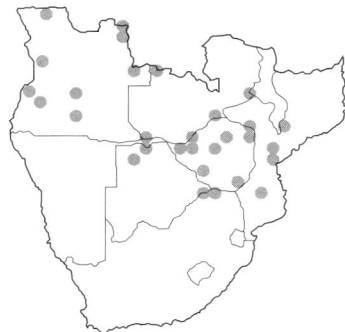

Fig. 74 *Hemisus guineensis*

DISTRIBUTION AND HABITAT (FIG. 74): This species is known from Mozambique, Zimbabwe, northern South Africa, northern Botswana, and Angola. It is found in grassland and open bush where temporary pans are formed in the rainy season.

ADVERTISEMENT CALL: The call is a long trill. The call has a duration of 1.8 s, consisting of 43 double notes with a dominant frequency of 3 kHz.

BREEDING: Unknown. Amplexing pairs were found in April in the Democratic Republic of the Congo.

TADPOLES: See the chapter on tadpoles.

NOTES: Specimens have been dug out of shallow burrows 6–10 cm deep.

KEY REFERENCE: Inger 1968.

Spotted snout-burrower
Hemisus guttatus (Rapp, 1842)
(Plate 5.7)

The specific name *guttatus* means "spotted."
Spotted shovel-nosed frog, spotted burrowing frog, eastern sharp-snouted frog.

Spotted Snout-Burrower

DESCRIPTION: The female may reach up to 80 mm in length and is the largest snout-burrower in the area. The toes are unwebbed, and the back pattern is quite distinct, being a number of yellow dots on a dark purple or brown background. The head is pointed and small, with very small eyes. The snout tip is hard, used for burrowing. The arms are muscular and the fingers are thick and strong. The inner metatarsal tubercle is shorter than the second toe.

DISTRIBUTION AND HABITAT (FIG. 75): This species has been recorded from the KwaZulu-Natal lowlands between Hluhluwe and Durban, through the interior of South Africa.

ADVERTISEMENT CALL: The advertisement call is a long, high-pitched buzz. It consists of a large number of pulses, produced at about 50/s, at an emphasized frequency of 2.1 kHz. The call may continue for more than 2 s.

BREEDING: Eggs are laid in chambers 15 cm below the surface. Each clutch consists of some 200 eggs. Each egg is 2.5 mm in diameter within 4-mm jelly capsules. The eggs are protected by a few top layers of empty jelly capsules.

TADPOLES: See the chapter on tadpoles.

KEY REFERENCE: Wager 1986.

Fig. 75 *Hemisus guttatus*

Marbled snout-burrower
Hemisus marmoratus (Peters, 1854)
(Plate 5.8)

The specific name refers to the mottled color of the back.
Mottled shovel-nosed frog, pig-nosed frog, mottled burrowing frog, marbled shovelnose frog. *Tsinidikae* in Setswana, *kaswanene* in Yao, *napûlo* in Cabaceira.

DESCRIPTION: This small to medium-sized frog (male up to 35 mm, female up to 55 mm long) is easily recognized by the sharp snout and transverse fold between and above the small eyes. It has an inner metatarsal tubercle shorter than the eye-nostril distance. The upper eyelid is longer than the eye-nostril distance. The front limbs are muscular, and the snout is hardened, enabling this species to dig nose-first into soft soil. The toes are slightly webbed. Coloration is variable, with dark gray or brown marbling or spots on a paler brown background. A light vertebral line is often present. Some individuals are uniformly colored.

DISTRIBUTION AND HABITAT (FIG. 76): These frogs have been found in savannas from most of sub-Saharan Africa, excluding rain forest, from Senegal to Eritrea, western Ethiopia, and Somalia, and south into southern Kenya and the northern and northeastern parts of South Africa.

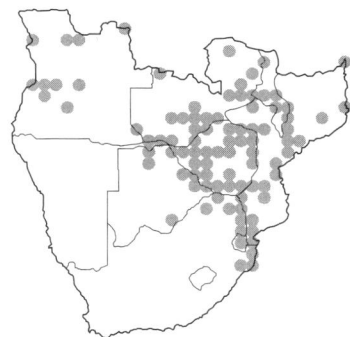

Fig. 76 *Hemisus marmoratus*

ADVERTISEMENT CALL: The male calls from a concealed site under vegetation at the edge of pools, usually on wet mud. The call is a long buzz, repeated frequently. Each call may last several seconds, at a pulse rate of 70–90/s, with most energy at 4 kHz. The pulses are double.

BREEDING: Breeding starts with the first rains. The males clasp the females and are dragged into the burrow, with the larger female digging. Females remain with the developing eggs, which are laid in a burrow or under a log or stone. Nests usually are found in wet soil under shade of vegetation or leaf litter. About 150–200 eggs are laid in a compact mass 25 × 13 mm, each egg 2–2.5 mm in diameter within a 3–4-mm capsule. Clutch sizes as small as 30–35 have been estimated. Many empty capsules protect the top of the clutch. The nest is situated a little back from the water. Continuing rains cause the ponds to fill, and the water rises to the level of the tadpoles and liberates them. They appear to be able to develop either when left in a moist mass or when in water.

TADPOLES: See the chapter on tadpoles.

NOTES: They are known to be eaten by fiscal shrikes and the sharp beaked snake *Rhamphiophis acutus*. They have been found in ground in which many tunnels exist, suggesting that the frogs forage underground. They eat nocturnal termites. In captivity they readily eat earthworms.

KEY REFERENCES: Loveridge 1942c, Bourquin 1985, van Dijk 1985b, Kaminsky et al. 1999.

De Witte's snout-burrower
Hemisus wittei Laurent, 1963

The specific name *wittei* refers to G.-F. de Witte, herpetologist at the Institut Royal des Sciences Naturelles in Brussels until 1951. Witte's shovelnose frog.

DESCRIPTION: This small burrowing frog, with the male up to 40 mm and the female up to 55 mm in length, differs from the marbled snout-burrower principally by a slightly rougher back and a

Fig. 77 *Hemisus wittei*

wide pale vertebral band. The pattern on the back is otherwise one of irregular blotches. The distance between the nostrils is greater than the snout-nostril distance. The tympanum is not visible. The vertebral line continues on to the thighs.

DISTRIBUTION AND HABITAT (FIG. 77): This frog is known from northeastern Zambia, extending northward.

ADVERTISEMENT CALL: The call is a long twittering, with a duration of a few seconds. The dominant frequency is at 2.7 kHz, with a pulse rate of 16/s.

BREEDING: Unknown.

TADPOLES: Unknown.

NOTES: Extensive fieldwork is required to discover the breeding biology of this little-known species.

KEY REFERENCE: Laurent 1963.

Tree Frogs—Family Hyperoliidae

Reed frogs, spiny reed frogs, banana frogs
The family consists of small to medium-sized frogs that are often brightly patterned. Many are adapted for climbing around in vegetation. They are found in dry and moist tropical areas throughout Africa, on the Seychelles and Madagascar Islands to the east, and on Sao Tome Island to the west. Six genera are known from southern Africa.

KEY TO THE GENERA, BASED ON ADULT MALES
1a. Pupil shape horizontal or round *Hyperolius*
1b. Pupil shape vertically elliptical (Fig. 78) 2

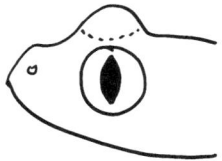

Fig. 78 Vertical pupil

2a. Throat gland absent *Leptopelis*
2b. Throat gland present (Fig. 79) 3

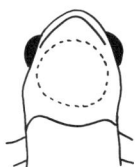

Fig. 79 Throat gland

3a. Throat gland overlies black pigmented vocal pouch 4
3b. No black pigment under throat gland *Afrixalus*

4a. Tympanum absent, adults up to 22-mm long   *Kassinula wittei*
4b. Tympanum present, adults may be up to 70-mm long   5

5a. Angle between second and third finger more than 45° (Fig. 80)
Semnodactylus wealii

Fig. 80   Finger angle

5b. Angle between second and third finger not more than 30°
Kassina

Spiny Reed Frogs—Genus *Afrixalus*

These small frogs are characteristically covered with small black spines on the back, from which the name "spiny reed frogs" derives. Many species are minute, often yellow, with longitudinal darker markings. There is no black pigment under the throat gland. Eggs are often attached to leaves near the water surface, and these leaves are usually glued together.

KEY TO THE SPECIES
1a. Adults over 29 mm long, webbing on hand reaching middle subarticular tubercle of outer finger   2
1b. Adults shorter than 29 mm, webbing not reaching subarticular tubercle of outer finger   3

2a. A dark vertebral band present (Fig. 81)   *Afrixalus fornasini*

Fig. 81   Dark band

2b. A pair of paravertebral bands meeting over the head, and a dark dorsolateral band behind eyelid   *Afrixalus wittei*

3a. Snout clearly rounded, almost bulbous (Fig. 82)
Afrixalus spinifrons

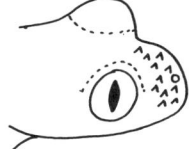

Fig. 82   Spines on snout

3b. Snout not as above   4

4a. The lumbar pattern in the form of a **U** (Fig. 83)
Afrixalus osorioi

Fig. 83   Lumbar pattern

4b. Pattern not as above   5

5a. A darker vertebral band usually present, with a dark stripe from the nostril through the eye to the groin (Fig. 84)
Afrixalus knysnae

Fig. 84   Stripe from nostril through eye to groin

5b. Markings not as above 6

6a. A light triangle on the head, with a pair of darker dorsolateral stripes (Fig. 85) *Afrixalus dorsalis*

Fig. 85 Dorsolateral stripes

6b. Markings not as above 7

7a. Dorsal pattern includes a pair of diverging paravertebral stripes, broadening posteriorly and continued on tibiae of folded legs as an oblique band spanning the full width of the limb
Afrixalus brachycnemis or *Afrixalus delicatus*
7b. Pattern not as above 8

8a. A dark patch present in the lumbar region of each side, and on the tibiae (Fig. 86) *Afrixalus aureus*

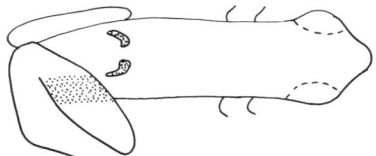

Fig. 86 Lumbar patch

8b. Markings, if present, in the form of elongated stripes
Afrixalus crotalus

Golden spiny reed frog
Afrixalus aureus Pickersgill, 1984
(Plate 6.1)

The specific name refers to the golden color of the back. Golden banana frog.

Golden Spiny Reed Frog

DESCRIPTION: The length of this frog reaches 23 mm in males and up to 24 mm in females. The belly is nearly smooth, while the throat gland is white with variable roughness. The snout is pointed. The head and snout are covered with many very small spines. These small spines are most strongly developed in summer between January and March. The rest of the back in males may be covered in slightly larger spines. The outer metatarsal tubercle is distinct. The tubercles beneath the two outer fingers are often double. The background color of the back varies from brown to yellow. Darker markings in the form of a patch are found on each side of the lower back, coinciding with a darker band on the lower leg. A dark band often with lighter speckles extends along the side from snout to groin, extending on to the back to include the upper eyelid.

DISTRIBUTION AND HABITAT (FIG. 87): This species has been collected from the north coast of KwaZulu-Natal through northeastern South Africa, Swaziland, and southern Mozambique. It is found in grassland at low altitudes and is listed as vulnerable in the South African Red Data Book.

ADVERTISEMENT CALL: The males form very high-density choruses and call from sunset to early the following morning. The call is a short trill, with a mean duration of 0.5 s. Six to 16 pulses are produced at a rate of 16–30/s. The emphasized frequencies are between 3.8 and 5.4 kHz.

BREEDING: About half of the males in a population do not call but wait near a calling male to intercept approaching females. This is known as satellite behavior and results in high levels of aggression between males. Breeding takes place during summer in temporary pans in dry grassland. The eggs are white and enclosed in vertically folded blades of grass, 40–60 mm above the water surface. Clutch size is 50.

TADPOLES: Unknown.

NOTES: The frog has been found in the leaf axil of water grass during the day and may spend time in direct sunlight.

KEY REFERENCES: Pickersgill 1984, Backwell & Passmore 1991.

Fig. 87 *Afrixalus aureus*

Short-legged spiny reed frog
Afrixalus brachycnemis (Boulenger, 1896)
(Plate 6.2)

The name *brachycnemis* means "short lower leg."
Short-legged banana frog, short-limbed banana frog, golden leaf-folding frog, Malawi banana frog. *Kachula kachena* in Nyungwe.

DESCRIPTION: The male reaches 25 mm and the female up to 27 mm in length. Small spines are present on the upper and lower surfaces of the male but only on the head of some females. A dark band with light speckling is present from snout to groin. The back pattern is a pair of darker dorsolateral stripes, sometimes with a patch between the eyes extending backward in a double band. These markings are, however, variable.

DISTRIBUTION AND HABITAT (FIG. 88): It has been found from Malawi to coastal Kenya and occurs in grassland and coastal forest.

ADVERTISEMENT CALL: The male calls from vegetation near flooded grass. The call is a "buzz," with a series of pulses produced for 4–9 s, at a pulse rate of about 33/s and a dominant midfrequency of 4.5 kHz.

BREEDING: The eggs are yellow, laid in leaf axils of grass a few centimeters above water. Unlike other spiny reed frogs, the eggs are not placed within glued leaves.

Fig. 88 *Afrixalus brachycnemis*

TADPOLES: Unknown.

NOTES: This frog has been found sitting on leaves in the sun during the day.

KEY REFERENCES: Stewart 1967, Schiøtz 1999.

Snoring spiny reed frog
Afrixalus crotalus Pickersgill, 1984
(Plate 6.3)

The name *crotalus* means "rattling."
Zimbabwe banana frog.

DESCRIPTION: The male reaches 22 mm and the female 24 mm in length. The chest and belly are smooth, but the throat disc has a few spines. There are minute spines on the head. The throat disc is large, semitriangular to oval with a curved rear edge. The back pattern is obscure or absent. The outer metatarsal tubercle is distinct. Tubercles beneath the outer two fingers are divided. The back is pale yellow, with a faint brown vertebral line. A dark side band with lighter speckles overlaps the upper eyelid. Sometimes the back is golden without markings.

DISTRIBUTION AND HABITAT (FIG. 89): This species has been collected from eastern Zimbabwe northward to southern Malawi and

Fig. 89 *Afrixalus crotalus*

eastward through central Mozambique to the coast. It is found in dry grassland.

ADVERTISEMENT CALL: The call is a series of distinct clicks, about 7/s, with maximum energy at 2.5 kHz.

BREEDING: Eggs are laid in folded glued leaves at the surface of standing water.

TADPOLES: Unknown.

KEY REFERENCE: Pickersgill 1984.

Delicate spiny reed frog
Afrixalus delicatus Pickersgill, 1984
(Plate 6.4)

The specific epithet *delicatus* refers to the delicate build of this species.
Pickersgill's banana frog.

DESCRIPTION: The male may reach up to 20 mm in length. The snout is pointed. Dark spines are present over the chest and belly in males but absent from the lower surface of the female. The throat disc has small spines. The disc is opaque and triangular, with a curved to straight edge. The outer metatarsal tubercle is weakly developed and rounded. Tubercles beneath the fingers usually are divided. The

Delicate Spiny Reed Frog

back is light brown to golden. Brown to black markings in the form of an indistinct head spot and middorsal line are present. A side band touches the upper eyelid. Divergent paravertebral stripes are usually present. The lower leg markings are sometimes in the form of an indistinct transverse stripe. The throat disc has an orange tinge.

DISTRIBUTION AND HABITAT (FIG. 90): This species is known from the coastal lowlands from Avoca in KwaZulu-Natal northward to Swaziland and Mozambique. It is found in short grass, near permanent or semipermanent pools.

ADVERTISEMENT CALL: Males form aggregations of 4–8 individuals that call from sunset to about midnight. The call consists of a "zip" sound followed by a longer trill. The zip is short, 0.2 s, with 12–25 pulses at a rate of 116–173/s, with an emphasized frequency between 4.4 and 5.8 kHz. The trill is longer, lasting up to 5.9 s, consisting of 13–55 pulses at a rate of 623/s, with an emphasized frequency between 4.9 and 5.8 kHz. Females are attracted to the trill call, while the zip part of the call functions in male-male spacing. Males wrestle, kick, and push as a spacing mechanism. About one-fourth of the males do not call but act as satellites. These satellite males wait near a calling male to intercept approaching females.

BREEDING: Eggs are deposited in leaves just at the surface of the water. The leaves are then folded lengthwise and glued. *Commelina*-

Fig. 90 *Afrixalus delicatus*

like plants are favored. Eggs also may be deposited on leaves above water, like those of *Polygonum pulchrum* or *Ludwegia stolonifera*. Up to three males may fertilize a single clutch, which is laid in 1–3 nests. The tadpoles drop into the pool and develop in water.

TADPOLES: Unknown.

NOTES: This frog has been found during the day in the leaf axils of arum lilies *Cyperus* and bulrushes. In captivity, one was eaten by the red-legged kassina *Kassina maculata*.

KEY REFERENCES: Backwell 1988, Backwell & Passmore 1990a, 1990b, 1991.

Striped spiny reed frog
Afrixalus dorsalis (Peters, 1875)
(Plate 6.5)

The name *dorsalis* refers to the characteristic pattern on the back. Cameroon banana frog, brown banana frog. *Tchimbota* (plural *olimbota*) in Angola, a name applied to more than one species.

DESCRIPTION: The male reaches 28 mm and the female 29 mm in length. The iris is golden, and the back is brown with a light triangle on the head and a band on either side of the back. The throat of the male is orange. The tibia has one light spot in Angolan frogs. This species is variable, however, and specimens in the population may show various back patterns. The webbing is well developed, with one joint or less free of webbing on the fourth and fifth toes.

DISTRIBUTION AND HABITAT (FIG. 91): This species has been collected from West Africa through the western lowlands to Angola. It is an inhabitant of forests.

ADVERTISEMENT CALL: The call consists of two sections, an initial short buzz and a series of about 8–60 clicks that may continue for up to 5 s. The initial buzz has a duration of about 0.2 s. Each click in turn consists of 3 pulses and is 0.03–0.05 s long. The clicks are produced at about 12/s, with a dominant frequency of 3.8 kHz. A presumed territorial call consists of a series of short harsh buzzes.

Fig. 91 *Afrixalus dorsalis*

BREEDING: The eggs are white, 2 mm in diameter, and deposited in small clumps of 20–30 on leaves. The female faces the plant stem to lay her eggs. More than one nest may be made. The leaves are folded by the female and glued together by the hind legs of the male. The eggs are laid just above the water, and the tadpoles drop in to the pool after about 10 days. Rain is not involved in the release of the tadpoles.

TADPOLES: See the chapter on tadpoles.

KEY REFERENCES: Schiøtz 1967, Amiet 1973, Van Berkom 1975.

Fornasini's spiny reed frog
Afrixalus fornasini (Bianconi, 1849)
(Plate 6.6)

This frog was named for Carlo Fornasini.
Greater leaf-folding frog, Mozambique banana-frog, silver-banded banana frog.

DESCRIPTION: The male may grow up to 38 mm long and the female, 40 mm. The back is covered with small black spines, each on a pale wart. The typical color pattern of this frog is distinctive—a darker brown vertebral band, with wide white or light brown bands on each side. The middle band begins between the eyes and continues over the vent. In some animals the back may be uniform brown, or uniform white in the northern areas into Tanzania. The upper halves of the femur and tibia are white, with dark lower halves. The contrast between the bands may be very slight at some times, as in other species, so caution is advised when using pattern to identify them. The fingers are webbed at the base, and the toes are webbed to the discs, except the fourth toe, which has one phalanx free.

DISTRIBUTION AND HABITAT (FIG. 92): This relatively large spiny reed frog has been collected from the tropical east coast of South Africa, northward through Mozambique, the eastern margins of Zimbabwe, and Malawi to East Africa. It is associated with deep ponds where reeds are growing.

ADVERTISEMENT CALL: The male calls from vegetation hanging low over water. The call is a very loud series of "clacks," about 7–12/s with a dominant frequency at 2.3–2.6 kHz, preceded by a short, quiet buzz. One male stimulates the next to call, resulting in a considerable overlap in the calls. There is some variation in the length of the two components of the call.

BREEDING: Breeding occurs during early to mid summer. The eggs are laid in vegetation up to 1 m above water. About 80 eggs are laid on a reed leaf, starting at the tip, the edges of which are folded toward one another and glued together. Sometimes the female deposits the eggs on more than one leaf. The eggs are white, 1.6 mm in diameter, and enclosed in a 3.5-mm jelly capsule.

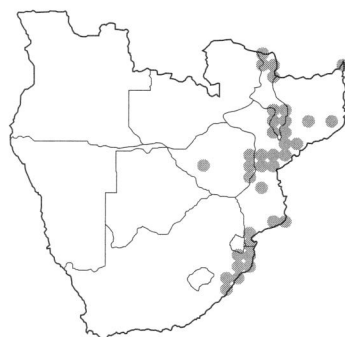

Fig. 92 *Afrixalus fornasini*

TADPOLES: See the chapter on tadpoles.

NOTES: The frog sits out on vegetation and when disturbed, drops into the water below. This frog has the unusual habit of eating the freshly laid eggs of the gray tree frog *Chiromantis xerampelina*. It finds the newly laid foam nest and sticks its head deep into the foam, to gulp a mouthful of eggs.

The skin contains small amounts of substances called *tachykinins*, which serve to detract mammal predators. Tachykinins are responsible for upsetting the normal heart beat. Fornasini's spiny reed frog is preyed upon at night by the marbled tree snake *Dipsadoboa aulica*.

KEY REFERENCES: Roseghini et al. 1988, Schneichel & Schneider 1988.

Knysna spiny reed frog
Afrixalus knysnae (Loveridge, 1954)
(Plate 6.7)

The specific name refers to Knysna on the south coast of South Africa, where the frog was first collected.
Knysna banana frog.

DESCRIPTION: This is a small frog, 25 mm long. The tubercles beneath the two outer fingers are distinct. Spines are uniformly scattered over the back and head. The background is yellow to brown with a darker vertebral band. A dark side stripe runs from the nostril through the eye to the groin.

DISTRIBUTION (FIG. 93): This species is known from the Eastern Cape Province of South Africa. It is found associated with ponds in the coastal lowlands.

ADVERTISEMENT CALL: The call is a high-pitched trill, lasting 8 s and longer. The pulses are produced at 25/s, with a dominant mid-frequency of 3.8 kHz.

BREEDING: This species breeds in shallow temporary pools. Eggs are laid in rows of 19–40 on the upper surface of submerged leaves. The

Fig. 93 *Afrixalus knysnae*

edges of the leaf are clasped between the hind limbs of the female and glued together. Eggs are 1 mm in diameter, slightly pigmented, within 2.5-mm capsules. It takes 6 weeks to metamorphosis.

TADPOLES: See the chapter on tadpoles.

KEY REFERENCE: FitzSimons 1946.

Osorio's spiny reed frog
Afrixalus osorioi (Ferreira, 1906)
(Plate 6.8)

This species was named for Balthazar Osorio.
Angola banana frog.

DESCRIPTION: The male may grow up to 31 mm SVL. The tympanum is small, and webbing extends nearly to the last joint of the fourth toe. The back is brown with small white spots and yellow ochre markings. The species is characterized by a lumbar pattern with a brown mark in the form of a U. The male has a yellow throat and small spines on the upper surfaces.

DISTRIBUTION AND HABITAT (FIG. 94): This species is known from Angola northward. It is associated with clearings and open spaces adjacent to forests.

Fig. 94 *Afrixalus osorioi*

ADVERTISEMENT CALL: The male calls from dense, low vegetation. The call is a brief deep trill, 0.4 s in duration, consisting of 12 pulses at a frequency of 2.5 kHz.

BREEDING: Unknown.

TADPOLES: Unknown.

KEY REFERENCES: Perret 1976b, Schiøtz 1982.

Natal spiny reed frog
Afrixalus spinifrons (Cope, 1862)
(Plate 7.1)

The specific name refers to the spines on the head.
Natal leaf-folding frog, Natal banana frog.

DESCRIPTION: This is a small, yellow or brown frog, with females growing up to 25 mm and males up to 20 mm. The pupil is vertical. It has a distinctive rounded snout, with many small black spines. One or two dark thin bands may be present on the back. A leg stripe is usually absent or inconspicuous. Distinct discs occur on the fingers and toes. Webbing is extensive. The throat disc of males is large and pale.

Fig. 95 *Afrixalus spinifrons*

DISTRIBUTION AND HABITAT (FIG. 95): It is known from the tropical east coast of South Africa and the KwaZulu-Natal midlands. It is found in the low vegetation around temporary pans.

ADVERTISEMENT CALL: The male calls from just above water level. The call consists of two components, a zip and a longer trill. The zip serves as a male-male interaction call, while the trill attracts females. The zip call consists of 8–23 pulses at a rate of 49–112/s. The zip call is short, lasting only 0.1–0.4 s. The mean emphasized frequencies are between 3.6 and 5.7 kHz. The trill call lasts 1.2–5.2 s and consists of 18–46 pulses at a rate of 4–13/s. Males form calling groups of up to 20 individuals.

BREEDING: This frog breeds from spring through to midsummer. The eggs are enclosed in a folded leaf, the edges of which are then glued. The leaves may be above water or submerged. The eggs are yellow, 1.2 mm in diameter, within 1.7-mm capsules. Clutch size varies from 10 to 50. Grass or *Phragmites* plants are selected for nest building. Most males call, but about 5% are satellites. Satellite males wait near calling males to intercept approaching females.

TADPOLES: See the chapter on tadpoles.

NOTES: They are reported to eat mosquitoes.

KEY REFERENCE: Backwell & Passmore 1991.

De Witte's spiny reed frog
Afrixalus wittei (Laurent, 1941)
(Plate 7.2)

The specific name refers to G.-F. de Witte, herpetologist at the Institut Royal des Sciences Naturelles in Brussels until 1951.
De Witte's leaping frog, Witte's banana frog.

DESCRIPTION: This is a small frog, although large for the genus, with the female growing up to 33 mm SVL. Small spines are present on the upper surface. A dark band is present along the side of the snout. A dark dorsolateral band without pale speckles reaches the back of the upper eyelid. Background color is golden yellow to brown. A pair of dark bands either side of the midline converges over the head.

DISTRIBUTION AND HABITAT (FIG. 96): This frog is found in tropical lowland savannas, known from eastern Angola, Zambia, and southwestern Democratic Republic of the Congo.

ADVERTISEMENT CALL: The male calls from grass blades over water. The call consists of a short buzz, followed by a rapid series of about 8 clicks. The duration of the buzz is 0.2 s, followed by the clicks, at a rate of 12/s. The duration of the call is about 0.8 s. The call has an emphasized frequency of 2.8 kHz.

Fig. 96 *Afrixalus wittei*

BREEDING: Unknown.

TADPOLES: Unknown.

KEY REFERENCE: Schiøtz 1975.

Reed Frogs—Genus *Hyperolius*

This genus consists of small to medium-sized (20–35-mm) climbing frogs that are often brightly colored. Living specimens (especially calling males) are surprisingly easy to identify, although preserved museum specimens are very difficult. The pupil is horizontal or round, the tympanum is indistinct, and the skin is smooth. There are no cornified spines on the female. The tips of the fingers and toes are expanded. Most species show a number of color patterns, and these often differ between the male and the female. Juveniles often have a color phase that becomes one of many adult phases. Eggs are laid on the surface or just above water level in vegetation. The eggs are small, 0.8–1.5 mm in diameter, with 100–500 or more per clutch. The lack of field information for many of these frogs results in uncertainty of the validity of many species names.

The genus is found in the savannas and forests of Africa south of the Sahara.

KEY TO MALES OF THE SPECIES OF *HYPEROLIUS*, EXCLUDING *HYPEROLIUS MARMORATUS*

This key is restricted to adult males. There is much variation in this genus, and a number of adult (calling) males should be examined. Where more than one species is indicated in the key, the species can be separated by examining the advertisement calls. *Hyperolius marmoratus* males display a range of color patterns and could be misidentified using the following key. The advertisement calls of the *H. marmoratus* complex are quite distinct, however, and this widespread group should be recognized easily. This genus is notorious for the lack of distinguishing characters that can be used in keys. Caution is required, using other clues besides the characters in these keys before arriving at an identification.

Check if the specimen could be *Hyperolius marmoratus* before using this key!

Tree Frogs—Family Hyperoliidae

1a. Belly dark with large pale spots (Fig. 97)
   Hyperolius steindachneri
1b. Belly not dark with large pale spots   2

Fig. 97   Belly spots

2a. Throat pouch turquoise   *Hyperolius kachalolae*
2b. Throat pouch not turquoise   3

3a. Throat flap with black spines (Fig. 98)   *Hyperolius spinigularis*
3b. Not as above   4

Fig. 98   Throat spines

4a. A pale triangle with base at level of eyes (Fig. 99)   5
4b. No pale triangle   6

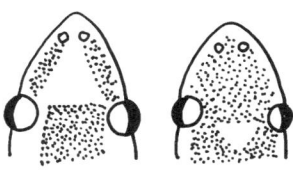

Fig. 99   Pale triangle

5a. Background color green   *Hyperolius ocellatus*
5b. Background color brown   *Hyperolius tuberilinguis* (part)

6a. Light heel spot present   7
6b. No light heel spot   8

7a. Pale brown dorsolateral stripe with a narrow dark border
   Hyperolius pickersgilli (part)

7b. White dorsolateral stripe with a broad dark border
Hyperolius mitchelli

8a. Green translucent belly skin, less than 25 mm   9
8b. Not as above   10

9a. Slender frogs, head width less than one-third of body length
Hyperolius nasutus or *Hyperolius poweri*
9b. Flat broad frogs, head width more than one-third of body length
Hyperolius pusillus

10a. Dorsolateral bands or rows of spots present   11
10b. No dorsolateral bands present   15

11a. Lateral bands darker than background   12
11b. Lateral bands lighter than background   18

12a. A lighter stripe present dorsal to the dark dorsolateral band
Hyperolius kivuensis
12b. No lighter stripe   13

13a. Dark bands converge behind eyes, eyes large
Hyperolius cinereus
13b. Dark bands do not converge behind eyes   14

14a. Head wider than one-third of body length, back green
Hyperolius vilhenai
14b. Head width less than one-third of body length
Hyperolius bocagei

15a. Back uniform green, head pointed
Hyperolius tuberilinguis (part)
15b. Back variously patterned   16

16a. Dorsal pattern consists of red and black reticulations on a cream background   *Hyperolius angolensis*
16b. Not as above   17

17a. An hourglass pattern on a brown background (Fig. 100)
Hyperolius major

Tree Frogs—Family Hyperoliidae 147

17b. Not an hourglass pattern
Hyperolius pictus or *Hyperolius puncticulatus* or *Hyperolius angolensis*

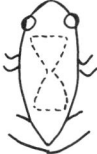

Fig. 100 Hourglass pattern

18a. Five light stripes on back (Fig. 101)
Hyperolius quinquevittatus
18b. Two dorsolateral bands or stripes present 19

Fig. 101 Five light stripes

19a. Pale dorsolateral bands with a dark border 20
19b. Pale dorsolateral bands without a dark edge 21

20a. One segment of fourth toe free of web (Fig. 102)
Hyperolius parkeri
20b. Two or more segments of fourth toe free of web
Hyperolius pickersgilli (part)

Fig. 102 One phalanx free

21a. Pale band runs from nostril to groin, through eye (Fig. 103)
Hyperolius argus
21b. Not as above 22

Fig. 103 Lateral band

22a. Distinct rows of dark spots on dorsum 23
22b. No distinct rows of dark spots 24

23a. Back green, up to 22-mm SVL   *Hyperolius nasutus* (part)
23b. Back brown, up to 43-mm SVL   *Hyperolius horstockii*

24a. Yellow bands from snout tip on a green background
    Hyperolius semidiscus
24b. Pale bands starting behind snout tip   25

25a. A light vertebral band present
    Hyperolius puncticulatus (part)
25b. No light vertebral band   *Hyperolius cinnamomeoventris*

Angolan reed frog

Hyperolius angolensis Steindachner, 1867
(Plate 7.3)

The specific name refers to Angola. A study in progress on the genetics of this and related frogs may lead to future changes in the status or name of this species.

DESCRIPTION: This is a medium-sized reed frog, with the female reaching 35 mm in length. It is similar to *H. marmoratus* morphologically. However, the color pattern of the back is quite distinct, consisting of red or brown markings, often with black, on a cream background. These markings are frequently interlinked. A finely vermiculated pattern is also common. The inside of the limbs, and the fingers and toes are red.

DISTRIBUTION AND HABITAT (FIG. 104): This species is known from Angola, western Zambia, southward to northern Namibia

Argus Reed Frog 149

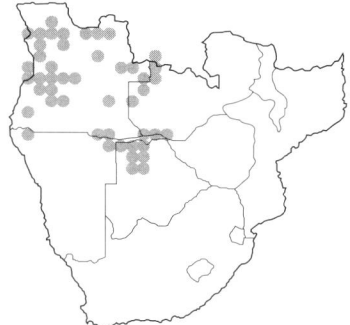

Fig. 104 *Hyperolius angolensis*

and northern Botswana. It occurs in savannas along rivers and streams.

ADVERTISEMENT CALL: The male calls from vegetation overhanging water, from early evening. The call is a brief whistle, 0.04 s in duration, at a frequency of 2.3 kHz. A chorus along a watercourse sounds like the tinkling of many drinking glasses.

BREEDING: The eggs are attached to submerged roots in small clumps. The eggs are pale yellow with a darker brown pole. The clutch size is about 200.

TADPOLES: The tadpoles are found in shallow water among vegetation.

NOTES: It is reported to be preyed upon by the bush snake *Philothamnus*.

KEY REFERENCE: Laurent 1954.

Argus reed frog
Hyperolius argus Peters, 1854
(Plates 7.4, 7.5)

This species is named for Argus the guardian of Io, the mythical being whose 100 eyes were given to the peacock.

Argus sedge frog, argus-eyed frog, argus-spotted sedge-frog, Boror reed frog.

DESCRIPTION: The male may be up to 34 mm long. The body is relatively wide, with a head width–body length proportion of 36%–42%. The sexes have different color patterns, with the male green or gray, often with small brown dots on the back, and thin light lateral bands. The female is light brown with a horseshoe-shaped pale band, with darker outline, over the snout and eyes. The bands on the back may be absent, or present as a series of wide dots.

DISTRIBUTION AND HABITAT (FIG. 105): This lowland species is recorded from Mozambique and the tropical northeast coastal plain of South Africa. It is found associated with temporary and permanent pools where water lilies are growing.

ADVERTISEMENT CALL: The male calls from vegetation growing in water, frequently on water lily leaves. The call is a rapidly repeated cluck, each call being only about 0.02 s long, with dominant harmonics between 3 and 4 kHz.

BREEDING: Breeding occurs around the edges and in the middle of shallow pans. These temporary pools formed in flat depressions are a favorite habitat for this species. It breeds from spring to summer after the rains have started. The eggs are 1 mm in diameter, within

Fig. 105 *Hyperolius argus*

4-mm capsules. Clutch size is about 200 eggs, laid in clusters of 30, each cluster being attached to vegetation hanging in water and up to 50mm below the surface.

TADPOLES: See the chapter on tadpoles.

KEY REFERENCE: Wager 1986.

Bocage's reed frog
Hyperolius bocagei Steindachner, 1867
(Plates 7.6, 7.7)

This species is named for the herpetologist J. V. Barboza du Bocage, who contributed greatly to the understanding of African frogs.
Katuti in Angola.

DESCRIPTION: This is a small frog, with the male up to 26mm SVL. The head is relatively broad, less than one-third of the body length. The main part of the webbing is level with the middle tubercle below the fourth toe, but forming a visible margin almost to the tip of the toe. The back is brown to green or yellow, with a darker dorsolateral line or series of spots in males. The back and upper limbs often have scattered dark spots. A dark line is often present on the side of the snout. Females in breeding are tomato red. This species is similar in overall morphology to the marbled reed frog *H. marmoratus* but distinguishable by its reduced webbing.

DISTRIBUTION AND HABITAT (FIG. 106): This species is known from Angola, southern Democratic Republic of the Congo, and western Zambia. It is associated with grassy pans.

ADVERTISEMENT CALL: The male calls from elevated positions in vegetation near water. Two calls may be heard, a harsh brief buzz at 3.5kHz with a duration of 0.03s, and a soft slower series of 4 or 5 clicks. The latter call may indicate male aggression.

BREEDING: Unknown.

TADPOLES: Unknown.

Fig. 106 *Hyperolius bocagii*

NOTES: It is believed in Angola that cattle die if they eat this species. The biology of this frog needs to be investigated in the field and involve finding the eggs and tadpoles.

KEY REFERENCE: Laurent 1964.

Ashy reed frog
Hyperolius cinereus Monard, 1937

The specific name *cinereus* means "ashy."
Monard's reed frog.

DESCRIPTION: The male grows up to 24 mm long and the female, 28 mm. Color (in preservative) is pale above and blue-gray below. The inner surface of the thigh is red. The male has two darker dorsolateral bands converging bluntly before reaching the level of the eyes. The eye is large, about 12% of body length.

DISTRIBUTION AND HABITAT (FIG. 107): This little-known frog has been recorded from a few localities in Angola. The preferred habitat is unknown.

ADVERTISEMENT CALL: Unknown.

BREEDING: Unknown.

Fig. 107 *Hyperolius cinereus*

TADPOLES: Unknown.

KEY REFERENCE: Monard 1937.

Cinnamon-bellied reed frog
Hyperolius cinnamomeoventris Bocage, 1866
(Plate 7.8)

The specific name *cinnamomeoventris* means "cinnamon colored belly."
Bragança reed frog.

DESCRIPTION: The male reaches 28 mm in length. The sexes have different color patterns, with the male brown or green with a light dorsolateral line and the female green above and pale yellow below, with an irregular dark line separating the two colors. The male may have darker spots on the back, with a yellow throat. The female does not have the pale dorsolateral lines, but a short dark line is present on the side of the snout. The skin of the back of both sexes is rather coarse.

DISTRIBUTION AND HABITAT (FIG. 108): This distinctive species is known from Cameroon, the Democratic Republic of the Congo, Uganda, Angola, and Kenya. It is found in both forests and savannas.

Fig. 108 *Hyperolius cinnamomeoventris*

ADVERTISEMENT CALL: The call consists of short clicks, each about 0.05 s long, with a dominant frequency of 3 kHz.

BREEDING: Unknown. The eggs are unpigmented.

TADPOLES: Unknown.

NOTES: This species is unusual in that it has been collected from both forests and savannas, and it would be very interesting to discover its biology.

KEY REFERENCES: Perret 1966, Inger 1968, Schiøtz 1975.

Horstock's reed frog
Hyperolius horstockii (Schlegel, 1837)
(Plate 8.1)

This frog was named for Hubertus B. van Horstock, who practiced medicine in Cape Town from 1826 to 1834. He collected for the Royal Museum of Natural History in Leyden.
Arum frog, arum lily frog, arum reed frog. *Arum-Frosch, Aronstab-Frosch* in German.

DESCRIPTION: This frog reaches 43 mm in length. The dorsal color is a pale yellow to a light brown. Very small dark spots are present on the back. A fine dark line runs along the side of the snout and

Horstock's Reed Frog

continues backward. Sometimes a series of small speckles separates the back color from a pale band on the side. The throat of the male is orange, and the hidden surfaces of the leg are red. The web and discs are also red-orange. The main webbing reaches or just passes the inner tubercle beneath the fourth toe.

DISTRIBUTION AND HABITAT (FIG. 109): Horstock's reed frog is found from the Tsitsikama National Park westward to Cape Town.

ADVERTISEMENT CALL: The male calls from the surface of the water, or up to a meter above water level, on vegetation growing in the water. The call is a long harsh bleat, about 0.4 s in duration, rising in frequency from 2.5 to 3.0 kHz.

BREEDING: Although this frog lives in a winter rainfall area, breeding takes place in early spring and summer. It is known to spawn from October to November. The eggs are 2 mm in diameter, inside 4-mm jelly capsules. They are cream with a brown hemisphere. Numerous clutches, 10–30 in size, are attached below water level to the roots of water plants.

TADPOLES: See the chapter on tadpoles.

NOTES: This frog usually is found during the day on sedges and other vegetation. This species was found breeding in the same ponds as the

Fig. 109   *Hyperolius horstockii*

marbled reed frog west of the Groot River Pass. The whiskered tern eats this frog.

KEY REFERENCES: Power & Rose 1929, Visser 1979, Wager 1986.

Kachalola reed frog
Hyperolius kachalolae Schiøtz, 1975
(Plate 8.2)

This frog was named for the town of Kachalola in Zambia, where the first specimens were collected.

DESCRIPTION: This frog reaches 29 mm in length. The back is smooth. Webbing is not extensive, one and one-half to one and three-fourths phalanges of the fourth toe are free of web. The sexes have different color patterns. The back is brown, green, or yellow in the male. A thin red line on the side of the snout continues backward as a dorsolateral stripe. This is sometimes broken into a series of small red spots. The upper surfaces of the female are tomato red. The discs and webbing are red. The underside is white. In males the throat flap is large, colored like the back, but the vocal sac is sometimes bright turquoise.

DISTRIBUTION (FIG. 110): This species is known from southern Malawi and the highlands of western and eastern Zambia. It is found in vegetation along the edges of small streams.

Fig. 110 *Hyperolius kachalolae*

ADVERTISEMENT CALL: Males call away from water, on grass, or high up in trees. The call is a short whistle 0.1 s long, with a dominant harmonic at 2.6 kHz. The call has an unusual, almost nasal, tonal quality.

BREEDING: Unknown.

TADPOLES: Unknown.

NOTES: Our knowledge of this species, like so many other reed frogs, is incomplete. Visitors to the area and residents would be able to make valuable contributions by observing and reporting details of natural history.

KEY REFERENCE: Schiøtz 1975.

Kivu reed frog
Hyperolius kivuensis Ahl, 1931
(Plate 8.3)

The specific name refers to Lake Kivu on the border between the Democratic Republic of the Congo and Rwanda.
Lake Kivu reed frog.

DESCRIPTION: The male reaches 33 mm in length. This species has a slender body with a long snout. The back is brown, silvery gray, or bright green. A dark stripe on the side of the snout passes backward through the eye to become a dark stripe on the side of the body. Sometimes a lighter line is present above the dark one. The underside is pale to gray. The parts of the legs and feet that are concealed when the animal is at rest are yellow to red.

DISTRIBUTION AND HABITAT (FIG. 111): This widely distributed reed frog is known from Angola, Zambia, Malawi, the Democratic Republic of the Congo, Burundi, Uganda, Tanzania, and Kenya. It is found in open bush.

ADVERTISEMENT CALL: The male calls from concealed positions high in vegetation. The call is a number of creaks. Each creak con-

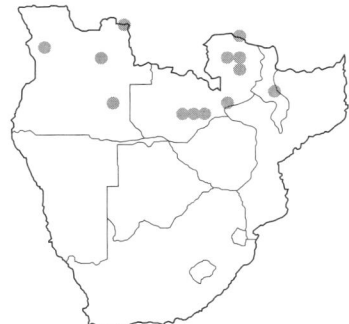

Fig. 111 *Hyperolius kivuensis*

sists of 5–8 pulses, with a duration of 0.1–0.18 s. The dominant harmonic is at 2.5 kHz.

BREEDING: The eggs are white with a dark pole. They are laid on vegetation.

TADPOLES: Unknown.

KEY REFERENCE: Ahl 1931.

Greater reed frog
Hyperolius major Laurent, 1957

The specific name *major* refers to the relatively large size of this species, compared to related frogs.

DESCRIPTION: The male may grow up to 30-mm long. The side of the face is curved, and the head width is 36%–41% of body length. The broad head gives the animal a flat-faced appearance. Webbing is moderate, extending at least up to the middle tubercle beneath the fourth toe. Two different color patterns are common. The first is a darker hourglass pattern on a brown background, sometimes with a pale triangle over the snout. The alternative pattern is a lighter band on the sides of the snout and body against a brown background.

Marmoratus Complex

Fig. 112 *Hyperolius major*

DISTRIBUTION AND HABITAT (FIG. 112): This forest species is only known from southern Democratic Republic of the Congo and northwestern Zambia.

ADVERTISEMENT CALL: Unknown.

BREEDING: Unknown.

TADPOLES: Unknown.

NOTES: Detailed field observations are needed for this little-known species.

KEY REFERENCES: Laurent 1957, Poynton & Broadley 1987.

Hyperolius marmoratus complex

This frog represents one of the puzzles of zoology. It is not known whether all the frogs placed in this species represent different color patterns of the same species, or whether they are actually a number of different, but similar-looking species. The frogs grouped into this species are termed a *complex*. This complex consists of a number of highly variable and very colorful reed frogs that have confused herpetologists for decades. Part of the confusion derives from the overlapping of color patterns in different localities. Additionally, each juvenile possesses one of a number of color patterns.

As it matures, it may retain the juvenile pattern or acquire one of a number of adult patterns. About 40 different color patterns are recognized in this complex. Genes control color patterns, and various populations appear to possess various combinations of color-pattern genes. This results in particular patterns being present in localized populations, for example, the striped forms common in northern KwaZulu-Natal. Various scientists have referred to these color forms as subspecies within one of three species: *H. parallelus*, *H. viridiflavus*, or *H. marmoratus*. Another opinion is that the forms intermingle and should be referred to as the species *H. marmoratus*.

The male advertisement call, which is unique to each species, and hence useful to distinguish species, is a very short whistle. The brevity of this call had made it difficult to analyze, before the recent availability of suitable computer programs. Some of the populations previously treated as subspecies or races of *H. marmoratus* have been found to have unique calls and have been recognized as distinct species. The Angolan reed frog *H. angolensis* is one example. Preliminary examination of *Hyperolius* calls recorded in southern and eastern Africa shows that at least three different call types are present. One is a short whistle at a constant frequency. The second is a longer whistle, rising initially through 300 Hz or more, before leveling off. The third call type is a short note that is often pulsed and not as harmonically pure as a whistle. Extensive fieldwork will be required to record natural calls at different temperatures and from as many different individuals in each population as possible. Detailed call analysis is required as part of the approach to understand the relationships in this complex.

The introduction of molecular biochemical techniques in recent years has enabled particular genes to be traced in populations. This has led to an understanding of the evolution and relationships of many species, some of which were difficult to identify using only external features. Preliminary biochemical studies of some populations of this group of reed frogs indicate that some subspecies are genetically identical and can confidently be placed in one species, while other subspecies are genetically isolated from neighboring populations and should be recognized as separate species.

The *H. marmoratus* complex presently consists of populations grouped by shared color patterns into subspecies. The biochemical work and the detailed call analyses indicate that the relationships and names within this complex should be revised. Until such an analysis is available, the present status should be maintained, with the caution that the taxonomy and systematics of this group are being revised. At the time of writing, a report was being prepared to split this complex into a number of species, based on differences in DNA sequences. The old classification is given here.

Marbled reed frog
Hyperolius marmoratus Rapp, 1842
(Plates 8.4, 8.5, 8.6, 8.7, 8.8)

The specific name *marmoratus* means "marbled" and refers to the color pattern.
Painted reed frog. *Kilowero* in Nyanja, *zonde* in Chewa, *marmorierter Riedfrosch* in German.

DESCRIPTION: This is a small to medium-sized frog, with the male reaching 43 mm in length. The side of the snout is curved, and the head width is 32%–38% of the body length. The main part of the webbing passes the middle tubercle beneath the fourth toe on the outer side. Various color patterns are found, some of which are listed below. These represent only broad classifications of pattern types, and many variations are known. Each color pattern description is followed by the current subspecies designation in parentheses.

1. Five light bands separated by four dark bands, with variations. These five bands are equal in width. This pattern is most common in southern Mozambique to northeastern South Africa, Swaziland, Zimbabwe, and Malawi. (*H. marmoratus taeniatus.*)
2. Three light bands, often with thin red lines along the center, separated by darker bands. The middle light band is about half the width of either black band adjoining it. This pattern is known from the eastern Zimbabwe area and western Mozambique. (*H. marmoratus marginatus.*)
3. A uniform brown back, with a darker margin. Darker spots are sometimes present. This pattern is known from eastern Zambia, northern Zimbabwe, western Malawi, and southeastern Tanzania. (*H. marmoratus marginatus.*)
4. Asymmetrical dark spots, marbling, or reticulation. The male often has a brown back with a light line behind each eye.

This form has been found in southern Zimbabwe and adjacent Mozambique. (*H. marmoratus swynnertoni.*)

5. A yellow or brown background, with lighter spots, each with a dark center. The underside has red marbling. This color pattern is known from south central Zambia. (*H. marmoratus pyrrhodictyon.*)

6. Red-brown spots on a light background. Sometimes the back is vermiculated. Dark spots are found around the vent and on the limbs. This pattern is known from northwestern Zambia, eastern Angola, and southern Democratic Republic of the Congo. (*H. marmoratus alborufus.*)

7. A dark red or brown back with a pale yellow stripe in the center of the back. A lateral light line separates the upper and lower surfaces. So far this is only known from northern Zambia. (*H. marmoratus argentovittis.*)

8. A yellow-brown back with an indistinct yellow dorsolateral line. Black spots are found on the sides and limbs. This form has been found from northeastern Zambia and southwestern Tanzania. (*H. marmoratus bitaeniatus.*)

9. A pale yellow back, often with small dark spots on the sides of the head. Sometimes a bright yellow dorsolateral band is present. This form is known in northern Zambia. (*H. marmoratus rhodoscelis.*)

10. Three light bands, with a central red line, separated by dark bands. The light and dark bands may be intermingled, to the extent that a reticulated pattern may be present. This pattern is found in central Zambia. (*H. marmoratus melanoleucus.*)

11. The back is black, with a pale yellow band. This form is found in southern Malawi and western Mozambique. (*H. marmoratus albofasciatus.*)

12. A pale brown background with black markings, sometimes forming irregular bands. This form is known from northern Malawi. (*H. marmoratus nyassae.*)

13. A brown or black background with lighter spots. This pattern is known from the southeastern Cape to southern Natal. (*H. marmoratus verrucosus.*)

14. Contrasting irregular patterns of light and dark, with yellows, browns, orange, and black being common colors. This pattern is found in KwaZulu-Natal. (*H. marmoratus marmoratus.*)

Marbled Reed Frog

DISTRIBUTION AND HABITAT (FIG. 113): This species complex is widely distributed in moist sub-Saharan Africa. It is found in savannas and open bush along streams and rivers, as well as in lowlands where temporary pools form during the rainy season.

ADVERTISEMENT CALL: The male calls from vegetation around pans and other water bodies. The following call details refer to populations on the South African east coast. The call is a short whistle, about 0.1 s long, with the emphasized frequency rising from 2.8 to 3.1 kHz. The call is very loud. Two males may call simultaneously but alternating with a third. The call is used to maintain male spacing at a minimum of about 50 cm, and the female selects an isolated male rather than a male calling close to another calling male. The female prefers a male with lower-frequency calls, implying that larger males are selected, as larger frogs make lower-pitched calls. The female also selects the male with the loudest call, providing that there is a reasonable difference between the calls. The male will return exactly to a previously used calling site on successive evenings.

BREEDING: A clutch consists of 150–650 small eggs, each 1.3–1.5 mm in diameter, within 2.5-mm capsules. Eggs are attached to submerged roots in small clumps of about 20. The eggs are pale yellow with a darker brown pole. Some eggs also have been reported as blue-green. Metamorphosis takes 64–100 days in captivity. A female has been reported to produce eggs (72–694/clutch) every 2 or 3 weeks for up to 14 months and longer in captivity, once sexual

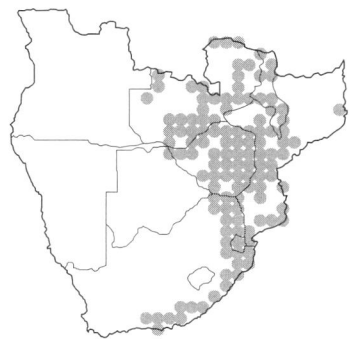

Fig. 113 *Hyperolius marmoratus*

maturity is reached. In the field the clutch size is also variable, as a female may lay a second clutch 15–60 days later, depending on the weather.

TADPOLES: See the chapter on tadpoles.

DEVELOPMENT OF COLOR POLYMORPHISM: The identification of this frog depends to a large extent on color pattern. Juveniles possess certain patterns and adults, others. The female and male color pattern develops differently. Some males retain the pattern they had as juveniles, yet others develop different patterns. The female pattern is usually completely different from the juvenile pattern. It has been shown that the adult color phase is developed when the animal reaches sexual maturity. When researchers bathed metamorphosing froglets in estrogen or testosterone (hormones normally only present at sexual maturity) for 1 minute a day, the juveniles developed precocious adult patterns. The natural potential for recombining the genes controlling color pattern is enormous. The amount of variation possible from a limited number of parents was illustrated by breeding six generations from one pair. The offspring showed an amazing variety of color patterns. If two individuals possess the genetic resources to create all these patterns, why do most populations in the field consist of one dominant pattern? Studies of the genetics of these frogs in the field would be very useful.

PROTECTION AGAINST DESICCATION: This frog spends time out in the bright sun and is at risk from drying out. Overall, however, it has a very low rate of water loss through the skin compared to other frogs. Water is further conserved in three main ways: by reducing activity, by reflecting sunlight, and by storing water in the bladder that is used for cooling when conditions become critical. During the dry season it reduces water loss by inactivity, remaining motionless on one leaf all day. It also reduces the loss of moisture by reducing the secretion from its skin glands. Above very high temperatures, like 42 °C, it makes use of body water stored in the bladder for cooling, by releasing it through the skin to permit evaporation. In the dry season the frog aestivates, a special form of dry-season "hibernation" that slows its metabolism down to 50% of the normal resting rate, which further reduces water loss. During the dry season the frog is white, especially at high temperatures. This reflective color derives

PLATE 1

1.1 *Arthroleptis francei*
France's squeaker (C. Tilbury), p. 43

1.2 *Arthroleptis reichei*
Reiche's squeaker (A. Pauw), p. 45

1.3 *Arthroleptis stenodactylus*
Common squeaker, p.45

1.4 *Arthroleptis wahlbergii*
Bush squeaker, p. 48

1.5 *Schoutedenella xenochirus*
Plain squeaker, p. 52

1.6 *Schoutedenella xenodactyloides*
Dwarf squeaker, p. 53

1.7 *Bufo amatolicus*
Amatola toad (M. Burger), p. 61

1.8 *Bufo angusticeps*
Sand toad, p. 63

PLATE 2

2.1 *Bufo* sp.
Solwezi toad, p. 57

2.2 *Bufo dombensis*
Dombe toad, p. 65

2.3 *Bufo fenoulheti*
Fenoulhet's toad, p. 66

2.4 *Bufo gariepensis*
Karoo toad, p. 70

2.5 *Bufo garmani*
Garman's toad, p. 72

2.6 *Bufo gutturalis*
Guttural toad, p. 74

2.7 *Bufo hoeschi*
Hoesch's toad, p. 77

2.8 *Bufo inyangae*
Inyanga toad, p. 78

PLATE 3

3.1 *Bufo kisoloensis*
Kisolo toad, male and female, p. 81

3.2 *Bufo lemairii*
Lemaire's toad, p. 82

3.3 *Bufo maculatus*
Flat-backed toad, p. 84

3.4 *Bufo nyikae*
Nyika dwarf toad (J. Bogart), p. 87

3.5 *Bufo pantherinus*
Western leopard toad, p. 89

3.6 *Bufo pardalis*
Leopard toad, p. 90

3.7 *Bufo poweri*
Power's toad, p. 91

3.8 *Bufo rangeri*
Ranger's toad, p. 93

PLATE 4

4.1 *Bufo robinsoni*
Paradise toad, p. 95

4.2 *Bufo taitanus*
Taita toad (A. Pauw), p. 96

4.3 *Bufo vertebralis*
Pygmy toad (M. Burger), p. 98

4.4 *Capensibufo rosei*
Rose's toad, p. 100

4.5 *Capensibufo tradouwi*
Tradouw's toad (M. Burger), p. 102

4.6 *Schismaderma carens*
Red toad, p. 103

4.7 *Stephopaedes anotis*
Chirinda toad, p. 105

4.8 *Heleophryne hewitti*
Hewitt's ghost frog (R. C. Boycott),
p. 109

PLATE 5

5.1 *Heleophryne natalensis*
Natal ghost frog, p. 111

5.2 *Heleophryne orientalis*
Eastern ghost frog (J. Visser), p. 112

5.3 *Heleophryne purcelli*
Purcell's ghost frog, p. 113

5.4 *Heleophryne regis*
Royal ghost frog (R. C. Boycott), p. 115

5.5 *Heleophryne rosei*
Rose's ghost frog (A. de Villiers), p. 117

5.6 *Hemisus* sp.
Barotse snout-burrower, p. 120

5.7 *Hemisus guttatus*
Spotted snout-burrower, p. 122

5.8 *Hemisus marmoratus*
Marbled snout-burrower, p. 124

PLATE 6

6.1 *Afrixalus aureus*
Golden spiny reed frog, p. 130

6.2 *Afrixalus brachycnemis*
Short-legged spiny reed frog, p. 132

6.3 *Afrixalus crotalus*
Snoring spiny reed frog, p. 133

6.4 *Afrixalus delicatus*
Delicate spiny reed frog, p. 134

6.5 *Afrixalus dorsalis*
Striped spiny reed frog (R. C. Drewes),
p. 136

6.6 *Afrixalus fornasini*
Fornasini's spiny reed frog, p. 137

6.7 *Afrixalus knysnae*
Knysna spiny reed frog (M. Burger),
p. 139

6.8 *Afrixalus osorioi*
Osorio's spiny reed frog (J. Vindum),
p. 140

PLATE 7

7.1 *Afrixalus spinifrons*
Natal spiny reed frog, p. 141

7.2 *Afrixalus wittei*
De Witte's spiny reed frog, p. 143

7.3 *Hyperolius angolensis*
Angolan reed frog, p. 148

7.4 *Hyperolius argus*
Argus reed frog, male, p. 149

7.5 *Hyperolius argus*
Argus reed frog, female, p. 149

7.6 *Hyperolius bocagei*
Bocage's reed frog, male, p. 151

7.7 *Hyperolius bocagei*
Bocage's reed frog, female, p. 151

7.8 *Hyperolius cinnamomeoventris*
Cinnamon-bellied reed frog (J. Vindum),
p. 153

PLATE 8

8.1 *Hyperolius horstockii*
Horstock's reed frog, p. 154

8.2 *Hyperolius kachalolae*
Kachalola reed frog, p. 156

8.3 *Hyperolius kivuensis*
Kivu reed frog, p. 157

8.4 *Hyperolius marmoratus*
Marbled reed frog, spotted type, p. 161

8.5 *Hyperolius marmoratus*
Marbled reed frog, speckled type, p. 161

8.6 *Hyperolius marmoratus*
Marbled reed frog, striped type, p. 161

8.7 *Hyperolius marmoratus*
Marbled reed frog, striped type, p. 161

8.8 *Hyperolius marmoratus*
Marbled reed frog, marbled type, p. 161

PLATE 9

9.1 *Hyperolius mitchelli*
Mitchell's reed frog, p. 165

9.2 *Hyperolius nasutus*
Long reed frog, p. 166

9.3 *Hyperolius nasutus*
Long reed frog, p. 166

9.4 *Hyperolius ocellatus*
Golden-eyed reed frog (M. Largen),
p. 168

9.5 *Hyperolius parkeri*
Parker's reed frog, p. 169

9.6 *Hyperolius pictus*
Variable reed frog, p. 172

9.7 *Hyperolius pictus*
Variable reed frog, p. 172

9.8 *Hyperolius poweri*
Power's reed frog, p. 173

PLATE 10

10.1 *Hyperolius puncticulatus*
Spotted reed frog, p. 175

10.2 *Hyperolius puncticulatus*
Spotted reed frog, p. 175

10.3 *Hyperolius pusillus*
Water lily reed frog, p. 176

10.4 *Hyperolius quinquevittatus*
Five-striped reed frog, p. 178

10.5 *Hyperolius semidiscus*
Yellow-striped reed frog (M. Burger),
p. 179

10.6 *Hyperolius spinigularis*
Spiny-throated reed frog, male, p. 180

10.7 *Hyperolius spinigularis*
Spiny-throated reed frog, female, p. 180

10.8 *Hyperolius steindachneri*
Steindachner's reed frog (W. Haacke),
p. 182

PLATE 11

11.1 *Hyperolius tuberilinguis*
Tinker reed frog, p. 183

11.2 *Kassinula wittei*
De Witte's clicking frog, p. 185

11.3 *Kassina kuvangensis*
Kuvangu kassina, p. 187

11.4 *Kassina maculata*
Red-legged kassina, p. 189

11.5 *Kassina senegalensis*
Senegal kassina, p. 191

11.6 *Semnodactylus wealii*
Weale's running frog, p. 193

11.7 *Leptopelis argenteus*
Silvery tree frog, p. 197

11.8 *Leptopelis bocagii*
Bocage's tree frog, p. 198

PLATE 12

12.1 *Leptopelis cynnamomeus*
Cinnamon tree frog, p. 200

12.2 *Leptopelis flavomaculatus*
Yellow-spotted tree frog, male, p. 201

12.3 *Leptopelis flavomaculatus*
Yellow-spotted tree frog, juvenile,
p. 201

12.4 *Leptopelis mossambicus*
Mozambique tree frog, p. 203

12.5 *Leptopelis natalensis*
Natal tree frog (M. Burger), p. 204

12.6 *Leptopelis xenodactylus*
Long-toed tree frog (M. Burger), p. 207

12.7 *Breviceps acutirostris*
Strawberry rain frog, p. 212

12.8 *Breviceps adspersus*
Common rain frog, amplexus, p. 213

PLATE 13

13.1 *Breviceps fuscus*
Black rain frog, p. 215

13.2 *Breviceps gibbosus*
Giant rain frog, p. 216

13.3 *Breviceps macrops*
Desert rain frog, p. 218

13.4 *Breviceps montanus*
Mountain rain frog, p. 219

13.5 *Breviceps mossambicus*
Mozambique rain frog, dark phase, p. 220

13.6 *Breviceps mossambicus*
Mozambique rain frog (M. Burger), p. 220

13.7 *Breviceps namaquensis*
Namaqua rain frog, p. 222

13.8 *Breviceps poweri*
Power's rain frog, pale phase, p. 223

PLATE 14

14.1 *Breviceps poweri*
Power's rain frog, dark phase, p. 223

14.2 *Breviceps rosei*
Rose's rain frog, p. 224

14.3 *Breviceps sylvestris*
Forest rain frog, p. 226

14.4 *Breviceps verrucosus*
Plaintive rain frog, p. 227

14.5 *Breviceps* sp.
Whistling rain frog (M. Burger), p. 228

14.6 *Phrynomantis affinis*
Spotted rubber frog, p. 231

14.7 *Phrynomantis annectens*
Marbled rubber frog, p. 232

14.8 *Phrynomantis bifasciatus*
Banded rubber frog, p. 234

PLATE 15

15.1 *Xenopus epitropicalis*
Southern tropical platanna (M. Largen),
p. 239

15.2 *Xenopus fraseri*
Fraser's platanna (H.-J. Herrmann),
p. 240

15.3 *Xenopus gilli*
Gill's platanna, p. 241

15.4 *Xenopus laevis*
Common platanna (M. Burger), p. 243

15.5 *Xenopus muelleri*
Müller's platanna, p. 247

15.6 *Xenopus petersii*
Peters' platanna, p. 248

15.7 *Afrana angolensis*
Angola river frog, p. 255

15.8 *Afrana dracomontana*
Drakensberg river frog, p. 257

PLATE 16

16.1 *Afrana fuscigula*
Cape river frog, p. 259

16.2 *Afrana inyangae*
Inyanga river frog, p. 260

16.3 *Afrana johnstoni*
Johnston's river frog (A. Pauw), p. 262

16.4 *Afrana vandijki*
Van Dijk's river frog, p. 263

16.5 *Amietia vertebralis*
Large-mouthed frog, p. 264

16.6 *Amnirana darlingi*
Darling's white-lipped frog, p. 266

16.7 *Amnirana galamensis*
Galam white-lipped frog, p. 268

16.8 *Amnirana lemairii*
Lemaire's white-lipped frog (M. Gadd),
p. 269

PLATE 17

17.1 *Amnirana* sp.
Hillwood white-lipped frog, p. 271

17.2 *Anhydrophryne rattrayi*
Rattray's frog, p. 272

17.3 *Anhydrophryne rattrayi*
Rattray's frog, red phase (J. Visser),
p. 272

17.4 *Arthroleptella bicolor*
Bainskloof moss frog, p. 275

17.5 *Arthroleptella drewesii*
Drewes' moss frog, p. 276

17.6 *Arthroleptella landdrosia*
Landdros moss frog, p. 279

17.7 *Arthroleptella lightfooti*
Lightfoot's moss frog, p. 280

17.8 *Arthroleptella ngongoniensis*
Ngongoni moss frog (M. Burger), p. 281

PLATE 18

18.1 *Arthroleptella villiersi*
De Villiers' moss frog, p. 283

18.2 *Aubria masako*
Masako fishing frog (J.-L. Amiet), p. 284

18.3 *Cacosternum boettgeri*
Boettger's dainty frog, gray phase, p. 287

18.4 *Cacosternum boettgeri*
Boettger's dainty frog, green phase, p. 287

18.5 *Cacosternum boettgeri*
Boettger's dainty frog, red phase (W. Branch), p. 287

18.6 *Cacosternum capense*
Cape dainty frog, p. 288

18.7 *Cacosternum namaquense*
Namaqua dainty frog (M. Burger), p. 290

18.8 *Cacosternum nanum*
Dwarf dainty frog (M. Burger), p. 291

PLATE 19

19.1 *Cacosternum platys*
Flat dainty frog, p. 292

19.2 *Hildebrandtia ornata*
Ornate frog, p. 294

19.3 *Hoplobatrachus occipitalis*
Crowned bullfrog, p. 295

19.4 *Microbatrachella capensis*
Micro frog (M. Burger), p. 298

19.5 *Natalobatrachus bonebergi*
Boneberg's fog (M. Burger), p. 299

19.6 *Nothophryne broadleyi*
Mongrel frog (C. Tilbury), p. 301

19.7 *Phrynobatrachus acridoides*
Eastern puddle frog, p. 304

19.8 *Phrynobatrachus mababiensis*
Mababe puddle frog (M. Burger), p. 305

PLATE 20

20.1 *Phrynobatrachus natalensis*
Natal puddle frog, striped phase, p. 307

20.2 *Phrynobatrachus natalensis*
Natal puddle frog, plain phase, p. 307

20.3 *Phrynobatrachus rungwensis*
Rungwe puddle frog, p. 311

20.4 *Poyntonia paludicola*
Montane marsh frog, p. 313

20.5 *Ptychadena anchietae*
Anchieta's ridged frog, p. 319

20.6 *Ptychadena bunoderma*
Rough ridged frog, p. 323

20.7 *Ptychadena grandisonae*
Grandison's ridged frog, p. 325

20.8 *Ptychadena guibei*
Guibe's ridged frog, p. 326

PLATE 21

21.1 *Ptychadena mapacha*
Mapacha ridged frog, p. 328

21.2 *Ptychadena mascareniensis*
Mascarene ridged frog, p. 329

21.3 *Ptychadena mossambica*
Mozambique ridged frog, p. 331

21.4 *Ptychadena oxyrhynchus*
Sharp-nosed ridged frog, p. 334

21.5 *Ptychadena porosissima*
Grassland ridged frog, p. 337

21.6 *Ptychadena schillukorum*
Schilluk ridged frog, p. 338

21.7 *Ptychadena subpunctata*
Spotted ridged frog, p. 340

21.8 *Ptychadena taenioscelis*
Small ridged frog, p. 341

PLATE 22

22.1 *Ptychadena upembae*
Upemba ridged frog, p. 342

22.2 *Ptychadena uzungwensis*
Udzungwa ridged frog, p. 344

22.3 *Pyxicephalus adspersus*
African bullfrog, p. 346

22.4 *Pyxicephalus adspersus*
African bullfrog, mottled phase, p. 346

22.5 *Pyxicephalus edulis*
Edible bullfrog, p. 349

22.6 *Strongylopus bonaespei*
Banded stream frog, p. 352

22.7 *Strongylopus fasciatus*
Striped stream frog (A. de Villiers),
p. 353

22.8 *Strongylopus fuelleborni*
Fülleborn's stream frog, p. 354

PLATE 23

23.1 *Strongylopus grayii*
Gray's stream frog, p. 356

23.2 *Strongylopus hymenopus*
Drakensberg stream frog, p. 357

23.3 *Strongylopus rhodesianus*
Chimanimani stream frog, p. 359

23.4 *Strongylopus springbokensis*
Namaqua stream frog, p. 360

23.5 *Strongylopus wageri*
Wager's stream frog, p. 362

23.6 *Tomopterna cryptotis*
Cryptic sand frog, p. 365

23.7 *Tomopterna delalandii*
Delalande's sand frog, p. 366

23.8 *Tomopterna krugerensis*
Knocking sand frog, p. 368

PLATE 24

24.1 *Tomopterna marmorata*
Marbled sand frog, p. 369

24.2 *Tomopterna natalensis*
Natal sand frog (M. Burger), p. 370

24.3 *Tomopterna tandyi*
Tandy's sand frog, p. 372

24.4 *Tomopterna tuberculosa*
Rough sand frog, p. 373

24.5 *Chiromantis xerampelina*
Gray tree frog, p. 375

24.6 *Scolecomorphus kirkii*
Kirk's caecilian (J. Visser), p. 382

24.7 *Thoraciliacus* sp.
Adult, p. 387

24.8 *Thoraciliacus* sp.
Tadpole, p. 387

from the food it consumes. Food wastes are converted to substances called *purines*. The pigment cells (iridiophores) of the skin possess small purine platelets that are arranged parallel to the surface. These crystals probably act as quarter-wavelength interference reflectors, reducing the heat load by reflecting sunlight.

The red skin on the inside of the thighs and the side of the belly is widely reported as functioning as a startle mechanism, as it is only visible when the animal jumps. However, this red skin is only half as thick as the belly skin and is well supplied with blood vessels, making it specialized for rapid water uptake. The frog would be able to make use of drops of dew or rain to replace water lost for cooling through this red skin.

NOTES: In parts of Angola it is believed that a cow swallowing this frog will die. Frog-eating bats *Nycteris grandis* will eat marbled reed frogs in captivity. Apart from bats it has been recorded as prey of the snake *Philothamnus angolensis*, water snakes *Lycodonomorphus*, fishing spiders, young crocodiles, birds like the woodland kingfisher, tree frogs *Leptopelis*, and the red-legged kassina *Kassina maculata*. It feeds on a range of small insects and is a known predator of the important citrus pest, the citrus psylla. Its longevity in captivity is at least 4 years 9 months.

KEY REFERENCES: Zimmerman 1975, 1979; Richards 1982; Kobelt & Linsenmair 1986; Dawson & Bishop 1987; Telford & van Sickle 1989; Schiøtz 1999 (as *Hyperolius viridiflavus*).

Mitchell's reed frog
Hyperolius mitchelli Loveridge, 1953
(Plate 9.1)

This frog was named for B. L. Mitchell who was in the Department of Game, Fish and Tsetse in Nyasaland (Malawi).

DESCRIPTION: The male may grow up to 27 mm long. The head width is about one-third of body length. The main part of the webbing reaches the middle tubercle beneath the fourth toe. A light band on the side of the snout continues over the upper eyelid as a pale, wider dorsolateral band. In many animals this white band has a black border. A light heel spot is usually present. Dark spots are often found

Fig. 114 *Hyperolius mitchelli*

on the limbs and back. The undersurfaces are yellow to orange in the male but only orange in the female.

DISTRIBUTION AND HABITAT (FIG. 114): This species is known from northeastern Tanzania, Malawi, to Mozambique. It is associated with water bodies in forest.

ADVERTISEMENT CALL: The male calls from vegetation beside streams. The call is a short chirp, about 0.05 s in duration, with dominant harmonics between 2.6 and 3.3 kHz.

BREEDING: Pale yellow eggs are laid on a leaf overhanging water, in clutches of 50–100. After 5 or 6 days the pale tadpole wriggles off the leaf into the water during rain.

TADPOLES: See the chapter on tadpoles.

NOTES: This species may be confused with the spotted reed frog *H. puncticulatus*, which has a clacking call.

KEY REFERENCES: Schiøtz 1975, De Fonesca and Mertens 1979, Channing and Crapon de Caprona 1987.

Long reed frog
Hyperolius nasutus Günther, 1864
(Plates 9.2, 9.3)

Long Reed Frog

The specific name *nasutus* means "large nosed" and refers to the long nose in this species.
Günther's sharp-nosed reed frog, sharp-and-blunt-snouted sedge-frog, longnose reed frog. *Thizunda, tchimbota* in Angola.

DESCRIPTION: This is a small green tree frog, with the male up to 25 mm and the females reaching 24 mm in length. The snout is elongated, pointed, and projecting beyond the mouth. The body is narrow, and the head width is 27%–31% of body length. The frog is grass green, with a translucent belly through which the internal organs may be seen. The internal organs are sheathed in white. The major pattern variations include (1) a uniform green back, (2) a pale dorsolateral band, or (3) light dorsolateral and paravertebral bands. Small dark dots may be present on the back and may form into longitudinal lines. The male has a bright yellow throat flap. The tympanum is not visible.

DISTRIBUTION AND HABITAT (FIG. 115): This common frog is found throughout Africa in suitable habitat. The southeastern boundary of this species is uncertain, owing to confusion with Power's reed frog *H. poweri*. This frog is frequently found on reeds growing in deep water, in pools, streams, and large rivers.

ADVERTISEMENT CALL: The male calls from grass or reeds often growing in waist-deep water. Calling begins just before sunset and continues until early morning. The call has been described as a high-

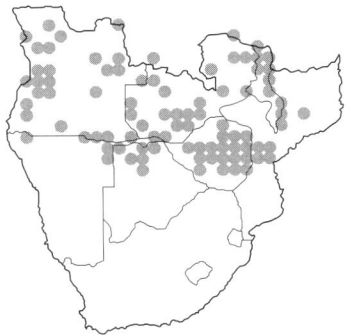

Fig. 115 *Hyperolius nasutus*

pitched scream or rasping creak. It consists of 11–14 pulses in 0.03 s, with a dominant frequency of 3.8–4.8 kHz.

BREEDING: The eggs are small, 0.8 mm in diameter, with a black upper pole and a white lower pole. They are laid in clutches of up to 200, attached to vegetation below water.

TADPOLES: See the chapter on tadpoles.

NOTES: The specimens referred to here as long reed frogs are separated by some authors into two species, *H. nasutus* and *H. benguellensis*. This is based on the fact that two juvenile color patterns are known: green ones are called *H. nasutus*, and reddish brown juveniles are named *H. benguellensis*. However, only one call is produced by both forms at Mare Dam in Zimbabwe, so I regard these two as merely color-pattern variants, as is found in many other species of reed frogs. However, the KwaZulu-Natal frogs do possess a quite different call, although they look the same as the long reed frog. The KwaZulu-Natal populations are identified as Power's reed frog *H. poweri*. There are probably other unrecognized but similar-looking species confused with the long reed frog.

These frogs are waterproof, but can only survive 2 weeks of dehydration, owing to their small size and minimal water reserves.

KEY REFERENCES: Schiøtz 1975, Withers, Hillman, Drewes, and Sokol 1982.

Golden-eyed reed frog
Hyperolius ocellatus Günther, 1859
(Plate 9.4)

The specific name *ocellatus* refers to the distinctive eye-like spots on the back of the females.
Ocellated reed frog.

DESCRIPTION: The male reaches 23 mm and the female, 30 mm in length. The sexes have different color patterns. The male is green with a pale silvery green triangle in front of the eyes, extending behind the eyes as dorsolateral stripes. The underside is white, but limbs and toes are green. The iris is golden. The female is silvery gray

Parker's Reed Frog

Fig. 116   *Hyperolius ocellatus*

with small black spots on the front half of the body. The belly is orange, with the lower surfaces of the limbs and toes pink.

DISTRIBUTION AND HABITAT (FIG. 116): This forest species just enters the area covered, in Cabinda. It is known from Nigeria, Uganda, and the Democratic Republic of the Congo.

ADVERTISEMENT CALL: The male calls from open vegetation at the edge of forests. The call is described as a fine twittering. It consists of 4–5 pulses, at a dominant frequency of 3.8–4.0 kHz, with a duration of 0.15 s.

BREEDING: Unknown. The eggs are pale green with a small dark gray-green pole.

TADPOLES: Unknown.

KEY REFERENCE: Schiøtz 1967.

Parker's reed frog
Hyperolius parkeri Loveridge, 1933
(Plate 9.5)

This frog was named for the herpetologist H. W. Parker, of the Natural History Museum in London during 1923–1957.
Brown-or-green sedge-frog.

DESCRIPTION: This is the only tree frog known where the male (24 mm) is substantially bigger than the female (21 mm). The snout projects beyond the mouth. Head width is 29%–33% of the body length. The back of the male is green, yellow, or brown, with a light band on the side of the snout and a dorsolateral band that has a dark border. The female is always green with scattered dark spots on the back. The breeding male has dark spines underneath the feet and body. The vocal sac is small. Webbing is extensive, with only one joint of the fourth toe free of web.

DISTRIBUTION AND HABITAT (FIG. 117): This species is known along the coastal lowlands from Kenya to Mozambique, and inland up to about 1000 m.

ADVERTISEMENT CALL: The male calls alongside streams in forests, or from grass in pools with standing water. Unlike other reed frogs, the male calls from a resting position, without raising the head. The call is a long loud trill, with an initial sound followed by up to 28 pulses at a dominant frequency of 4.2 kHz. The duration of the call is about 1.5 s.

BREEDING: The white eggs are attached to sedges or the underside of reed leaves just above water level. Clutch size is 36–110.

TADPOLES: Unknown.

Fig. 117 *Hyperolius parkeri*

Pickersgill's Reed Frog

NOTES: This frog is quite different from other reed frogs in call position and in the large size of the male, and it has been suggested that it be placed in another genus.

KEY REFERENCES: Loveridge 1933, Schiøtz 1975.

Pickersgill's reed frog
Hyperolius pickersgilli Raw, 1982

This species was named for the collector, Martin Pickersgill.
Avoca reed frog.

DESCRIPTION: The male may grow to 22 mm and the female 30 mm in length. The tympanum is not visible. Webbing is well developed, with two to three joints of the fourth toe free of web. Head width is less than one-third of the body length. The sexes have different color patterns. The male is brown above, with a pale stripe on the side of the snout that continues over the eye backward to the groin. The dorsolateral stripe is edged with darker brown. Sometimes a pale spot is present on the heel. The hidden parts of the limbs are yellow. The female is bright lime-green above with no dorsolateral stripes. The side and belly are yellowish to white. A dark stripe on the side of the snout may be present.

DISTRIBUTION AND HABITAT (FIG. 118): This frog is known from the coastal lowlands of KwaZulu-Natal in South Africa. This species

Fig. 118 *Hyperolius pickersgilli*

is found among dense stands of the razor edge–leafed sedge *Cyperus immensus* that grows in stagnant water about half a meter deep. Many of the coastal localities where this sedge grows are being drained in order to build houses, and habitat destruction has become a serious threat to this frog. This species is listed as endangered.

ADVERTISEMENT CALL: The male calls from spring to late summer from dense vegetation about a meter above the water surface. The call is quiet, insect-like, with a dominant frequency of 3.0 kHz. Call duration is about 0.7 s, with a rate of pulses at 100/s.

BREEDING: Mating and egg laying take place just above water level. Clutch size is about 50. Eggs are 1 mm in diameter, with brown animal poles. The tadpole wriggles into the water about a week after the eggs are laid.

TADPOLES: See the chapter on tadpoles.

KEY REFERENCE: Raw 1982.

Variable reed frog
Hyperolius pictus Ahl, 1931
(Plates 9.6, 9.7)

The specific name *pictus* means "painted," referring to the back pattern.
Variable montane sedge frog, Ahl's painted reed frog.

DESCRIPTION: The male grows up to 29 mm and the female, 38 mm in length. The side of the snout is curved, with a blunt tip. The head is 32%–35% of the body length. This is a short-legged frog, with variable markings in brown and green. The back may be uniform, or with light longitudinal bands, or with irregular longitudinal dark brown or green bands. The underside is yellow to orange. The limbs are orange and the discs reddish. Several different adult patterns are known.

DISTRIBUTION AND HABITAT (FIG. 119): This frog is known from the highlands of southwestern Tanzania, northern Malawi, and adjoining Zambia. It is found around water bodies on the highlands.

Fig. 119 *Hyperolius pictus*

ADVERTISEMENT CALL: The call is a two-part croak. The two parts may be alternated. One part consists of 15 pulses at a rate of 30/s with a duration of 0.5 s. The second part consists of about 12 pulses at a rate of 100/s. The croaks may be slower or may speed up. The dominant frequency is 2.7 kHz.

BREEDING: Breeding takes place during the summer rainy season. Eggs are laid in gelatinous clusters on vegetation above water level at the water's edge. Each 75-mm cluster contains 60–100 eggs, each egg being 2 mm in diameter within a 5-mm capsule. The egg is white with a gray upper half. Eggs may drop into the water where they sink. Tadpoles hatch after 18 days and may be flooded into the pools by rain. Time to metamorphosis is 3–4 months.

TADPOLES: Unknown.

NOTES: Various color patterns may resemble those of the spotted reed frog *H. puncticulatus*.

KEY REFERENCES: Stewart & Wilson 1966, Stewart 1967, Schiøtz 1975.

Power's reed frog
Hyperolius poweri Loveridge, 1938
(Plate 9.8)

The specific name refers to the collector J. H. Power, herpetologist at the museum in Kimberley.

DESCRIPTION: This frog is similar in shape to the long reed frog *H. nasutus*. The male is up to 22 mm long. The body is narrow, elongated, with a sharp overhanging snout. Snout-eye distance is slightly greater than eye diameter. The tympanum is hidden. The disc of the fourth toe, and two joints are free of web. The back varies from green to brown. In the male, white stripes may be present on the side of the snout and continue over the eyes backward as dorsolateral stripes. These lines may be edged by a slight darkening. The female does not have these stripes. Small black dots on the back may form a vertebral line. Numerous small black points are present on the nostrils and the palms and soles. The belly is translucent and silvery. The breeding male has a yellow throat disc.

DISTRIBUTION AND HABITAT (FIG. 120): At present, this species is only known from the eastern seaboard of South Africa. The northern boundary of this species and the southern boundary of the long reed frog *H. nasutus* are not yet established. This frog occurs in pans along the coastal lowlands where the vegetation is dense.

ADVERTISEMENT CALL: The call is a harsh chirp, with about 6 pulses following an initial buzz. The duration is 0.2–0.3 s, with a dominant frequency of 6.0 kHz.

Fig. 120 *Hyperolius poweri*

BREEDING: The eggs are white with a greenish-gray pole, about 1 mm in diameter within a 2.2-mm capsule. Clutch size is 200, with the eggs being laid in clusters of 2–20. The eggs are deposited on vegetation below water level.

TADPOLES: See the chapter on tadpoles.

NOTES: The males are aggressive toward other calling males. This species is distinguished from the long reed frog *H. nasutus* by the higher-pitched call with more distinct pulses.

KEY REFERENCES: Loveridge 1938, Wager 1986.

Spotted reed frog
Hyperolius puncticulatus (Pfeffer, 1893)
(Plates 10.1, 10.2)

The specific name *puncticulatus* means "spotted".
Golden sedge frog, southern broad-striped sedge-frog, coastal reed frog. *Koti* in Misuku.

DESCRIPTION: The male is up to 33 mm and the female 43 mm long. The snout is blunt with straight sides, and the head width is 35–38% of the body length. The feet are moderately webbed, with one joint free of web on the fourth toe. The back is yellowish brown, with a light band on the snout continuing over the eye to a narrow dorsolateral band. The dorsolateral band may continue only as far as the arm or may continue as a series of spots. A series of light middorsal spots or a continuous band may also be present. Other patterns include (1) reddish brown back with a broad yellow stripe on the side of the snout and body, a black line surrounding the light stripe, and an orange undersurface; and (2) Black back with light yellow spots, yellow undersurface, and orange throat.

DISTRIBUTION (FIG. 121): This species is known from Malawi and northward into Tanzania. It is associated with forests.

ADVERTISEMENT CALL: The male calls from above ground in vegetation around the edge of forest pools. The call is a series of brief clacks. Each clack is short, 0.02 s, with a dominant frequency of

Fig. 121 *Hyperolius puncticulatus*

2.0 kHz. The clacks are spaced half a second apart when the males are excited.

BREEDING: Breeding takes place in midsummer. Clutch size is unknown, although in captivity a female deposited 19 eggs, each 2.5 mm in diameter within 5-mm capsules. The eggs are white and laid in a 25–50-mm cluster on submerged vegetation.

TADPOLES: Unknown.

NOTES: Known predators include the savanna white-lipped snake *Crotaphopeltis hotamboeia*.

KEY REFERENCE: Stewart 1967.

Water lily reed frog
Hyperolius pusillus (Cope, 1862)
(Plate 10.3)

The specific name *pusillus* means "very small."
Water lily frog, transparent pigmy sedge-frog, translucent reed frog, dwarf reed frog.

DESCRIPTION: The male reaches 21 mm in length. Head and body are broad and flat. The snout is blunt and curved, and the head width is 34%–39% of the body length. Webbing is reduced, with one to slightly more joints of the fourth toe free of web. It is translucent

Water Lily Reed Frog

green, often with a darker line on the side of the snout. Dark spots may be present on the back. The male throat is white. The feet and discs are sometimes yellow, otherwise green. Many specimens are translucent, and the internal organs can be seen through the body wall of the belly. The eyes are golden, in contrast to the body, with black horizontal pupils.

DISTRIBUTION AND HABITAT (FIG. 122): This species occurs along the eastern coastal lowlands in open grassy pans, also in northwestern Botswana and in Malawi. This frog is often found on floating vegetation like lily leaves.

ADVERTISEMENT CALL: Males call from vegetation at the water surface. The call is a series of soft flat clicks, 0.02 s long, with dominant frequency between 4.5 and 5.4 kHz.

BREEDING: Breeding takes place during summer. Mating occurs on the water surface, and batches of 20–120 eggs are laid in a single layer between overlapping lily leaves. Total clutch size varies from 216 to 313. The eggs are white or light green and small, 0.8 mm in diameter, in 2-mm capsules.

TADPOLES: See the chapter on tadpoles.

NOTES: The tissue fluid of this species is green. They are known to eat ants and flying termites. Predators include the yellow-billed egret.

KEY REFERENCE: Power 1935.

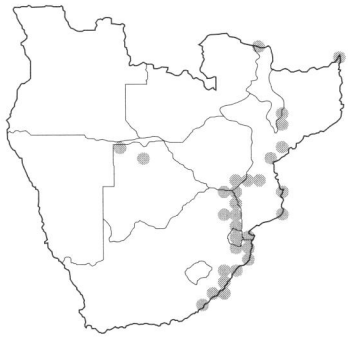

Fig. 122 *Hyperolius pusillus*

Five-striped reed frog
Hyperolius quinquevittatus Bocage, 1866
(Plate 10.4)

The specific name means "five stripes" and refers to the common color pattern.
Black-striped sedge frog, tropical reed frog.

DESCRIPTION: The male is up to 28-mm long. The side of the snout is straight, and head width is 29%–33% of body length. The legs are short, with the tibia length being less than half the length of the body. The adults have two color patterns: (1) five light stripes, with green vertebral and side stripes and golden brown dorsolateral stripes, separated by darker brown areas; white belly; and red or pink limbs and toes. (2) a green back and sides with two dark brown dorsolateral stripes; white belly; and red limbs and toes.
Older specimens are believed to become more uniformly patterned.

DISTRIBUTION AND HABITAT (FIG. 123): This species is known from Angola, southern Democratic Republic of the Congo, southern Tanzania, northern Zambia, and Malawi. It is found in open savannas at higher altitudes.

ADVERTISEMENT CALL: The male calls from grass stems in marshy places, frequently within 100 mm of the ground. The call consists of a short creak, 0.01 s in duration, with 10 pulses and a dominant fre-

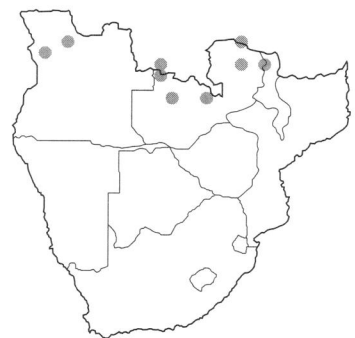

Fig. 123 *Hyperolius quinquevittatus*

quency of 3.5 kHz. It sounds like the long reed frog *H. nasutus* but is harsher.

BREEDING: Unknown.

TADPOLES: Unknown.

NOTES: This species resembles the long reed frog in shape, call, and preferred habitat, but it occurs at a higher altitude.

KEY REFERENCE: Schiøtz 1975.

Yellow-striped reed frog
Hyperolius semidiscus Hewitt, 1927
(Plate 10.5)

The specific name *semidiscus* means "half-disc" and refers to the incomplete throat disc.
Hewitt's reed frog.

DESCRIPTION: This frog may reach 35 mm in length. The side of the snout is curved, and the tip is blunt. Webbing reaches the distal tubercle beneath the fourth toe. The back is a uniform green with a yellow band from the tip of the snout, through the eye, and continuing as a dorsolateral band to the lower back. In some specimens the stripe from the snout tip to the eye is absent. A slightly darker narrow edging to the pale band is often present.

DISTRIBUTION AND HABITAT (FIG. 124): This species occurs along the east coast of southern Africa as far north as Swaziland. It is found in dense reeds and vegetation along river courses and standing water in lowland savannas.

ADVERTISEMENT CALL: The male calls from a meter or so above the water. The call has two parts, with a longer creak, followed by a short creak. The first part is 0.1 s long at a pulse rate of 190/s, followed by a 0.05-s call at the same pulse rate, both at a dominant frequency of 2.8 kHz.

BREEDING: It breeds from spring to summer after the rains have

Fig. 124 *Hyperolius semidiscus*

started. The eggs are 1mm in diameter, within 4-mm capsules. Clutch size is about 200. The eggs are laid in clusters of 30, each cluster being attached to vegetation hanging in water, and up to 50mm below the surface.

TADPOLES: See the chapter on tadpoles.

KEY REFERENCE: Wager 1986.

Spiny-throated reed frog
Hyperolius spinigularis Stevens, 1971
(Plates 10.6, 10.7)

The specific name *spinigularis* means "spiny throat."
Spiny reed frog, Mulanje reed frog.

DESCRIPTION: The male reaches 24mm and the female, 28mm in length. The snout is blunt with straight sides. Head width is 34%–36% of body length. The eyes are noticeably protruding. Webbing is well developed, with the main part level with the middle tubercle beneath the fourth toe. The species gets its name from the black spines on the male throat gland. There are also spines on the lower surface and the underside of the leg in the male. Both sexes have small spines on the back. The back is green or brown, with snout stripes and dorsolateral stripes edged with brown. An alternative pattern includes a pale triangle on the snout with a broken dorsolateral band.

Spiny-Throated Reed Frog

DISTRIBUTION AND HABITAT (FIG. 125): This species is known from Mulanje in Malawi (Ruo Estate and Chisambe Tea Estate) and the Uluguru and Usambara Mountains, Tanzania. Both habitats are at a medium altitude in forests. The frogs prefer overgrown marshes, where they select broad-leaved perches.

ADVERTISEMENT CALL: In captivity the males make a weak, rasping, high-pitched "tcheek-tcheek" call, believed to serve a territorial function. The advertisement call is unknown and may not be present. They breed in ponds together with many other calling species.

BREEDING: It breeds from the end of December to the middle of March. A single mass of 150–200 unpigmented eggs is laid among grass stems or on leaves above water. The eggs are 1.8–2 mm in diameter in 3.5-mm capsules. Egg masses have been recorded up to 5 m above water level. The female has been reported to return on two successive nights to wet the eggs.

TADPOLES: See the chapter on tadpoles.

NOTES: The male differs from all other reed frogs by prominent black spines covering the throat disc, chest, abdomen, and undersurface of hind limbs, although the female has no spines.

KEY REFERENCE: Stevens 1971.

Fig. 125 *Hyperolius spinigularis*

Steindachner's reed frog
Hyperolius steindachneri Bocage, 1866
(Plate 10.8)

This frog was named for the Austrian herpetologist Franz Steindachner.

DESCRIPTION: The male is up to 29 mm long, and the larger female reaches 33 mm. This species has heavy fingers and moderate discs. The ventral coloration is characteristic, consisting of large white or pale yellow spots on a black background. The back is a uniform olive to brown.

DISTRIBUTION AND HABITAT (FIG. 126): This species is known from Zambia, through Angola to southwestern Democratic Republic of the Congo. This frog occurs in vegetation along the edges of water bodies. It has been found in association with the long reed frog *H. nasutus* and the marbled reed frog *H. marmoratus*.

ADVERTISEMENT CALL: Unknown.

BREEDING: Unknown.

TADPOLES: Unknown.

KEY REFERENCE: Laurent 1954.

Fig. 126 *Hyperolius steindachneri*

Tinker reed frog
Hyperolius tuberilinguis Smith, 1849
(Plate 11.1)

The specific name *tuberilinguis* means "bump on tongue," referring to a papilla on the tongue.
Yellow-green reed frog, green reed frog, straw-or-green sedge-frog, Smith's reed frog.

DESCRIPTION: This is a medium-sized frog, but it is relatively large for the genus. The male is up to 33 mm in length. The snout is pointed with straight sides. Head width is more than 33% of body length. The adult is often a uniform yellow or green but sometimes brown with a backward-pointing light triangle between the eyes.

DISTRIBUTION AND HABITAT (FIG. 127): This distinctive species is known along the eastern lowlands from Kenya to the eastern coast of South Africa. It is found in lowland savannas, often in temporary pools with dense vegetation.

ADVERTISEMENT CALL: The male calls from above ground level in vegetation. The call is a sharp click or tap, at an emphasized frequency of 3 kHz. The male uses calls as spacing cues, although both vocalizations and combat serve to maintain the distance between males. There are up to 6 clicks in each call, although the female has

Fig. 127 *Hyperolius tuberilinguis*

been shown to prefer calls with 2 or 3 clicks. The male also produces a creaking aggression call.

BREEDING: The eggs are laid in a mass a short distance above the surface of the water, attached to vegetation. The egg mass is very sticky. Each egg is white or yellow, 1.5 mm in diameter within a 4-mm capsule. Clutch size is 236–400.

TADPOLES: See the chapter on tadpoles.

NOTES: It is preyed upon at night by the marbled tree snake *Dipsadoboa aulica*.

KEY REFERENCES: Wager 1986, Pallett & Passmore 1988.

De Vilhena's reed frog
Hyperolius vilhenai Laurent, 1964

This species was named for E. De Vilhena, deputy administrator of the Diamond Company of Angola.
Luita River reed frog.

DESCRIPTION: De Vilhena's reed frog is known only from one juvenile, 21 mm long. The body is squat, and the snout is blunt, just overhanging the lower jaw. Head width is 37% of body length. The specimen is well webbed, with one or less joints of the fourth toe free of web. The back is pale green, with a darker pigment in the form of a band reaching the tip of the snout through the posterior edge of the upper eyelid, passing the nostrils along the edge of the snout. The most remarkable character of this species is the extent of webbing of the fourth toe, with only two-thirds of the last phalanx free of web.

DISTRIBUTION AND HABITAT (FIG. 128): This species is known only from the type locality, "Cuilo, along the Luita River," in Angola. It occurs in gallery forests.

ADVERTISEMENT CALL: Unknown.

BREEDING: Unknown.

De Witte's Clicking Frog

Fig. 128 *Hyperolius vilhenai*

TADPOLES: Unknown.

NOTES: This little-known Angolan frog would be very interesting to study in the field.

KEY REFERENCE: Laurent 1964.

Clicking Frog—Genus *Kassinula*

There is only one species in this genus of small terrestrial frogs.

De Witte's clicking frog
Kassinula wittei Laurent, 1940
(Plate 11.2)

The specific name *wittei* refers to G.-F. de Witte, herpetologist at the Institut Royal des Sciences Naturelles in Brussels until 1951.
Witte's running frog.

DESCRIPTION: The female reaches 22 mm and the male, 21 mm in length. The pupil is vertical. The tympanum is not visible. The tips of the fingers and toes are expanded into small discs. The fifth toe has a small tubercle underneath, at its base. The color pattern consists of a dark vertebral band and dark paravertebral bands, with intervening light bands that have a fine dark line along

Fig. 129 *Kassinula wittei*

the middle. The underside is white. The male has a circular throat gland.

DISTRIBUTION AND HABITAT (FIG. 129): This little-known frog is found in southern Democratic Republic of the Congo and the uplands of western and northern Zambia. It occurs in flooded grasslands and temporary pools.

ADVERTISEMENT CALL: The call consists of a series of double metallic clicks, 0.1 s apart. Each pair of clicks is separated by 0.2 s. The dominant frequency is 4.2 kHz. The male calls from the base of flooded grass tufts.

BREEDING: Unknown.

TADPOLES: Unknown.

NOTES: This frog is very common in flooded grassy areas throughout the highlands. When disturbed, it escapes underwater.

KEY REFERENCE: Schiøtz 1975.

Kassinas—Genus *Kassina*

This group includes medium-sized to large ground-living frogs. The pupil is vertical, and teeth are present on the front of the roof of the mouth. Some species possess discs on the fingers and toes. The angle between the second and third fingers is 23°–30°. The eggs are laid in water, and the large tadpoles develop with characteristically high fins. The genus is found throughout sub-Saharan Africa. All kassinas are known as *chikwarikwari* in Shangaan.

KEY TO THE SPECIES

1a. Tips of fingers and toes expanded into discs, which are broader than the width of the subarticular tubercles (Fig. 130)
Kassina maculata
1b. Expanded discs absent 2

Fig. 130   Toe discs

2a. Width of inner metatarsal tubercle greater than width of subarticular tubercle of first toe (Fig. 131)   *Kassina kuvangensis*
2b. Width of inner metatarsal tubercle not exceeding width of subarticular tubercle of first toe   *Kassina senegalensis*

Fig. 131   Tubercles

Kuvangu kassina
Kassina kuvangensis (Monard, 1937)
(Plate 11.3)

The specific name refers to Kuvangu in Angola, where this species was first found.
Kuvangu running frog.

DESCRIPTION: The male reaches 51 mm in length, while the normally larger female has only been recorded up to 49 mm. No discs are present on fingers or toes. The inner metatarsal tubercle is large, greater than width of subarticular tubercle of first toe, equal to the distance between the nostrils. The male throat gland is circular without a free rear flap. The back is uniformly dark gray-brown, sometimes with irregular markings arranged in rows along the body. The underside of the leg is marbled red and gray, while the belly is white to yellow or orange. Both male and female have a vent directed downward. Two pairs of frilled lobes surround the female vent. The male has a glandular area on the inner side of the forearm.

DISTRIBUTION AND HABITAT (FIG. 132): This species is known from northern and western Zambia and southern Angola. It is found in marshes and along slow-flowing streams inside dense vegetation and in flooded grasslands.

ADVERTISEMENT CALL: At nightfall the males start calling from holes and in depressions under grass. The call is a series of fast rising "quoiks." The duration of the call is 0.03 s, and calls can be 0.15 s apart. The dominant frequency rises from an initial 0.6 kHz through 1.5 kHz.

BREEDING: Unknown. The female lays 130 eggs in a sticky clump. The eggs are greenish with a dark pole, 2 mm in diameter.

TADPOLES: See the chapter on tadpoles.

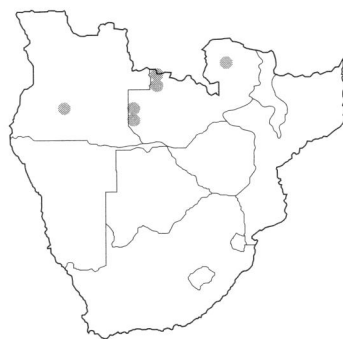

Fig. 132 *Kassina kuvangensis*

NOTES: Although many species may co-occur in an area, the Kuvangu kassina has not yet been reported to call with other kassinas. They are common in marshes in the western part of northern Zambia. When threatened, the frogs may arch forward into a ball with the eyes flattened. As a further defense against being eaten, the skin contains trypargine, a poison that kills small mammals by respiratory failure and paralysis.

KEY REFERENCES: Schiøtz 1975, Yasuhara et al. 1981, Channing & Broadley 1992.

Red-legged kassina
Kassina maculata (Duméril, 1853)
(Plate 11.4)

The specific name *maculata* means "spotted," referring to the color pattern of the back.
Red-legged pan frog, red-blotched black frog, spotted running frog. Known by the Nyungwe as *chula*, a general term for other species of frogs as well.

DESCRIPTION: The male grows up to 65 mm and the female, 68 mm. Head and body are stocky. The eyes are large and protruding. The tympanum is half of the eye diameter. Discs are present on tips of fingers and toes that are wider than the subarticular tubercles. The male throat flap is circular, and the female vent is directed downward and surrounded by simple lobes covered with small spines. The back is gray with large black spots. A thin pale line surrounds each spot. All concealed parts of the limbs are red with black spots.

DISTRIBUTION AND HABITAT (FIG. 133): This species is known from Kenya along the coastal lowlands to the tropical east coast of South Africa. It is found in deep temporary pools. It is able to climb well and will seek shelter in leaf axils.

ADVERTISEMENT CALL: The call resembles the noise of bursting bubbles. The male calls from vegetation at the water surface in deep water. The call is a very short, rising note. Call length is less than 0.03 s, with the dominant frequency rising rapidly from 0.3 to 1.3 kHz.

Fig. 133 *Kassina maculata*

BREEDING: The eggs are attached to submerged plants in small groups. Each egg is 1.5 mm in diameter, within a 2.5-mm capsule.

TADPOLES: See the chapter on tadpoles.

SKIN TOXINS: The skin contains at least three kinds of defensive chemicals. The first is a peptide that stimulates the large intestine of some animals. The second group of peptides found in the skin is called *tachykinins*. At least two different tachykinins are present, Glu^2, Pro^5-kassinin and hylambatin. Both of these are responsible for lowering the blood pressure and increasing the heart rate. The third kind of peptide is known as Leu^5-cerulein. This has a potent action on the gallbladder and stimulates pancreatic juice, which is rich in enzymes but poor in bicarbonate. The effect of these peptides is to make any mammal that eats the frog, or even tastes the skin, violently ill, hopefully protecting the frog against any future attacks. These chemical defenses are very effective, as only a few millionths of a gram of secretion per kilogram of predator is effective.

NOTES: The male is difficult to approach, as it stops calling and disappears below the surface of the water when it detects the swell caused by the movement of the observer. Known prey includes the marbled reed frog *Hyperolius marmoratus*, and the golden-backed spiny reed frog *Afrixalus aureus*. Despite the skin toxins, they are eaten by the yellow-billed egret and the vine snake *Thelotornis*.

KEY REFERENCES: Nakajima 1981, Roseghini et al. 1988.

Senegal kassina
Kassina senegalensis (Duméril & Bibron, 1841)
(Plate 11.5)

The specific name *senegalensis* refers to Senegal, where the species was first discovered.
Senegal frog, running frog, bubbling kassina, Senegal running frog. *Senegal-Streifenfrosch* in German, *borrelvleipadda* in Afrikaans.

DESCRIPTION: Both sexes are about the same size, up to 49 mm in length. Small swellings are present at the tips of the fingers and toes. The toes are very slightly webbed. Inner metatarsal tubercle length is less than the distance between the nostrils. The subarticular tubercle of the first toe is wider than the inner metatarsal tubercle width. The male throat gland is paler than the vocal sacs and is elongated without a free posterior edge. The vent is directed downward and in females is surrounded by two pairs of lobes without spines. The back pattern is a dark vertebral band with a pair of paravertebral bands. This is usually distinct on a yellowish brown to gray background. The color pattern varies somewhat geographically, as is found in many other widespread species of frogs, being a series of dorsal spots in western Zambia and Angola.

DISTRIBUTION AND HABITAT (FIG. 134): This common frog occurs widely in sub-Saharan Africa, in moist and arid savannas, into West Africa.

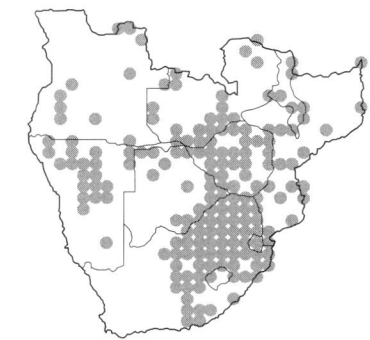

Fig. 134 *Kassina senegalensis*

ADVERTISEMENT CALL: The male calls from under vegetation away from water but sometimes calls in shallow water providing that enough cover is available. The call consists of a rising note that sounds like a bursting bubble. Individuals in a chorus may call very rapidly in succession, producing an effect as if the calls were moving across the breeding site. Males form calling aggregations, with 3–10 males in a group. The call of one male triggers another male to call. Males call in single bouts, with a chorus leader setting the pace, being answered by one or more others. Different males may serve as chorus leaders. Each call is short, 0.1–0.2 s. The dominant frequency increases from 0.4 kHz to 1.5 or 2.0 kHz.

BREEDING: The female is attracted to the male at the calling site away from the water. The male clasps the female, and then the female leads the way to the water. The eggs are laid in shallow water. They are pale blue-green, 1.4–1.8 mm in diameter, in jelly capsules 3 mm in diameter. Eggs are laid singly or in groups of 1–20, every 30 cm. The female dives to grasp an underwater object and touches her vent to it while depositing an egg. The eggs sink and are soon difficult to see. Clutch size is 260–400. Development to metamorphosis takes 52–90 days.

TADPOLES: See the chapter on tadpoles.

NOTES: This species possesses a territorial call, which is trilled with a duration of 0.2 s and dominant energy at 0.4–1.6 kHz. This call is often heard early in the evening when the males are closely spaced.

Food is restricted to small insects and other arthropods. The frogs have been found underground in the burrows of the giant girdled lizard *Cordylus giganteus* and in termite mounds. Maximum recorded longevity in captivity is 5 years 5 months.

KEY REFERENCES: Guibé & Lamotte 1958, Schiøtz 1967, Wickler & Seibt 1974, Branch & Patterson 1975, Fleischack & Small 1979.

Running Frog—Genus *Semnodactylus*

There is only one species in this genus. The angle between the second and third finger is 46°, considerably more than the similar-looking species of *Kassina*.

Weale's running frog
Semnodactylus wealii (Boulenger, 1882)
(Plate 11.6)

The species was named for F. M. Weale of Kaffraria.
Rattling kassina, Weale's frog. *Langtoon-vleipadda* or *ratelpadda* in Afrikaans.

DESCRIPTION: The male reaches 44 mm in length. The markings on the back consist of three dark stripes, on a yellow-brown to gray background. Each stripe has a light center. A dark stripe is often present on the side. The throat disc in the male is darkly pigmented. The hands and feet are yellow. The arms and legs are thin and long, and the frog moves by walking or running.

DISTRIBUTION AND HABITAT (FIG. 135): Weale's running frog has been collected in southern and eastern South Africa. It is found in open short grasslands where sedges are growing, even at high altitudes.

ADVERTISEMENT CALL: The male often calls while clinging to vertical stems, 10–30 cm above the ground. It has been found calling from a variety of sites, however, including exposed sites on banks, or concealed within aquatic vegetation some distance from the edge. A

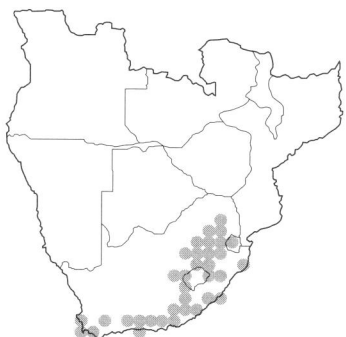

Fig. 135 *Semnodactylus wealii*

male calling from vegetation at the water surface arches his back and lifts his head. The call sounds like the creak of a cork being removed from a bottle. The call has two parts, with an initial rapidly pulsed sound, followed by a number of slower pulses. The initial sound is about 0.1 s, within the total duration 0.4–0.5 s. The initial pulse rate is 80/s, with the slower phase at 15/s. The dominant frequency is 2.1 kHz. Advertisement calls of different males are separated in time. This is achieved by the call of one male triggering the call of a second. In this way the calls of different males do not overlap and confuse the approaching female.

BREEDING: Eggs are laid from September to October on the Cape peninsula. The eggs are deep yellow, hatching into tadpoles after 9 days. The eggs are 1.7 mm in diameter, in a 2.4-mm capsule, attached singly or in small groups to submerged vegetation. Clutch size is 100–300.

TADPOLES: See the chapter on tadpoles.

NOTES: The skin contains small amounts of peptides called cerulein and tachykinin. See the species account on red-legged kassina *K. maculata* for the effects of these skin defenses. The maximum longevity record is 9 years in captivity.

KEY REFERENCES: Channing 1976b, Bishop 1984, Wager 1986, Roseghini et al. 1988.

Tree Frogs—Genus *Leptopelis*

Most of these frogs live above ground in vegetation, but some live in burrows, and eggs are laid in shallow nests near water. The tadpoles have elongated tails with which they wriggle to the water. Nine species are found here, with others farther north.

KEY TO THE SPECIES
1a. Large discs present on fingers and toes   3
1b. Discs small, just wider than fingers, back predominantly green (Fig. 136)   2

Tree Frogs—Family Hyperoliidae

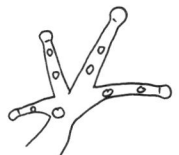

Fig. 136 Finger discs

2a. A dark blotch extending from the anterior of each leg insertion into the lighter dorsal color, which is otherwise uniform.
Leptopelis anchietae
2b. Not as above *Leptopelis xenodactylus*

3a. Fingers without web, or with only very little 5
3b. Web reaching or passing inner tubercle of outer finger (Fig. 137) 4

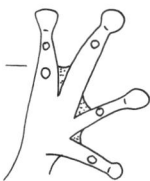

Fig. 137 Two phalanges free

4a. Webbing reaching outer tubercle of outer finger (Fig. 138)
Leptopelis natalensis
4b. Webbing not reaching outer tubercle of outer finger
Leptopelis flavomaculatus

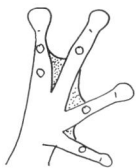

Fig. 138 One phalanx free

5a. Disc of fourth toe wider than distal subarticular tubercle 6
5b. Width of disc not greater than width of subarticular tubercle 8

6a. Metatarsal tubercle more than 80% length of inner toe 7

6b. Metatarsal tubercle less than length of inner toe
                                                  Leptopelis cynnamomeus

7a. Width of tympanum greater than half of eye diameter (Fig. 139)
                                                 Leptopelis mossambicus
7b. Width of tympanum less than half of eye diameter
                                                 Leptopelis argenteus

Fig. 139 Tympanum width–eye diameter comparison

8a. Interorbital distance 36% or more of distance from nostril to tympanum   *Leptopelis parbocagii*
8b. Interorbital distance less than 36% of distance from nostril to tympanum   *Leptopelis bocagii*

Anchieta's tree frog
Leptopelis anchietae (Bocage, 1873)

This species was named for J. d'Anchieta, the collector.
Huila forest treefrog.

DESCRIPTION: This is a medium-sized frog, up to about 50 mm in length. The back is light brown with darker sides. The side of the head is dark. There are pale spots on the arms and legs. Pectoral glands are present on males. The toes are without large discs and there is no webbing.

DISTRIBUTION AND HABITAT (FIG. 140): This species is known from Angola, in the Mount Chininga region, between 1200 and 1700 m. It is a savanna species.

ADVERTISEMENT CALL: Unknown.

BREEDING: Unknown.

Fig. 140 *Leptopelis anchietae*

TADPOLES: Unknown.

KEY REFERENCE: Bocage 1873.

Silvery tree frog
Leptopelis argenteus (Pfeffer, 1893)
(Plate 11.7)

The specific name *argenteus* means "silvery."
Broadley's tree frog, Bagamoyo forest treefrog.

DESCRIPTION: This is a medium-sized frog, with the male up to 45 mm and the female reaching 52 mm in length. The width of the disc of the fourth toe is 133%–162% the width of the outer tubercle beneath the fourth toe. The length of the inner metatarsal tubercle is 84%–98% the length of the inner toe, which is spade-like. The male does not possess pectoral glands. The tympanum is small, with a diameter less than half the eye diameter. The back is light brown, with a darker triangle between the eyes that points backward. A pair of darker bands may separate over the lower back. A dark line along the snout often continues behind the eye. Male and female patterns are similar. This widespread species has previously been considered as two species, with the southern *L. broadleyi* present as far north as Malawi. I regard this as a polymorphic species as the populations have the same advertisement call.

Fig. 141 *Leptopelis argenteus*

DISTRIBUTION AND HABITAT (FIG. 141): This species is known from Tanzania, Kenya, Malawi, and Mozambique, to the eastern highlands of Zimbabwe. It has been found on trees and grass in lightly wooded wet savanna.

ADVERTISEMENT CALL: The male calls from dense bushes or high grass or sedge, up to 2 m above ground level. Three different calls are produced, 2 short croaks and a longer whine. The croak may precede or follow 2 or 3 of the longer whines, or either may be uttered alone. The croaks are less than 0.1 s long with dominant frequencies between 1.5 and 2.0 kHz, while the other croak is 0.2 s long, with dominant energy at 1.8 kHz. Often a croak is followed immediately by 2 whines, sounding as if two different species are calling.

BREEDING: Unknown.

TADPOLES: Unknown.

NOTES: This is a widespread variable species. Although it is common, nothing is known of its biology.

KEY REFERENCES: Stevens 1974, Schiøtz 1975, Howell 1981.

Bocage's tree frog
Leptopelis bocagii (Günther, 1864)
(Plate 11.8)

Bocage's Tree Frog

This species was named for the herpetologist J. V. Barbosa du Bocage, director of the National Museum in Lisbon, known as the Museu Bocage.

Bocage's frog, Bocage's burrowing frog, horseshoe forest treefrog. *Finye* in Chewa, Ngoni, and Nyanga; *katuti* in Cazomba and Lwena; and *calungurano* in some other parts of Angola.

DESCRIPTION: The male is up to 50 mm and the female, 58 mm in snout-vent length. The width of the disc of the fourth toe is 80%–100% the width of the outer tubercle below the toe. The metatarsal tubercle is 105%–140% the length of the inner toe and is spade-like to assist with digging. The male has pectoral glands. The tympanum is large, and the horizontal diameter is at least half the eye diameter. The discs are small, not exceeding the width of the digits. The markings are a dark n-shaped area on a lighter brown background, sometimes with a vertebral band. Irregular lines are present on the snout and sides of the body. Various markings occur between the eyes. A population in Kakamega, Kenya, is a green-backed form, with typical markings and call. It can be separated from the similar *L. parbocagii* by the ratio of the distance between the eyes, divided by the nostril to tympanum distance, which is 36% or less.

DISTRIBUTION AND HABITAT (FIG. 142): This largely ground-dwelling tree frog is known from northeastern South Africa through to the Caprivi Strip and Zimbabwe, northward. It occurs in open savannas.

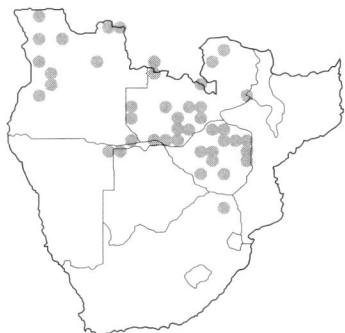

Fig. 142 *Leptopelis bocagii*

ADVERTISEMENT CALL: The male calls mostly from ground level but also from within mammal burrows and even a meter or two above ground in reeds or other vegetation. The call is a slow "quaak." Often 2 calls are uttered in succession. The duration of each call varies from 0.2 to 0.4 s, at a dominant frequency of 0.6 kHz.

BREEDING: The male holds on to the female by a sticky secretion from glands underneath his body. The eggs are laid during rain in deep holes in the ground.

TADPOLES: Unknown.

NOTES: Food items include earthworms, snails, arthropods, and frogs. They are eaten by the night adder *Causus rhombeatus*. This is one of the few African frogs known to form a thin cocoon to prevent desiccation during dry weather. The others are the African bullfrog *Pyxicephalus adspersus* and the giant rain frog *Breviceps gibbosus*.

KEY REFERENCES: Schiøtz 1975, Dudley 1978.

Cinnamon tree frog
Leptopelis cynnamomeus (Bocage, 1893)
(Plate 12.1)

The name *cynnamomeus* means "like cinnamon," referring to the color of the back.
Triad tree frog, Angola forest treefrog.

DESCRIPTION: The male grows up to 40 mm. The width of the disc of the fourth toe is 125%–164% the width of the outer tubercle beneath the toe. The metatarsal tubercle is 59%–80% the length of the inner toe, but only slightly spade-like. The male has weakly developed pectoral glands. The tympanum is large, with a horizontal diameter about half as large as the diameter of the eye. The discs are large. The pattern on the back consists of a darker bar between the eyes, which may extend as a triangle backward to join a pair of diverging side bands. The ground color is brown. A dark line runs from the tip of the snout continuing backward a short distance behind the eye.

Fig. 143 *Leptopelis cynnamomeus*

DISTRIBUTION AND HABITAT (FIG. 143): This frog is known from southeastern Democratic Republic of the Congo and northwestern Zambia to southern Angola. It is found in well-wooded savannas.

ADVERTISEMENT CALL: Males call a meter above ground. The call consists of 3 short notes, preceded by a short buzz. The first note appears to follow the buzz without a pause. The call is frequency-modulated, with a dominant frequency between 1.0 and 2.0 kHz. The buzz is 0.2 s in duration, and the short notes are about 0.2 s apart.

BREEDING: It breeds from the first heavy rains. The male makes a shallow pit while holding the female. A pair has been found in amplexus 50 mm below the surface. Eggs were found in the soil after the parents had vacated the burrow.

TADPOLES: Development to the tadpole stage takes up to 30 days, and to metamorphosis, 4 months.

NOTES: The young are first bright green before turning brown.

KEY REFERENCES: Linden 1971, Schiøtz 1975.

Yellow-spotted tree frog
Leptopelis flavomaculatus (Günther, 1864)
(Plates 12.2, 12.3)

The specific name *flavomaculatus* refers to the yellow spots found on the back of many young individuals.

Johnston's tree frog, brown forest treefrog.

DESCRIPTION: The male is up to 50 mm and the female, 70 mm in length. The width of the disc of the fourth toe is 120%–170% the width of the outer tubercle beneath the toe. The metatarsal tubercle is about equal in length to the first toe. The male has pectoral glands. The horizontal diameter of the tympanum is more than half the diameter of the eye. The toes are webbed, with the broad web between fourth and fifth toes reaching or passing the outer tubercle of the fifth toe. Juveniles are green with yellow spots, and adults may be green with white heels (in males) or brown. The typical n-shaped markings on the back and dark bar between the eyes are present in brown individuals.

DISTRIBUTION AND HABITAT (FIG. 144): The yellow-spotted tree frog is known from coastal Kenya, southward through Malawi to eastern Zimbabwe. This is a forest form, also found in small, dry forest remnants.

ADVERTISEMENT CALL: The male selects dense and high vegetation from which to call, making him difficult to observe. The male sometimes calls from a burrow, or from vegetation up to 4 m above ground. The call is a soft drawn-out cry, 0.3–0.7 s long, consisting of closely spaced harmonics at 0.75, 1, 1.25, 1.5, 1.75, and 2 kHz. The call shows

Fig. 144 *Leptopelis flavomaculatus*

slight frequency modulation, with a small rise in the beginning and a drop in frequency afterward. The soft call is very difficult to locate. A calling male 5 m away sounds as if it is 200 m further. It will call from sunset through to dawn.

BREEDING: Unknown.

TADPOLES: Unknown.

NOTES: In Zimbabwe they have been recorded calling with *L. mossambicus*.

KEY REFERENCES: Schiøtz 1975, De Fonesca & Jocque 1979.

Mozambique tree frog
Leptopelis mossambicus Poynton, 1985
(Plate 12.4)

The specific name *mossambicus* is derived from Mozambique. Brown-backed tree frog.

DESCRIPTION: The male reaches 52 mm and the female, 63 mm in length. The width of the disc of the fourth toe is 104%–140% of the width of the outer tubercle beneath the toe. The metatarsal tubercle is spade-like, 90%–130% the length of the first toe. The male has pectoral glands. The tympanum is large, with a horizontal diameter more than half the diameter of the eye. The juvenile is green, while the adult is brown with the typical *Leptopelis* n-shaped darker marking on the back. Darker patches may be present above each eye.

DISTRIBUTION AND HABITAT (FIG. 145): This tree frog is known from southern Malawi, through the lowlands of Mozambique, Zimbabwe, and Swaziland, into northern and eastern South Africa. It is found in savannas.

ADVERTISEMENT CALL: The call consists of 2 notes aptly described as "wala." The dominant energy is between 0.5 and 1.5 kHz, and the duration of both notes together is less than 0.2 s. The male calls while clinging to grass stems or low bushes about a meter off the ground, and they have been recorded calling up to 2.4 m above ground.

Fig. 145 *Leptopelis mossambicus*

BREEDING: It breeds from the first heavy rains. The male digs a shallow nest while holding the female. The eggs are laid in a muddy nest and left to hatch into tadpoles, which must then wriggle to the water.

TADPOLES: At False Bay Park they were found in a dark muddy water pool with a thick substrate of leaf detritus.

NOTES: In captivity one ate a chameleon its own size.

KEY REFERENCES: Schiøtz 1975, Wager 1986.

Natal tree frog
Leptopelis natalensis (Smith, 1849)
(Plate 12.5)

The specific name *natalensis* refers to the province of Natal, where the species was first found (now KwaZulu-Natal in South Africa). Forest tree frog.

DESCRIPTION: The length is up to 65 mm. The eyes are large, reddish or golden. Webbing reaches the outer tubercle of the outer finger. The disc on the fourth toe is over twice the width of the outer tubercle beneath the toe. The color pattern is typically a uniform green back, although pale brown frogs without a darker pattern are common. A third color pattern consists of emerald green blotches,

Natal Tree Frog

sometimes outlined with a delicate dark line, on a golden brown background.

DISTRIBUTION AND HABITAT (FIG. 146): This frog is known only from the KwaZulu-Natal lowlands. It occurs in coastal forest.

ADVERTISEMENT CALL: The male calls from trees and is usually difficult to locate. The call consists of a single short "quack" 0.05 s long, sometimes with 2 or 3 repeated in quick succession. The quacking notes may be preceded by a buzz, up to 0.5 s long.

BREEDING: The eggs are laid in a muddy nest near water or among decaying leaves. Each egg is 3 mm and yellow. Clutch size is 185.

TADPOLES: Tadpoles have been found in a muddy black pool. The tadpole hatches after 2 weeks, although it can delay hatching until the weather is wet. It wriggles toward the water, moving over stones and twigs. The drive to get to water is so strong that a tadpole is able to wriggle up the side of a container in captivity. It comes to the surface when disturbed and wriggles in the soft mud. The tadpole also is able to jump forward by flicking its tail. Metamorphosis takes 6 weeks. The tadpole is able to survive dry spells for weeks by taking up water through a well-developed capillary network on the belly.

NOTES: During the day the adult can be found up in vegetation clinging to leaves or branches or in shady spots under leaf litter.

Fig. 146 *Leptopelis natalensis*

KEY REFERENCES: Wager 1931, Wager 1986.

Cryptic tree frog
Leptopelis parbocagii Poynton & Broadley, 1987

The specific name *parbocagii* means "near *bocagii*," as this species is very similar to *L. bocagii*.
Lake Upemba forest treefrog.

DESCRIPTION: These are medium-sized to large tree frogs, with the male up to 54 mm and the female up to 64 mm in length. The discs are small. The width of the disc of the fourth toe is 80%–108% of the width of the outer tubercle beneath the toe. The metatarsal tubercle is spade-like for digging, 106%–134% the length of the first toe. The male has pectoral glands. The tympanum is large. The horizontal diameter of the tympanum is half or more of the diameter of the eye. When young, this green tree frog has a black line along the side of the white-tipped snout. The dorsal pattern is a dark **n**- or **m**-shaped marking, or a darker dorsal patch extending on to the head. It can be separated from the similar *L. bocagii* by the ratio of the distance between the eyes, divided by the nostril to tympanum distance, which is 36% or more.

DISTRIBUTION AND HABITAT (FIG. 147): This species is found in Malawi and Mozambique, northern Zambia, southern Tanzania, and the Democratic Republic of the Congo. It is known from savanna.

Fig. 147 *Leptopelis parbocagii*

ADVERTISEMENT CALL: Unknown. This is a burrowing frog that may climb vegetation to call.

BREEDING: Unknown.

TADPOLES: Unknown.

KEY REFERENCES: Stewart 1967 (as *L. bocagii*), Poynton & Broadley 1987.

Long-toed tree frog
Leptopelis xenodactylus Poynton, 1963
(Plate 12.6)

The specific name *xenodactylus* means "strange toe," referring to the long toes without discs.
Weza forest treefrog.

DESCRIPTION: The male grows to 50 mm and differs from most other *Leptopelis* by the lack of enlarged discs. The toes and fingers are long, with very little webbing between the toes. The tympanum is slightly less than half the diameter of the eye. The inner metatarsal tubercle is slightly spade-like. The back is a uniform green.

DISTRIBUTION (FIG. 148): This little known species has been collected only from the southern KwaZulu-Natal highlands. It occurs

Fig. 148 *Leptopelis xenodactylus*

in marshy areas with high grass polls. This species is listed as endangered.

ADVERTISEMENT CALL: The call is produced while the male is concealed at the base of a grass tussock or underground. Each call is a short croak, 0.1 s long, with the dominant frequency between 3.0 and 4.0 kHz. Like other species in the genus, the call is sometimes preceded by a soft buzz.

BREEDING: Unknown.

TADPOLES: Unknown.

NOTES: It is known to climb vegetation, although it has often been found at ground level. More needs to be discovered of the natural history of this interesting frog.

KEY REFERENCE: Passmore & Carruthers 1995.

Rain Frogs, Rubber Frogs—Family Microhylidae

The frogs making up this family are also known as *narrow mouthed toads*. Adults of the southern African species are small-mouthed and narrow-headed. The legs are moderately built, as most species walk, burrow, or climb. Tadpoles of the rubber frogs are midwater filter feeders, without jaw sheaths or labial teeth. There is no tadpole stage in two of the three genera covered here.

KEY TO THE GENERA
1a. Inner metatarsal flattened and spade-like, frogs squat (Fig. 149)
Breviceps
1b. Inner metatarsal tubercle not flattened 2

Fig. 149 Body shape

2a. Dorsum rough, color brown or gray without red markings
Probreviceps rhodesianus
2b. Dorsum smooth, with red or orange markings *Phrynomantis*

Rain Frogs—Genus *Breviceps*

Local names include *isiNana*, and *Kurzmaule-fröschen* in German. All *Breviceps* species are known as *chinani* in Shangaan and are believed to herald rain. This group of burrowing frogs possesses a number of features that enable it to be successful in the underground habitat. All the species in this genus burrow backward while scooping away the sand by means of a spade-like metatarsal tubercle on the foot. The forelimbs and hind limbs are short, and the body is globular. This body shape and the ability to inflate the body while buried in soil are characteristic of burrowing frogs.

The male is smaller than the female yet has to remain with the female during amplexus so as to be in the underground nest to fertilize the eggs. Mating is very unusual in these frogs, as the male is too small to be able to clasp the female in the way other frogs do. The small male overcomes the size difference by gluing himself on to the back of the female. The glue persists for some days and is strong enough to permit the female to burrow backward and construct a nest without dislodging the male. Eggs develop directly into small froglets, without a free-swimming feeding tadpole stage. When conditions start to dry out, the frog is able to secrete a mucous coating that waterproofs the skin and blocks all the body orifices. With the body inflated, presumably to increase the surface area for oxygen uptake through the skin, especially the well-vascularized skin on the lower belly, the frog is able to survive long periods of dryness underground.

There are probably many more species of rain frogs than are presently recognized.

KEY TO THE SPECIES

Note: There are species in this genus that have not been described at the time of writing, and this key will not be useful to identify them.

1a. Tympanum visible, sometimes partly concealed   2
1b. Tympanum not visible   3

2a. Glandular ridges on back   *Breviceps verrucosus*
2b. Glandular ridges not present, back usually reddish
    Breviceps acutirostris

3a. Basal subarticular tubercles double (Fig. 150)
    Breviceps namaquensis
3b. Basal subarticular tubercles single or not developed   4

Fig. 150   Double tubercles

4a. A pair of dorsal paravertebral ridges   *Breviceps sylvestris*
4b. Dorsum without skin ridges   5

5a. Feet paddle-like with fleshy webbing (Fig. 151)
                                               Breviceps macrops
5b. Feet unwebbed, tubercles present   6

Fig. 151   Paddle-like foot

6a. Outer toe short, not longer than wide (Fig. 152)   7
6b Outer toe longer than wide   9

Fig. 152   Small outer toe

7a. Outer toe minute, only a tubercle   *Breviceps poweri*
7b. Outer toe length about equal to width   8

8a. Two isolated black longitudinal patches on the throat
                                               Breviceps adspersus
8b. Throat uniformly darkened   *Breviceps mossambicus*

9a. Back rough, densely granular   11
9b. Back not covered with pitted granules   10

10a. Back a uniform brown to black, with small conical tubercles
$\qquad$ *Breviceps fuscus*
10b. Back patterned, covered with fine granules
$\qquad$ *Breviceps montanus*

11a. Belly densely granular, dorsal granules pitted
$\qquad$ *Breviceps gibbosus*
11b. Belly smooth or slightly granular $\qquad$ *Breviceps rosei*

Strawberry rain frog
Breviceps acutirostris Poynton, 1963
(Plate 12.7)

The specific name refers to the sharp snout.
Cape short-headed frog.

DESCRIPTION: The female reaches 40 mm and the male, usually less than 25 mm in length. Both upper and lower surfaces are granular. The snout is sharp, and the distance between the eyes is about equal to the length of the upper eyelid. The tympanum is usually not visible. The inner and outer toes are longer than they are wide. The back and sides are frequently reddened, with darker warts. The lower surface is purple with cream spots.

DISTRIBUTION AND HABITAT (FIG. 153): The strawberry rain frog is found along the southern Cape Fold Mountains in South Africa. It prefers thick forests, or grasslands at a high altitude.

ADVERTISEMENT CALL: The male calls from ground level. The call is a short whistle, 1.9 kHz with a duration of 200 ms. The calls may be produced rapidly in succession.

BREEDING: Unknown. These interesting frogs would be worthwhile subjects for field observations.

NOTES: The male may call within meters of the black rain frog *Breviceps fuscus*. The possible interactions between these two species will be interesting to discover.

KEY REFERENCE: Passmore & Carruthers 1979.

Fig. 153 *Breviceps acutirostris*

Common rain frog
Briceps adspersus Peters, 1882
(Plate 12.8)

The specific name *adspersus* means "sprinkled," referring to the markings on the back.
Peters' rain frog, South African short-head, Transvaal short-headed frog. *Senatswii* in Setswana; *iSinana* in Zulu; *unocebeyi*, *isele lendyebo* (the frog that brings wealth), *inkosazana* ("princess," a respectful term to induce it to bring rain while people are hoeing), *unomadambatane*, *chinana* in Kalanga; *chinani* in Shangaan; *tsininikae* in Tswana. These names are also used for other species of *Breviceps*. *Bosveld-reënpadda* in Afrikaans.

DESCRIPTION: This is a medium-sized frog, with the male up to 47 mm and the female up to 60 mm long. The tympanum is not visible. The lower surface is smooth, but the back is usually rough. The arms and legs are very short. The inner metatarsal tubercle is large and flattened and used by the frog for digging backward into the soil. The inner and outer toes are as long as they are wide. The pattern on the back is variable but mostly includes paired light patches on a brown background. Darker markings including a brown or black stripe running from the eye toward the armpit are also present. The undersurface is white, with darker mottling often on the throat. Two isolated black longitudinal patches are present on the throat.

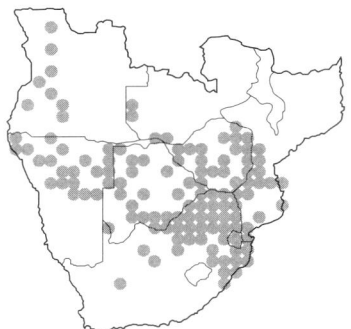

Fig. 154 *Breviceps adspersus*

DISTRIBUTION AND HABITAT (FIG. 154): It is known from Angola across to southern Mozambique, southward to central Namibia and the interior of South Africa. This species may be found in the Kalahari sand dunes and across the dry savanna of southern Africa.

ADVERTISEMENT CALL: The call usually is produced underground in burrows, or at the base of vegetation. Males emerge after dark and move to a calling position about a meter from the burrow. These calling positions are often just depressions in the ground and are used on successive nights. The call is a short chirp or whistle, 0.1 s in duration, at a dominant frequency of 2 kHz. The calls are repeated rapidly in groups of 3 or more.

BREEDING: The smaller male glues on to the lower back of the female. The female digs backward with the male attached, producing a burrow in which the eggs are laid. The eggs are 5 mm in diameter within 10-mm capsules. It appears that the male alone produces the glue that attaches the male to the female during amplexus. Evidence for this comes from an incident when a male rain frog became attached to a sand frog in a plastic bag. Although it is not known if the female also produces glue, both species have skin richly supplied with glands.

TRADITIONAL BELIEFS: This species prefers sandy moist soil and often occupies gardens and fields, where it may be accidentally dug out while a gardener or worker is hoeing. Traditional beliefs in Eastern Cape Province of South Africa direct that a few corn grains should be inserted in its hiding place and the earth put back over the frog. The many common names listed for these well-known frogs demonstrate that they are held in respect.

NOTES: Up to 24 individuals have been found hibernating communally in the roots of an *Acacia* tree in winter. They are known to eat termites and can be found during day and night at the mouth of termite nests feeding on winged forms when these swarm. Enemies include the black backed jackal *Canis mesomelas* and the fiscal shrike, which has been observed impaling one through the head on a thornbush. Other predators are the olive thrush *Turdus olivaceus* and the hadeda ibis *Bostrychia hagedash*, which locates the frogs underground by probing with its long beak.

KEY REFERENCES: Hewitt 1937, Milstein 1967.

Black rain frog
Breviceps fuscus Hewitt, 1925
(Plate 13.1)

The specific name *fuscus* refers to the dark color of the frog. Plain rain frog, brown short-headed frog.

DESCRIPTION: The female grows up to 51 mm long. The tympanum is hidden, and the back is covered with small conical tubercles, fairly widely spaced. The eye is small. The inner and outer toes are longer than they are wide. The back is brown to black, with no markings. The undersurface is smooth and dark, although some animals have light spots.

DISTRIBUTION AND HABITAT (FIG. 155): The black rain frog is known from the forested slopes and plateaus of the southern Cape Fold Mountains.

ADVERTISEMENT CALL: The males may call from within a burrow or from vegetation, 30 cm above ground level. The male also calls from within the burrow while guarding eggs. The call is a short chirp, 0.2 s long, at a dominant frequency of 1.8 kHz.

Fig. 155 *Breviceps fuscus*

BREEDING: Breeding takes place during summer from October. The eggs are yellow, 5 mm in diameter within 8-mm capsules and are laid in a chamber 30 or 40 mm below the surface. The eggs form a sphere about 30 mm across, with a layer of empty egg capsules on top. The size of the clutch in two nests from George was 42 and 43 eggs, each with additional 25–30 empty egg cases. Each nest had a 15-mm opening to the surface. The male remains with the eggs and continues to call.

NOTES: Breeding tunnels about 150 mm deep have been recorded from the forests of the Western Cape Province in South Africa. This frog is known to be eaten by the bushpig *Potamochoerus porcus* in the forests of the Eastern Cape Province, with 18 specimens being recorded from the stomach of one pig. Males of the black and strawberry rain frogs may be heard calling within meters of each other on the edges of indigenous forest.

KEY REFERENCES: Visser 1979, Palmer 1982.

Giant rain frog
Breviceps gibbosus (Linnaeus, 1758)
(Plate 13.2)

The specific name refers to the swollen-looking body.
Cape short-head, Cape rain frog, South African short-headed frog.

Giant Rain Frog

DESCRIPTION: The female reaches 60 mm and the male, 52 mm in length. The tympanum is not visible, and the upper and lower surfaces are rough. The toes are small, with the length of the inner toe being equal to its width. The back is brown with paler patches and darker granules. A dark patch extends backward from the eye. The underside is off-white with brown markings.

DISTRIBUTION AND HABITAT (FIG. 156): This frog is known from Piketberg to the Stellenbosch area, with a population in Newlands in Cape Town. It is found in sandy areas. This species is listed as near threatened.

ADVERTISEMENT CALL: The male calls from below ground or from the mouth of a burrow at 45°, at least 150 mm deep. The burrows are often placed under vegetation, which makes locating calling males very difficult. The call is a long chirp, 0.5 s, with the dominant harmonic being 1.1 kHz. The pulse rate is about 50/s. Males may be heard calling from late April with the first autumn rains.

BREEDING: Breeding is initiated by the onset of the heavy winter rains in June. Despite the large size of this frog, the male is glued on to the back of the female, and the pair burrow backward into the soil. Nests have been found containing a pair plus eggs, or up to 22 young.

Fig. 156 *Breviceps gibbosus*

NOTES: This frog has the distinction of being the first frog species described from Africa, as *Rana gibbosa* by Gerstener in 1550, predating the major work of Linnaeus that appeared in 1758.

This species is able to produce a thin cocoon around itself, with the nostrils plugged. The body is inflated and the ventral skin shows large red blood vessels. In this condition the frog is able to survive long periods underground.

KEY REFERENCES: McLachlan 1978, de Villiers 1988c.

Desert rain frog
Breviceps macrops Boulenger, 1907
(Plate 13.3)

The name *macrops* refers to the large eyes of this species. Boulenger's short-headed frog. *Melkpadda* ("milk frog") in Afrikaans, referring to the pale color of the back; also *blaas-op*, *Jan Blom*, *donderpadda*.

DESCRIPTION: The female reaches 50 mm in length. The tympanum is not visible. The eyes are large, and the space between the eyes is about half the eye diameter. The hands and feet are paddle-like, with fleshy webbing and reduced or absent tubercles. The back is pale, almost white, sometimes with darker markings. The lower surface is white, with a transparent window in the midbelly region where pigment is lacking. Usually the pattern of the back is concealed by a layer of sand attached to the skin, which renders this animal perfectly camouflaged against the sand dunes on which it lives.

DISTRIBUTION AND HABITAT (FIG. 157): The desert rain frog is known along the Namaqualand coast from Kleinsee to Lüderitz in Namibia, up to 8 km inland. It is listed as near threatened.

ADVERTISEMENT CALL: The call is a subdued rising whistle, heard throughout the year when conditions are misty. The dominant energy is at 1.3 kHz, rising from 1.2 to 1.4 kHz. The duration of each quiet whistle is just over 200 ms. The male calls in the open, sometimes only a meter or so from another male. A chorus structure is evident, where one male initiates a bout of calling and is followed by other males in a regular pattern.

Fig. 157 *Breviceps macrops*

BREEDING: Unknown: Presumably the female lays eggs in burrows in the damp sand.

NOTES: This frog is found on the white sands of the coast of Namaqualand, from just beyond the splash line of the beach. It emerges after dark and runs around on the sand, gathering with others at dung where they feed on beetles and moths. It is active during both misty and clear nights. The interactions between this species and the Namaqua rain frog *B. namaquensis*, if they indeed do overlap in distribution, would be interesting to discover.

KEY REFERENCE: de Villiers 1988a.

Mountain rain frog
Breviceps montanus Power, 1926
(Plate 13.4)

The specific name *montanus* refers to the mountainous habitat where this species is found.
Mountain short-headed frog.

DESCRIPTION: The female only reaches 31 mm in length. The tympanum is not visible, and the upper and lower surfaces are rough like sandpaper, covered with granules. The inner and outer toes are as long as they are wide. The color pattern is a brown vertebral band on a

Fig. 158 *Breviceps montanus*

darker background. Darker markings occur in the band, which has irregular edges. A dark eye stripe runs from the eye to in front of the arm. Coloration below is variable, with darker markings.

DISTRIBUTION AND HABITAT (FIG. 158): This frog is known from the western Cape Fold Mountains and Table Mountain, found at high altitudes on the slopes and plateaus. They are often found sheltering under stones.

ADVERTISEMENT CALL: The male calls while concealed under ground or sheltered at the base of vegetation or between stones. The call is a short whistle, with a duration of 0.1 s and an emphasized frequency of 2.2 kHz.

BREEDING: Unknown. Breeding apparently occurs during summer, with calls recorded in January and females with large eggs collected in October.

KEY REFERENCE: Visser 1979.

Mozambique rain frog
Breviceps mossambicus Peters, 1854
(Plates 13.5, 13.6)

The specific name *mossambicus* refers to the island of Mozambique where the species was first discovered.

Mozambique Rain Frog

Flat faced frog, Mozambique short-headed frog. *Mopskopffrosch* in German, *chibawatiko* in Ngoni, *kaswanene* in Yao, *lukumba* in Misuku, *nantusi* in Manganja, *nasanene* in Njanja, *finye* in Cholo and Cewa, *ciswenene* in Yao, *mbulundu* in Sena, *injactumbâsi* on Mozambique island, *talango* in Biballa, *kavumba-njimi* in Cazumbo and Lwena, *caralilacema* in Quissange and Quimbundo.

DESCRIPTION: The female grows to 52 mm SVL. The outer finger reaches the outer tubercle beneath the fourth finger. A darkened area of the throat may be continuous with the dark stripe from eye to forearm. Very similar to *B. adspersus*, from which it is distinguished by color pattern, *B. mossambicus* having dark dorsal flecks and *B. adspersus* possessing white dorsal patches. However, the dorsal color pattern is very variable from region to region.

DISTRIBUTION AND HABITAT (FIG. 159): The Mozambique rain frog is known from Southern Tanzania, the Mozambique coastal plain westward to Malawi and Zimbabwe and southward to the eastern Cape. It is essentially a savanna form.

ADVERTISEMENT CALL: The male calls from beneath leaf litter or while well concealed at ground level. The call is a short chirp, 0.05 s long at a dominant frequency of 2.6 kHz.

BREEDING: Each egg is 0.6 mm in diameter within a 12-mm capsule. About 20 eggs are laid in a spherical chamber or nest which is often

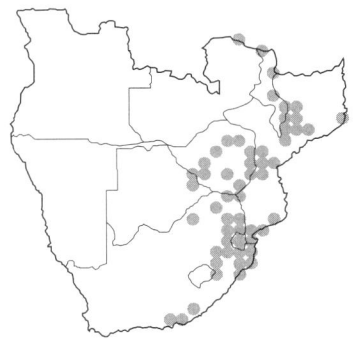

Fig. 159 *Breviceps mossambicus*

under a stone. The female then leaves the nest and burrows nearby. The eggs hatch after 6–8 weeks, first developing into nonswimming and nonfeeding tadpoles that move around in the softened jelly and then into dark juvenile froglets, 8–9 mm long.

NOTES: It has been found under leaf litter in wooded areas. This frog is preyed upon by the vine snake *Thelotornis kirtlandii*, the white lipped snake *Crotaphopeltis hotamboeia*, and the night adder *Causus rhombeatus*.

KEY REFERENCE: FitzSimons & Van Dam 1929.

Namaqua rain frog
Breviceps namaquensis Power, 1926
(Plate 13.7)

The specific name *namaquensis* refers to Namaqualand in South Africa, the area where this species is found.
Namaqualand short-headed frog.

DESCRIPTION: The female reaches 45 mm. The eyes are large, with the distance between the eyes about half the horizontal diameter of the eye. The tubercles beneath the toes are well developed and double. The inner toe is about as long as it is wide. The dark brown back has lighter sides. A short dark eye stripe extends backward but does not reach the arm. The lower surface is smooth and white.

DISTRIBUTION AND HABITAT (FIG. 160): This frog is known along the Namaqualand coast to the adjacent inland mountains. It occurs in arid sandy habitats that are well covered with vegetation.

ADVERTISEMENT CALL: Males call beneath vegetation. The call is a whistle, 0.15 s long, rising from 1.3 to 1.5 kHz. Calls are produced at a rate of about 2/s.

BREEDING: Unknown.

NOTES: This species is preyed upon by the Cape cobra *Naja nivea*.

Fig. 160 *Breviceps namaquensis*

KEY REFERENCE: Passmore & Carruthers 1979.

Power's rain frog
Breviceps poweri Parker, 1934
(Plates 13.8, 14.1)

This species was named for the herpetologist J. H. Power, director of the McGregor Museum in Kimberley, 1947–1958.
Power's short-headed frog. *Kavumbula ndimi* ("found when digging") in Lunda.

DESCRIPTION: The female grows up to 50 mm long. The tympanum is not visible. The fourth finger just reaches the inner tubercle beneath the third finger. The inner metatarsal tubercle is often continuous with the spade-like outer metatarsal tubercle. The outer toe is minute. The back is tan to dark brown or brick red with darker mottling. A light line joining the feet along the posterior hind limbs is continuous with a characteristic light spot above the vent. Sometimes a light vertebral line is present, reaching the pale spot. A series of orange spots is present along the side of the back, together with irregular lighter blotches on the sides. A dark eye stripe reaches the shoulder.

DISTRIBUTION AND HABITAT (FIG. 161): Power's rain frog is known from Zambia, southern Tanzania, Malawi, and Mozam-

Fig. 161 *Breviceps poweri*

bique. It is found in Mopane and Brachystegia woodlands up to 1300 m.

ADVERTISEMENT CALL: The male calls from a slight depression in the open. This depression is about 1 m from its burrow. The call is a series of rolling notes. Between 7 and 12 notes are produced per call. Each note is a whistle, 0.4 s long, produced about 2/s. Each whistle rises slightly in pitch, with the peak frequency at 1.5 kHz.

BREEDING: Unknown.

NOTES: This frog is reported to be eaten by the Mozambique spitting cobra *Naja mossambica*.

KEY REFERENCE: Stewart 1967.

Rose's rain frog
Breviceps rosei Power, 1926
(Plate 14.2)

The frog was named for the dentist and naturalist Walter Rose. Sand rain frog, Rose's short-headed frog.

DESCRIPTION: The female is up to 36 mm SVL, but the male is generally shorter than 15 mm. The tympanum is not visible. The outer

Rose's Rain Frog

toe reaches the inner tubercle of the fourth toe. The inner and outer toes are about as long as they are wide. The back is mostly dark brown, with pale blotches along the side. Sometimes a thin vertebral stripe is present, with a thin line joining foot to foot through the vent. This line is very variable, however, and is frequently interrupted. A dark eye stripe joins eye to armpit. The throat is granular and slightly darkened in males. The underside is pale with brown flecks smooth or slightly granular.

DISTRIBUTION AND HABITAT (FIG. 162): This frog is known from the Cape Flats and other low-laying sandy areas along the southwestern Cape coast. It is associated with dense sedges and other low coastal vegetation.

ADVERTISEMENT CALL: Breeding starts in spring, although the male may call from midwinter in July, continuing sporadically to summer in January. The male calls from an elevated position, from 30 cm to a merte above ground, often climbing fallen sedges. The call is a short whistle, 0.1 s long at a dominant frequency of 2.1 kHz. The male calls day and night after heavy rain.

BREEDING: The female approaches the male at ground level. Amplexus lasts for 4 or 5 days, and the male assists the female during burrowing by making digging movements with his hind feet. I dug up a pair that had burrowed in captivity, and found both male and female "waterproofed" by a mucous cocoon. The following night

Fig. 162 *Breviceps rosei*

the male was still glued to the female. Eggs are unknown in this species.

NOTES: The calling male will quietly drop out of vegetation when disturbed. However, it often gets entangled in dense sedge stems and can be found worming its way to the ground.

KEY REFERENCE: FitzSimons 1946.

Forest rain frog
Breviceps sylvestris FitzSimons, 1930
(Plate 14.3)

The specific name *sylvestris* refers to the forest habitat where this species is found.
Transvaal forest rain frog, forest short-headed frog.

DESCRIPTION: The female reaches 50 mm in length. The tympanum is not visible. The back is granular, with small conical tubercles, and a ridge runs from behind each eye, often converging over the shoulder region and then running parallel to the midline. The length of the inner toe is equal to its width, while the outer toe is longer than wide. The back pattern consists of lighter patches between the pair of paravertebral skin ridges, with a dark eye stripe running from eye to armpit. The lower surface is white with brown speckles.

DISTRIBUTION AND HABITAT (FIG. 163): This frog occurs in the northeastern forests of South Africa, where it lives beneath leaf litter. It is classified as near threatened.

ADVERTISEMENT CALL: This is a brief whistle, 0.2 s at a dominant frequency of 1.7 kHz.

BREEDING: Breeding takes place in early summer, and the young emerge about 8 weeks later. The eggs are laid in a nest at the base of a rock or below roots. About 56 eggs are laid, along with a top layer of empty capsules. The female stays near the eggs. The developing tadpoles move actively, creating a froth.

KEY REFERENCE: Wager 1986.

Fig. 163 *Breviceps sylvestris*

Plaintive rain frog
Breviceps verrucosus Rapp, 1842
(Plate 14.4)

The specific name *verrucosus* means "warty."
Natal short-headed frog. *Klaende reënpadda* in Afrikaans.

DESCRIPTION: The female may reach 53 mm in length. The tympanum is usually visible, although it may be covered by granules in some specimens. The outer toe is long, extending beyond the basal tubercle of the fourth toe. The upper and lower surfaces are granular, with the granules pitted. There are glandular ridges on the back. The coloration of the back is variable, usually a tan to dark brown background with black markings, often with two lighter stripes running posteriorly from the head.

DISTRIBUTION (FIG. 164): This frog is known from the eastern escarpment of South Africa. It occurs in forested areas and in places that previously were covered with forest.

ADVERTISEMENT CALL: The male calls from a burrow, in the open, or 10–40 cm above ground level on vegetation or rock. The call is a long whistle, up to 0.6 s, at a dominant frequency of 2.0 kHz.

BREEDING: Unknown.

Fig. 164 *Breviceps verrucosus*

NOTES: This species has been found in residential areas adjoining forest.

KEY REFERENCES: Pickersgill 1975, Poynton & Pritchard 1976.

Whistling rain frog
Breviceps sp.
(Plate 14.5)

DESCRIPTION: The male may grow to 40 mm long. The tympanum is not visible. The back is rough although smoother in some specimens. Many different color patterns are known. Commonly, it has a dark eye stripe running to the arm. The back is tan to brown, with two rows of paler patches. Small black markings are interspersed with darker areas. The sides are lighter, and the underside is pale. Some specimens may have a thin vertebral stripe.

DISTRIBUTION AND HABITAT (FIG. 165): This frog is known from the eastern parts of South Africa. It is found in well-wooded sandy areas.

ADVERTISEMENT CALL: The call is a long soft whistle. It is repeated regularly. Each whistle may be up to 1.5 s long, at an emphasized frequency of 3.2 kHz.

BREEDING: Unknown.

Highland Rain Frog

Fig. 165 *Breviceps* sp.

NOTES: This frog and the Mozambique rain frog call together from the same habitat.

KEY REFERENCE: Passmore & Carruthers 1995.

Rain Frogs—Genus *Probreviceps*

Only one species occurs in the area covered by this work, with another three species in Tanzania.

Highland rain frog
Probreviceps rhodesianus Poynton & Broadley, 1967

The species was named for Rhodesia (now Zimbabwe) where it was discovered.
Forest rain frog, Zimbabwe big-fingered frog.

DESCRIPTION: The male is known to be up to 35 mm and the female, 49 mm long. The metatarsal tubercles and tubercles beneath the toes are well developed. The tympanum is visible. The back is very rough, pale brown to gray with darker, purple spots. The underside is mottled. The vent is directed downward.

DISTRIBUTION AND HABITAT (FIG. 166): This species is only known from the eastern highlands of Zimbabwe. It may be more widely distributed than the map suggests. The highland rain frog

Fig. 166 *Probreviceps rhodesianus*

is found in evergreen mountain forest, usually under rotten logs or under piles of leaf litter, from areas of steep slope. Its proposed conservation status is vulnerable.

ADVERTISEMENT CALL: Unknown, although they scream when disturbed. A valuable contribution could be made by anyone with the opportunity to record the advertisement call and other natural history details of this interesting species.

BREEDING: Eggs are laid in a burrow, consisting of a hollow in humus beneath a layer of dead leaves. Clutch size is 20, and each egg is 5 mm in diameter.

KEY REFERENCE: Poynton & Broadley 1967.

Rubber Frogs—Genus *Phrynomantis*

Rubber frogs are known from Central Africa southward to Namibia, and the eastern parts of South Africa. There are four species, including one in West Africa. The species are distributed in moist and dry tropical regions, with one species endemic to the Namib Desert. Tadpoles are large, midwater filter feeders, without jaw sheaths or labial teeth. Three species occur in this area.

Spotted Rubber Frog

KEY TO THE SPECIES

1a. Dorsal pattern consists of two broad orange to red bands from the snout back to the hind limbs, with a separate patch of color over the rear (Fig. 167) *Phrynomantis bifasciatus*
1b. Dorsal pattern consists of spots or blotches, never two broad bands 2

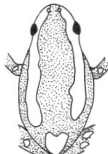

Fig. 167 Dorsal pattern

2a. Tips of fingers without discs, dorsal pattern of small spots *Phrynomantis affinis*
2b. Tips of fingers expanded, dorsal pattern of irregular blotches (Fig. 168) *Phrynomantis annectens*

Fig. 168 Finger discs

Spotted rubber frog
Phrynomantis affinis (Boulenger, 1901)
(Plate 14.6)

The specific name *affinis* means "neighboring" and refers to the similarity of this frog to *P. bifasciatus*.
Pweto snake-neck frog. *Wendelhalsfrosch* in German.

DESCRIPTION: The female reaches 65 mm in length. The tips of the fingers and toes are without discs. The pattern on the back consists of orange or red spots on a dark brown or black background. The arms are short and stout, and the animal moves by walking.

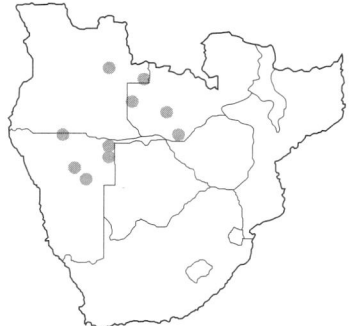

Fig. 169 *Phrynomantis affinis*

DISTRIBUTION AND HABITAT (FIG. 169): The spotted rubber frog is known from southern Tanzania, western Zambia, eastern Angola, and northern Namibia. It is found in sandy areas.

ADVERTISEMENT CALL: Unknown.

BREEDING: Unknown.

TADPOLES: Unknown.

NOTES: This species feeds on ants but will take other insects in captivity. This species is rarely encountered, although widespread.

Marbled rubber frog
Phrynomantis annectens (Werner, 1910)
(Plate 14.7)

The specific name *annectens* means "to connect with," but Werner's reason for selecting this name is obscure.
Cape snake-neck frog. *Engmaulfrosch* in German.

DESCRIPTION: This is a small frog, with the female reaching 40 mm in length. The body is flattened. The toes have a trace of webbing. The fingers and toes possess small discs. The horizontal diameter of the eye is about equal to the distance between the tip of the snout and the eye. The back is smooth, with red, pink, yellow, orange,

Marbled Rubber Frog

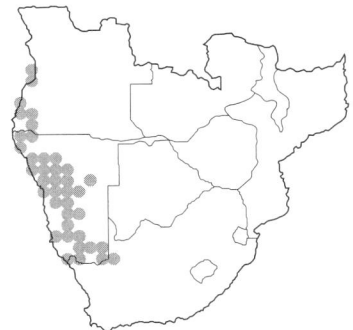

Fig. 170 *Phrynomantis annectens*

silver, or golden patches on a black or silver background. The underside is pale.

DISTRIBUTION AND HABITAT (FIG. 170): This desert-adapted frog is known from South Africa in the Richtersveld, the Augrabies area, and Aggenys on the southern bank of the Gariep River northward through the Namib Desert into Angola, and on the rocky mountains of central Namibia. It is found in very dry areas, always associated with rock outcrops.

ADVERTISEMENT AND AGGRESSION CALL: The male calls from the edge of a rock pool. It may call while sitting partly in the water or while concealed under a rock. The advertisement call is a long trill lasting up to 12 s, at a dominant frequency of around 2.2 kHz. If an intruder male approaches within about 100 mm of a calling male, the latter produces an aggression call (a series of shorter notes) and attacks the intruder. The fight consists of face-to-face wrestling, usually in deep water. Fights last about 6 s, with the established male winning all the fights in 25 observed cases.

BREEDING: Each female lays 80–100 eggs, deposited in small groups of 2–8. Eggs are laid on submerged rock or attached to vegetation 5–30 cm below water level. Eggs hatch into free-swimming tadpoles within 18–36 hours.

TADPOLES: See the chapter on tadpoles.

NOTES: Although this frog is found in very dry areas, it breeds in deep rock pools that keep water for a long time, as the tadpole is a relatively slow developer. The tadpole eats unicellular algae and diatoms. The adult frog can appropriately be called a crevice creeper. It retires into the narrow cracks found in the granite, shale, and schists in the drier areas. In the Namib Desert it occurs on granite domes, where, despite the low precipitation, the large rock surface collects sufficient water in which it can breed.

KEY REFERENCES: Gradwell 1974, Channing 1976a.

Banded rubber frog
Phrynomantis bifasciatus (Smith, 1847)
(Plate 14.8)

The specific name *bifasciatus* refers to the two orange or red stripes on the back.
Red-banded frog, red-banded rubber frog, South African snake-neck frog. *Bindenfrosch* in German, *rooibandrubberpadda* in Afrikaans.

DESCRIPTION: The male grows up to 53 mm and the female reaches 65 mm in length. The skin is smooth. The head is flat and narrow, with a tympanum just smaller than the eye. The toes and fingers have small discs, which are truncated, and very little webbing. As in many climbing frogs, the last segment is not in line with the rest of the finger or toe. The coloration of the back consists of an orange or red patch over the base, and two broad bands of the same color running from in front of the eyes to the leg. The lower surface is smooth, with a gray background and white spots and blotches.

DISTRIBUTION AND HABITAT (FIG. 171): This frog is known from the moist savannas of Kenya east to Angola and southward to Namibia and northern South Africa. It has been found in small mammal burrows and beneath the sheath leaves of banana plants, and will climb into any small crevice during the day.

ADVERTISEMENT CALL: The male calls from the water's edge or while concealed under vegetation, down rodent holes, or often inside

Banded Rubber Frog

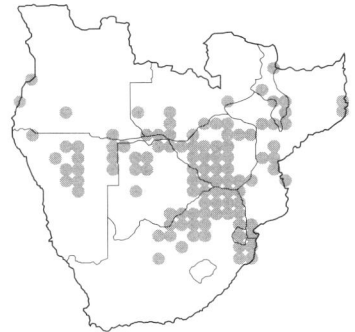

Fig. 171 *Phrynomantis bifasciatus*

logs. The call is a long melodious trill, lasting up to 3 s, with emphasized frequencies at 1.2 and 2.4 kHz. Each note lasts only 0.02 s, with a similar interval between notes. The call can be heard for some distance.

BREEDING: It breeds during the rainy season in summer. The eggs are laid at the bottom of temporary muddy pools. Even the smallest water bodies are used for depositing eggs. It is not uncommon to find tadpoles in water trapped in animal prints in mud, especially those of elephants. Each egg is 1.3 mm in diameter, in a 4-mm capsule. The eggs either are deposited in a 75-mm mass on vegetation or are sunk. Clutch size is 300–1500. The tadpole hatches after 4 days.

TADPOLES: See the chapter on tadpoles.

SKIN TOXINS: When disturbed, the frog inflates and arches its body, with the head tucked in. The bright contrasting color of the back is believed to serve as a warning to predators. It is accompanied by a skin toxin that causes irritation, although these frogs can be handled with no ill effects. Handling of this frog by a person with scratches on the hands has resulted in painful swellings, with difficult breathing, headache, faster heart rate, and nausea. These symptoms only last about 4 hours, but water from the aquarium that had contained these frogs later produced further mild symptoms when splashed onto scratches.

NOTES: This attractive frog is well known by keepers in the pet trade. It was imported into Germany for this purpose before 1931. It is eaten by hammerkops *Scopus umbretta*. Maximum recorded longevity in captivity is 6 years 7 months.

KEY REFERENCES: Power 1927c, Jaeger 1971, Wager 1986, Colley 1987.

Platannas—Family Pipidae

These frogs spend nearly their whole life in water and are adapted to an aquatic existence. They are smooth, streamlined, with large webbed feet and sensory lateral-line organs. Calling, feeding, and breeding take place in water. They are nearly the only frogs in the region that feed on aquatic prey. They feed on their own tadpoles, making indirect use of the algal food supply in the water on which the tadpoles feed. They do not possess a tongue, unlike most other frogs. This family has a very good fossil record. The earliest fossils are known from the Lower Cretaceous of the Middle East 120 million years ago.

Two genera are found in Africa: *Hymenochirus* and *Xenopus*. *Xenopus laevis* has become a standard laboratory animal, on which many physiological, embryological, and genetic investigations are based, and its aquatic nature makes it an easy animal to keep and breed in captivity. The common platanna *X. laevis* was used from the 1930s extensively for pregnancy testing, because the female would produce eggs when injected with the urine of a pregnant woman.

The frogs in this subfamily are found in all kinds of water bodies, from rivers and lakes to ditches. Many are known to have a courtship behavior that involves the clasped pair swimming in loops. The eggs are deposited at the top of the loop while the pair is inverted.

Platannas—Genus *Xenopus*

The name *Xenopus* means "strange foot," referring to the claws on three of the five toes. There are only six species in this area. All the species of *Xenopus* are adapted for a life in water, being smooth with large webbed feet and strong legs for swimming. The head is small and flattened, and the eyes are on top of the head. Sensory organs that look like "stitches" are arranged around the eyes and along the sides. The attachment of the legs to the body, the pelvic girdle, is able to slide. This mechanism increases the efficiency of movement, by increasing the swimming stroke. The body can be shortened as an escape mechanism, or lengthened to enhance the ability to quickly swim away from a predator.

KEY TO THE SPECIES
1a. Three claws on each hind foot 2
1b. A fourth "claw" on the metatarsal tubercle (Fig. 172) 5

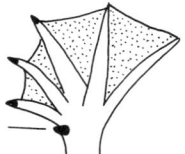

Fig. 172 Fourth "claw"

2a. Subocular tentacle less than half the eye diameter 3
2b. Subocular tentacle equal to or more than half the eye diameter, 14 or less sense organs around the eye (Fig. 173) *Xenopus muelleri*

Fig. 173 Subocular tentacle

3a. Ventral surface heavily speckled or blotched on a yellow background (Fig. 174) 4
3b. Ventral surface unmarked or lightly speckled, 17 sense organs around eye *Xenopus laevis*

Fig. 174 Belly pattern

4a. Adults with less than 40-mm SVL, subocular tentacle absent, restricted to the southwestern tip of Africa *Xenopus gilli*

4b. Adults with more than 40-mm SVL, 14 sense organs around the eye, found in northern areas   *Xenopus petersii*

5a. Subocular tentacle long, 8 sense organs around each eye
    Xenopus fraseri
5b. Subocular tentacle very short, 6–14 sense organs around each eye
    Xenopus epitropicalis

Southern tropical platanna
Xenopus epitropicalis Fischberg et al., 1982
(Plate 15.1)

The specific name *epitropicalis* means "outside *Xenopus tropicalis*." This species was discovered at Kinshasa in the Democratic Republic of the Congo, south of the range of *X. tropicalis*.
Equatorial clawed frog, Cameroon clawed frog. *Äquator-Krallenfrosch* in German.

DESCRIPTION: The male grows to 50 mm in length. It resembles the common platanna closely and is difficult to distinguish. It has 6–14 stitchlike sense organs around the eye.

DISTRIBUTION AND HABITAT (FIG. 175): This species is found from the Congo River basin northward to Cameroon, in permanent water in lowland rain forest.

Fig. 175 *Xenopus epitropicalis*

ADVERTISEMENT CALL: The advertisement call is a repeated trill uttered underwater. Each trill is 0.3 s long, consisting of a mean of 9 pulses. The calls are repeated rapidly, three or four times per second. The series of calls may continue for 8 s or more. The call is low-pitched, with the dominant harmonic below 1 kHz.

BREEDING: Unknown.

TADPOLES: Unknown.

NOTES: This species is visible at the surface of the water during the day.

KEY REFERENCES: Loumont 1983, Tinsley & Kobel 1996.

Fraser's platanna
Xenopus fraseri Boulenger, 1905
(Plate 15.2)

The species was named for Louis Fraser who collected for the Natural History Museum in London.
Fraser's clawed frog. *Fraserscher Krallenfrosch* in German.

DESCRIPTION: This frog grows to 51 mm. A protective membrane covers the lower half of the eye. This frog has a characteristic fourth "claw" on the foot, which is a metatarsal tubercle with a hard black point. There are 18–21 lateral-line organs. Overall, the back is light, with a dark band behind the eyes. The subocular tentacle is long with 8 sense organs around each eye.

DISTRIBUTION AND HABITAT (FIG. 176): Fraser's platanna is known from northern Angola to West Africa. It is found in permanent water bodies in lowland rain forest.

ADVERTISEMENT CALL: The advertisement call has a mean length of 1 s, with 173 pulses/s. The dominant energy of these calls is around 3 kHz. These are long weak trills, resembling "ien in in, ien in in," with 1 call every second or two.

BREEDING: The male utters a "tick tick" call during amplexus. The eggs are 1.0 mm in diameter, chocolate brown, and are laid singly.

Fig. 176 *Xenopus fraseri*

They sink or end up on water plants. Breeding occurs after dark in captivity.

TADPOLES: See the chapter on tadpoles.

NOTES: This species has been found in gallery forest in Angola.

KEY REFERENCES: Senfft 1939, Laurent 1954, Arnoult & Lamotte 1968, Vigny 1979a, Tinsley & Kobel 1996.

Gill's platanna
Xenopus gilli Rose & Hewitt, 1927
(Plate 15.3)

The specific name commemorates E. L. Gill, director of the South African Museum in 1926.
Gill's frog, Cape clawed frog, Cape platanna. *Gills Krallenfrosch, Zwerg-Krallenfrosch*, and *Kap-Krallenfrosch* in German.

DESCRIPTION: This is a small platanna, less than 40 mm long. The head is pointed rather than rounded when viewed from above. There is no tentacle below the eye. There are 20–24 lateral-line organs. The back pattern usually consists of three light longitudinal markings, one middorsal and a less distinct marking on each side, on an olive green background. Numerous pale flecks and larger, darker marks

Fig. 177 *Xenopus gilli*

cover the back. Underneath the frogs are gray with some yellow markings.

DISTRIBUTION AND HABITAT (FIG. 177): Gill's frog is presently known from dark water ponds on the sandy flats between the Cape peninsula and Cape Agulhas, and on ponds on the Cape peninsula. This species is endangered (see Conservation below).

ADVERTISEMENT CALL: The call is a series of buzzes, produced underwater. It calls during the day and night. Mean duration is 0.12 s, with up to 20 pulses/call at a rate of 173/s. The emphasized frequency is 2.8 kHz.

BREEDING: Gill's frog is known to spawn in July and early October, at the beginning and end of the winter rains. Mating is protracted, lasting up to a day. The eggs are 1.3 mm in diameter and chocolate brown. Clutch size is 300–600.

Successful breeding can occur in acid black-water ponds, at a pH above 3.8. The jelly layers of the eggs may act as a buffer to acid stress. In contrast, the common platanna, which is regarded as a threat to Gill's platanna owing to the ability of the two species to hybridize, is unable to breed below pH 5 under the same conditions.

TADPOLES: See the chapter on tadpoles.

CONSERVATION: Gill's platanna is listed as endangered in the South African Red Data Book. This species is one of the most endangered in southern Africa, owing to the loss of habitat caused by housing, and the danger of hybridization with the common platanna. No known population of Gill's platanna is without hybrids. Hybrids with the common platanna are known, although Gill's platanna is able to avoid competition in dark water ponds with a low pH. In December 1984 a concrete wall was erected around one pond containing Gill's platanna in the Cape Point Nature Reserve, to prevent the common platanna from entering the pond.

NOTES: In captivity they have been recorded to live for up to 9 years. This suggests that captive populations could be used to breed individuals to restock natural areas. Recorded food items include mainly aquatic invertebrates, such as dragonfly larvae, beetle larvae and adults, midge fly larvae, copepods, ostracods, mites, beach fleas, bugs, mayflies, but also snails, platanna eggs, tadpoles, and smaller frogs. During the rainy season they are able to migrate up to 1.5 km between ponds.

The skin contains large amounts of the peptide cerulein. This is part of the defense system against predators. See species account for the common platanna, for the action and effects of this skin peptide.

KEY REFERENCES: Fielding 1979, Vigny 1979a, Simmonds 1985, Roseghini et al. 1988, Baard 1989, Picker & de Villiers 1989a, Picker et al. 1993.

Common platanna
Xenopus laevis (Daudin, 1802)
(Plate 15.4)

The specific name *laevis* refers to the smooth skin.
Platanna, clawed frog, common clawed frog, upland clawed frog, African clawed frog. *Plathander* (early use) or *klaupad* in Dutch; *gewone platanna* in Afrikaans; *ngova*, *udlela* in Xhosa; *Krallenfrosch*, *glatter Spornfrosch*, *grosser Krallenfrosch*, *glatter Krallenfrosch* in German; *tchimbota* in Kimbundu and Muanha, the name being applied to many species; *muzapo* at Alto Cuilo; *kololo* in Nyngwe; *namwonde* in Yao.

DESCRIPTION: The common platanna is normally up to 130 mm long although an exceptional female measured 147 mm. The female is larger than the male and has flaps bearing papillae around the vent. The body is flattened, and the head is pointed. The eyes are small, round, and situated on top of the head. The tympanum is not visible. The front limbs are small and short with thin fingers, while the hind legs are long and muscular with large toes and webbing. Three toes have hard black claws. Coloration below is usually pale, sometimes with some yellow. Darker belly markings are uncommon. The back is dark gray with darker blotches. The tentacle below the eye is minute. There are 23–31 lateral-line bars between eye and vent. These lateral-line bars are sensory organs.

DISTRIBUTION AND HABITAT (FIG. 178): This very common species occurs widely in sub-Saharan Africa in savanna. It is found in many types of water bodies and is always found associated with people. This species occupies a very wide range of habitats, from temporary ponds in arid areas to permanent rivers. Specimens are known from cave systems, 500 m from the entrance.

ADVERTISEMENT CALL: Both males and females call. The male advertisement call consists of alternating fast- and slow-pulsed elements. Up to five frequencies may be stressed, and there are individual variations in the emphasis of different bands. The slow component has 24–42 pulses/s; the rapid component, 43–66/s. The duration of the slow element is 0.34–0.9 s, while the fast element has

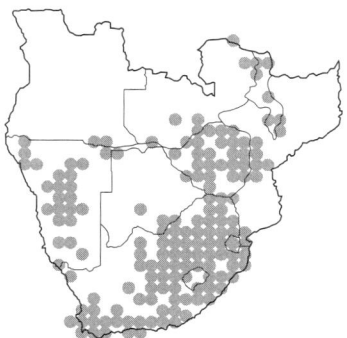

Fig. 178 *Xenopus laevis*

a duration of 0.18–0.6 s. Calling continues for a number of minutes, with frequencies up to 2.3 kHz being stressed.

BREEDING: Breeding is triggered by a rise in water level associated with an influx of fresh water. In the Western Cape Province they spawn during the winter rainfall months of June and July, and after heavy rains in summer. The males have a soft amplectant call while clasping. About 1000 eggs are laid in a clutch, and this can be repeated after a month. One pair laid 29 clutches, between 280 and 2123 eggs at a time, over a period of 2 years. Eggs are 1.1–1.2 mm diameter, within a 1.6-mm capsule. The eggs are pale brown. Eggs may be attached firmly to the stalk of aquatic vegetation or other objects under water. The time to metamorphosis is 49–64 days.

TADPOLES: See the chapter on tadpoles.

UNDERWATER LIFE: The adult is well suited to underwater life. It shows the best swimming performance at a preferred temperature of 27°C. If it spends up to 1 hour underwater, the blood becomes more acid, enabling more oxygen to be supplied to the tissues. The frog often breeds in ponds that are created by runoff from agricultural lands. The tadpole is extremely sensitive to pollutants in the form of insecticide, herbicide, and fungicide, and could serve as a monitor of pollutants in water. Soft-skinned animals like frogs that live in water are a target for bacterial infection. The skin produces antimicrobial peptides, the magainins, which inhibit the growth of numerous bacteria and fungi. These are already being commercialized.

FOOD: The adult finds prey by the use of its lateral-line organs, with which it detects vibrations set up by the prey moving. It can also locate food by detecting the odor. Adults have been recorded taking a wide range of prey, like common river frogs *Afrana angolensis*, platanna juveniles and tadpoles, insects, young birds and mice that fall into the water, as well as small fishes. It can take winged insects by leaping from the surface of the pond. Young frogs are voracious eaters of mosquito larvae.

PREDATORS: Yellow-billed egrets, reed cormorants, white-breasted cormorants, gray herons, fish eagles, serrated terrapins *Pelusios sinuatus*, water snakes *Lycodonomorphus mlanjensis*, clawless otters, and largemouth bass *Micropterus salmoides* prey upon this frog.

The frogs have a chemical defense against many animals. The skin contains a number of substances, one of which is a peptide called xenopsin. Xenopsin is known to cause contraction in the rat stomach. Another peptide found in the skin is cerulein. This causes spasms in the gallbladder and stimulates the pancreatic juice. Together these skin defenses cause the predator to vomit and feel ill for some time. Predators soon learn to exclude *Xenopus* species from their diet.

COLONIZING: Juveniles and adults will migrate in swarms away from the breeding pond, especially if the pond is drying and the weather is wet. I have seen hundreds moving across land in the same direction on many occasions. They are able to rapidly colonize newly created water bodies. Feral populations are known in the United Kingdom, California, Europe, and South America. The success of this frog as a colonizer has been attributed to its great reproductive potential, cannibalism, and predator-avoidance strategies. However, recent evidence from some parts of southern California suggests that extended drought and predaceous fish have resulted in marked declines in feral populations.

NOTES: This species is able to withstand 25% seawater indefinitely. The maximum recorded longevity is 30 years, 4 months, and 27 days in captivity. The frog can be attracted to ponds fertilized with fowl manure. This stimulates the frog to breed and encourages algal growth. The tadpoles hatch into ponds with an algal bloom and so have plenty of food. It seems that the adult is attracted by the fertilizer and not by the subsequent algal bloom. Fish farmers find that this frog is difficult to keep out of breeding ponds, and it consumes both fish and fish food. During the dry season it burrows into mud at the bottom of a pond.

KEY REFERENCES: Van Bergeijk 1954, Wheeler 1956, Araki et al. 1973, Anderson & Prahlad 1976, Vigny 1979a, Picker 1980, Katz et al. 1981, Boutilier 1986, Baker & White 1987, Tinsley & Kobel 1996.

Müller's platanna
Xenopus muelleri (Peters, 1844)
(Plate 15.5)

This species is named for the anatomist Johannes Müller of the Friedrich-Wilhelms University in Berlin.
Mueller's clawed frog, Müller's smooth clawed frog, tropical platanna, northern tropical platanna. *Müllers Krallenfrosch* in German, *cam usónde* in Tete and Sena, *geelpensplatanna* in Afrikaans, *kololo* in Nyungwe, *namwonde* in Yao.

DESCRIPTION: This is a large frog. Although the male is smaller, the female may be up to 90 mm long. Dorsal coloration is gray with darker blotches. Ventral coloration is frequently variable, pale to darkly marked, with some yellowing. The tentacle below the eye is at least half as long as the eye diameter. A protective membrane covers more than half of the eye. There are 22–27 lateral-line bars between eye and vent. The inner metatarsal tubercle is small and pointed.

DISTRIBUTION AND HABITAT (FIG. 179): Müller's platanna occurs widely in the tropical savanna areas, from northeastern South Africa, northern Namibia, and Botswana, extending northward.

ADVERTISEMENT CALL: The call consists of only one component, with a duration of 0.2 s, consisting of 5–7 pulses at a rate of 26–32/s. The emphasized frequency is 774–1182 Hz.

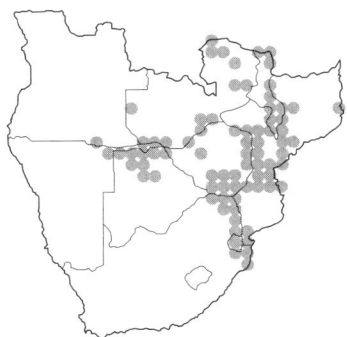

Fig. 179 *Xenopus muelleri*

BREEDING: Unknown. The eggs are small, 1.0 mm, and dark gray.

TADPOLES: See the chapter on tadpoles.

NOTES: The adult eats toad tadpoles and fish but is in turn preyed upon by the hammerkop, the snake *Rhamphiophis oxyrhynchus rostratus* in Malawi, and the green water snake *Philothamnus hoplogaster*. This snake also takes the tadpole. These frogs may be restricted to permanent ponds during the dry season. When the rains come, the frogs move into temporary water bodies where conditions for breeding are better. The skin is known to contain cerulein, a defense mechanism against predators. See the species account for the common platanna for details. In captivity they have been known to live for 9 years.

KEY REFERENCES: Arnoult & Lamotte 1968, Roseghini et al. 1988, Tinsley & Kobel 1996.

Peters' platanna
Xenopus petersii Bocage, 1895
(Plate 15.6)

This species was named for the herpetologist W. C. H. Peters, director of the Zoologisches Museum of the Friedrich-Wilhelms University of Berlin.
Peters' clawed frog, Angola smooth clawed frog. *Muzapo* at Alto Cuilo, *chimboto* in Angola, *t'chuila* at Cassange, *tchimbotwe* in Lwena, *Peters' Krallenfrosch* in German.

DESCRIPTION: This is a large frog, with the female up to 80 mm long. Peters' platanna is similar in overall morphology to the other species. The tentacle below the eye is very small, less than half the eye diameter. There are less than 25 lateral-line bars between eye and vent and 14 sense organs around the eye. Coloration below consists of a dark yellow background with dark markings in the form of small speckles or larger blotches.

DISTRIBUTION AND HABITAT (FIG. 180): This species is widely distributed in a broad belt from Angola and Namibia eastward to Tanzania. It is found in savannas and coastal lowlands.

Peters' Platanna

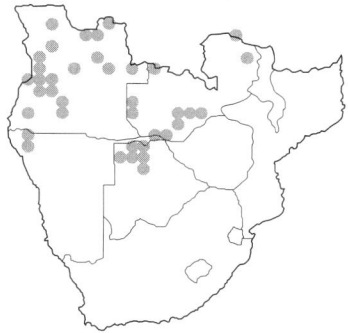

Fig. 180 *Xenopus petersii*

ADVERTISEMENT CALL: The call is a series of short, metallic chirps. The chirps are produced at a rate of 3/s. Each chirp consists of 5 pulses at a rate of 70/s. The dominant harmonics are at 2 kHz.

BREEDING: Unknown.

TADPOLES: Unknown.

NOTES: This species is known from permanent water bodies.

KEY REFERENCES: Vigny 1979a, Tinsley & Kobel 1996.

Common Frogs—Family Ranidae

Common frogs are found worldwide. The smallest and largest frogs in Africa are in this family. There are 64 species in the area covered here. Fossils have been found in many parts of the world, including North Africa.

KEY TO THE GENERA

1a. Vomerine teeth present on the roof of the mouth (Fig. 181a)   9
1b. Vomerine teeth absent   2

2a. A raised area behind each eye, also white stripes from eye to jaw (Fig. 181b)   *Poyntonia paludicola*
2b. Not as above   3

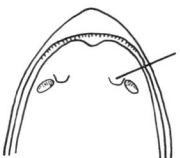 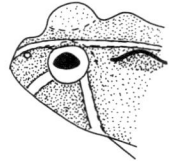

Fig. 181a Teeth on roof of mouth   **Fig. 181b** Eye-jaw stripes

3a. A tubercle present midway along the tarsus (Fig. 182)   *Phrynobatrachus*
3b. No midtarsal tubercle   4

Fig. 182 Tarsal tubercle

Common Frogs—Family Ranidae 251

4a. Males with a pale, hardened snout tip
                                                        Anhydrophryne rattrayi
4b. Male snout tip not hardened   5

5a. Digital discs present, sometimes very small   6
5b. Digital discs absent   7

6a. Discs on fingers large and truncated (Fig. 183)
                                                        Natalobatrachus bonebergi
6b. Discs small, rounded   *Nothophryne broadleyi*

Fig. 183 Truncated discs

7a. Webbing present   *Microbatrachella capensis*
7b. Webbing absent   8

8a. Belly with discrete dark blotches or spots (Fig. 184)
                                                                    Cacosternum
8b. Belly flecked, overall dark, or immaculate   *Arthroleptella*

Fig. 184 Belly markings

9a. Belly dark with pale spots   *Aubria masako*
9b. Belly white or with dark flecks   10

10a. Outer metatarsals separated from rest of sole by a web (Fig. 185)
                                                                                     11

Fig. 185 Toes free

10b. Outer metatarsals bound into a fleshy sole, inner metatarsal tubercle flanged (Fig. 186) 16

Fig. 186 Toes bound

11a. Vomerine projections between the internal nostrils and not reaching their margins 12
11b. Vomerine projections abutting onto anterior margins of internal nostrils (Fig. 187) *Ptychadena*

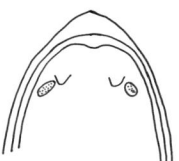

Fig. 187 Vomerine teeth

12a. Foot at least as long as distance from tip of urostyle to tympanum (Fig. 188) *Strongylopus*
12b. Foot shorter than distance from tip of urostyle to tympanum
13

Fig. 188 Foot-urostyle length comparison

Common Frogs—Family Ranidae 253

13a. Transverse skin groove behind eyes (Fig. 189)
Hoplobatrachus occipitalis
13b. No transverse skin groove behind eyes 14

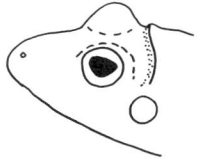

Fig. 189   Transverse groove

14a. A broad golden, green or brown band with a light margin running from snout to vent   *Amnirana*
14b. No broad band running from snout to vent 15

15a. No pupillary umbraculum present   *Afrana*
15b. Pupillary umbraculum present (Fig. 190)   *Amietia vertebralis*

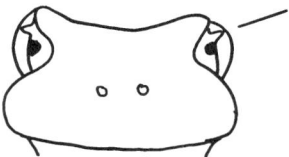

Fig. 190   Umbraculum

16a. Longitudinal light and dark bands on throat (Fig. 191)
Hildebrandtia ornata
16b. No longitudinal banding on throat 17

Fig. 191   Throat markings

17a. Lower jaw with two sharp bony cusps (Fig. 192)   *Pyxicephalus*
17b. Lower jaw without sharp cusps   *Tomopterna*

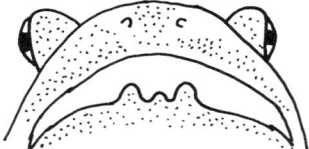

Fig. 192 Jaw cusps

River Frogs—Genus *Afrana*

This genus was erected for species in Africa previously included in the cosmopolitan genus *Rana*. The word *Afrana* is derived from Africa and *rana*, Latin for "frog". The word *rana* in turn comes from a much older root, the Sanskrit or Aryan *ru* or *rau*, meaning "one who makes a noise." They are known as *xlamgwa* in Shangaan, a term that includes the ridged frogs *Ptychadena*. This group of large frogs has strong legs and well-developed webbing between the toes.

KEY TO THE SPECIES

1a. Tympanum visible (Fig. 193)   2
1b. Tympanum not visible, or partially obscured   *Afrana vandijki*

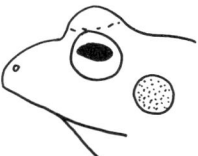

Fig. 193 Tympanum visible

2a. Tympanum less than half the eye diameter (Fig. 194)   3
2b. Tympanum more than half the eye diameter   4

Fig. 194 Small tympanum

3a. Head wide: head width–tibia length ratio 66–76% (Fig. 195)
Afrana johnstoni
3b. Head width moderate: head width–tibia length ratio 58–67%
Afrana inyangae

Fig. 195   Tibia

4a. Two segments of fourth toe free of web (Fig. 196)
Afrana angolensis
4b. Less than two segments of fourth toe free of web   5

Fig. 196   Two phalanges free

5a. Head wide: head width–tibia length ratio 65–85% (Fig. 197)
Afrana fuscigula
5b. Head moderate: head width–tibia length ratio 60–66%
Afrana dracomontana

Fig. 197   Tibia

Angola river frog
Afrana angolensis (Bocage, 1866)
(Plate 15.7)

The specific name refers to Angola, where this species was first found.

Common river frog, common rana, Angola frog. *Kasanda* in Misuku, *nachidive* in Nyanja, *kazoli* in Lwena.

DESCRIPTION: The female exceptionally reaches 90 mm in length. Head width–foot length ratio is 0.6 or less. The tympanum is more than half the eye diameter. The legs are long. Usually two segments of the fourth toe are free of web, although this varies from population to population. The skin has fine longitudinal ridges, which tend to be more continuous in the northwest of their range. Color is variable, usually darker blotches on a light brown background, but green to dark brown backgrounds with or without patterning are known. The lower surface is pale, sometimes with a darker mottling on the throat. During the breeding season the top of the male thumb develops into a dark swollen nuptial pad.

DISTRIBUTION AND HABITAT (FIG. 198): This species is widespread, from Ethiopia south to Angola and South Africa. It is found in most permanent water bodies in the range.

ADVERTISEMENT CALL: The male calls from the water's edge. The call has two parts, consisting of a short series of 6–7 frequency modulated clicks, followed by a short croak. The mean duration of the clicking phase is 0.35 s, and the mean duration of the croak is 0.54 s. The dominant harmonic of the clicking phase rises from 2.7 to 2.9 kHz, while the dominant harmonic of the croak is 0.8 kHz.

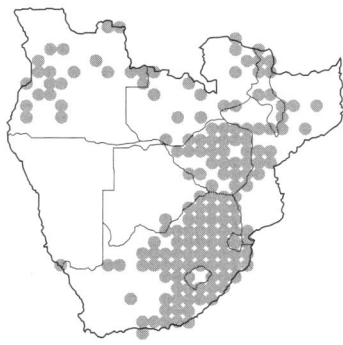

Fig. 198 *Afrana angolensis*

BREEDING: Breeding may occur during most months of the year, although it peaks in spring and autumn. The eggs are laid in shallow water near the edge of streams. Eggs are 1.1–1.2 mm in diameter in a 4-mm capsule. They soon accumulate debris and become quite difficult to see.

TADPOLES: See the chapter on tadpoles.

NOTES: They are preyed upon by the serrated terrapin *Pelusios sinuatus*, which sneaks up from behind and drags the frog down by a leg, which it tears off and eats. The terrapin will return later to eat the other leg and then the rest of the frog. Sometimes several frogs are found with legs missing. Other known predators include the green water snake *Philothamnus hoplogaster*, the white-lipped snake *Crotaphopeltis hotamboeia*, and the water snake *Lycodonomorphus rufulus*. The skin contains peptides called bradykinins, which mimic mammalian hormones, serving to deter mammalian predators by slowing down their heartbeat and making them nauseous. This frog feeds on earthworms, snails, arthropods, and other frogs. They are eaten by villagers in West Africa as *bengwele*.

KEY REFERENCES: Wager 1986, Roseghini et al. 1988, Channing 1979 (all as *Rana angolensis*).

Drakensberg river frog
Afrana dracomontana (Channing, 1978)
(Plate 15.8)

The specific name refers to the Drakensberg Mountains, where the species was discovered.
Drakensberg frog, Sani Pass frog.

DESCRIPTION: The female grows to 65 mm, and the male up to 56 mm. It is a typical water frog with long, well-muscled legs. The tympanum is smaller than the eye. The ratio of head width to body length is 32%–39%. Two segments of the fourth toe are free of webbing on the outside, but only one is free on the inside. Color is variable, usually darker blotches on a light brown background, but green to dark brown backgrounds with or without patterning are known. The ventral surface is pale, sometimes with a darker mottling on the throat. Superficially this species resembles *A. angolensis* and *A. fuscigula*, and shares a number of color patterns with both these species. This species can be distinguished from the two similar species only by determining the shape of the body as measured by ratios, for example, head width vs. body length and head width vs. tibia length. However, for all practical purposes this species can be distinguished easily from *Amietia vertebralis*, and as these are the only two species of large frog on the Lesotho plateau, identification is easy. The advertisement call is also distinctive.

DISTRIBUTION AND HABITAT (FIG. 199): This species is only known from the Lesotho plateau, found along permanent streams.

ADVERTISEMENT CALL: The male calls either at the water's edge or some distance away. The call consists of a series of clicks followed by a short croak. The clicks are produced at a rate of 9–19/s, with a duration of 0.8–1.3 s. After a short interval of about 100 ms, the croak follows, rapidly pulsed (42–46/s) with a duration of 143–603 ms. Dominant harmonics occur at around 1.8 kHz for the clicking phase but lower (1.1 kHz) for the second phase, which is somewhat frequency-modulated.

BREEDING: Eggs are laid in shallow, calm water, about 150 in a clutch. They are small, dark, in a 5-mm capsule, deposited singly or in small clumps. Eggs are recorded from October to February.

Fig. 199   *Afrana dracomontana*

TADPOLES: See the chapter on tadpoles.

KEY REFERENCE: Channing 1979 (as *Rana dracomontana*).

Cape river frog
Afrana fuscigula (Duméril and Bibron, 1841)
(Plate 16.1)

The specific name *fuscigula* refers to the dark mottling on the throat. Dusky-throated frog, brown-throated frog. *Kaapse rivierpadda* in Afrikaans.

DESCRIPTION: This is a large stocky frog, with the male up to 75 mm long and the female reaching 125 mm. These frogs are similar in overall appearance to most other species of the genus but separated by the wide head (head width–tibia length ratio more than 65%; head width = 40% of body length). The tympanum is large, and webbing is extensive, with only one or half a segment of the fourth toe free of web. This species shares a number of color patterns with the other river frogs, but green or brown backgrounds, with darker blotches and a lighter vertebral stripe, are common. The undersurface, especially the throat region, is usually darker.

DISTRIBUTION AND HABITAT (FIG. 200): This species is known from northern and eastern South Africa to the Western Cape Province and Namaqualand, with an apparently isolated population in the

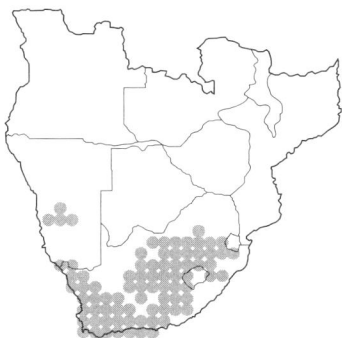

Fig. 200 *Afrana fuscigula*

Naukluft Mountains, and another along the Fish River in southern Namibia. This frog is found in permanent water. By creating suitable habitat, the construction of storage dams has been beneficial to this species.

ADVERTISEMENT CALL: The male calls from vegetation in water, often from very deep water in dams. The call has two parts, a slow clicking followed by a short croak. The clicking part probably serves a male spacing function. The short croak is often the only call heard, especially in the west of the range. At Naukluft the males may produce 1–6 croaks after a series of clicks. The clicking phase may last 8–50 s, at a rate of 3.7–9.5/s. Clicking sequences do not overlap appreciably, suggesting that this call inhibits other males from clicking. The croak is 37–302 ms long, at a pulse rate of 110–265/s. The dominant harmonics for both call types are about 1.0–1.5 kHz. The males in a chorus call louder, higher, and more rapidly once the chorus starts. The calls build to a crescendo and then fade in about 3 minutes. The call can be heard day and night.

BREEDING: Populations breed during the winter rains in June and July to September in the winter rainfall region, and from November to January in the summer rainfall areas. In Bainskloof I watched a female approach a calling male, in 40-mm-deep water. She moved slowly, covering only 50 cm in 5 minutes until they made contact. Eggs are laid at the bottom of quiet pools or attached to weeds and stones. The eggs are small, 1.5 mm in diameter in 3.5-mm capsules. One pair laid 900 eggs one night and 1080 the next.

TADPOLES: See the chapter on tadpoles.

NOTES: Apart from a range of small insects, it is recorded to take caterpillars, millipedes, and crabs. There is also a record of one taking a mouse.

KEY REFERENCES: Rose 1929, Channing 1979, Wager 1986 (all as *Rana fuscigula*).

Inyanga river frog
Afrana inyangae (Poynton, 1966)
(Plate 16.2)

Inyanga River Frog

The specific name *inyangae* refers to the district of Inyanga on the eastern highlands of Zimbabwe.
Inyanga frog.

DESCRIPTION: The stocky male grows to 59 mm SVL. It is distinguished from the similar Johnston's river frog on the basis of body proportions: head width–tibia length ratio of 58–67%; head width–foot length ratio of 55% or more. The head is acutely pointed, and the tympanum is less than half the eye diameter. The back is green to gray, with darker markings.

DISTRIBUTION AND HABITAT (FIG. 201): This species is known only from the eastern highlands of Zimbabwe, where it is found in rocky, fast-flowing streams.

ADVERTISEMENT CALL: Unknown.

BREEDING: Eggs are laid in shallow rocky pools. The clutch consists of 40–80 eggs, each 2.5 mm in diameter within 7-mm capsules. They are laid as a compact mass adhering to strands of vegetation, just below the surface of the water.

TADPOLES: See the chapter on tadpoles.

Fig. 201 *Afrana inyangae*

KEY REFERENCE: Lambiris 1985b (as *Rana johnstoni inyangae*).

Johnston's river frog
Afrana johnstoni (Günther, 1893)
(Plate 16.3)

This frog was named for H. A. Johnston, C. B. (later Sir Harry Johnston), explorer in Uganda and central Africa.
Johnston's rana, Tshiromo frog.

DESCRIPTION: The female grows to 64 mm SVL. It is distinguished from the similar Inyanga river frog on the basis of body proportions: head width–tibia ratio of 66–76%; head width–foot length ratio of 60%. The tympanum is small, not exceeding half the eye diameter. This is an aquatic species, with extensively webbed feet. Less than two segments of the fourth toe are free of web. The back is grayish green with darker markings. The underside is marbled.

DISTRIBUTION AND HABITAT (FIG. 202): This species is known only from Mount Mulanje in Malawi, above 2000 m. It is found in deep pools and along rocky torrents, as well as in the small streams at high altitudes.

ADVERTISEMENT CALL: Unknown.

Fig. 202 *Afrana johnstoni*

Van Dijk's River Frog

BREEDING: Unknown.

TADPOLES: The tadpoles are always found in two age classes, the smaller from the current year and the bigger tadpoles from the previous year. This indicates that they remain in the water for two seasons before metamorphosing.

KEY REFERENCE: Stevens 1974 (as *Rana johnstoni*).

Van Dijk's river frog
Afrana vandijki Visser & Channing, 1997
(Plate 16.4)

This species is named for D. E. (Eddie) van Dijk of Stellenbosch.

DESCRIPTION: This is a heavy-bodied frog, reaching a length of 54 mm in the male and 56 mm or slightly longer in the female. Although at first glance it appears similar to other river frogs, this species has a large pale marking in the middle of the back, and the upper part of the tympanum is obscured by a prominent skin fold that runs from the back of the eye to the arm. In many specimens the tympanum is not visible. The fourth toe has two or three segments free of webbing.

DISTRIBUTION AND HABITAT (FIG. 203): This species is known from the mountains of the southern part of the Western Cape Province, South Africa, including the Swartberg and the Boosmans-

Fig. 203 *Afrana vandijki*

bos Wilderness Area. It is found in fast-flowing rocky streams in well-vegetated valleys.

ADVERTISEMENT CALL: The call consists of two phases: a series of clicks, followed by a croak. The croak is the more common call, as the series of clicks probably serves as a call to space the males. The first phase consists of 13 clicks (10–15) uttered in 0.8 s. The croak call is harsh note with distinct pulses, about 0.25 s long.

BREEDING: Breeding takes place after the streams have slowed, from October to December.

TADPOLES: See the chapter on tadpoles.

NOTES: *A. vandijki* may represent the southernmost species of a group of high-altitude frogs found on the mountains from Rwanda southward.

KEY REFERENCE: Visser & Channing 1997.

Large-Mouthed Frog—Genus *Amietia*

There is one species in this genus, which is restricted to the Drakensberg Mountains in South Africa and Lesotho.

Large-mouthed frog
Amietia vertebralis (Hewitt, 1927)
(Plate 16.5)

The specific name *vertebralis* refers to the markings along the back. Aquatic river frog, ice frog.

DESCRIPTION: This is a very large frog, reaching 145 mm in length. The head is very wide, equal to half the body length in adults, with a head width–tibia length ratio of over 100%. The adult spends most of the time in water and has a flattened head and fully webbed feet. The eye has an umbraculum, which is a protective outgrowth of the iris, found in many high-altitude animals, which serves to block harmful UV radiation. The back is mostly gray-brown, with darker blotches.

Large-Mouthed Frog

Fig. 204 *Amietia vertebralis*

DISTRIBUTION AND HABITAT (FIG. 204): The large-mouthed frog is known from Lesotho and the foothills of the Drakensberg Mountains. It is only found in cold flowing streams.

ADVERTISEMENT CALL: The call consists of a very long series of clicks, followed by a short croak. The clicks are uttered at a rate of 6.2–8.4/s, for a duration of 3–11 s. The croak lasts 0.03–0.57 s, exceptionally up to 3 s. The dominant harmonics are very low, 0.1 and 0.4 kHz.

BREEDING: Eggs have been found from October through January. They are dark, within capsules 5 mm in diameter, and found in quiet pools or slow-moving streams.

TADPOLES: See the chapter on tadpoles.

NOTES: The adult can be seen in pools with just the head protruding. When disturbed, it dives under rocks or hides in the bottom mud. It eats a range of arthropods, will devour smaller frogs without hesitation, and appears to be a specialist feeder on crabs, which it catches and eats underwater.

KEY REFERENCE: Lambiris 1988g (as *Rana vertebralis*).

White-Lipped Frogs—Genus *Amnirana*

These robust frogs usually have a broad golden-brown or green band running the length of the body. Many species have pale upper jaws, leading to the name white-lipped frogs. They resemble typical river frogs, but breeding males have a glandular area on the front of the upper arm. Four species are known from this area, with an additional undescribed species from northwestern Zambia.

KEY TO THE SPECIES

1a. Tips of fingers and toes expanded into discs 2
1b. No discs on fingers and toes 3

2a. Internarial distance less than one and a half times snout to nostril distance (Fig. 205) *Amnirana parkeriana*
2b. Internarial distance more than one and a half times snout to nostril distance *Amnirana lemairii*

Fig. 205 Snout-nostril–internarial distance comparison

3a. No skin ridges bordering broad vertebral band 4
3b. Flattened skin ridges bordering broad vertebral band
Amnirana galamensis

4a. Side of body dark brown or black *Amnirana darlingi*
4b. Side of body green *Amnirana* sp.

Darling's white-lipped frog
Amnirana darlingi (Boulenger, 1902)
(Plate 16.6)

This species was named for J. ffoliott-Darling of Mashonaland in Zimbabwe.
Golden-backed frog.

Darling's White-Lipped Frog

DESCRIPTION: The female reaches 72 mm in length and the male, 55 mm. The distance between the eyes is less than the distance from nostril to eye. Tips of fingers and toes are not expanded into discs. Webbing is moderate, with two to three segments of the fourth toe free of web. The broad golden band over the back has lighter edges. The sides of the body are dark. A distinct white line runs from the nostrils, below the eye and tympanum to above the arm insertion.

DISTRIBUTION AND HABITAT (FIG. 206): This species is found from Mozambique across to Angola. It is common in southern Zambia around Livingstone. This frog occurs in savannas and lowland evergreen forests.

ADVERTISEMENT CALL: The male calls while floating in shallow water among vegetation. The call consists of a low-pitched rapid snore. If a few males are calling in the same pond, the calling becomes faster and faster for a few seconds, reaching a peak just before calling stops. The initial call consists of about 17 pulses at a rate of 35/s. The pulse rate can increase to 50/s, and the number of pulses in each call may decrease to 10. The calls start about 0.5 s long, decreasing to 0.2 s as the males compete. The emphasized frequency is 550 Hz.

BREEDING: Unknown.

TADPOLES: Unknown.

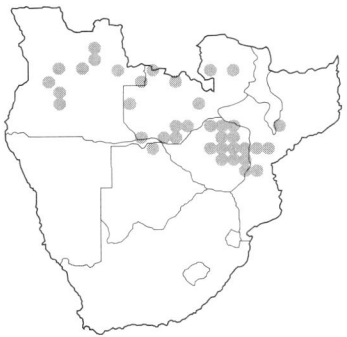

Fig. 206 *Amnirana darlingi*

NOTES: This frog is preyed upon by the water monitor *Varanus niloticus*, the boomslang *Dispholidus typus*, and the vine snake *Thelotornis*.

KEY REFERENCE: Poynton & Broadley 1985b (as *Hylarana darlingi*).

Galam white-lipped frog
Amnirana galamensis (Duméril & Bibron, 1841)
(Plate 16.7)

The specific name *galamensis* refers to Lake Galam in Senegal. Golden-backed frog, marble-legged frog.

DESCRIPTION: The male grows to 78 mm and the female, up to 86 mm long. The distance between the eyes is equal to the distance from nostril to eye. The tips of fingers and toes are not expanded. Webbing is moderate, with two and a half to three segments of the fourth toe free of web. The breeding male has a pair of baggy throat pouches opening through a pair of slits parallel to the lower jaw. The color pattern is attractive; dark sides border a broad golden vertebral band. The golden brown band is bordered by a pair of flattened ridges running from eye to leg. The upper lip is lighter than the lower.

DISTRIBUTION AND HABITAT (FIG. 207): This frog has been found from Mozambique to northern Zambia and northward to

Fig. 207 *Amnirana galamensis*

Somalia, then westward to Senegal. It is found in permanent ponds.

ADVERTISEMENT CALL: The call is described as a noise like a tire deflating or a muffled doglike bark that is difficult to locate. The males gather in permanent pools, calling within 75 cm of one another. The call resembles a nasal bleat, 0.6 s long, with emphasized frequencies between 2 and 3 kHz.

BREEDING: Unknown.

TADPOLES: Unknown.

NOTES: This frog uses termitaria as refuges during the dry season, and has been found emerging at the start of the rains. The local villagers in West Africa eat this species. The skin contains bradykinins, substances that mimic mammalian hormones by slowing the heart rate and making any mammal predator feel very ill.

KEY REFERENCES: Stevens 1974, De Fonesca & Jocque 1979, Roseghini et al. 1988, Simbotwe 1988 (all as *Hylarana galamensis*).

Lemaire's white-lipped frog
Amnirana lemairii (Witte, 1921)
(Plate 16.8)

This species was named for the Lemaire expedition to Africa. Lofoi frog.

DESCRIPTION: The male is up to 66 mm and the female, 76 mm long. The distance between the eyes is equal to the distance from nostril to eye. The internarial distance is more than one and a half times snout to nostril distance. The tips of the fingers and toes are expanded into discs. Webbing is extensive, with two to two and a half segments of the fourth toe free of web, although a thin margin of web is present along the toe. The foot length (measured from the base of the inner metatarsal tubercle to the tip of the fourth toe) is less than half the body length. The throat pouch is small. A pair of skin ridges down the back border a brown band running from head to leg. The upper lip is white, with a pale line running from nostrils to above the arm.

Fig. 208 *Amnirana lemairii*

DISTRIBUTION AND HABITAT (FIG. 208): This frog is known from northern Angola, northern Zambia, and adjacent Democratic Republic of the Congo. It is found in permanent water bodies.

ADVERTISEMENT CALL: Unknown.

BREEDING: Unknown. It breeds throughout the year, with a peak at the end of the wet season.

TADPOLES: Unknown (see Fig. 322).

NOTES: Like most of the species of *Amnirana*, extensive field observations are required. These could be done by anyone prepared to spend some time observing these frogs at night during and after rain.

KEY REFERENCE: Schmidt & Inger 1959 (as *Rana albolabris lemairii*).

Parker's white-lipped frog
Amnirana parkeriana (Mertens, 1938)

This species is named for H. W. Parker, herpetologist at the Natural History Museum in London from 1923 to 1957.
Congolo frog.

Hillwood White-Lipped Frog

Fig. 209 *Amnirana parkeriana*

DESCRIPTION: The female reaches 82 mm and the male, 74 mm in length. The internarial distance is less than one and a half times snout to nostril distance. The snout is prominent and pointed. The fingers and toes have small discs with distinct circummarginal grooves. The webbing is extensive, reaching the discs as a thin margin to the toes. The foot length is less than half the body length.

DISTRIBUTION AND HABITAT (FIG. 209): This species is only known from western Angola, in forested country and in swamps along the coast.

ADVERTISEMENT CALL: Unknown.

BREEDING: Unknown.

TADPOLES: Unknown.

KEY REFERENCE: Schmidt & Inger 1959 (as *Rana parkeriana*).

Hillwood white-lipped frog
Amnirana sp.
(Plate 17.1)

DESCRIPTION: This undescribed species is similar to *A. darlingi* but has different body proportions. The body is a metallic green with a reddish sheen on the legs. A pale flattened glandular ridge runs from

Fig. 210 *Amnirana* sp.

the nostril, over the eye to the vent. The tympanum is as large as the eye. Breeding males have a nuptial pad in the form of a black ring around the third toe.

DISTRIBUTION AND HABITAT (FIG. 210): This species is presently known only from northwestern Zambia. It is probably widespread in marshes in high-altitude grasslands.

ADVERTISEMENT CALL: Unknown.

BREEDING: Unknown.

TADPOLES: Unknown.

Rattray's Frog—Genus *Anhydrophryne*

There is only one species in this genus. The small frog is restricted to certain forests of the eastern Cape and is characterized by the hard snout of the male that is used to dig nests in the damp soil.

Rattray's frog
Anhydrophryne rattrayi Hewitt, 1919
(Plates 17.2, 17.3)

The species was named for George Rattray, the principal of Selbourne College for 27 years, who was the first to collect this unusual small frog.
Hogsback frog.

Rattray's Frog

DESCRIPTION: The female of this small frog may reach 22 mm in length. The tubercles on the hands and feet are poorly developed. The outer metatarsal tubercle is absent or very reduced. The male possesses a hardened tip to the snout, which is pale and flat. Webbing is absent. The back is brown, with darker markings, and a darker horizontal stripe through the eye. The ventral surface is white with brown marbling.

DISTRIBUTION AND HABITAT (FIG. 211): This species is only known from the Amatola and Katberg Mountains, Stutterheim, and Peddie in eastern Cape, South Africa. It is found adjacent to streams in thick vegetation. This frog is threatened by the clearing of forest to build houses and by the planting of exotic pine trees, and is listed as near threatened.

ADVERTISEMENT CALL: The male calls from a concealed site on the forest floor, near streams or water. The call is a short high-pitched ping, 0.05 s in duration at 3.5 kHz. The call may be repeated rapidly. The male calls during misty or wet nights during the summer rains, from October to February.

BREEDING: A few large eggs are laid in a hollowed-out nest in damp soil under leaf litter. The male makes the nest, using its hardened snout. About 11–20 eggs are laid in a spherical, 25-mm nest. Each egg

Fig. 211 *Anhydrophryne rattrayi*

is 2.6 mm in diameter in a 6-mm capsule. The eggs are white with a tinge of yellow. Rattray found the nests on a watershed between two streams. Development in captivity takes 26 days. The eggs develop directly into froglets, without a free-swimming tadpole stage.

NOTES: Adults are recorded as eating forest floor arthropods such as springtails and woodlice.

KEY REFERENCES: Hewitt 1919, Wager 1986.

Moss Frogs—Genus *Arthroleptella*

These small frogs live in wet mossy places. The eggs are laid in vegetation and develop directly into small froglets. There are seven species, associated with mountains in southern and eastern South Africa.

KEY TO THE SPECIES

The southwestern Cape species are very similar and difficult to tell apart but are easily distinguished on the basis of the male advertisement call. This key makes use of call characters and distributional cues.

1a. Known from KwaZulu-Natal Province of South Africa   2
1b. Found in the Western Cape Province of South Africa   3

2a. Outer metatarsal tubercle absent or feebly developed; male call a number of single notes, each note 0.03 s long at a dominant frequency of 2.2–2.7 kHz   *Arthroleptella hewitti*
2b. Male has a trilled 55 ms long cricket-like call with 10 pulses, with 5.5 kHz midpoint frequency.   *Arthroleptella ngongoniensis*

3a. Male advertisement call a very brief chirp, less than 0.2 s.   4
3b. Male advertisement call a series of individual clicks, longer than 0.3 s   5

4a. Call of 3 notes, between 3.1 and 3.4 kHz; known from Table Mountain and the Cape peninsula   *Arthroleptella lightfooti*
4b. Call of 4–5 notes, between 3.8 and 4.1 kHz; known from the mouth of the Palmiet Valley across to Franschhoek
                                                            Arthroleptella villiersi

5a. Call an irregular series of clicks in 0.3 s, 4.1–4.6 kHz, known from the mountains around Wellington *Arthroleptella bicolor*
5b. Call a series of clicks, longer than 0.5 s   6

6a. Call a series of evenly spaced clicks, 0.7 s long, 3.5–4.1 kHz, known from the mountains near Hermanus
Arthroleptella drewesii
6b. Call a series of clicks over 1 s long, known from the Jonkershoek Mountains to Betty's Bay   *Arthroleptella landdrosia*

Bainskloof moss frog
Arthroleptella bicolor Hewitt, 1926
(Plate 17.4)

The specific name refers to a common color pattern that consists of a dark brown background with pale sides.

DESCRIPTION: The frog may reach 22 mm in length. The limbs are thin and spindly, with an outer metatarsal tubercle that is well developed. The ventral surface is white in the female but darker in the male, which also has a black throat. The back of the thigh has scale-like corrugations of the skin. Color varies, in shades of brown, and the animal is able to become very pale or very dark.

This species is impossible to distinguish from Lightfoot's moss frog *A. lightfooti*. Both species possess unique advertisement calls, however.

DISTRIBUTION AND HABITAT (FIG. 212): This species is restricted to the mountains north of Wellington and the Riviersonderend Mountains in Western Cape Province, South Africa. It is found on slopes where water is seeping and along small streams.

ADVERTISEMENT CALL: The call consists of an irregular series of clicks, which run together into a chirping call. The duration of each call is about 0.3 s, with 5–7 notes or clicks. In a typical call, there is an initial pair of notes, followed after a short interval by a burst of 3–5 notes, and concluded after another interval by a single note. The dominant energy is between 4.1 and 4.6 kHz.

Fig. 212 *Arthroleptella bicolor*

BREEDING: Eggs are laid in small numbers (8–10) under moss or similar vegetation in seepage zones. The eggs develop directly into 4-mm froglets.

NOTES: The males often remain and call near clutches of eggs.

KEY REFERENCE: Channing, Hendricks, and Dawood 1994.

Drewes' moss frog
Arthroleptella drewesii Channing et al., 1994
(Plate 17.5)

The species was named for the collector of the type specimen, R. C. Drewes of the California Academy of Sciences.

DESCRIPTION: This is a small frog, just exceeding 20 mm in length. A broken glandular ridge extends from the upper lip at the angle of the jaw to the arm insertion. The toes possess a trace of webbing at the base, and each toe has rounded subarticular tubercles. The inner metatarsal tubercle protrudes distinctly, while the outer metatarsal tubercle is a small ridge. Toe tips are slightly expanded and rounded. The backs of the thighs of the male are joined by a swollen glandular area. The eyelids are warty, and there is a row of black warts running backward from each eye to the sacral region and an irregular series of warts from there to the vent. The dorsal warts are black

Fig. 213 *Arthroleptella drewesii*

against a brown background. Arms and legs are darkly marked with brown blotches on a pale background. The pigmentation covers most of the paler background but is lighter in parts. The ventral surface is darkly marked against a pale background, which is nearly obscured. The soles of the hands and feet are similarly marked. Very small white tubercles are present on the front of the vocal pouch, extending backward to below the angle of the jaw.

DISTRIBUTION AND HABITAT (FIG. 213): This species is only known from the Fernkloof Nature Reserve in Hermanus in Western Cape Province, South Africa, and adjacent wet areas above 200 m. It is found under stones on grassy slopes in the vicinity of seepages and waterfalls. Its conservation status is near threatened.

ADVERTISEMENT CALL: The call consists of a series of more or less evenly spaced clicks. Five to 7 single or double clicks are produced in 0.6 s. The dominant energy in the call is between 3.5 and 4.1 kHz. Males call from ledges on moss-covered slopes, often concealed under vegetation. Males call in large numbers day and night during the rainy season from June through September.

KEY REFERENCE: Channing, Hendricks, and Dawood 1994.

Hewitt's moss frog
Arthroleptella hewitti FitzSimons, 1947

Fig. 214 *Arthroleptella hewitti*

This species was named for John Hewitt of the Albany Museum in Grahamstown.
Chirping frog, yellow bandit frog. *Natalse kwetterpadda* or *Hewitt se mospadda* in Afrikaans.

DESCRIPTION: The female reaches 36 mm in length. The outer metatarsal tubercle is absent or weakly developed. The dorsal coloration is brown with darker markings, with a dark stripe through the eye. The ventral surface is white or mottled.

DISTRIBUTION AND HABITAT (FIG. 214): This frog is known from the midlands and lower escarpment slopes of the Drakensberg in KwaZulu-Natal, South Africa. It is found on well-vegetated slopes near streams.

ADVERTISEMENT CALL: Males call from moss near water along streams. The call is a series of short, high-pitched notes. Each note is 0.03 s long at a dominant frequency of 2.2–2.7 kHz. Sometimes males only produce 1 note after long intervals, while during a chorus, calls are produced in quick succession.

BREEDING: This species breeds during spring and early summer (September to December). Eggs were found in a small hollow, 150 mm deep, in black earth under a fern that was growing against rock. The clutch consisted of 33 eggs, each 3 mm in diameter, cream-colored, in a double row in a jelly string 75 mm long. Clutches vary from 14 to 40 eggs, and these may be laid in a scooped-out nest in wet mud or under vegetation or rock. Metamorphosis takes less than 3 weeks.

NOTES: This species is associated with forest or remnants of forest.

KEY REFERENCE: FitzSimons 1947.

Landdros moss frog
Arthroleptella landdrosia Dawood & Channing, 2000
(Plate 17.6)

The specific name refers to the locality where it was first found, near the Landdroskop hut on the Hottentots Holland Mountains.

DESCRIPTION: The male reaches 15 mm in length. The internarial distance is 80% of the distance between the anterior corners of the eyes. There is no glandular ridge running from the upper lip to the arm insertion. The back is smooth. Dorsal background coloration is a gray. A pale patch behind the head extends backward as a vertebral line. Four to five small white spots are present on each eyelid. These extend to the sides and tip of the snout. Darker dorsal markings include a triangle with its base between the eyes, facing backward. The sides of the body are underlain with a reddish brown infusion.

DISTRIBUTION AND HABITAT (FIG. 215): This species has been found in the coastal strip near Rooi Els, and the adjoining Hottentots Holland mountain range in Western Cape Province, South Africa. It occurs in seepages where the vegetation offers good cover. Its conservation status is near threatened.

ADVERTISEMENT CALL: Males call from moss near water along streams. The call consists of a series of about 8 notes in 1.3 s. The first note is single, followed by a note of 4 pulses, then 3 double clicks, terminating in 3 slower, more energetic, notes, each consisting of 2 closely spaced pulses. The dominant frequency is 4.4 kHz. This call is twice as long as that of *A. drewesii*, the species with the next longest call.

Fig. 215 *Arthroleptella landdrosia*

BREEDING: This species breeds during spring and early summer (September to December). Details of eggs are unknown.

NOTES: This species occurs together with De Villiers' moss frog.

KEY REFERENCE: Dawood & Channing 2000.

Lightfoot's moss frog
Arthroleptella lightfooti (Boulenger, 1910)
(Plate 17.7)

This frog was named for R. M. Lightfoot, a clerical and scientific assistant at the South African Museum from 1888 to 1921.
Cape chirping frog, brown bandit frog.

DESCRIPTION: The female reaches 22 mm in length. The limbs are thin and spindly, with an outer metatarsal tubercle that is well developed. The back is variable, from light tan, through red-brown to black. Ventral surface is white in females but darker in males, which have a black gular region.

DISTRIBUTION AND HABITAT (FIG. 216): This species is known only from Table Mountain and other slopes on the Cape peninsula, South Africa. It is found at the base of grass tussocks and beneath mats of moss. Its conservation status is near threatened.

Fig. 216 *Arthroleptella lightfooti*

ADVERTISEMENT CALL: The male calls from concealed sites at the base of vegetation, or from a nest below moss. The call is a high-pitched chirp of 3 notes, 0.1 s long at a dominant frequency between 3.1 and 3.4 kHz. It can be heard calling during the day on the top of Table Mountain for much of the year.

BREEDING: Lightfoot's moss frog breeds from July through November. The eggs are laid in small clutches (5–12), on damp soil under vegetation or exposed. Each 4-mm egg is covered by an 8-mm jelly capsule. In the eggs tadpoles develop into young froglets, without a free-swimming stage. In fact, the tadpoles are unable to swim, although they may wriggle around in damp moss. The eggs only require from a week to 10 days before the young frogs hatch out.

NOTES: Eggs frequently are found on damp slopes, particularly near waterfalls. Calling males are frequently found near eggs under moss.

KEY REFERENCE: Power & Rose 1929.

Ngongoni moss frog
Arthroleptella ngongoniensis Bishop & Passmore, 1993
(Plate 17.8)

The specific name refers to the Acocks vegetation type (Ngongoni veld) in which this species is found.
Natal bandit frog.

DESCRIPTION: This is a very small frog. The male may be up to 18 mm and the female, 22 mm long. Webbing is absent. The tympanum is visible and just over half the eye diameter. The back is sandy brown. Four indistinct dorsal stripes are present, extending on to the arms and legs. A dark brown stripe passes from the tip of the snout, through the nostril, eye, and tympanum to the arm. The underside is white without markings, and the throat and limbs are pale yellow.

DISTRIBUTION AND HABITAT (FIG. 217): This very rare frog is known only from the Ixopo area of KwaZulu-Natal, South Africa. All the specimens found so far come from only three localities, all within a radius of 11 km. They are known from grassland on watered slopes.

ADVERTISEMENT CALL: Males call on misty days, from concealed positions at the base of vegetation. At night they climb 50 cm up grass and call a little below the tips of the grass stems. The trilled 55 ms long cricket-like call has 8–10 pulses, with 5.5-kHz midpoint frequency. The call is repeated three or four times with an interval of a second between calls. The call is quiet and difficult to locate.

Fig. 217 *Arthroleptella ngongoniensis*

De Villiers' Moss Frog

BREEDING: Eggs are laid at the base of grass tussocks. There are 11–14 eggs/clutch, each 2 mm in diameter. The eggs are unpigmented, and no tadpole stage is present. Small froglets, 4 mm long, are reported to emerge from the eggs 27 days after being laid.

NOTES: This species is found in an area that is under extreme pressure from forestation. It has been recommended that the conservation status of this species be listed as critically endangered.

KEY REFERENCE: Bishop & Passmore 1993.

De Villiers' moss frog
Arthroleptella villiersi Hewitt, 1935
(Plate 18.1)

This species was named for Con de Villiers of the Zoology Department at the University of Stellenbosch.

DESCRIPTION: The female may reach 22 mm in length. The limbs are thin and spindly, with an outer metatarsal tubercle that is well developed. The back is variable, from light tan, through red-brown to black. The belly is white in females but darker in males, which also have a black throat region.

DISTRIBUTION AND HABITAT (FIG. 218): This species has been found in the coastal strip near Rooi Els and the adjoining Hottentots

Fig. 218 *Arthroleptella villiersi*

Holland mountain range, South Africa. It occurs in seepages where the vegetation offers good cover.

ADVERTISEMENT CALL: Males call from concealed positions under moss and other vegetation in damp spots. The call is a brief, high-pitched ticking. The call lasts only 0.07–0.11 s, with 4 or 5 notes at an emphasized frequency of 3.8–4.1 kHz.

BREEDING: Eggs have been found from July to November. An average of 11 eggs is laid in a small jelly mass, about 30 mm across, often found at the base of a wet moss-covered rock, where vegetation is growing and humus-rich soil has accumulated. Each egg is 3 mm in diameter, and metamorphosis occurs after 10–14 days, or longer in captivity. The froglets start feeding before the tail is fully resolved.

NOTES: Eggs have been found lightly concealed under overhanging grass on wet slopes and the sides of road cuttings. This species is found together with the Landdros moss frog.

KEY REFERENCE: Channing, Hendricks, and Dawood 1994.

Fishing Frogs—Genus *Aubria*

This genus of forest-dwelling frogs is found in the dense forests of West and Central Africa. One species gets into this area.

Masako fishing frog
Aubria masako Ohler & Kasadi, 1990
(Plate 18.2)

This species is named for the Masako Forest, near the village of Batibongena, 15 km from Kisangani in the Democratic Republic of the Congo.
Brown ball frog.

DESCRIPTION: This is a large species, with the male reaching 81 mm and the female over 90 mm SVL. The tympanum is distinct and large. A patch of glandular tissue is present behind the thigh, close to the knee. The feet are not completely webbed, with two and one-half to

Masako Fishing Frog

three segments of the fourth toe free of web. The back is brown and faintly marked with dark spots. Many specimens have a pale stripe down the middle of the back. The throat, chest, and belly have whitish spots on a dark maroon background. This pattern may become less obvious in large adults, although the throat retains the markings. The sexes cannot be determined externally.

DISTRIBUTION AND HABITAT (FIG. 219): This frog is found in the Congo River basin, on the Cameroonian highlands to the northwest, and in adjacent areas to the south in Angola. Details of the habitat where a single specimen was collected in Kakindo in Angola are not available. This species is associated with closed-canopy rain forest, open swamp forest, and swamps. Adults burrow during the day.

ADVERTISEMENT CALL: I am grateful to J.-L. Amiet for kindly providing me with his unpublished recording of the call. The call consists of a series of about 14 short, low-pitched whoops that start softly and get louder before fading away. The whoops are produced at a rate of 14/10 s. Each whoop has a duration of about 0.3 s, with pulses at a rate of 90/s. The emphasized harmonics are at 200 and 300 Hz.

BREEDING: Unknown, other than that the eggs are laid in strings.

TADPOLES: See the chapter on tadpoles.

Fig. 219 *Aubria masako*

NOTES: This frog sits on the edge of the pond and snaps up small fish, mostly *Epiplatys*, that leap out of the water. Other food items are arthropods, young fishing frogs, and Boettger's dwarf clawed frog *Hymenochirus boettgeri*.

KEY REFERENCES: Knoepffler 1976, Ohler 1996.

Dainty Frogs—Genus *Cacosternum*

These small frogs are typically slender with thin limbs and dark spots or blotches on the belly. Five species are known. A number of other cryptic species may be present also. At the time of writing a study to determine the status of these species was in progress.

KEY TO THE SPECIES

1a. Inner metatarsal tubercle shorter than first segment of inner toe (Fig. 220)   2
1b. Inner metatarsal tubercle longer than first segment of inner toe   3

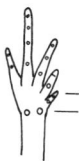

Fig. 220   Metatarsal tubercles

2a. Markings present on belly, palmar tubercles smaller than tubercles of fingers   4
2b. No markings on belly, palmar tubercles larger than tubercles on fingers (Fig. 221)   *Cacosternum nanum*

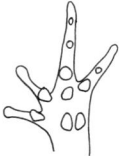

Fig. 221   Palmar tubercles

3a. A large pair of glands at rear of body and on flanks (Fig. 222)
Cacosternum capense
3b. No large glands at rear of body   *Cacosternum namaquense*

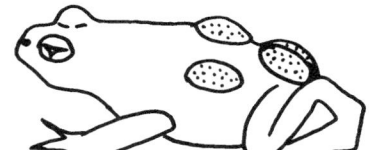

Fig. 222 Dorsal glands

4a. Call a series of clicks that speed up, found along the Western Cape lowlands   *Cacosternum platys*
4b. Call consists of regularly spaced clicks, found in the dry interior, northward   *Cacosternum boettgeri*

Boettger's dainty frog
Cacosternum boettgeri (Boulenger, 1882)
(Plates 18.3, 18.4, 18.5)

This frog was named for O. Boettger, unsalaried herpetologist at the Senckenberg Museum from 1875 to 1910.
Boettger's metal frog. *Gewone blikslanertjie* in Afrikaans.

DESCRIPTION: This small frog is not known to exceed 23 mm in length. The body shape is characteristic, with a narrow head widening to the belly region. The arms and legs are thin and long. The feet are unwebbed. The back pattern is very variable, from green to brown, with spots or stripes. The lower surface has discrete small gray or black spots.

DISTRIBUTION AND HABITAT (FIG. 223): This small frog is widespread in southern Africa, excluding the winter rainfall region of the Western Cape Province. It is found in grassland but rarely on slopes.

ADVERTISEMENT CALL: The male calls from water level. Usually it is concealed in cracks or under vegetation. The call is a rapid series of high-pitched clicks, about 10 clicks/s, the series lasting about a second, at an emphasized frequency of 5.2 kHz. The males have a

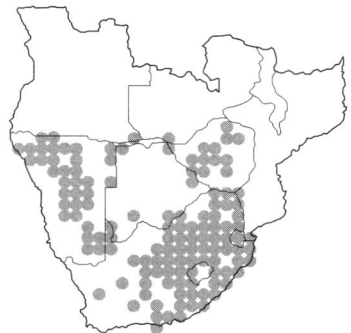

Fig. 223 *Cacosternum boettgeri*

simple chorus organization. Calling occurs in a bout, or set sequence. The same individual in a group usually starts the calling bouts. During the early rains the males call day and night.

BREEDING: This species breeds in flooded depressions, especially where grass is growing. Breeding takes place from October to February in the summer rainfall area. Amplexus is axillary. The eggs are laid under water, attached to grass stems, with some eggs sinking to the bottom. Each egg is 0.6 mm in diameter. Clutch size is 250.

TADPOLES: See the chapter on tadpoles.

NOTES: This little frog is known to spend the winter underground at the end of the burrows of the sungazer lizard *Cordylus giganteus* and in termite mounds. It has been found up to 3 m from the burrow entrance and feeds on small insects. It is preyed upon by yellow-billed egrets *Egretta intermedia* and the snake *Psammophylax rhombeatus*. Apart from the advertisement call, a second call type consisting of a faster trill has been reported, and may be a male-male interaction call.

KEY REFERENCES: Balinsky 1957, Van den Elzen & Van den Elzen 1977, Douglas 1970.

Cape dainty frog
Cacosternum capense Hewitt, 1926
(Plate 18.6)

Cape Dainty Frog

The specific name *capense* means "of the Cape" and refers to the locality where it was discovered.
Cape metal frog.

DESCRIPTION: Although this species is the largest in the genus, the female only reaches 39 mm in length. The inner metatarsal tubercle is flattened and flange-like. A characteristic pair of large skin glands is present on the flanks, and another behind on the midline. Many smaller glands are also present on the back. The back is pale brown with flecks of white, black, and darker brown. The belly is white with large gray, greenish, or black mottles.

DISTRIBUTION AND HABITAT (FIG. 224): The Cape dainty frog presently occurs in the area from Stellenbosch to Malmesbury, in the southern Western Cape Province, South Africa. Although it was described from Rondebosch Common in Cape Town, the frogs can no longer be found there. This species is absent from sandy soils, apparently preferring heavy clay and loam.

ADVERTISEMENT CALL: Males call from the edge of flooded grassy areas. The call is a creak, 0.2 s long. The pulse rate is 100/s, and the emphasized frequency rises from 2 kHz to 2.6 kHz.

Fig. 224 *Cacosternum capense*

BREEDING: This frog is known to breed during the winter rains, from June to August. Clutch size is 57–400 eggs. Each egg is 1 mm in diameter, white with a black hemisphere, and within a 3-mm capsule. Groups of 30–40 eggs have been observed attached to submerged vegetation.

TADPOLES: Unknown.

NOTES: This species is able to survive in the wheatlands, despite the extensive agricultural activity. The glands in the skin presumably secrete substances noxious to other frogs, as other species die when placed in the same vivarium. This species is listed as vulnerable.

KEY REFERENCE: de Villiers 1988d.

Namaqua dainty frog
Cacosternum namaquense Werner, 1910
(Plate 18.7)

The specific name refers to Namaqualand, where this species is common.
Namaqua metal frog.

DESCRIPTION: The female reaches a length of 25 mm. The inner metatarsal tubercle is distinct but narrow. The outer metatarsal tubercle is reduced or absent. Two large characteristic skin glands occur on the lower back, which has a pale or dark brown background, with light and darker markings, and a pale triangle between the eyes and the tip of the snout. The lower surface is smooth, with dark markings that tend to become smaller toward the sides.

DISTRIBUTION AND HABITAT (FIG. 225): This species is found from southern Namibia throughout Namaqualand, and as far west as the Karoo National Park in central South Africa. It is associated with rocky areas.

ADVERTISEMENT CALL: The male calls in vegetation at water level, or just away from the water. The call is a creak, which rises slightly in pitch. Call duration is 0.3 s; pulse rate is 75/s at a dominant fre-

Dwarf Dainty Frog

Fig. 225 *Cacosternum namaquense*

quency of 2.5 kHz. Males call alternately so that a continuous sound is produced.

BREEDING: This species breeds in temporary pools formed in rock tanks or pools in riverbeds. Two clutches counted had 43 and 69 eggs.

TADPOLES: See the chapter on tadpoles.

NOTES: The male fights off other intruding males. It has a clicking territorial call that is uttered when another male is less than 50 cm away.

KEY REFERENCE: Branch 1988b.

Dwarf dainty frog
Cacosternum nanum Boulenger, 1887
(Plate 18.8)

The specific name *nanum* means "dwarf."
Mozambique metal frog. *Koperblikslanertjie* in Afrikaans.

DESCRIPTION: The female is up to 25 mm long. The inner metatarsal tubercle is small. The pattern of the back is variable, usually a brown background with darker flecks. A dark stripe is present from the nostril, through the eye, nearly to the arm. A pale vertebral line is sometimes present. The lower coloration is white with various

Fig. 226 *Cacosternum nanum*

amounts of darker gray mottles. The throat is gray. The palmar tubercles are smaller than the tubercles on the fingers.

DISTRIBUTION AND HABITAT (FIG. 226): This frog is known from the eastern and southern parts of South Africa. It occurs in grasslands and savannas and is often found where shallow water is flowing slowly.

ADVERTISEMENT CALL: The male calls from water level while concealed in vegetation. The call is a short creak, consisting of 3–5 notes/s, each note 0.03 s long at a dominant frequency of 3.5 kHz.

BREEDING: Eggs are laid in shallow ponds. They are attached in clusters of 8–25 on vegetation below water level. Each egg is 0.9 mm in diameter within a 1.4-mm capsule. The developing embryos are yellow and smaller than the head of a match.

TADPOLES: See the chapter on tadpoles.

NOTES: In captivity this frog will take mosquitoes. Two or more species may presently be confused under this name.

KEY REFERENCE: Wager 1986.

Flat dainty frog
Cacosternum platys Rose, 1950
(Plate 19.1)

Flat Dainty Frog

The name *platys* refers to the flat appearance of this species.

DESCRIPTION: This small frog is not known to exceed 22 mm in length. The body shape is characteristic, with a narrow head widening to the belly region. The arms and legs are thin and long. The feet are unwebbed. The back pattern is very variable, from gray through brown, with spots or stripes. The lower surface has discrete small gray or black spots.

DISTRIBUTION AND HABITAT (FIG. 227): This species is found in the winter rainfall region of Western Cape Province of South Africa. It occurs in flooded grassland and seepages, at all altitudes.

ADVERTISEMENT CALL: The male calls from water level beneath emergent vegetation. The call resembles the sound of a marble falling to a hard floor—a series of clicks that starts slowly and accelerates. Each call is around 0.2 s long, with 7–9 clicks at a dominant frequency of 7.5–8 kHz.

BREEDING: Unknown.

TADPOLES: Unknown.

Fig. 227 *Cacosternum platys*

NOTES: This species is confused under *C. boettgeri* in earlier publications.

KEY REFERENCE: Rose 1950.

Ornate Frogs—Genus *Hildebrandtia*

This medium-sized frog is stocky and brightly patterned, with greens, golds, pinks, blacks, and browns being the dominant colors. It is found throughout moist savannas. There are two species, of which only one occurs in the area covered by this book.

Ornate frog
Hildebrandtia ornata (Peters, 1878)
(Plate 19.2)

The specific name *ornata* refers to the elaborate pattern on the back. Ornate burrowing frog, Hildebrandt's burrowing frog, African ornate frog.

DESCRIPTION: This stocky frog may reach up to 65 mm in length in the male and 70 mm in the female. Webbing is not extensive, just reaching the middle tubercle beneath the fourth toe. The inner metatarsal tubercle is longer than the first toe and flattened for digging. The frog is very beautifully marked, with a broad golden brown or green band down the back. Other green, golden, or brown patterns are common. A pair of characteristic Y-shaped light bands is found on the throat, against a dark background.

DISTRIBUTION AND HABITAT (FIG. 228): The ornate frog has been collected from West Africa, around the rain forest to Mozambique, Zambia, Angola, Botswana, northeastern South Africa, and Namibia. It is a savanna frog, breeding in shallow pans.

ADVERTISEMENT CALL: The male starts calling later than most species during the evening, often not before 22 h 30 min. It calls from shallow pans or some meters from the edge of water. The call is a harsh bellow, with a duration of 0.3–0.4 s, and a dominant harmonic at 1 kHz rising to 1.8 kHz, with a second frequency-modulated emphasis at 2.5 kHz rising to 2.8 kHz. Each call consists of very

Crowned Bullfrog

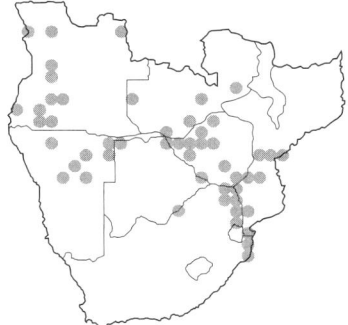

Fig. 228 *Hildebrandtia ornata*

rapidly pulsed notes. Although this species usually is found calling from shallow pans, it has been recorded calling from tanks on top of granite inselbergs in Mozambique.

BREEDING: The eggs are 1.4 mm in diameter in 3-mm capsules, and are scattered singly in shallow water.

TADPOLES: See the chapter on tadpoles.

NOTES: It is preyed upon by the hammerkop.

KEY REFERENCES: Inger 1968, Wager 1986.

Crowned Bullfrogs—Genus *Hoplobatrachus*

This large frog is similar in shape to the bullfrogs and fishing frogs. At least two species are known, of which only one reaches central Africa.

Crowned bullfrog
Hoplobatrachus occipitalis (Günther, 1859, "1858")
(Plate 19.3)

The name *occipitalis* refers to the transverse pale groove behind the eyes.

Groove-crowned bullfrog, giant swamp frog, African tigrine frog, African Peters frog. *Bengwele* in Hausa.

DESCRIPTION: This large robust frog may grow in length to 135 mm. A characteristic skin groove passes across the head just behind the eyes. The well-webbed feet and delicate hands show the aquatic nature of this frog, similar to those of the platanna *Xenopus*. The male has a small round opening to each vocal pouch, situated near the angle of the jaw. This vocal pouch opening is approximately the same size as the eye. The back is generally a shade of gray with darker markings. The underside is white with large dark irregular spots. There is sometimes a greenish tinge in the layer of mucus on the skin. This is especially noticeable in older specimens, which might be bright green. This green rubs off, however, and consists of chains of spherical algae.

DISTRIBUTION AND HABITAT (FIG. 229): This frog is known from northern Angola and Zambia, the Sudan, and across to Senegal. It is found in lakes, deep permanent ponds, swamps, and rivers.

ADVERTISEMENT CALL: The call consists of a series of deep notes, each 0.15 s long with emphasized harmonics at 0.8 and 2.5 kHz. The internote interval is 0.2 s.

BREEDING: This frog breeds throughout the year. Each female produces 469–3752 eggs, white with a black pole, measuring from 2.9 to

Fig. 229 *Hoplobatrachus occipitalis*

3.7 mm. The eggs are deposited in huge rafts in the backwaters of large rivers.

TADPOLES: See the chapter on tadpoles.

NOTES: This large frog with well-webbed, strong feet is able to escape disturbance by bounding rapidly across the surface of the water into vegetation on the opposite side of the pool. Like many large river frogs, the adult basks alongside rivers, sometimes in the lower branches of trees, jumping into the river when disturbed. As it jumps, it produces a characteristic warning whistle. When in water, this frog spends most of the time floating with its eyes protruding above the water. The adult is recorded feeding on earthworms, crustaceans including land crabs, spiders, other arthropods, snails, fish, frogs, tadpoles, snakes, lizards, and birds. This is one of the few frog species in Africa for which detailed ecological information is available. Work done in West Africa showed that this species can reach a biomass of 30.5–44.4 kg/ha. This is about half as much as Müller's platanna *Xenopus muelleri*, for which the density was calculated to have between 400 and 1550 individuals/ha. The two species together produced peaks of 108,100 tadpoles/ha at a biomass of 324.3 kg/ha at Bangui. This significant biomass indicates that tadpoles play an important part in the food web of tropical ponds. When the rains arrive in savanna areas, the frogs move out of riverbeds into temporary pools, covering up to 1.4 km in a single night.

In West Africa local villagers eat these frogs. Their skin is known to contain small amounts of bradykinins, substances that mimic mammalian hormones and slow down the heartbeat of small mammal predators, making them feel ill and hopefully deterring them from eating other crowned bullfrogs. Maximum recorded longevity in captivity is 10 years 11 months.

KEY REFERENCES: Sanderson 1936b, Lamotte & Züber-Vogeli 1954, Guibé & Lamotte 1958, Schiøtz 1963, Inger 1968, Micha 1975, Spieler & Linsenmair 1998 (as *Rana occipitalis* or *Dicroglossus occipitalis*).

Micro Frog—Genus *Microbatrachella*

The single species in this genus is endemic to low-lying seepage areas in the southwestern Cape.

Micro frog
Microbatrachella capensis (Boulenger, 1910)
(Plate 19.4)

The specific name *capensis* refers to the Cape of Good Hope. Cape Flats frog.

DESCRIPTION: This is a very small frog. The female may reach a length of 18 mm. The toes are slightly webbed. The pupil is horizontal. The back is brown, although sometimes greenish or black, with darker markings, often with a thin pale vertebral stripe. Sometimes broader lateral stripes may be present. The legs are thin and short, with the tibia less than half the body length. The belly may be mottled to varying degrees. The throat region of males is pigmented but not mottled.

DISTRIBUTION AND HABITAT (FIG. 230): The known range of this frog is the sandy flats of the southwestern Cape, where it is confined to a dozen or so seepage pools in the Betty's Bay and Kleinmond area, near Aghulas, and some relict patches of vegetation in Cape Town. This species is abundant where it occurs.

ADVERTISEMENT CALL: Males call from among vegetation at water level. The call is short, 0.1 s long, consisting of 5–6 pulses, with a dominant frequency of 4.9 kHz. Calls have been heard during the winter rainy season, from May to August.

Fig. 230 *Microbatrachella capensis*

BREEDING: Breeding starts with the onset of the winter rains in May or June. Eggs are attached in clusters of about 20, to vegetation just below the surface.

TADPOLES: See the chapter on tadpoles.

NOTES: This species prefers semipermanent water where little disturbance has occurred. This frog is listed as critically endangered. Extensive housing developments on the Cape Flats have destroyed the habitat where this species once flourished. The threat to this frog is taken so seriously that during construction of a new road near Betty's Bay, the road was moved slightly so as to avoid a breeding pond. This species is sometimes found in association with the threatened Cape platanna *Xenopus gilli*.

KEY REFERENCES: Hewitt 1926a, Rose 1929, De Villiers 1988b, Baard 1989.

Boneberg's Frog—Genus *Natalobatrachus*

There is only one species in this genus, known from forested slopes in southeastern South Africa.

Boneberg's frog
Natalobatrachus bonebergi Hewitt & Methuen, 1913
(Plate 19.5)

The specific name honors Father P. Boneberg of the Marianhill Mission, the collector of the first specimens.
Kloof frog, Natal diving frog.

DESCRIPTION: The female reaches 37 mm in length. The pupil is horizontal. The fingers possess large truncated discs, while the toes have smaller discs. The snout is long, overhanging the mouth. The toes are slightly webbed. The back has elongated skin ridges, with brown coloration, usually with a vertebral stripe. A distinct dark stripe from the tip of the snout runs through the lower part of the eye backward to the arm. The back pattern consists mainly of browns, with small pale spots.

Fig. 231 *Natalobatrachus bonebergi*

DISTRIBUTION AND HABITAT (FIG. 231): This species is restricted to forests along the southeastern and eastern coasts. Recent housing developments and sugar cane planting along the coast have destroyed much of the habitat where this species once occurred.

ADVERTISEMENT CALL: The male calls from the open, or while in holes or hidden in rock cracks, from 1 to 2 m above water. The call is a soft click, with a dominant frequency of 3.6 kHz.

BREEDING: Breeding takes place from October to May. This frog breeds near shallow (30–40 cm) narrow streams with low banks, with overhanging vegetation. Most eggs are attached to vegetation overhanging water, with one-third of the clutches examined encircling a stem or leaf. Eggs are sometimes attached to rock faces overhanging water. Twenty clutches have been reported above one pool. Clutch size is 75–108. Eggs may be placed from a few centimeters to 2 or more m above water, with a reported mean of 58 cm. Each egg is 1.5–2 mm in diameter, in 4-mm capsules. The tadpoles develop partly and then drop into the water below.

TADPOLES: See the chapter on tadpoles.

NOTES: The adults are frequently found within a meter of an egg mass.

KEY REFERENCES: Wager 1986, Kok & Seaman 1988, 1989.

Mongrel Frog—Genus *Nothophryne*

There is only one species in this genus, known from Mount Mulanje in Malawi.

Mongrel frog
Nothophryne broadleyi Poynton, 1963
(Plate 19.6)

This species was named for D. G. Broadley of the Natural History Museum in Bulawayo, who collected the first specimens.
Broadley's mountain frog.

DESCRIPTION: The female is up to 28 mm long. The toes are unwebbed. The body is flattened, with the fingertips slightly expanded into discs. The back is brown with a light interocular bar, edged behind by a darker line. Other lighter markings include a patch in the middle of the back and a light vertebral line. The belly has irregular dark blotches. The male vocal pouches expand through slits near the angle of each jaw.

DISTRIBUTION AND HABITAT: (FIG. 232): This species is only known from Mount Mulanje in southern Malawi, but it may occur on nearby mountains. It is found on rocky areas from 1200 m upward.

Fig. 232 *Nothophryne broadleyi*

ADVERTISEMENT CALL: The call is a weak chirp but has yet to be recorded.

BREEDING: Clutch size is about 30. Eggs, 1.5 mm in diameter, are laid in damp moss where there is seepage over rocks.

TADPOLES: Unknown.

NOTES: The tadpoles have been seen but not yet collected. A trip to the top of Mount Mulanje with a tape recorder and camera would yield valuable natural history information on the mongrel frog.

KEY REFERENCES: Poynton & Broadley 1985a.

Puddle Frogs—Genus *Phrynobatrachus*

This is a large genus of small brown frogs. They are common in practically all damp habitats in the warmer areas and are an important component of the tropical ecosystems, as they breed continuously and reach maturity at 5 months. Many different color patterns are known. Savanna species share a set of color patterns, while rain forest species share a different set of color patterns. The shared color patterns in different habitats probably serve as camouflage against common predators. This is the only genus which has a small tubercle midway along the tarsus.

KEY TO THE SPECIES

1a. Fingers and toes expanded into small discs (Fig. 233)   2
1b. Toes not expanded into discs, although tips may be swollen   5

Fig. 233 Small discs

2a. Broad web reaching distal subarticular tubercle of third toe (Fig. 234)   3

2b. Webbing not reaching distal subarticular tubercle of third toe
4

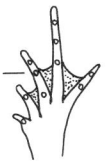

Fig. 234 Webbing

3a. A continuous glandular fold running from eye at least to scapular region (Fig. 235)   *Phrynobatrachus acridoides*
3b. No continuous skin fold from eye to scapular region   *Phrynobatrachus perpalmatus*

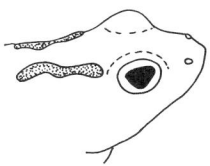

Fig. 235 Glandular fold

4a. Broad web passing proximal subarticular tubercle of fourth toe, at least on one side   *Phrynobatrachus rungwensis*
4b. Broad web not passing proximal tubercle of fourth toe
Phrynobatrachus mababiensis (Misuku form)

5a. Broad web passing proximal subarticular tubercle of fourth toe, at least on one side   6
5b. Broad web not passing proximal tubercle of fourth toe (Fig. 236)
7

Fig. 236 Minimal web

6a. Broad web just reaching distal subarticular tubercle of third toe
Phrynobatrachus natalensis

6b. Broad web extending two-thirds or less of distance between subarticular tubercles of third toe   *Phrynobatrachus stewartae*

7a. Upper and lower jaws barred, barring confluent
Phrynobatrachus mababiensis
7b. Jaws darkened, or with faint barring on upper jaw
Phrynobatrachus parvulus

Eastern puddle frog
Phrynobatrachus acridoides (Cope, 1867)
(Plate 19.7)

The specific name *acridoides* means "cricket-like."
Small puddle frog, East African puddle frog, Zanzibar puddle frog, Zanzibar river frog.

DESCRIPTION: The male reaches 28 mm and the female, 30 mm in length. The male has small folds in the vocal pouch running parallel to the jaw. The back is gray-brown with darker markings, sometimes with a pale or green vertebral band. The tympanum is visible. Small discs are present as swellings. Webbing is variable, but the main web reaches the outer tubercle beneath the third toe, without passing the middle tubercle of the fourth toe. The upper jaw has light speckling. The male has an evenly shaded throat region, which is speckled in the female. A pale stripe occurs on the back of the thigh. The belly is white with a yellowish tinge in the groin. A glandular ridge runs from each eye back to the shoulder region, sometimes continuing backward as a border to the dorsal band. Other paired warts may occur on the back.

DISTRIBUTION AND HABITAT (FIG. 237): This species is known from West Africa to Somalia and southward to northeastern South Africa. It is found in savannas and forests wherever there is permanent water.

ADVERTISEMENT CALL: The call is a harsh creak repeated continuously day and night. The male calls while resting on vegetation at water level in a shallow pool. Each call has a duration of about 0.9 s, with a pulse rate of 50/s. The emphasized frequency is 2 kHz.

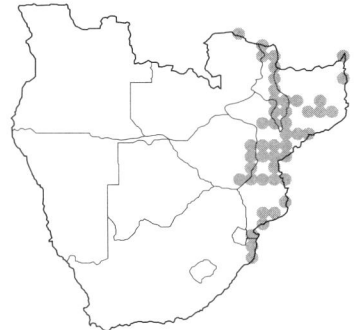

Fig. 237 *Phrynobatrachus acridoides*

BREEDING: Calling is known from January to May in Malawi, depending on the availability of pools. The eggs are small, dark, 0.8 mm in diameter. The eggs are laid in a small mat, which floats just below the surface.

TADPOLES: Unknown.

NOTES: This frog has been recorded as the food of the sand snake *Psammophis sibilans* and the vine snake *Thelotornis capensis*. The small discs may enable this species to move over soft mud.

KEY REFERENCES: Stewart 1967, Dudley 1978.

Mababe puddle frog
Phrynobatrachus mababiensis FitzSimons, 1932
(Plate 19.8)

The specific name *mababiensis* refers to the Mababe Depression in Botswana, where this frog was first collected.
Dwarf puddle frog, common cricket frog, Mababe river frog.

DESCRIPTION: This is a very small frog. The male grows up to 19 mm and the female is slightly longer at 21 mm. The throat sac of the male has a transverse fold. Glands are present on the upper leg. The toes and fingertips are swollen, but discs are not present. Broad web reaches the inner tubercle beneath the third toe and usually reaches the inner tubercle of the fourth toe. The tubercle of the heel is prominent. The back is mainly brown with darker and lighter markings. Many small warts are present on the back. The light and dark barring on the upper and lower jaws corresponds. Many different color patterns are known, with vertebral stripes or bands being common.

DISTRIBUTION AND HABITAT: (FIG. 238): This small frog is known from Angola and Tanzania south to Namibia and eastern South Africa. It occurs in savannas at high and low altitudes. This species is found in wet areas with emergent vegetation, like roadside ditches and grassy fields.

ADVERTISEMENT CALL: The male calls from a concealed position at the base of grass near pools and small bodies of water. The call consists of a number of long buzzes, typically interspersed with a few separate clicks. The buzzing may continue for seconds, at a pulse rate of 80/s and an emphasized frequency of 4.1 kHz.

BREEDING: This frog breeds in summer, although some calling may be heard for most months of the year. The small black eggs are 0.9 mm in diameter in 1.1-mm capsules. They are laid in a single layer, about 50 mm across, which floats on the surface.

TADPOLES: See the chapter on tadpoles.

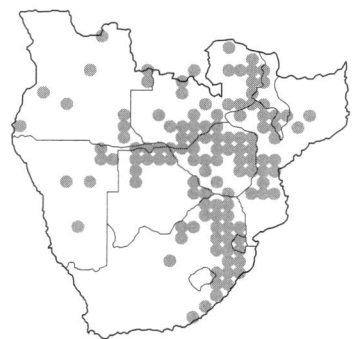

Fig. 238 *Phrynobatrachus mababiensis*

NOTES: In captivity this frog has been reported to eat mosquitoes. It is eaten by the Herald snake *Crotaphopeltis hotamboeia*, the swamp viper *Atheris nitschei*, and the cattle egret. Frogs from the Misuku Mountains in northern Malawi have more enlarged toe tips and have been suggested to be a different species, the Ukinga puddle frog *Phrynobatrachus ukingensis*.

KEY REFERENCES: Stewart 1967, Wager 1986.

Natal puddle frog
Phrynobatrachus natalensis (Smith, 1849)
(Plates 20.1, 20.2)

The specific name *natalensis* refers to the province of Natal (now KwaZulu-Natal, South Africa) where this species was first discovered.
Puddle frog, Smith's frog, snoring puddle frog, Natal river frog. *Kikvors* in Dutch, *Tchimbotwe* in Lwena, *Mbovu* in Chewa and Ngoni, *Snorkmodderpadda* in Afrikaans.

DESCRIPTION: The male reaches 34 mm and the female, 40 mm in length. Male throat sacs have longitudinal folds. Femoral glands are absent. There are no discs on fingers and toes, although a slight swelling may be present. Webbing in this species is quite variable. Broad web reaches the outer tubercle below the third toe, passes midway between inner and middle tubercle of the fourth toe, and reaches the outer tubercle of the fifth toe. Coloration is variable. A rich brown background is typical, although a thin vertebral stripe, darker speckling, and a pale dorsal band are some of the more common patterns.

DISTRIBUTION AND HABITAT: (FIG. 239): This frog is widely distributed in all the countries covered, excluding the very arid Kalahari sand area and the winter rainfall region of the southern tip of Africa. It is found in grasslands and thorn savannas.

ADVERTISEMENT CALL: The male calls during day and night in wet weather. The call is a slow quiet snore. The dominant harmonic is at 2 kHz, with a pulse rate of about 60/s–80/s and a duration of 0.5 s. Two or more males may call in chorus, but more commonly

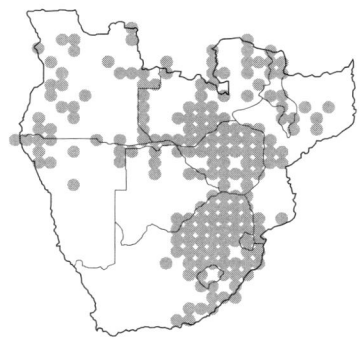

Fig. 239 *Phrynobatrachus natalensis*

the calls are heard without pattern from around small bodies of water.

BREEDING: Breeding takes place from spring through summer. The mating pair swim while depositing eggs. The eggs are small, 0.6–1.0 mm in diameter, and dark brown on top. They float on the surface of the water in a single-layer mat. About 200 eggs are laid in each clutch. Eggs may be laid in deep water or very shallow water, frequently associated with emergent vegetation. Metamorphosis occurs after 27–40 days.

TADPOLES: See the chapter on tadpoles.

NOTES: This frog is found at both low and moderate altitudes, often breeding in small temporary pools remote from other water. The maximum recorded longevity in captivity is 5 years. It eats earthworms, snails, arthropods, and other frogs. In turn, it is preyed upon by the black-necked spitting cobra *Naja nigricollis*.

KEY REFERENCES: Power 1927a, Inger 1968, Stewart 1974.

Dwarf puddle frog
Phrynobatrachus parvulus (Boulenger, 1905)

The specific name *parvulus* means "very small."
Loanda river frog.

Dwarf Puddle Frog

DESCRIPTION: The male in this species grows to 16 mm and the female, up to 25 mm. The male has a throat sac with a transverse fold and a flattened gland on the upper leg. Digital discs are absent. Webbing is not extensive, with the broad web only reaching the inner tubercle below the third toe and not or only just reaching the inner tubercle of the fourth toe. The heel tubercle is rounded with a conical profile. The back is mostly brown, with a lighter band below the tympanum that runs from eyelid to arm. The back of the thigh has a lighter band running from knee to knee.

DISTRIBUTION AND HABITAT (FIG. 240): This frog is widely distributed in northern Botswana, northeastern Zimbabwe, Malawi, Zambia, and Angola. It is found in the higher nonforested areas.

ADVERTISEMENT CALL: The call is reported as a "long, buzzy, cricket-like trill, sometimes ending in a 'chip'." The call has not yet been recorded for analysis.

BREEDING: These small frogs breed during the wet seasons and probably throughout the year. Details on eggs are unknown.

TADPOLES: Unknown.

NOTES: Food items that have been reported include earthworms, snails, and arthropods.

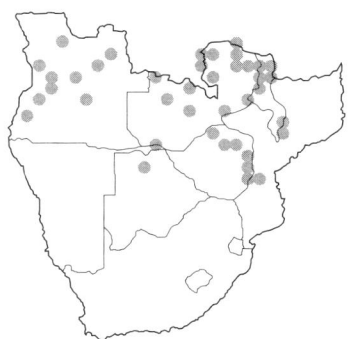

Fig. 240 *Phrynobatrachus parvulus*

KEY REFERENCE: Stewart 1967.

Webbed puddle frog
Phrynobatrachus perpalmatus Boulenger, 1898

The specific name *perpalmatus* means "much webbing."
Mondo in Nyungwe, Lake Mwero river frog.

DESCRIPTION: This is a small frog, with the male up to 25 mm and the female up to 29 mm long. No femoral glands are present in the male. The throat sac of the male is unpigmented, without distinct folds. Small discs are present on fingers and toes. The webbing is well developed, with the broad web extending past the distal subarticular tubercle of the third toe and middle tubercle of the fourth toe. The heel tubercle is flap-like. A pale band below the vent runs from knee to knee, with a second band interrupted at the vent. The skin is quite smooth.

DISTRIBUTION AND HABITAT (FIG. 241): This species is reported from Sudan to northern Zambia, Malawi, and adjacent Mozambique. It is found in permanently wet sites.

ADVERTISEMENT CALL: Unknown.

BREEDING: Unknown.

Fig. 241 *Phrynobatrachus perpalmatus*

TADPOLES: Unknown.

NOTES: This aquatic frog is found in flooded grass and reeds. This species eats earthworms, snails, and arthropods. The sand snake *Psammophis sibilans* and the vine snake *Thelotornis capensis* eat it.

KEY REFERENCE: Loveridge 1933.

Rungwe puddle frog
Phrynobatrachus rungwensis (Loveridge, 1932)
(Plate 20.3)

The specific name refers to Mount Rungwe in southern Tanzania. Rungwe river frog.

DESCRIPTION: The male of this small species reaches 23 mm in length. Glands are present on the upper leg. The throat sac in the male is folded behind. Small discs are present on the tips of the middle toes, but the fingers are only slightly swollen. Webbing is not extensive. The broad web reaches midway between the tubercles below the third toe and reaches the proximal subarticular tubercle of the fourth toe. The tarsal tubercle is conical, with no transverse fold. No light band is present below the tympanum. A light band on the back of the thigh is edged with a dark border. The back is brown with darker markings. The skin glands on the back are not arranged in longitudinal rows.

DISTRIBUTION AND HABITAT (FIG. 242): This small frog is known from southern Democratic Republic of the Congo, southwestern Tanzania and northern Malawi. It has been found in open grasslands.

ADVERTISEMENT CALL: Unknown.

BREEDING: Unknown.

TADPOLES: Unknown.

KEY REFERENCE: Loveridge 1932.

Fig. 242 *Phrynobatrachus rungwensis*

Stewart's puddle frog
Phrynobatrachus stewartae Poynton & Broadley, 1985

This species was named for the collector, Margaret Stewart of the State University of New York, Albany.
Stewart's river frog.

DESCRIPTION: The male is up to 21 mm and the female, 23 mm long. The male throat sac has a flap at the back. The glands on the upper leg are yellow, elongated, and flattened. Discs are absent. Webbing is moderate, with the broad web extending midway between the tubercles beneath the third toe and passing the inner tubercle of the fourth toe on the inside. The heel tubercle is spurlike on a fold. There is no light band below the tympanum. The back is brown, with a darker triangle between the eyes. The warts on the back are edged with black.

DISTRIBUTION AND HABITAT (FIG. 243): This frog is known only from Rumpi, in Malawi. It is restricted to grassy areas with vegetation in water.

ADVERTISEMENT CALL: Calling takes place under vegetation in marshy areas. The call is similar to that of the Mababe puddle frog *P. mababiensis*, but is louder, faster and longer. It consists of a long, buzzy, low cricket-like trill followed by a crisp "chip," the chip repeated one or more times. The call has yet to be recorded and analyzed.

Montane Marsh Frog

Fig. 243 *Phrynobatrachus stewartae*

BREEDING: Unknown.

TADPOLES: Unknown.

NOTES: The only known female contained eggs that were 0.6 mm in diameter and darkly pigmented. More observations are required of this interesting frog.

KEY REFERENCES: Stewart 1967, Poynton & Broadley 1985.

Marsh Frog—Genus *Poyntonia*

This genus was erected to accommodate a species of small brown frog. There is only one species.

Montane marsh frog
Poyntonia paludicola Channing & Boycott, 1989
(Plate 20.4)

The specific name *paludicola* means "marsh dwelling."
Kogelberg reserve frog.

DESCRIPTION: The female grows to 30 mm, although the male is smaller. The female has a relatively narrower head and shorter tibia than the male. The tympanum is not visible. The pupil is horizontal. The toes are long, with broad webbing almost reaching the outer tubercle below the third toe and midway between the inner and middle tubercles below the fourth toe, at least on the inside. The back is gray brown and extremely granular. A raised area behind the eye resembles the parotid gland in toads. A distinct glandular ridge runs from the top of the head, behind the eye, then diagonally backward to the angle of the jaw. A pale to reddish thin vertebral stripe is present in many individuals. A pale ridge runs from the eye back to the angle of the jaw, and a short white stripe is present from the tip of the snout to the jaw. One to three equally spaced white stripes may be present between the tip of the snout and the angle of the jaw, running from the eye to the upper lip.

DISTRIBUTION AND HABITAT (FIG. 244): This frog is found only on slopes of the Cape Fold Mountains at the southern tip of Africa. It is restricted to areas that receive between 2000 and 3000 mm of rainfall per year. The habitat where these frogs have been found consists of shallow seepage zones, shallow streams along rock outcrops, and marshy areas away from larger watercourses. Its conservation status is near threatened.

ADVERTISEMENT CALL: Males call from late summer to late winter and may call throughout the year during suitable weather. The call consists of 1–6 notes, each note with a duration of 159–184 ms, with a dominant harmonic at 2.2 kHz.

BREEDING: Unknown.

Fig. 244 *Poyntonia paludicola*

Common Frogs—Family Ranidae

TADPOLES: See the chapter on tadpoles.

NOTES: Although this frog occurs in an area that is well visited, it was not found until relatively recently. This suggests that there are many other new species of frogs waiting to be discovered.

KEY REFERENCE: Channing & Boycott 1989.

Ridged Frogs—Genus *Ptychadena*

This is a large group of specialist jumping frogs. All *Ptychadena* species are known as *munzabwa*, "the great jumper" in Lunda.

KEY TO THE SPECIES

1a. At least two dark bands below vent from knee to knee (Fig. 245)
                                    Ptychadena subpunctata
1b. One or no bands below vent   2

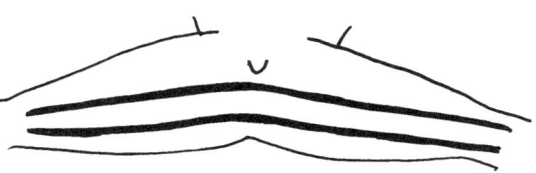

Fig. 245 Two bands

2a. A light triangle on snout (Fig. 246)   3
2b. No light triangle (light vertebral band may be present)   5

Fig. 246 Pale triangle

3a. Snout projecting, distance from nostril to tip of snout more than internarial distance, posterior thigh mottled (Fig. 247)
                                    Ptychadena oxyrhynchus

3b. Nostril to snout distance not more than internarial distance, thigh not mottled 4

Fig. 247 Snout-nostril distance

4a. Posterior face of thigh with light and dark longitudinal bands, no row of tubercles under fourth metatarsus (Fig. 248)
Ptychadena anchietae
4b. No dark bands on posterior thigh, a row of tubercles under fourth metatarsus *Ptychadena obscura*

Fig. 248 Thigh bands

5a. Two to two and one-third phalanges of fourth toe free of web (Fig. 249) *Ptychadena mascareniensis*
5b. Two and one-third or more phalanges of fourth toe free of web 6

Fig. 249 Webbing

6a. Foot length more than half of body length (Fig. 250) 7
6b. Length of foot less than half of body length 17

Common Frogs—Family Ranidae 317

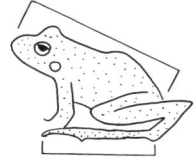

Fig. 250 Foot-body length comparison

7a. Posterior face of thigh with contrasted light and dark longitudinal bands (Fig. 251) 14

Fig. 251 Contrasting bands

7b. Posterior face of thigh mottled (Fig. 252) 8

Fig. 252 Mottled thigh

8a. Light line on upper surface of tibia (Fig. 253)
Ptychadena porosissima
8b. No light tibial line 9

Fig. 253 Tibial line

9a. Not more than three phalanges of fourth toe free of web 10
9b. More than three phalanges of fourth toe free of web 12

10a. Snout with skin ridges 11
10b. Snout without skin ridges *Ptychadena grandisonae*

11a. A pair of ridges on snout and another in interorbit
Ptychadena broadleyi
11b. Snout ridges continuous with paravertebral ridges (Fig. 254)
Ptychadena uzungwensis

Fig. 254 Dorsal ridges

12a. Paravertebral skin folds hugely developed, bumpy
Ptychadena bunoderma
12b. Dorsal skin folds evenly developed 13

13a. Nostril midway between eye and snout, or closer to eye
Ptychadena ansorgii
13b. Nostril closer to snout than to eye *Ptychadena perplicata*

14a. Continuous dark band from knee to knee below vent (Fig. 255)
Ptychadena taenioscelis
14b. No continuous dark band transverse below vent 15

Fig. 255 One continuous band

15a. Middorsal pair of skin folds divergent, not reaching rear of body
(Fig. 256) *Ptychadena guibei*
15b. Middorsal skin folds continuous from head to vent 16

Fig. 256 Skin folds

16a. Less than three and one-half phalanges of fourth toe free of web
Ptychadena upembae
16b. At least three and one-half phalanges of fourth toe free of web
Ptychadena keilingi

17a. Paravertebral folds continuous from head to midback
Ptychadena mossambica
17b. Skin folds interrupted between head and midback (Fig. 257)
18

Fig. 257 Skin folds

18a. Pale ridge running backward from upper lip to arm insertion broken *Ptychadena schillukorum*
18b. Pale ridge running backward from upper lip to arm insertion not broken (some specimens may have a discrete posterior spot) (Fig. 258)
Ptychadena mapacha

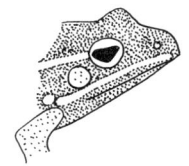

Fig. 258 Pale ridge

Anchieta's ridged frog
Ptychadena anchietae (Bocage, 1867)
(Plate 20.5)

This species was named for J. d' Anchieta.
Savanna ridged frog, plain grass frog., *Zonde* in Chewa and Ngoni, *nyankanzondo* in Nyungwe.

DESCRIPTION: These are small to medium-sized frogs, with males up to 51 mm and females up to 62 mm long. The distance from the nostril to snout tip is equal to the distance between the nostrils. Throat pouch slits end level with the lower edge of the arm. The tympanum is slightly smaller than the eye and edged with white. No row of tubercles is present under the fourth metatarsus. One and a half to two segments of the fourth toe are free of web. The top of the snout is light, forming a pale triangle. There is no light vertebral band, nor light line on the upper surface of the tibia. The back of the thigh shows light and dark parallel longitudinal bands. The back is often uniform brown without markings. A dark stripe runs from the nostril through the eye and the tympanum to the arm.

DISTRIBUTION AND HABITAT (FIG. 259): This species is known from Ethiopia to Angola and eastern South Africa. It is a savanna form, usually found in grassland near water.

ADVERTISEMENT CALL: The males call from open ground near water. The call is a high-pitched trill, repeated rapidly. Each trill consists of 10–12 pulses, with a duration of about 0.2 s, and harmonics at 1.8 and 3.5 kHz, rising respectively to 1.9 and 4 kHz by the end of

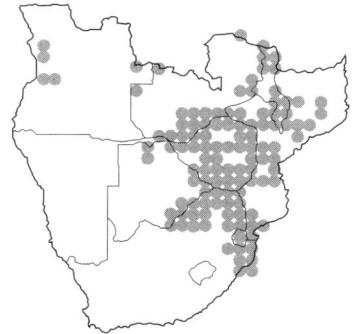

Fig. 259 *Ptychadena anchietae*

the call. The duration of the call is 0.25 s. This species also possesses a faster chorus call and a harsher territorial call.

BREEDING: It breeds during the summer rainy season. Mating and egg laying take place in shallow temporary ponds. The eggs float in a single layer on the water surface, with up to 300 eggs in a raft. Each egg is white with a gray top half, 1 mm in diameter, and within a 3-mm capsule.

TADPOLES: See the chapter on tadpoles.

NOTES: It is preyed upon by the sand snake *Psammophis sudanensis*, cattle egrets, and yellow billed kites. Perhaps the most remarkable predator on these frogs is the large slit-faced bat *Nycteris grandis*, which finds the male frog by listening for its advertisement call. The bat is tuned in only to the call of this species, as it does not take the Mozambique ridged frog *P. mossambica* even though both frogs may be present in the same pond. Unlike many other *Ptychadena* species, this one jumps away from water when disturbed.

KEY REFERENCE: Lamotte & Perret 1961b.

Ansorge's ridged frog
Ptychadena ansorgii (Boulenger, 1905)

This species is named for W. J. Ansorge.

DESCRIPTION: The distance between the nostrils is equal to the distance from snout to nostril. The nostril is situated midway between the tip of the snout and the eye. The throat pouch slits are level with the lower edge of the arm. An outer metatarsal tubercle is absent. Three to three and a half segments of the fourth toe are free of web. A pale vertebral line is usually present, but there is no light line on the upper surface of the tibia. The back of the thigh has longitudinal rows of light spots. The lower jaw is not banded.

DISTRIBUTION AND HABITAT (FIG. 260): This frog has been collected in Angola, northern Zambia, and Malawi. It is found in forests and savannas.

Fig. 260 *Ptychadena ansorgii*

ADVERTISEMENT CALL: The male calls from concealed positions in dense vegetation from swamps or slow-flowing streams. The call is a squeaky "tink-tink." The tinks are produced at a rate of about 8/s, with harmonics at 2.0 and 4.0 kHz. A rapid buzz consisting of about 20 pulses at a rate of 50/s may precede the series of tinks.

BREEDING: The breeding biology of this species is unknown.

TADPOLES: Unknown.

KEY REFERENCE: Poynton & Broadley 1985b.

Broadley's ridged frog
Ptychadena broadleyi Stevens, 1972

This species is named for D. G. Broadley of the Natural History Museum in Bulawayo.

DESCRIPTION: This is a moderately sized frog, with the male reaching 41 mm and the female 48 mm in length. The distance between the nostrils is equal to the distance from snout tip to nostril, which is midway between eye and snout tip. Throat pouch slits end level with the lower edge of the arm. A row of tubercles is present under the fourth metatarsal tubercle. Between two and three segments of the fourth toe are free of web. A pair of short skin folds is found anterior to the upper eyelids, another pair is found between the eyes, and

Fig. 261 *Ptychadena broadleyi*

a third pair behind the eyes. These may be continuous with the skin folds on the back. A light line is present from snout to vent. No longitudinal light line occurs on the tibia. The back of the thigh is variable, with two longitudinal series of light spots, or bands.

DISTRIBUTION AND HABITAT (FIG. 261): This frog is only known from Zomba plateau and Mount Mulanje in Malawi. It is associated with woodland clearings and exposed rock and has been found on granite outcrops. Its proposed conservation status is vulnerable.

ADVERTISEMENT CALL: The advertisement call is described as a soft nasal "pwaak." Visitors to Zomba would be in a good position to record the call of this frog, so that it can be analyzed.

BREEDING: The frogs breed in seeps on granite outcrops. Details of breeding are unknown.

TADPOLES: See the chapter on tadpoles.

KEY REFERENCE: Stevens 1972.

Rough ridged frog
Ptychadena bunoderma (Boulenger, 1907)
(Plate 20.6)

The specific name *bunoderma* means "bumpy skin."

DESCRIPTION: This is a medium-sized frog, with males up to 45 mm long. The internarial distance is less than the distance from snout tip to nostril. Gular pouch slits end level with the lower edge of the arm insertion. A row of tubercles is present under the fourth metatarsal. Four joints of the fourth toe are free of web. The upper surface of the tibia has no light line, and the posterior face of the thigh has scattered light spots. Overall the coloration is uniform dark brown or green, and the back is very bumpy due to the presence of huge paravertebral skin folds.

DISTRIBUTION AND HABITAT (FIG. 262): This species is known from Angola and northwestern Zambia, from flooded grassland.

ADVERTISEMENT CALL: Males call from beneath grass tussocks some meters from the water. The call is a soft, short "wawk." The duration of the call is 150 ms, with emphasized harmonics at 1.4 and 2.8 kHz. A chuckle call also may be heard.

BREEDING: Nothing is known about the breeding biology of this species.

TADPOLE: Unknown.

KEY REFERENCE: Boulenger 1907.

Fig. 262 *Ptychadena bunoderma*

Grandison's ridged frog
Ptychadena grandisonae Laurent, 1954
(Plate 20.7)

This species is named for A. G. C. Grandison of the Natural History Museum in London.

DESCRIPTION: These are medium-sized frogs, females up to 50 mm and males up to 44 mm long. Nostrils are situated midway between eye and snout tip. The gular pouch slits end below the level of the arm insertion. A row of tubercles is present under the fourth metatarsal, and three phalanges of the fourth toe are free of web. A light dorsal line is usually present between snout and vent. The posterior face of the thigh usually has a longitudinal series of light spots, but the pattern can be variable. The lower jaw is marbled.

DISTRIBUTION AND HABITAT (FIG. 263): This species is found from Rwanda, southward to Angola and Zambia in open savannas.

ADVERTISEMENT CALL: Males call from flooded grass. The call is a slow-rising "wauk." The duration of the call is 310 ms, with an initial emphasized frequency of 2.4 kHz, rising to 3.0 kHz. A chuckle call is also produced.

BREEDING: Breeding takes place during the summer months but details are unknown.

TADPOLES: See the chapter on tadpoles.

Fig. 263 *Ptychadena grandisonae*

KEY REFERENCE: Laurent 1954.

Guibe's ridged frog
Ptychadena guibei Laurent, 1954
(Plate 20.8)

This species was named for J. Guibé, director of the Paris Museum. Yellow-bellied ridged frog, Guibe's yellow-bellied grass frog. *Mazupa* in Dundo, *kazoli* in Cazombo.

DESCRIPTION: These are small to medium-sized frogs, with males up to 36 mm and females 43 mm long. Internarial distance is equal to the distance from snout tip to nostril. Nostrils are placed midway between snout tip and eye. The gular pouch openings end level with the lower edge of the arm insertion. A row of tubercles is usually present under the fourth metatarsal. Three or three and a half phalanges of the fourth toe are free of web. The paravertebral folds separate before reaching the tip of the urostyle, and a shorter pair of folds inside them runs to the tip of the urostyle. A light broad dorsal band runs from snout to vent. The front of the upper arm is black. The posterior face of the thigh has regular light and dark bands. The posterior part of the ventral surface is yellow.

DISTRIBUTION AND HABITAT (FIG. 264): They are known from the Democratic Republic of the Congo, southward to Mozambique and westward to Angola in grassland.

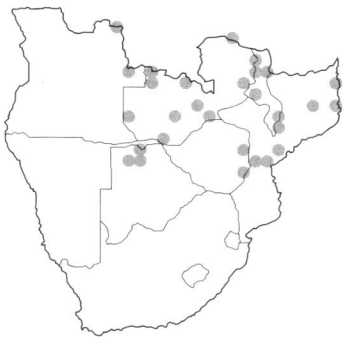

Fig. 264 *Ptychadena guibei*

ADVERTISEMENT CALL: Males call from concealed positions in thick grass or under debris within half a meter of shallow water in pans. The call consists of 3 pulses, repeated rapidly. Each group of 3 pulses is 0.1 s long, with dominant energy at 1.8 kHz.

BREEDING: Breeding starts in November at the beginning of the wet season. No details of breeding are available.

TADPOLES: Unknown.

KEY REFERENCES: Schmidt & Inger 1959, Laurent 1964, Stewart 1967.

Keiling's ridged frog
Ptychadena keilingi (Monard, 1937)

This species was named for the missionary R. P. Keiling of Cubango in Angola.

DESCRIPTION: The internarial distance is equal to the distance from nostril to snout tip. Nostrils are closer to the eye than to the tip of the snout. A row of tubercles is present under the fourth metatarsal. Webbing is very reduced, with three and two-thirds or more joints of the fourth toe free of web. The posterior face of the thigh is irregularly banded. A light vertebral band is present, and the throat is spotted.

DISTRIBUTION AND HABITAT (FIG. 265): This little-known frog has been collected in Angola and northwestern Zambia, in flooded grassland.

ADVERTISEMENT CALL: Males call from damp ground in the open. The call is a short trill, 0.15 s long, at a dominant frequency of 3.6–4.3 kHz. Each trill consists of 7–10 pulses. Different males call almost simultaneously, producing a confusion of sound.

BREEDING: Nothing is known about the breeding biology of this species.

TADPOLES: Unknown.

Fig. 265 *Ptychadena keilingi*

KEY REFERENCE: Monard 1937.

Mapacha ridged frog
Ptychadena mapacha Channing, 1993
(Plate 21.1)

The specific name *mapacha* refers to the area near Katima Mulilo in the Caprivi Strip, Namibia, where this species was discovered.

DESCRIPTION: These are small to medium-sized frogs, with the SVL in males up to 31 mm. They resemble both *P. mossambica* and *P. schillukorum* in having short legs and dark markings on the dorsum. This species is distinguishable from both by the unbroken ridge extending from the upper lip, below the tympanum, back to the arm insertion. The tympanum is equal in size to the eye. The toes are partially webbed, with two and two-thirds to three phalanges of the fourth toe free. The longitudinal skin ridges are interrupted and indistinct, with nine ridges across the dorsum at the widest part. The posterior face of the thigh has a number of small white spots. The dorsum is olive brown with dark spots. The ridges along the upper lip and running back from the eye are cream, while reddish brown infusions are present behind the tympanum and on the tibia.

DISTRIBUTION AND HABITAT (FIG. 266): This species is presently only known from Katima Mulilo and surrounding areas in northern

Mascarene Ridged Frog

Fig. 266 *Ptychadena mapacha*

Namibia, in wooded savannas. Further fieldwork is required to establish the geographical range of this species.

ADVERTISEMENT CALL: Males call from concealed positions under vegetation, while sitting in shallow water. The call consists of a short whistle, repeated at a rate of 6/s. Each note rises in pitch with the emphasized frequency at 1.6 kHz, and harmonics at 2.0 and 3.8 kHz.

BREEDING: Nothing has been reported of the breeding biology of this species.

TADPOLES: Unknown.

KEY REFERENCE: Channing 1993b.

Mascarene ridged frog
Ptychadena mascareniensis (Duméril & Bibron, 1841)
(Plate 21.2)

The specific name *mascareniensis* derives from the Mascarene Islands, where this frog was first found.
Mascarene frog, Mascarene grass frog. *Sodumbra* at St. Salvador in Angola, *sononga* at Caconda, *bengwele* or *likotsi* in West Africa, *Nilfrosch* in German.

DESCRIPTION: These are medium-sized frogs, with the SVL in males up to 46 mm and in females up to 58 mm. Internarial distance is equal to the distance from nostril to snout. Nostrils are situated midway between snout tip and eye. The gular pouch slits end above the level of the arm insertion. The outer metatarsal tubercle is absent. There is no row of tubercles under the fourth metatarsal. Two phalanges of the fourth toe, sometimes two and one third, are free of web. The back is generally dark brown with a broad vertebral stripe, which may range from green, through yellow to brown. A light line is present on the upper surface of the tibia. A dark band runs from knee to knee below the vent. The posterior face of the thigh is banded.

DISTRIBUTION AND HABITAT (FIG. 267): This species occurs widely from West Africa to eastern South Africa. This species is interesting as it is also found on Madagascar, Seychelles, and the Mascarene Islands off East Africa. It is found along streams and in temporary and permanent standing water.

ADVERTISEMENT CALL: Males call from the edge of water, sometimes from emergent vegetation. The call is a series of clucking sounds, repeated rapidly. Each call is 0.2–0.3 s long, consisting of 16–24 pulses, with dominant harmonics at 0.7–1 kHz, and a higher harmonic starting at 2.1 kHz, rising to 3 kHz. They call antiphonally, and males may form a dense calling group of six to eight in a small area of flooded grass. They use their vocal pouch for the advertisement call but produce a "chuckle" call, presumably a male-male interaction call, by vibrating their flanks.

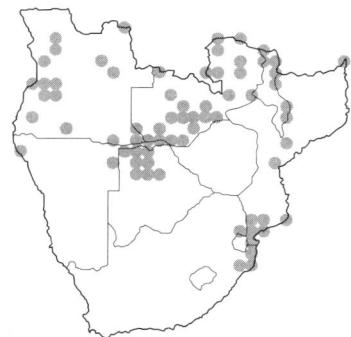

Fig. 267 *Ptychadena mascareniensis*

BREEDING: Breeding takes place during the summer rainy season. The eggs are small and white with a black upper half. Eggs were laid at the edge of Lake Chilwa during rain. The lake is slightly brackish, but the lake edge is relatively fresh during the rains.

TADPOLES: See the chapter on tadpoles.

NOTES: This frog is associated with swamps and marshes in open savannas. It escapes from disturbance by jumping away from water. It feeds on earthworms, snails, arthropods, and other frogs and is in turn preyed upon by sharp-nosed snakes *Rhamphiophis oxyrhynchus*. Local tribes in West Africa eat these frogs. When captured, they have a "foam and moan" display, where they produce skin secretions and make a moaning call while they adopt a rigid posture. Although this behavior is an attempt to distract predators, they are ready to escape by jumping at every opportunity. Maximum recorded longevity in captivity is 6 years 7 months.

KEY REFERENCES: Lamotte & Perret 1961a, Stewart 1967, Amiet 1974, Passmore 1977a.

Mozambique ridged frog
Ptychadena mossambica (Peters, 1854)
(Plate 21.3)

The specific name *mossambica* refers to Mozambique, where this species was first found.
Mozambique grass frog. *Zonde* in Chewa and Ngoni.

DESCRIPTION: These are medium-sized frogs. Males grow up to 44 mm and females, 53 mm in length in Mozambique but only 29 and 42 mm in western Zambia. Internarial distance is greater than the distance from nostril to tip of snout. Gular pouch slits end level with the lower edge of the arm insertion. A row of tubercles is present under the fourth metatarsal. Two and two-thirds to three phalanges are free of web (in the eastern part of the range), but only two to two and a third are free in the western part. This character must be treated with caution when identifying this species. Paravertebral folds are replaced behind by a pair of para-urostylar folds. This is a variable species in terms of markings. A light line is often present on the tibia,

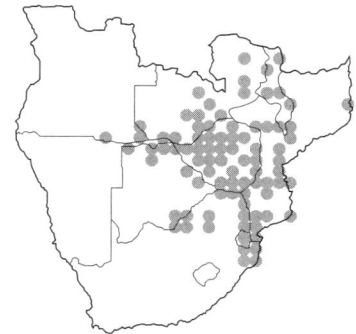

Fig. 268 *Ptychadena mossambica*

with a characteristic broad light vertebral band. The back is green or brown with dark brown markings.

DISTRIBUTION AND HABITAT (FIG. 268): They are known from Somalia south to Namibia, Botswana, and Natal, preferring open savanna.

ADVERTISEMENT CALL: Males call while well concealed. In Swaziland the call is a repeated quacking, 0.1 s long, with dominant energy at 0.8 kHz and a rising harmonic starting at 2.3 kHz and increasing to 3 kHz. The chorus call is a series of discrete clucks at 2.8 kHz. The territorial call is a complex series of notes. In the west, at Popa Falls, the call is similar but with emphasized harmonics at 1 kHz and between 3 and 4 kHz.

BREEDING: The breeding biology has not been reported. It would be quite easy for someone to observe the breeding behavior of this common frog, and record the number and size of the eggs and how they are laid.

TADPOLES: Unknown.

NOTES: This appears to be a very variable species, with the east-west difference in size associated with differences in webbing, with intermediates in both size and webbing. The calls are also slightly different, with the western calls being of a higher frequency. It is possible that two related species are being confused under one name. Extensive fieldwork and a molecular study are required to evaluate the present taxonomy. Specimens from the west with extensive webbing may key out as *P. schillukorum*.

KEY REFERENCES: Passmore 1977a, Poynton & Broadley 1985b.

Dark ridged frog
Ptychadena obscura (Schmidt & Inger, 1959)

The specific name *obscura* means "dark" or "obscure."

DESCRIPTION: These are medium-sized frogs, with males up to 38 mm and females up to 45 mm long. The nostril is closer to the eye than to the tip of the snout. Gular pouch slits end level with the lower edge of the arm insertion. A row of tubercles is present under the fourth metatarsus, and two to three phalanges of the fourth toe are free of web. A pale triangle is present on top of the snout, but a vertebral stripe is absent. A continuous middorsal pair of skin folds runs from the back of the head to the vent. No light line is present on the tibia. The posterior face of the thigh has no longitudinal dark bands.

DISTRIBUTION AND HABITAT (FIG. 269): This species is known from northern Zambia and the Upemba National Park in the Democratic Republic of the Congo, in grasslands above 750 m.

Fig. 269   *Ptychadena obscura*

ADVERTISEMENT CALL: The advertisement call is unknown.

BREEDING: Breeding takes place during the rainy season. No details of breeding biology are known.

TADPOLES: Unknown.

KEY REFERENCE: Schmidt & Inger 1959.

Sharp-nosed ridged frog
Ptychadena oxyrhynchus (Smith, 1849)
(Plate 21.4)

The specific name *oxyrhynchus* means "sharp snout."
Sharp-nosed ridged frog, sharp-nosed frog, sharp-nosed grass frog. *Zonde* in Chewa and Ngoni; *nyankamzondo* in Nyungwe; *bengwele* in West Africa where they are eaten; *sononga* at many Angolan localities, apparently a general term for many species; *môme* at Mozambique; *nya-idiwe* at Quellimane; *nyadschidwe* in Sena; *schûri* at Tete; *maye-kokuta* on Inhambane; *ma-hillam-scha* in Maputo; *umJamu* in Zulu; *kasoto* in Misuku; *mome* in Botswana.

DESCRIPTION: These are medium-sized frogs, with the SVL in males up to 62 mm and in females up to 85 mm. Internarial distance is less than the distance from nostril to snout tip. The tympanum is as large as the eye. Gular pouch slits end level with the lower edge of the arm insertion. There is no row of tubercles under the fourth metatarsal. The feet are extensively webbed, with only one and a half to two phalanges of the fourth toe free of web. The tibia is longer than the foot. There is a distinct pale triangle on top of the snout, not continued backward as a pale band. A thin pale vertebral stripe may be present. The back is brown, with reddish infusions on the skin ridges. A narrow dark stripe passes backward from the snout, through the nostril. It widens behind the eye to include the tympanum and then continues to the leg as a dark broken band. The posterior face of the thigh is mottled.

DISTRIBUTION AND HABITAT (FIG. 270): This species is widely distributed in savannas from Senegal to the eastern Cape.

Sharp-Nosed Ridged Frog

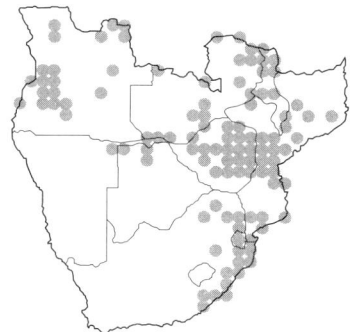

Fig. 270 *Ptychadena oxyrhynchus*

ADVERTISEMENT CALL: Males call from open ground away from water, or along the water's edge. The call consists of a loud trill, repeated rapidly. Each trill consists of 10–15 pulses and is frequency-modulated. The dominant harmonic starts at 1 kHz, rising to 1.5 kHz, before dropping slightly at the end. The duration of each trill is 0.4–0.5 s. A second less emphasized harmonic rises to 3 kHz. West African frogs show some variation, with calls only 0.2 s long, with 8 pulses, and with a lower dominant frequency at 0.5 rising to 0.7 kHz.

BREEDING: These frogs breed during the summer rainy season. Amplexus is axillary. The eggs are 1 mm in diameter in 3-mm capsules. They are laid on water in short strings (75–200 mm long) that break up, permitting the eggs to float away. The eggs are whitish with a dark brown pole. The size of one clutch was counted as 3476.

TADPOLES: See the chapter on tadpoles.

NOTES: This species has been recorded breeding in rock pools. They occur with *Afrana angolensis* in Angola. Sexual maturity is reached 8–9 months after metamorphosis, when females may reach 59 mm. In West Africa the local villagers eat these frogs. The tadpoles are efficient insect predators, judging by the very high levels of dieldrin that accumulates in their tissues when their habitat is sprayed with 2% dieldrin to control mosquitoes! This species is reported to be capable of very long jumps and was once the holder of the long jump record in *Guinness Book of Records*, before the giant African *Conraua goliath* was available. They are preyed upon by the water snake *Lycodonomorphus mlanjensis*, the snake *Rhamphiophis oxyrhynchus rostratus*, the boomslang, vine snakes, and the water monitor *Varanus niloticus*. Maximum recorded longevity in captivity is 8 years 11 months. Perhaps two species, one from West Africa and one from eastern and southern Africa, are confused under one name.

KEY REFERENCES: Stewart 1967, Inger 1968, Passmore 1977a, Barbault & Rodriques 1978.

Many ridged frog
Ptychadena perplicata Laurent, 1964

The specific name *perplicata* means "many folds," referring to the dorsal skin folds that characterize this genus.

DESCRIPTION: These frogs are medium-sized, with the female holotype 33 mm long, resembling *P. guibei*. The snout is blunt, with nostrils closer to the snout than to the eye. Internarial distance is greater than the interorbital space. The tympanum is smaller than the eye. The distance between eye and tympanum is about one-third the eye diameter. Fingers and toes are without swellings. The tibia is more than half the body length. Webbing is reduced, with more than three phalanges of the fourth toe free of web. Inner and outer metatarsal tubercles are present, although the outer metatarsal tubercle is not well developed. The dorsal skin is smooth, but the skin folds are rough and the posterior face of the thigh is granular. A pale band runs from the top of the snout to the vent. There are six distinct dark bands, the middle pair running from the interorbital region to the vent, and the lateral pairs from the upper eyelid to the origin of the tibia. Color pattern is similar to that of *P. guibei*, with distinct dorsal spots. Pigmentation is barred on the lower jaw. The posterior face of the thigh is covered partly with longitudinal pale lines. The anterior face of the thigh and tarsus have dark crossbars.

DISTRIBUTION AND HABITAT (FIG. 271): This species is known from Angola and northern Zambia.

Fig. 271 *Ptychadena perplicata*

ADVERTISEMENT CALL: Unknown.

BREEDING: Unknown.

TADPOLES: Unknown.

NOTES: The coloration is also similar to that of *P. porosissima*.

KEY REFERENCE: Laurent 1964.

Grassland ridged frog
Ptychadena porosissima (Steindachner, 1867)
(Plate 21.5)

The specific name *porosissima* means "spotted."

DESCRIPTION: These are medium-sized frogs, with males up to 43 mm and females up to 49 mm long. The internarial distance is equal to the distance from nostril to tip of snout. Gular pouch slits end level with the lower edge of the arm insertion. Three phalanges of the fourth toe are free of web. Dorsal color is brown, with darker spots arranged along the dorsal skin ridges. A pale vertebral stripe is present, often with a lateral stripe on each side. The posterior face of the thigh has longitudinal rows of light spots. A pale tibial line is present.

DISTRIBUTION AND HABITAT (FIG. 272): They are widely distri-

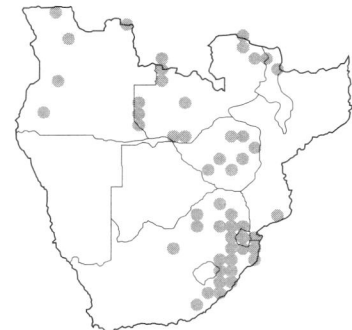

Fig. 272 *Ptychadena porosissima*

buted from Ethiopia to Eastern Cape Province of South Africa, in higher moist areas including forest.

ADVERTISEMENT CALL: Males call from beneath grass and other vegetation in shallow water. The calls are typically *Ptychadena*-like, a high-pitched short buzz, 0.1–0.2 s long, with dominant harmonics at 2 and 4 kHz. Each call consists of 10–12 pulses.

BREEDING: Breeding starts with the rainy season. The eggs are 1 mm in diameter in 5-mm capsules. The eggs float and are laid in shallow grassy pools.

TADPOLES: See the chapter on tadpoles.

NOTES: Recorded food items include earthworms, snails, arthropods, and other frogs. They are eaten by the ornate green snake *Philothamnus ornatus*.

KEY REFERENCES: Inger & Marx 1961, Wager 1965, Passmore 1977a.

Schilluk ridged frog
Ptychadena schillukorum Werner, 1907
(Plate 21.6)

This species is named for Schilluk, the area and people of the Sudan, west of the Nile between 9° and 11° north.
Nyamkandeli in Nyungwe.

Schilluk Ridged Frog

Fig. 273 *Ptychadena schillukorum*

DESCRIPTION: These are small frogs with short legs. Males may reach 48 mm and females 49 mm in length. Internarial distance is greater than the distance from nostril to tip of snout. Gular pouch slits end at the middle of the arm insertion. There is no row of tubercles under the fourth metatarsal. Webbing is reduced, with only two to three phalanges of the fourth toe free of web. Dorsal skin folds are not continuous from head to sacrum. The posterior face of the thigh usually has fine vermiculations. The lower jaw is marbled.

DISTRIBUTION AND HABITAT (FIG. 273): This species is found from West Africa to Ethiopia and south to Mozambique.

ADVERTISEMENT CALL: Males call while floating in a spread-eagled manner, from very dense vegetation at the edge of shallow pools. The call is a series of clicks at 1.7 kHz, the clicks being repeated at a rate of about 8/s.

BREEDING: Nothing is known about the breeding biology of this species.

TADPOLES: Unknown.

KEY REFERENCE: Channing 1993b.

Spotted ridged frog
Ptychadena subpunctata (Bocage, 1866)
(Plate 21.7)

The specific name *subpunctata* means "spotted underneath." Spotted frog, Bocage's grass frog.

DESCRIPTION: This is a large species, with males up to 55 mm and females up to 68 mm long. Interorbital distance is less than the distance from snout tip to nostril. Gular pouch slits end level with the middle or lower arm insertion. There is no row of tubercles under the fourth metatarsal. Webbing is extensive, with only one and a half to two phalanges of the fourth toe free of web. The top of the snout is light. A pale line runs along the upper surface of the tibia. The posterior face of the thigh has two or more dark longitudinal lines running from knee to knee. The lower surface is speckled.

DISTRIBUTION AND HABITAT (FIG. 274): This frog is known from Namibia, Botswana, Angola, Zambia, and southern Republic of the Congo. It is associated with deep permanent water in savannas.

ADVERTISEMENT CALL: Males call from the edge of deep pans. The call consists of soft croaks and loud clucks. The clucks are brief, with emphasized frequencies from 750 Hz to 3.5 kHz. Clucks may be uttered singly or in various combinations. The croaks are 230–380 ms long, with an emphasized harmonic at 800 Hz. There are less energetic, frequency-modulated harmonics rising from 1.2 and 1.9 kHz.

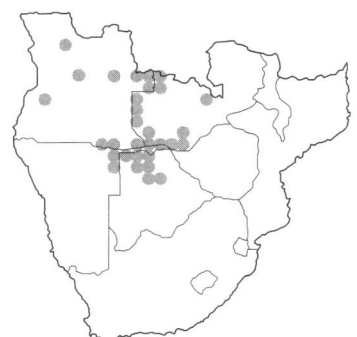

Fig. 274   *Ptychadena subpunctata*

The croaks are produced in rapid succession, interspersed with clucks. The pattern of these two components results in a call that is similar to that of many *Afrana* species.

BREEDING: Eggs are 1.2 mm in diameter within 3-mm capsules. They are scattered around in shallow water, with about 1 egg/cm^2. Clutch size is estimated at 1000, but it is difficult to count when the eggs are widely scattered over and between leaves.

TADPOLES: Unknown.

NOTES: This frog resembles *Afrana angolensis* in form, color patterns, behavior, and call. When disturbed, it escapes by jumping into water and then quickly jumping back onto land, often repeating the maneuver.

KEY REFERENCE: Channing & Griffin 1993.

Small ridged frog
Ptychadena taenioscelis Laurent, 1954
(Plate 21.8)

The specific name *taenioscelis* means "banded leg."
Spotted-throated ridged frog, dwarf grass frog. *Kazuázu* at the Luachimo River, *tchizunda* in Cameia.

DESCRIPTION: These are small frogs, with males up to 35 mm and females up to 40 mm long. Internarial distance is less than the distance from nostril to tip of snout. Gular pouch openings end at the middle of the arm insertion. There is no row of tubercles under the fourth metatarsal. Three phalanges of the fourth toe are free of webbing. A pair of dorsal skin folds extends onto snout. A pale ridge runs under the eye to the arm. The tympanum is smaller than the eye. Coloration is brown dorsally, with darker rectangular markings on a lighter background. There are three thin pale lines on the back. The posterior face of the thigh possesses longitudinal bands, one of which runs below the vent from knee to knee.

DISTRIBUTION AND HABITAT (FIG. 275): This species is distributed in a band across the continent from Tanzania and eastern South Africa to Angola, in grasslands.

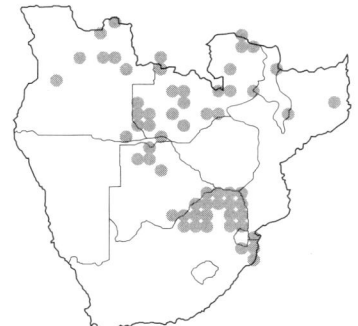

Fig. 275 *Ptychadena taenioscelis*

ADVERTISEMENT CALL: Males call from short flooded grass, sitting in water. The call is a rapid chirp, 0.1–0.3 s long, with dominant energy at 2.8–3.5 kHz. Each call consists of 22–25 rapid pulses. The pitch rises slightly during the call. Three to eight males congregate in calling units. Apart from the advertisement call, a chorus call (a harsher call probably used to space males) and a territorial call (a clucking uttered when males are within 200 mm of each other) are known.

BREEDING: Males call in the early evening, and amplexus follows a cautious creeping approach by the male. The amplexing pair deposits eggs over a 3-hour period, moving up to 8 m in the process. Two to ten eggs are deposited at a time, in shallow water where they sink.

TADPOLES: Unknown.

NOTES: The West African *Ptychadena pumilio* has been confused with *P. taenioscelis*, but the call of *P. pumilio* is quite different.

KEY REFERENCES: Laurent 1964, Passmore 1976.

Upemba ridged frog
Ptychadena upembae (Schmidt & Inger, 1959)
(Plate 22.1)

Upemba Ridged Frog

The specific name *upembae* refers to the Upemba National Park, in the Democratic Republic of the Congo, where the species was first discovered.

DESCRIPTION: These are medium-sized frogs, with males up to 44 mm and females up to 51 mm long. Internarial distance is equal to distance from snout tip to nostril. Gular pouch openings end level with the lower edge of arm insertion. A row of tubercles is found under the fourth metatarsal. Three phalanges of the fourth toe are free of web. A light vertebral stripe is present. Darker spots are arranged along the longitudinal skin ridges. A large white dorsolateral fold runs from the tympanum almost to the top of the leg. There is no light line on the upper surface of the tibia. A dark longitudinal band is present on the posterior face of the thigh, at least on one leg.

DISTRIBUTION AND HABITAT (FIG. 276): This species is known from Mozambique, Malawi, Zambia, the Democratic Republic of the Congo, and Angola.

ADVERTISEMENT CALL: Males call from the base of grass tussocks in deep flooded areas. The call is a harsh trill, 0.3 s long, with a pulse rate of 40/s. The call rises to a peak with emphasized harmonics at 1.6 and 3.5 kHz, before tapering off.

Fig. 276 *Ptychadena upembae*

BREEDING: No details of the breeding biology are available.

TADPOLES: Unknown.

NOTES: These frogs escape disturbance by jumping away from water into vegetation.

KEY REFERENCE: Stewart 1967.

Udzungwa ridged frog
Ptychadena uzungwensis (Loveridge, 1932)
(Plate 22.2)

The name *uzungwensis* refers to the Udzungwa Mountains, a forested region of southern Tanzania renowned for its high biological diversity.
Uzungwe grass frog.

DESCRIPTION: These are medium-sized frogs, with males up to 42 mm and females up to 48 mm long. The internarial distance is less than the distance from nostril to tip of snout. Gular pouch slits end at the middle of the arm insertion. There is a row of tubercles under the fourth metatarsal, and three phalanges of the fourth toe are free of web. A pair of short skin folds runs from the upper eyelid toward the snout. Ridges on the snout are continuous with the paravertebral ridges. A light vertebral stripe is present, and the outer dorsolateral fold is a white ridge. The posterior face of the thigh has a row of light spots, although sometimes this is replaced by a light band. The dorsal pattern consists of dark spots along the skin ridges, which may fuse in some individuals and almost obscure the ground color. The underside is white, while the throat and groin of males are deep yellow.

DISTRIBUTION AND HABITAT (FIG. 277): These frogs are known to occur from Rwanda southward to Angola and northern South Africa, in high-altitude grasslands.

ADVERTISEMENT CALL: Males call from seepages in shallow water. The call is a typical trill, with males calling antiphonally.

BREEDING: Unknown.

Udzungwa Ridged Frog

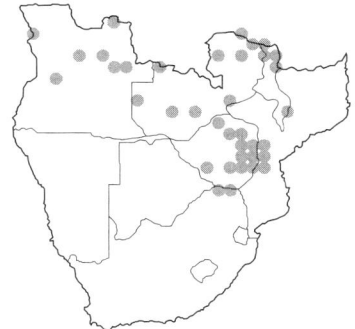

Fig. 277 *Ptychadena uzungwensis*

TADPOLES: Unknown.

NOTES: These frogs have been found near shallow pools on the Chimanimani Mountains. They are known to eat snails, arthropods, and other frogs. Individuals may show a defensive behavior when captured, by bowing the body, stiffening and straightening the hind legs, and squeaking.

KEY REFERENCE: Stewart & Wilson 1966.

Bullfrogs—Genus *Pyxicephalus*

This genus includes the largest frog in the area. The lower jaw has two sharp cusps. Bullfrogs are a food source to many people, after they emerge following heavy rain. Two species are recognized in this area.

KEY TO THE SPECIES

1. Distance between tympanum and eye equal to eye width (Fig. 278)
Pyxicephalus edulis

Fig. 278 Tympanum-eye distance compared to eye width

1b. Distance between tympanum and eye greater than eye width
(Fig. 279) *Pyxicephalus adspersus*

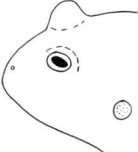

Fig. 279 Tympanum-eye distance compared to eye width

African bullfrog
Pyxicephalus adspersus Tschudi, 1838
(Plates 22.3, 22.4)

The specific name *adspersus* means "sprinkled" (with markings). Giant bullfrog, Tschudi's African bullfrog. *Grabfrosch, Ochsenfrosch, Gespenkelter Grabfrosch* in German; *isanyankomo* ("sucking a cow"), *indubule, ikuxla* in Shangaan; *letlametlo* (plural *matlametlo*) in Pedi and Setswana, who also use the name *mekadi* for the fat of the bullfrog, a local delicacy; *mafina* in Humbe in Angola; *lentsoeta* in Sesuto; *tshetshe*, or *dzetshe* in Kalanga; *groot brulpadda* in Afrikaans.

DESCRIPTION: This very large robust frog, with its weight recorded at 1.075 kg, is unmistakable by its size and the presence of two razor-sharp projections on the lower jaw. The male may grow up to 230 mm, with a jaw 90 mm wide. The female is smaller than the male. There is no outer metatarsal tubercle, and the inner metatarsal tubercle is spade-like. The distance between the eye and the tympanum is greater than the width of the tympanum. The back has distinct longitudinal skin folds. Coloration is variable, mostly with a brown or dark green background, but a bright green component is usually present. Even blue patterns are known. The side of the body around the arm is often deep yellow, especially in breeding males. The newly metamorphosed juvenile is bright green with a vertebral stripe.

DISTRIBUTION AND HABITAT (FIG. 280): The large bullfrog is widely distributed in the drier savannas, reaching the northeastern coastal plain. It is found wherever there are large pans that fill with water during the rains.

African Bullfrog

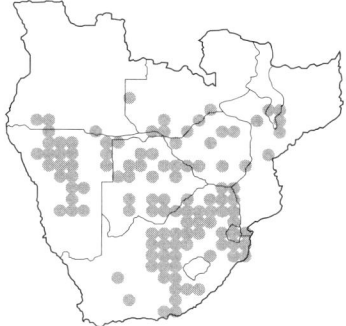

Fig. 280 *Pyxicephalus adspersus*

ADVERTISEMENT CALL: The male calls from shallow water. The very low-pitched "whoop" call resembles the bellowing of cattle, hence, the name *bullfrog*. The call is quite soft for a large frog and is up to 2.0 s long, with an emphasized harmonic between 200 and 250 Hz. The males utter a snorting call when fighting, but this is not always distinct.

BREEDING: Unlike most frogs, this bullfrog only emerges and starts breeding after exceptionally heavy rain, usually well after the start of the season. Breeding is initiated by 65 mm of rain over the previous day or two. Breeding takes place during daytime, with spawning happening from 7h00min through to 16h00min. There are two slightly different breeding strategies, depending on the age of the male. Younger males are not as aggressive as the full-grown males.

Younger (smaller) males congregate in a small area, perhaps only 1 or 2 m^2, in shallow water. The larger males occupy the center of these breeding arenas or leks and attempt to chase off other males. A female approaches the group of males by swimming along at the surface until she is within 3 m or so of the group of males. The female then dives and reappears on the surface in the middle of the male group. She is soon grasped by one of the large males, and mating ensues. Eggs are laid in the shallow edge of the pond, but fertilization takes place above water level—the female arches her back to position her vent above the surface. The eggs are fertilized before they reach the water. The spent female then shakes her head from side to side, and the clasping male releases her. Eggs are

1.1–1.3 mm in diameter, inside 4-mm capsules. The females are attracted to the same area where the males are calling and chasing one another. All egg laying occurs in this small area, and all the tadpoles presumably hatch together, ready to form the characteristic large schools.

The full-grown males are much more aggressive. The males fight, causing injury and even killing one another. The dominant male attempts to prevent other males from participating in breeding. Most of the females are mated by the dominant male, in his territory. This dominant male remains in the pool, and he is the individual that takes care of the tadpoles (see below).

TADPOLES: See the chapter on tadpoles.

PARENTAL CARE: An adult male is often found near the eggs, and in or near a school of tadpoles. Much speculation was generated about whether the male was eating the tadpoles or whether the male was positioned to care for the young by attacking predators. For example, a bullfrog was reported to have attacked a human bending down to touch the tadpoles. Perhaps a large bullfrog is just naturally belligerent. However, the dominant male remains in the pool after breeding and may take care of the tadpoles. Schools of tadpoles that were isolated at the edges of a drying pond were able to reach the main body of water by following a channel dug by the attendant male. When investigators built an earth dam around a tadpole school, the male would break a channel through the wall to release the tadpoles. This provides experimental evidence of parental care. Channels over 15 m long are known.

NOTES: Newly metamorphosed frogs eat anything that moves, even siblings. It is not uncommon to find two newly emerged bullfrogs swallowing a third, one from each end! The adult is known to eat bullfrog tadpoles and young frogs. Bullfrogs are voracious, with one recorded eating 17 young rinkhals (spitting cobras) and a small chicken. They are known to feed on termites, red toads *Schismaderma carens*, river frogs *Afrana*, snout-burrowers *Hemisus*, and toads *Bufo*. A 170-mm frog was able to eat large snakes up to 760 mm long, by holding the snake near the head, centering the snake with the fore limbs and fingers, and then lunging forward with a wide gape. They eat a lot and they grow rapidly.

Like other frogs that spend the dry season underground, the bullfrog forms a cocoon of old skin around itself, which serves as waterproofing. The adults have been found during the dry season buried under the sand of a dry riverbed. It reaches full size after 28 years, and the maximum longevity for an African bullfrog in captivity was estimated at 45 years.

It is eaten by various peoples in Africa, including the Batswana, the Sena of Port Herald District, and the bushmen. Bullfrogs have long been used as food in Africa, as remains of bullfrogs have been found at Stone Age sites in Namibia.

Birds are major predators of bullfrogs. Records of predators include the pink backed pelican, saddlebill, white headed vulture, yellow billed kite, tawny eagle, fish eagle, bateleur, lesser spotted eagle, and the yellow billed egret. Turtles *Pelusios* prey on tadpoles, holding them in their jaws and ripping them with clawed fore limbs. Tadpoles are also preyed upon by the Nile monitor *Varanus niloticus*, which eats mouthfuls of swarming tadpoles in shallow water.

Young juveniles will approach to attack anything small enough to eat, but if faced with something too large, will chirp and retreat.

Its conservation status is near threatened.

KEY REFERENCES: Balinsky & Balinsky 1954, Grobler 1972, Loveridge 1979, Cruz-Uribe & Klein 1982/83, Paukstis & Reinbold 1984, Kok et al. 1989, Van Wyk et al. 1991, Channing, Passmore, and Du Preez 1994.

Edible bullfrog
Pyxicephalus edulis Peters, 1854
(Plate 22.5)

The specific name *edulis* refers to the fact that this species is eaten by humans.
Beira bullfrog, Peters' bullfrog, eastern burrowing-bullfrog. Many of the local names apply to both species of bullfrogs: *Tess* in Sena and Ndau; *thesi* in Chikwawa, Cewa, and Sena; *lithesi* in Yao; *mafima* at Humbe; *sesi* in Nyungwe; *kwee* in Khoisan (Hietsware); *txe* in !Kung.

DESCRIPTION: This is a large robust frog, up to 120mm long. It resembles a small African bullfrog but can be distinguished from it

Fig. 281 *Pyxicephalus edulis*

by the narrower head (some females resembling large river frogs). The back does not have continuous elongated longitudinal folds, although it may be rough with short folds or bumps. The tympanum is placed about one eye width behind the eye. The breeding male is bright green, while the female is duller and brownish. The back has dark spots, often with a pale vertebral stripe.

DISTRIBUTION AND HABITAT (FIG. 281): This species is known mostly from the eastern coastal plain, from northern South Africa to Kenya. It is found in marshy areas and occurs together with the African bullfrog *P. adspersus*, for example, at Nylsvlei in South Africa and at Beira in Mozambique. Further fieldwork is required to determine the range of this species.

ADVERTISEMENT CALL: The male calls at night after even light rain early in the season. The call sounds like the barking of a small dog. The male calls from vegetation in the water, and his white vocal pouch flashes with reflected moonlight as he calls. The call is short, 0.19 s, and frequency-modulated, with the highest frequencies reached in the middle of the call. The emphasized harmonic reaches 450–600 Hz, measured at the peak, typically with closely spaced lower and higher harmonics present.

BREEDING: Breeding takes place in shallow water early in the rainy season. The frogs breed at night after rain, and males may be found

Edible Bullfrog

in amplexus with the smaller females throughout the pond. No leks are formed. Eggs are scattered.

TADPOLES: Unknown.

NOTES: This frog is well known by the local tribes in Mozambique. Many people eat both species of bullfrog and believe that the smaller edible bullfrog *P. edulis* that is present early in the season grows into the large African bullfrog *P. adspersus*, which is only found later in the season after heavy rains.

KEY REFERENCE: Channing, Passmore, and Du Preez 1994.

Stream Frogs—Genus *Strongylopus*

This genus is characterized by extremely long toes and reduced webbing. All the species are able to move rapidly through grass.

KEY TO THE SPECIES
This genus is fairly variable, so more than one specimen should be keyed out to confirm the species identification.

1a. More than two phalanges of fourth toe free of web   3
1b. Less than two phalanges of fourth toe free of web   2

2a. Foot length less than two and a half times head width
                                         Strongylopus hymenopus
2b. Foot length more than two and a half times head width
                                         Strongylopus wageri

3a. Head narrow, less than 35% of SVL   4
3b. Head wider, more than 35% of SVL   5

4a. Dark paravertebral stripes paired, not continuous
                                         Strongylopus bonaespei
4b. Dark paravertebral stripes distinct, continuous   7

5a. Foot length less than twice the head width, snout sharp
                                         Strongylopus springbokensis
5b. Foot length more than twice the head width   6

6a. Head width less than 84% of fourth toe length
             Strongylopus rhodesianus
6b. Head width more than 84% of fourth toe length
               Strongylopus grayii

7a. Head width–tibia length ratio more than 52%
              Strongylopus fuelleborni
7b. Head width–tibia length ratio less than 52%
               Strongylopus fasciatus

Banded stream frog
Strongylopus bonaespei (Dubois, 1980)
(Plate 22.6)

The specific name *bonaespei* is Latin for the Cape of Good Hope. Cape grass frog, Jonkersberg frog.

DESCRIPTION: This slender frog has a sharp snout. The male reaches 35 mm in length. The fourth toe is very long, extending past the hand when the species is sitting. Fine longitudinal skin ridges are present. A small projection, called a *coruncle*, is seen at the front of the eye where the upper lid joins. Back patterns are variable. Generally these consist of dark and light longitudinal stripes on the back, in gold and browns, with barred markings on the thigh. A white line runs from below the eye, below the tympanum to the arm.

DISTRIBUTION AND HABITAT (FIG. 282): This species occurs on the mountains of the southwestern tip of Africa. It lives in open grasslands.

ADVERTISEMENT CALL: The male calls from seepage areas and from the edge of small pools. The call consists of a squawk or two, followed by a fast cackle. The squawk is 0.1 s long, and each note of the cackle is 0.05 s long. The emphasized frequency is around 2.5 kHz.

BREEDING: This frog breeds from winter (June) to early summer. A clutch of 39 eggs was recorded on waterlogged moss and earth, 60 mm from the water's edge. The eggs are laid singly or in 60–70-mm rows. Each egg is encased in a 7-mm capsule.

Striped Stream Frog

Fig. 282 *Strongylopus bonaespei*

TADPOLES: Unknown.

NOTES: This species is partly diurnal. The skin is known to contain bradykinins, substances that mimic mammalian hormones and affect the heart rate and blood pressure. These serve as a defense against small mammal predators, by making them ill, but not killing them, so they can learn that frogs are unpleasant to eat, and hopefully teach this to their young.

KEY REFERENCES: Greig et al. 1979, Roseghini et al. 1988 (as *Rana montana*).

Striped stream frog
Strongylopus fasciatus (Smith, 1849)
(Plate 22.7)

The specific name *fasciatus* refers to the stripes on the back.
Striped long-toed frog, striped frog, long-toed frog. *Gestreepte langtoonpadda* in Afrikaans.

DESCRIPTION: The male is up to 37mm and the female up to 50mm long. It is slender with a sharp head. Head width-tibia length ratio is less than 52%. The tympanum is more than half of the eye diameter. Webbing is present only at the base of the toes. The extreme length of the toes and feet is characteristic of this species, along with the distinctive markings. These consist of a yellow to orange band

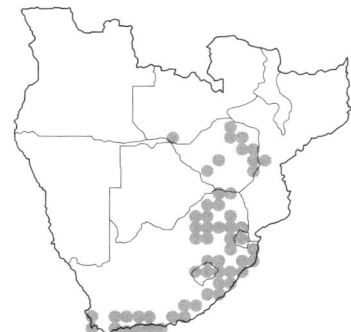

Fig. 283 *Strongylopus fasciatus*

down the back, bordered by dark stripes, on a silvery background. The back is smooth, except for ridges that underlie the dark stripes either side of the midline. Other longitudinal stripes may be divided or broken up. The thigh is also striped lengthwise.

DISTRIBUTION AND HABITAT (FIG. 283): This frog is known from Southern South Africa, along the east coast to Zimbabwe, Mozambique, and Zambia. It is associated with grasslands.

ADVERTISEMENT CALL: The male calls from within grass or other vegetation. The call is a single, short, high-pitched note that may be repeated. A chorus gives a rippling effect. Each note has a duration of 0.02 s, with maximum energy at 3.3–3.6 kHz. The ripple may continue for up to 8 s.

BREEDING: This frog breeds throughout the year. Eggs are 1.4 mm in diameter within 5-mm capsules. They are laid in shallow grassy pools and streams. They become covered with sand particles and are difficult to see.

TADPOLES: See the chapter on tadpoles.

KEY REFERENCE: Greig et al. 1979 (as *Rana fasciata*).

Fülleborn's stream frog
Strongylopus fuelleborni (Nieden, 1910)
(Plate 22.8)

Fülleborn's Stream Frog

This frog was named for Friedrich Fülleborn, a physician and naturalist in German East Africa, now Tanzania.
Long-toed grass frog.

DESCRIPTION: The male is up to 40 mm and the female up to 53 mm long. It is a slender frog with very long toes, with characteristic longitudinal markings on a yellow background. The head width–tibia length ratio is more than 52%. The skin is smooth, with slight ridges under the dark bands. Webbing is nearly absent, with only a little webbing at the base of the toes. A dark band passes from the snout, backward through the eye to the arm. Malawian frogs have a dark longitudinal bar on the front of the upper arm. The back of the thigh is without markings.

DISTRIBUTION AND HABITAT (FIG. 284): This species is found on the highlands of Malawi and the mountains of southern Tanzania. It occurs in grasslands.

ADVERTISEMENT CALL: This species is reported calling from October until July on the Nyika plateau. It may call during the day in winter. The call is similar to that of the striped stream frog *S. fasciatus*, being a short high-pitched note. However, the pitch is lower, with dominant energy at 2.8 kHz. The duration of each note is about 0.025 s.

Fig. 284 *Strongylopus fuelleborni*

BREEDING: Eggs are laid in clusters just above water level underneath dense vegetation, from mid-February to mid-March in Malawi. There are 1–14 eggs in each cluster. Each egg is 2–3 mm in diameter within a firm 4–6.5-mm capsule. The capsules remain firm even after the tadpoles hatch and enter the water. See the description of terrestrial development in the Namaqua stream frog *S. springbokensis*.

TADPOLES: Unknown.

NOTES: It is active throughout the year in Malawi.

KEY REFERENCES: Stewart 1967, Stevens 1974 (as *Rana fasciata fuelleborni*).

Gray's stream frog
Strongylopus grayii (Smith, 1849)
(Plate 23.1)

This frog was named for John Gray of the Natural History Museum in London.
Gray's frog, clicking stream frog, spotted stream frog, Gray's spotted frog. *Klik-langtoonpadda* in Afrikaans.

DESCRIPTION: The male grows to 35 mm and the female, up to 64 mm. The toes are long, with very little webbing. Head width is more than 84% of fourth toe length. The pattern on the back is typically a series of small darker markings on a brown background. However, a broad pale or reddish stripe is also a common variant.

DISTRIBUTION AND HABITAT (FIG. 285): It occurs in the south and east of South Africa, south of the Limpopo River. Animals were released in 1855 on the island of St. Helena by Miss Phoebe Moss, from specimens collected in South Africa. This species is very tolerant of poor-quality water and will breed in flooded refuse pits and even within the spray zone along the coast.

ADVERTISEMENT CALL: Calling starts with onset of cold weather on the Cape peninsula, before the winter rains. The male calls from

Drakensberg Stream Frog

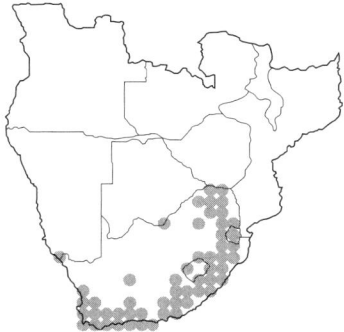

Fig. 285 *Strongylopus grayii*

the base of vegetation near small puddles. The call is a short (6-ms) click, with dominant energy around 2.3 kHz.

BREEDING: This species spawns in June and July during the winter rains. The eggs are laid singly or in small groups, usually just above water level in damp places. Often the eggs are laid in crevices under rocks or below leaves. Clutch size is 250–350 eggs. Each egg is in a capsule 4 mm in diameter. Hatching into tadpoles can be arrested by dry weather.

TADPOLES: See the chapter on tadpoles.

NOTES: This species calls during winter. Along the southern coast, calling is initiated by a drop in temperature rather than rainfall. Like other species of this genus, the eggs can remain viable on damp soil, with development arrested, awaiting the rise of the water level after rains. The eggs can remain for 51 days before being placed in water, at which time the tadpoles hatch and continue development. The skin contains bradykinins, which act by making small mammal predators feel ill, to deter them from eating frogs.

KEY REFERENCES: de Villiers 1929a, Barbour 1934, Roseghini et al. 1988 (as *Rana grayii*).

Drakensberg stream frog
Strongylopus hymenopus (Boulenger, 1920)
(Plate 23.2)

The specific name *hymenopus* refers to the webbed feet.
Berg stream frog, Natal Drakensberg frog. *Drakensberg-langtoonpadda* in Afrikaans.

DESCRIPTION: The male grows to 60 mm in length. The toes are only slightly webbed, but the webbing is variable, with two to three segments of the fourth toe free. The toes are not as long as the toes of other species of the genus. Foot length less than two and a half times head width. They do not pass the hand when the frog is sitting. The snout is rounded, and the back is covered with fine warts. The back has darker speckles on a brown background, and the legs are barred.

DISTRIBUTION AND HABITAT (FIG. 286): This frog is known from the slopes and plateau of the Drakensberg Mountains, where it frequents rocky stream banks.

ADVERTISEMENT CALL: The call is a rough trill, consisting of 1 or more notes, strung together in various combinations. The duration varies from 1 pulse (7.5 ms) to a sequence of pulses of 53 ms. It appears that the calls get longer as more males join the chorus. The mean pulse rate is 209/s, with an emphasized harmonic between 0.9 and 1.2 kHz.

Fig. 286 *Strongylopus hymenopus*

BREEDING: It breeds in or near mountain streams. Eggs are attached to rock in flowing water, or deposited away from the current in shallow pools. Clutch size is 200–500, with the eggs sometimes laid in groups of 7–15. The eggs are large, with capsules up to 10 mm.

TADPOLES: See the chapter on tadpoles.

NOTES: It has been suggested that two species from the Drakensberg are being confused under the name *S. hymenopus*. This suggestion was based on finding two distinct kinds of tadpoles. Further fieldwork is required.

KEY REFERENCES: Channing 1979, Wager 1986 (as *Rana hymenopus*).

Chimanimani stream frog
Strongylopus rhodesianus (Hewitt, 1937)
(Plate 23.3)

The specific name refers to Rhodesia, now Zimbabwe.
Hewitt's long-toed frog.

DESCRIPTION: This is a medium-sized frog, with the female up to 50 mm long. It is slender with long toes and reduced webbing. Head width is less than 84% of fourth toe length. The color pattern is often uniform brown or orange dorsally, although thin dark longitudinal lines are common.

DISTRIBUTION AND HABITAT (FIG. 287): This species occurs on the eastern highlands of Zimbabwe and the Gorongoza Mountain in Mozambique. It is found in dense grass near streams and rivers.

ADVERTISEMENT CALL: The call is a high-pitched trill, consisting of about 6 notes. The duration of the call is around 0.4 s, at a pulse rate of 14/s. Emphasized frequency is 3.2 kHz.

BREEDING: Unknown.

TADPOLES: See the chapter on tadpoles.

Fig. 287 *Strongylopus rhodesianus*

KEY REFERENCE: Lambiris 1985a (as *Strongylopus grayi rhodesianus*).

Namaqua stream frog
Strongylopus springbokensis Channing, 1986
(Plate 23.4)

This species was named for the town of Springbok in Namaqualand. Springbok frog.

DESCRIPTION: This frog is similar in color pattern and overall shape to Gray's stream frog *S. grayii*. The back is yellowish brown, with darker markings edged with dark brown. A narrow vertebral stripe is present in many specimens. The snout is sharper in profile than that of Gray's stream frog. The foot length is less than twice the head width. A breeding male has small sharp spines along the back of the legs, and the fingers develop a paddle-like appearance due to the development of a margin of web.

DISTRIBUTION AND HABITAT (FIG. 288): This frog is confined to the mountainous areas of Namaqualand, in South Africa, north of the Knersvlakte and south of the Gariep River. It is able to survive the harsh climate by remaining near springs and seeps.

ADVERTISEMENT CALL: The male calls from a concealed site, usually some distance from water. The call consists of a series of 2–7 notes. Each note has a duration of 0.11 s, with a pulse rate of 185/s

Namaqua Stream Frog

Fig. 288 *Strongylopus springbokensis*

and emphasized frequencies of 0.8, 2.6, and 3.6 kHz. The total duration of the call varies from 0.22 (2 notes) to 1.17 s (7 notes). Two other calls are known. The aggression call is produced when one calling male gets too close to another calling male. It consists of a single sharp note with emphasized harmonics from 0.4 to 1.8 kHz. The male release call consists of a long series of squeaking calls that may last up to 3 s.

BREEDING: Breeding begins at the start of the winter rains. Eggs are laid above water level, often under rocks, or otherwise concealed in crevices. The calling male remains with the eggs in tunnels in vegetation, in cracks in rock, or inside old rodent burrows, with hundreds of eggs lining the walls and roof. The eggs develop to the stage when the tadpoles' eyes and tail are well formed, without hatching. They remain at that stage until they are flooded, presumably by rising water or a very heavy rainfall. The tadpoles then hatch rapidly and continue their development in the water.

TADPOLES: See the chapter on tadpoles.

NOTES: Rain can be infrequent in the arid areas of Namaqualand. This species is able to breed successfully by depositing eggs out of water. The eggs develop, but the tadpoles remain within the eggs until they come into contact with water. This is an unusual but effective strategy to synchronize tadpole development with the short time that water may be in the pools.

One of the disadvantages of a life restricted to small isolated pools is that genetic defects can become established in the population. A survey of one such permanent spring in Namaqualand showed that 13 adults were resident, of which 2 were blind in the left eye. Follow-up studies will be necessary to determine if this was a genetic effect or merely the results of coincidental accidents.

KEY REFERENCE: Channing 1986.

Wager's stream frog
Strongylopus wageri (Wager, 1961)
(Plate 23.5)

The specific name refers to the collector, V. A. Wager, a plant pathologist and naturalist who studied many South African frog species. Wager's frog, plain stream frog, Natal uplands frog. *Gewone langtoonpadda* in Afrikaans.

DESCRIPTION: This frog grows to 48 mm. The toes are long, with three segments of the fourth toe free of web. Foot length is more than two and a half times head width. The back is generally without markings, being a plain reddish brown to green. A characteristic broad black stripe runs from the nostril, through the eye, and back to the arm. In many animals this stripe continues behind the arm, although it is less distinct. A white line borders the upper lip.

DISTRIBUTION AND HABITAT (FIG. 289): This species is known from the foothills and high slopes of the Drakensberg Mountains. It is a forest frog at lower altitudes, and occurs in grassland on the mountains.

ADVERTISEMENT CALL: The quiet call consists of a series of notes, repeated at a rate of 14/s. Each note is 0.05 s long, with frequency-modulated harmonics, rising rapidly. Mean emphasized harmonics are at 1.5 and 2.1 kHz, but these harmonics rise in pitch from 1.2 to 1.6 kHz and from 1.6 to 2.3 kHz. The male can call while submerged.

BREEDING: Eggs are laid in clutches of 120–250, sometimes in smaller batches. The eggs are attached to vegetation, frequently to overhanging branches or stems that are touching the water. Eggs

Fig. 289   *Strongylopus wageri*

are 2.8 mm in diameter within 6-mm capsules and hatch after 10 days.

TADPOLES: See the chapter on tadpoles.

NOTES: Breeding occurs during the dry winter or autumn when pools have stabilized. The areas where this frog breeds are subjected to the scouring action of floods during the rainy season. This species is associated with the Natal ghost frog *Heleophryne natalensis*. Its conservation status is least concern.

KEY REFERENCES: Wager 1986 (as *Rana wageri*), Boycott 1987.

Sand Frogs—Genus *Tomopterna*

This is a genus of small, robust, burrowing frogs, often found burrowed in sandy riverbeds. They are adapted for burrowing by possessing a large flattened flange on the heel that enables them to rapidly burrow backward into the ground. Identification of these frogs is not easy, and calls are probably the most reliable means of identifying some species. The genus is present throughout the subcontinent, with some populations even able to exist in the Namib Desert. A number of undescribed species are not included here. Many of these come from north of South Africa, and identifications in these countries should be particularly cautious and must be based on call analysis or DNA sequences.

KEY TO THE SPECIES

1a. Outer metatarsal tubercle distinctly elevated (Fig. 290)
   Tomopterna delalandii or *Tomopterna tandyi*
1b. Outer metatarsal tubercle small or absent   2

Fig. 290   Outer metatarsal tubercle

2a. Inner metatarsal tubercle greater than 140% the length of second toe (Fig. 291)   3
2b. Inner metatarsal tubercle less than 120% the length of second toe
   5

Fig. 291   Inner metatarsal tubercle

3a. Webbing reaching middle tubercle below fourth toe and outer tubercle of fifth (Fig. 292)   *Tomopterna marmorata*
3b. Webbing not as extensive   4

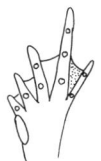

Fig. 292   Webbing

4a. Subarticular tubercles of first finger single
   Tomopterna cryptotis
4b. Proximal tubercles of first finger double (Fig. 293)
   Tomopterna krugerensis

Cryptic Sand Frog

Fig. 293   Double tubercle

5a. Webbing just passing the inner metatarsal tubercle of fourth toe, not reaching middle tubercle   *Tomopterna tuberculosa*
5b. Webbing reaching middle tubercle beneath fourth toe (Fig. 294)
Tomopterna natalensis

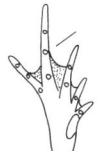

Fig. 294   Webbing

Cryptic sand frog
Tomopterna cryptotis (Boulenger, 1907)
(Plate 23.6)

The specific name *cryptotis* means "hidden ear," as the tympanum is difficult to see.
Tremolo sand frog, pyxie, striped pyxie, Catequero bullfrog. *Klein Grabfrosch* in German, *trillersandpadda* in Afrikaans.

DESCRIPTION: This is a small, robust frog, with the male up to 45 mm and the female up to 58 mm in length. The length of the tibia is equal to the head width. A glandular ridge is present below the tympanum. The inner metatarsal tubercle, used for digging, is flattened and large. Up to three and a half segments of the fourth toe are free of webbing. The subarticular tubercles of the first finger are single. The back is variable, with various lighter and darker markings. Grays, reds, and white are common colors. A thin vertebral stripe is sometimes present, and a lighter head patch is common.

DISTRIBUTION AND HABITAT (FIG. 295): This species occurs in the central highlands of South Africa and in Angola, Zambia, Malawi,

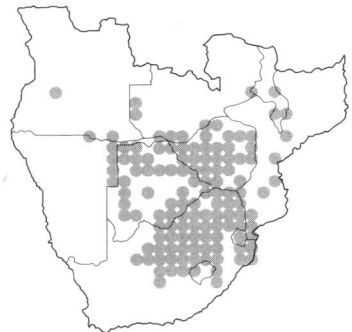

Fig. 295 *Tomopterna cryptotis*

Mozambique, Namibia, Botswana, Zimbabwe, Swaziland, and Lesotho. Due to confusion with *T. tandyi*, the extent of its distribution is unknown. It is associated with sandy soils and occurs along drainage lines.

ADVERTISEMENT CALL: The male calls from the edge of temporary pools. Often these are muddy, and the frogs sit on the mud at the water's edge. The call is a long series of short notes. The emphasized harmonics are 3.2–3.7 kHz. Each note is 0.03 s long, and the call rate is 10–12/s.

BREEDING: The eggs are laid singly in shallow water. Clutch size is 2000–3000. Each egg is 1.5 mm, in a 3-mm capsule.

TADPOLES: See the chapter on tadpoles.

NOTES: It is mostly impossible to distinguish this species from the knocking sand frog or Tandy's sand frog, unless the calls have been heard. Known predators include the hammerkop and the barn owl. The tadpole is preyed upon by the fishing spider. Adults may retreat into termite mounds during the day.

KEY REFERENCE: Wager 1986.

Delalande's sand frog
Tomopterna delalandii (Tschudi, 1838)
(Plate 23.7)

Delalande's Sand Frog

This species was named for Pierre-Antoine Delalande, a French naturalist and explorer. He was the son of an employee of the Natural History Museum in Paris and made three trips to the Cape.
Delalande's dwarf bullfrog, Cape sand frog, Delalande's frog, African bullfrog, Delaland's burrowing frog.

DESCRIPTION: This is a small robust frog, with the female up to 50 mm long. The arms and legs are short but well built, and the enlarged metatarsal tubercle is flattened and used for digging. Three segments of the fourth toe are free of webbing. The row of glands below the tympanum are not fused to form a ridge. The background color is gray, with darker and lighter patches. There is often a light patch in the head region. A pale vertebral stripe is usually present, with thin pale stripes on either side.

DISTRIBUTION AND HABITAT (FIG. 296): This species is known from the Cape peninsula eastward to St. Francis Bay, and northward to Springbok in Namaqualand. It occurs in sandy flat areas.

ADVERTISEMENT CALL: The male calls from muddy banks at the edge of temporary water bodies, although it also calls and breeds along watercourses. The call is a series of short notes, like many others in this genus. Each note is about 0.025 s long, with a 0.2-s

Fig. 296 *Tomopterna delalandii*

interval. The emphasized frequencies are 1.9–2.3 kHz. The call is lower-pitched than that of adjacent species.

BREEDING: Breeding takes place during winter in the winter rainfall area and during summer in the summer rainfall areas. At the southern tip of Africa, various populations may breed from June to October, with calling heard through to summer. Eggs are laid from June to August in the winter rainfall area. The eggs are deposited in small, slimy masses, or singly with joined capsules. The eggs have a strongly disagreeable odor. The clutch size is 2500.

TADPOLES: See the chapter on tadpoles.

NOTES: Specimens have been found hiding in a molehill during the day. The maximum recorded longevity in captivity is 7 years 7 months.

KEY REFERENCE: Power 1927b (as *Pyxicephalus delalandi*).

Knocking sand frog
Tomopterna krugerensis Passmore & Carruthers, 1975
(Plate 23.8)

This frog was named for the Kruger National Park, where it was first discovered.
Sandveld pyxie, Kruger bullfrog.

DESCRIPTION: The male grows up to 51 mm and the female, up to 58 mm SVL. It is robust, with a large, flattened inner metatarsal tubercle. The head width is equal to the tibia length. A glandular ridge runs below the tympanum. The proximal tubercles of the first finger are double, or at least divided. Up to three and a half segments of the fourth toe are free of web. In the field, calling males are similarly patterned to the cryptic sand frog, although they are slightly larger. Coloration is variable, with grays, browns, and white predominating. Vertebral stripes are not as common as in the other species.

DISTRIBUTION AND HABITAT (FIG. 297): This species is found in a broad belt from southern Mozambique and northeastern South

Marbled Sand Frog

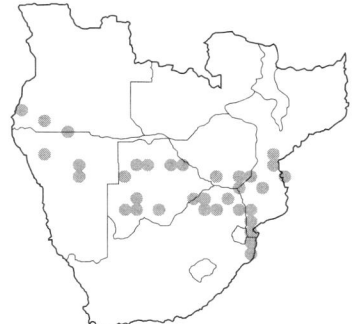

Fig. 297 *Tomopterna krugerensis*

Africa, through Botswana to Namibia and Angola. It occurs in sandy savannas. The distribution of this frog is not yet fully known.

ADVERTISEMENT CALL: The call of this species is quite different from all other calls in this genus. It is a loud knocking. Each note is 0.01 s long, with the emphasized frequency at 2.4 kHz.

BREEDING: Clutch size is 5000. The eggs are 1.2 mm in diameter, in 3-mm capsules. They are creamy yellow.

TADPOLES: Unknown.

KEY REFERENCE: Passmore & Carruthers 1975.

Marbled sand frog
Tomopterna marmorata (Peters, 1854)
(Plate 24.1)

The specific name refers to the marbled pattern on the back.
Marmorate pyxie, Mozambique dwarf bullfrog, russet-backed sand frog, marbled bullfrog.

DESCRIPTION: This medium-sized, robust, frog has a prominent flange on the heel. The male grows to 45 mm and the female, to 55 mm. Webbing is moderate, reaching the middle tubercle below the fourth toe, with three segments of the fourth toe free of web. A glandular ridge below the tympanum is absent. Coloration is variable,

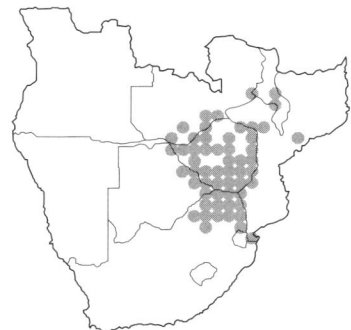

Fig. 298 *Tomopterna marmorata*

with grays and browns common, but a reddish tinge is often present. A pale head patch is usually present. A light vertebral stripe is uncommon.

DISTRIBUTION AND HABITAT (FIG. 298): This species is known from northeastern South Africa, Botswana, Zambia, Zimbabwe, Malawi, and Mozambique.

ADVERTISEMENT CALL: The call is similar to all others in the genus, being a rapidly repeated series of short notes. There are harmonics at 1.4, 2.3, and 4.0 kHz, with a duration of 0.05 s.

BREEDING: Clutch size is 150. The eggs are laid singly. They are 2 mm within 3.2-mm capsules. They sink to the bottom and become covered with mud.

TADPOLES: Unknown.

NOTES: Reliable identification is only possible for calling males.

KEY REFERENCES: Stewart 1967, Lambiris 1989.

Natal sand frog
Tomopterna natalensis (Smith, 1849)
(Plate 24.2)

Natal Sand Frog

The specific name *natalensis* refers to the province of KwaZulu-Natal, where this species was first discovered.
Natal pyxie, Natal bullfrog. *Natalse sandpadda* in Afrikaans.

DESCRIPTION: This is a robust frog, with the male up to 39 mm and the female 44 mm in length. A large flange on the inner metatarsal tubercle is used for digging. Webbing is very reduced, sometimes just reaching the middle tubercle beneath the fourth toe, usually with three and a half segments of the fourth toe free. Head width is less than tibia length. A glandular ridge runs from the eye, over the tympanum to the arm, where it joins another glandular ridge extending back from the upper lip. The back is variable, often with a darker bar between the eyes and blotches of grays and brown. Dark spots are present on the lower back. Some individuals have a pale vertebral stripe.

DISTRIBUTION AND HABITAT (FIG. 299): This species occurs from southern Mozambique southward to Eastern Cape Province and westward to the central highlands of South Africa. It is found in savannas.

ADVERTISEMENT CALL: The male calls after the first rains. The call is a series of short notes, repeated incessantly. Each note is 0.08 s long, with emphasized frequencies between 1.3 and 1.6 kHz.

Fig. 299 *Tomopterna natalensis*

BREEDING: Eggs are 0.6–1.2 mm in diameter within 2.5-mm capsules. This species breeds in streams but not dams. The eggs are found scattered in groups of two to six, in considerable numbers. The eggs are soon covered with bits of material from the bottom of the pond and are difficult to see.

TADPOLES: See the chapter on tadpoles.

NOTES: This species is reported to be eaten by the brown house snake.

KEY REFERENCE: Balinsky 1957 (as *Pyxicephalus natalensis*).

Tandy's sand frog
Tomopterna tandyi Channing & Bogart, 1996
(Plate 24.3)

This species is named for Mills Tandy, who collected the first specimens.
This species originated a long time ago by hybridization between two species of sand frogs. The evidence for this is a double set of chromosomes produced by the combination of genes from the parental species.

DESCRIPTION: It is indistinguishable from Delalande's sand frog and the cryptic sand frog. The arms and legs are short but well built, and the enlarged metatarsal tubercle is flattened and used for digging. Three segments of the fourth toe are free of webbing. The row of glands below the tympanum are not fused to form a ridge. The background color is gray, with darker and lighter patches. There is often a light patch in the head region. A pale vertebral stripe is usually present, with thin pale stripes on either side. The color patterns may be slightly different in some individuals from the Eastern Cape Province—a dark background with distinct elongated white markings, as well as black spots.

DISTRIBUTION AND HABITAT (FIG. 300): This species is known from Angola, Namibia, Botswana to western South Africa, and northward to Kenya. Records for *T. cryptotis* in many countries may actually be *T. tandyi*. It occurs in sandy flat areas where pans form. Farm dams provide a man-made habitat.

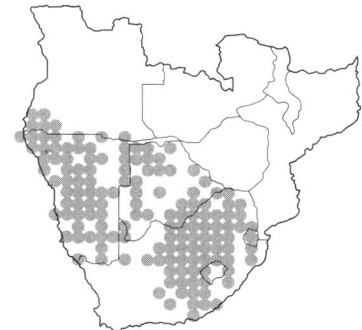

Fig. 300 *Tomopterna tandyi*

ADVERTISEMENT CALL: The male calls on the muddy edges of newly formed pools. It may also call from under vegetation in flooded areas. The call is a series of notes with emphasized harmonics at 2.6–2.8 kHz. The note repetition rate is temperature-dependent, but at a typical evening temperature of 19 °C the notes are produced at a rate of 8/s.

BREEDING: Unknown.

TADPOLES: See the chapter on tadpoles.

NOTES: The distribution of this species is presently not well known, and field studies are required.

KEY REFERENCE: Channing & Bogart 1996.

Rough sand frog
Tomopterna tuberculosa (Boulenger, 1882)
(Plate 24.4)

The specific name *tuberculosa* refers to the tubercles on the back. Beaded pyxie, warty frog, beaded dwarf bullfrog, tuberculate sand frog, Angolan burrowing frog, Angola bullfrog. *Gimboto* or *kimboto* in Angola.

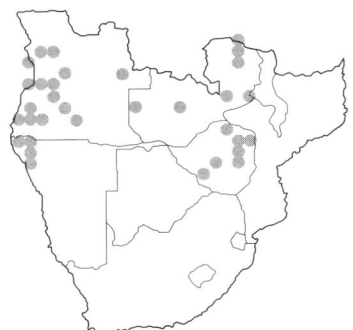

Fig. 301 *Tomopterna tuberculosa*

DESCRIPTION: This is a robust frog, with the male up to 40 mm and the female 45 mm in length. A digging flange is present on the inner metatarsal tubercle. Webbing is reduced, just passing the inner metatarsal tubercle of the fourth toe. The width of the head is usually less than the length of the tibia. The back has numerous warty ridges. The coloration of the back is variable, from a uniform brown in the west to blotched with a light vertebral stripe in the east. A light bar between the eyes separates two darker markings.

DISTRIBUTION AND HABITAT (FIG. 301): This species is known from Namibia and Angola eastward to the Democratic Republic of the Congo and Zimbabwe. It occurs in dry savannas.

ADVERTISEMENT CALL: The male calls from the edge of water, often camouflaged among pebbles. The call is a continuous fast rattle. The notes are produced at a rate of 13/s, and each note is brief, with an emphasized frequency of 2.6 kHz.

BREEDING: Unknown.

TADPOLES: Unknown.

KEY REFERENCE: Lambiris 1989.

Foam Nest Frogs—Family Rhacophoridae

This family of tree frogs is represented in Africa only by three species of *Chiromantis*, of which only one occurs within the area covered by this book. The other members of the family are tree frogs of Asia.

Gray tree frog
Chiromantis xerampelina Peters, 1854
(Plate 24.5)

The specific name *xerampelina* means "dry vine leaves," referring to the color of the frog.
Great gray tree frog, African gray tree frog, foam nest frog, grey foam-nest tree frog, southern foam-nest tree-frog. *Ruderfrosch* in German, *schûre* in Tete and Sena, *zhulankombe* in Kalanga, *chikwarikwari* in Shangaan.

DESCRIPTION: The male reaches 72 mm and the female, 85 mm in length. It is distinguishable from other frogs in the area by the pairs of opposable fingers, with which it can cling on to thin branches. Although a common color is gray, it can be almost white, through shades of gray and brown, with darker markings. The throat may be lightly speckled to heavily marked in black. The skin is roughly textured, and the eyes are large and protruding with horizontal pupils. The fingers and toes have large adhesive discs. Both toes and fingers are webbed.

DISTRIBUTION AND HABITAT (FIG. 302): The gray tree frog is found in northeastern South Africa, eastern Botswana, to Kenya and west to Angola. It occurs in lowland wooded savannas.

ADVERTISEMENT CALL: The breeding season coincides with the early rains in October to January, and breeding may occur after each rain. The male calls from above ground level, in grass, low bushes,

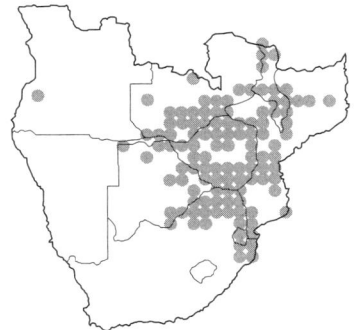

Fig. 302   *Chiromantis xerampelina*

or trees next to water. The calls vary, often being a very toadlike croaking. Males gather at call sites and tend to move toward each other while calling. Unlike nearly all other frogs, the male is not aggressive toward other breeding males. The dominant frequency varies between 1.2 and 2.2 kHz, with 4 or 5 equally spaced pulses in each call. The pulse rate may vary from 20/s to 44/s. The females approach the calling males by climbing through the trees, sometimes 2–3 m above ground.

BREEDING: The gray tree frog has a remarkable breeding strategy. The male selects a suitable site on a branch, rock, or in other vegetation overhanging water and starts to call. The site can be grass growing on the edge of a pool, although it seems to prefer a sturdy shrub or tree branch when this is available. The advertisement call attracts other males, and soon up to eight males can be calling nearby. The female arrives a little later, approaching by moving above ground level where there is adequate cover.

A male clasps the female, and she starts to produce a secretion that she beats into foam by paddling with her legs. She deposits eggs into the foam. The eggs are fertilized by the amplexing male, who places his cloaca next to that of the female.

Often extra males clasp the amplexing pair. From one to seven extra males gather around the pair and compete with each other and the amplexed male to fertilize the eggs. To test whether peripheral males play a role in fertilization, investigators prevented the primary male from fertilizing the eggs. Many of the eggs still developed, showing that the peripheral males were responsible for fertilizing a proportion of the eggs in the nest.

The female is unable to produce sufficient foam for one nest without rehydrating. The male releases her, and she climbs down to the pool where she absorbs water through her belly skin. She then returns to continue building the nest. She may return and mate with the same male or another male. On average it takes nearly two and a half sessions to complete a nest.

From 500 to 1226 eggs are deposited in each nest. The female may return to a nest the night following its construction, to add more foam but no new eggs. One pair in captivity produced a new foam nest on three successive nights. The tadpoles rely initially on the bubbles in the foam nest for oxygen. The outside of the nest dries, and the eggs develop into small black tadpoles. After 3–5 days the bottom of the nest gives way, probably owing to the action of enzymes produced by the developing tadpoles, and the whole mass of tadpoles drops into the water below.

TADPOLES: See the chapter on tadpoles.

NOTES: This frog is a master of surviving the dry hot African savanna. It conserves water by tucking the limbs under the body to reduce the amount of exposed skin. Also, during the dry season it forms a waterproof cocoon by secreting fluid under the outer layer of skin. In addition it is uricotelic, which means that it excretes uric acid as a mechanism to concentrate wastes and conserve water. Overall, this frog is very efficient at water conservation; it loses water at a rate as slow as reptiles.

This frog may spend the day exposed to direct sunlight without ill effects. At ambient temperatures between 39 and 43°C, the frog is able to maintain a body temperature 2–4° below ambient temperatures by adjusting the rate of evaporative water loss using nervous (sympathetic) control. The blood of the gray tree frog is adapted to carry oxygen at high temperatures.

As a final strategy it is able to survive 6 months or more without food or water. It is preyed upon by the boomslang *Dispholidus typus*. I have been disconcerted tracking down a gray tree frog, only to find a large boomslang doing the same thing from the other side of the bush. It is also fed on by the vine snake *Thelotornis capensis*, and the large slit-faced bat *Nycteris grandis* will take this frog in captivity.

Even the bullfrog is reported to eat it. Samango monkeys will eat the foam nests containing eggs. Perhaps one of the most bizarre egg predators is Fornasini's spiny reed frog *Afrixalus fornasini*, which locates fresh nests before the outside has hardened. It sticks its head deep into the foam nest and takes a mouthful of eggs and foam.

KEY REFERENCES: Loveridge 1970, Damstra 1983, Kaul & Shoemaker 1989, Jennions & Passmore 1993, Seymour & Loveridge 1994.

Species Accounts
ORDER GYMNOPHIONA

Caecilians are limbless amphibians that resemble worms. They burrow into soft soil and leaf litter. The eyes are present but covered. Two families of caecilians occur in Africa, and representatives of both families are known from Malawi.

KEY TO THE FAMILIES

1a. Tentacle about midway along upper jaw; a second, inconspicuous row of teeth in the lower jaw — Caeciliidae

1b. Tentacle close to the front of the upper jaw, a single row of teeth in the lower jaw — Scolecomorphidae

Family Scolecomorphidae

The scolecomorphids are legless amphibians that spend their life below the surface of forest litter and soft tropical soils. This family of caecilians is restricted to Africa and differs from other caecilians in details of skull morphology. They are usually only discovered after very heavy rain, and so very little is known of their biology. There is only one genus with seven species. The only species in this area comes from Malawi.

Genus *Scolecomorphus*

This genus has been found in the forests of eastern and central Africa. Eyespots are visible in young animals but lost in older individuals as the skull grows. A short tentacle that fits into a socket is present on each side of the head. Only one species is known from the area covered here.

Kirk's caecilian
Scolecomorphus kirkii Boulenger, 1883
(Plate 24.6)

This species is named for Sir John Kirk (1832–1922) who was vice-consul at Zanzibar and a keen naturalist.
Lake Tanganyika caecilian.

DESCRIPTION: It has a large, earthworm-like body, 185–451 mm long, with a diameter of 7–20 mm. The body has 131–152 rings, and the posterior end is blunt. The snout tip projects forward of the mouth. Small nostrils are present at the sides of the snout. A short sensory tentacle, only about 1 mm long, is present below each nostril. The small dark eyespots are visible only in young individuals. The vent is a longitudinal slit near the posterior end on the ventral surface. The adults are purple or black above, with brown

Kirk's Caecilian

Fig. 303 *Scolecomorphus kirkii*

sides. The undersurface is white in front, becoming pink toward the back.

DISTRIBUTION AND HABITAT (FIG. 303): This little-known amphibian has been recorded only from high-elevation forests in Malawi above 1400 m, and the Ubena highlands in Tanzania.

BREEDING: Unknown.

NOTES: All the specimens collected so far emerged after heavy rain. They emerge and feed on earthworms on the surface. Extensive observations during heavy rain would be very valuable, to discover more of the biology of this animal.

KEY REFERENCE: Stewart 1967.

Family Caeciliidae

This family is widespread, with representatives in India, the Seychelles, Africa, and Central and South America. Only one genus occurs in this area.

Genus *Boulengerula*

This genus is known from equatorial Africa south to Malawi. There are five species, of which only one is known from this area.

Changamwe caecilian
Boulengerula changamwensis Loveridge, 1932

This caecilian was named for Changamwe, near Mombassa, Kenya, where it was first found.
Changamwe lowland caecilian.

DESCRIPTION: This wormlike caecilian has a vertical keel on the terminal shield. The coloration is an even livid pink. There are 140–148 rings along the body. It can be distinguished from Kirk's caecilian by the absence of a small sensory tentacle below the nostril.

DISTRIBUTION AND HABITAT (FIG. 304): This species is known from western Kenya and southern Malawi. The Malawi record is based on one specimen collected from Mount Zomba or Mount Mlanje.

BREEDING: Unknown.

NOTES: This caecilian is known to eat termites. Anyone with the opportunity to spend time in the high-altitude forests of central

Changamwe Caecilian

Fig. 304 *Boulengerula changamwensis*

Africa during the rains should be on the lookout for this interesting but little-known animal.

KEY REFERENCE: Loveridge 1936.

Fossil Frogs

Many fossil frogs have been recovered in southern Africa. Most of these belong to the family Pipidae or to ancestors of that family. Fossils provide a perspective on the anatomy of ancestral frogs and allow inferences to be made about the direction and rate of change of anatomical characters. These data will be useful to an understanding of the relationships of living species.

Geological Background

Kimberlite pipes, which are vertical structures of an igneous origin that were formed by the cooling of molten rock, are fairly common in central and southern Africa. They are known from Zambia, Tanzania, Botswana, Angola, the Democratic Republic of the Congo, Mali, and South Africa. Kimberlite is relatively soft and weathers with time, often forming a crater. The craters become filled with water and are ideal sites for frogs to breed in. Over the years the lakes are filled in and become perfect sites where fossilization can occur.

Kimberlite is the parent rock from which African diamonds are derived. This has advantages and disadvantages for a study of fossil frogs. On the one hand, the location of all of the pipes is mapped, and they are investigated by means of trenches and boreholes. This intensive examination uncovers many frog fossils. On the other hand, however, there is high security where diamonds may be concerned. Geologists working for companies exploring for diamonds are often unwilling to disclose the location of kimberlite pipes or any details about their investigations.

Fossilization

In order for a fossil to be formed, the remains of the frog have to be covered by a layer of fine silt, and then left undisturbed while successive layers of sediment accumulate. The bones are replaced gradually by silica, or the impressions left by the body are filled in slowly. Terrestrial species, or those that only enter temporary pools to breed, are rarely in an environment that is suitable for fossil formation. Clearly *Xenopus* species and their relatives, which spend their life in water, might find themselves in water bodies where sediments are slowly forming. Lakes are ideal sites. Old crater lakes, along with dolomitic caves, provide many of the known fossils. Cave breccias often contain fragments of frog bones that were mostly brought into the cave by predators, often small mammals.

The crater lakes would have been oases of freshwater, with abundant plant and animal life. Successive heavy rains would bring new sediment into the lake, creating the necessary conditions for fossilization to occur. Catastrophic die-off of complete lake faunas caused by poisoning of the water by volcanic ash, or temperature shock, might explain why many fossils are often found together.

Although the earliest amphibian fossils are known from the lower Triassic 250 million years ago, the modern families of frogs are poorly represented in fossil collections. Seventeen fossil families are known worldwide, with the pipoids known from sediments older than 100 million years. In Africa, practically all the best-known frog fossils can be classified as belonging to the pipoids, a group that includes the modern family Pipidae. Examples of a fossil tadpole and adult of the genus *Thoraciliacus* from a crater lake in Namaqualand are illustrated (Plates 24.7, 24.8).

Tadpoles

Identification of Tadpoles

Tadpoles are very easy to identify to the level of family, and often to genus. Unlike adults, which are normally secretive during the day, tadpoles can be found and collected from most water bodies. The identification relies on anatomical features of the mouth, vent, spiracle, and certain body proportions. These are best seen through a stereomicroscope, although a good hand lens can be used for all but the smallest tadpoles.

Characters Used for Identification

Tadpoles should be examined carefully under a microscope or hand lens in order to check the features listed below. Pale structures like papillae around the mouth, and the spiracle opening are best seen if the tadpole is lightly stained—food coloring works well. Tadpole identification may be supported by behavioral data. Some species of tadpoles school, some live in midwater, while many are bottom dwellers. Most frogs will lay their eggs only in particular habitats, so the tadpoles will be found only in those places. In the keys that follow, an indication is given of the likely habitat and behavior of the tadpoles. These keys will enable tadpoles to be identified to genus, and sometimes to species. The tadpoles of many of the species are unknown or undescribed. In the species accounts I have indicated the species for which no information is available. Check the distribution of these unknown tadpoles to be aware of their possible presence when attempting to identify specimens. Tadpoles are frequently very similar within a genus. For this reason an illustration of only a typical tadpole for each genus has been provided.

Tadpole identification in the field is not a problem, as for each area the species maps will often quickly establish a list of expected tadpoles, which will only be a small subset of the species in this book. Tadpoles remain a very interesting part of the biology of frogs, and hopefully this book will stimulate the discovery and description of all the remaining unknown species.

Finally, the identification of a tadpole can be established without doubt only if either the tadpole is reared from the eggs laid by known parents or the tadpole is permitted to grow and metamorphose into a frog that can be identified.

Terminology Used in the Keys and in Descriptions of Tadpoles (Figs. 305, 306)

Body length. A straight line measured laterally from the tip of the snout to the junction of the tail muscles.

Dorsal. The upper surface of the body.

Jaw sheaths. Serrated keratinized sheaths overlying upper and lower cartilages that serve as cutting or abrasive structures.

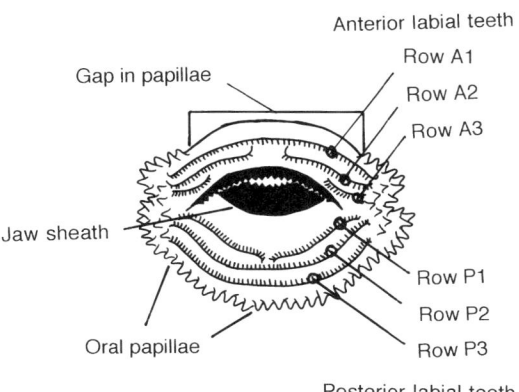

Fig. 305 Tadpole mouthparts. This example of *Strongylopus* has an upper gap in the papillae, and three anterior rows of labial teeth, with only the most anterior row (A1) complete. There are three posterior rows, with only the first row (P1) incomplete. The labial tooth row formula is 3(2 − 3)/3(1). The dark biting mouthparts are the keratinized jaw sheaths

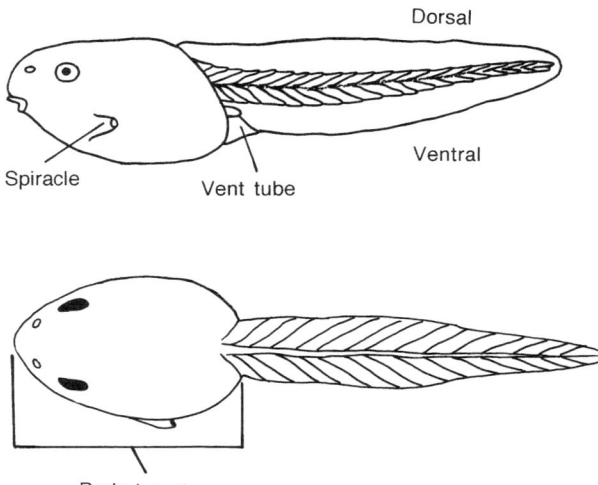

Fig. 306 Tadpole body parts. The body is measured from the snout to the start of the caudal muscles. The tubelike structure on the left side of the body is the spiracle

Labial tooth row. A line of small labial teeth embedded in a tooth ridge.

Labial tooth row formula. A notation for designating the number of tooth rows on the upper and lower labia, and the position of rows with medial gaps. Upper rows are numbered from the lip to the mouth, and lower rows are numbered from the mouth posteriorly. Numbers in parentheses indicate rows with medial gaps. A formula of 3(2 – 3)/3(1) indicates that there are 3 upper rows, with the 2 rows closest to the mouth having medial gaps, and 3 posterior rows, of which the row closest to the mouth has a medial gap.

Medial gap. A break in the middle of a labial tooth row.

Oral angle. The sides of the mouth.

Oral disc. The structures around the mouth, including upper and lower labia, usually with transverse rows of labial teeth, and papillae on the face and margin of the disc.

Oral papilla (plural papillae). A fleshy projection on the face or margin of the oral disc.

Spiracle. One or two openings of different shapes and positions for the exit of water that has been pumped through the buccopharynx for respiration and feeding.
Tail length. Measured laterally from the junction of the tail muscles with the body, to the tip of the tail.
Tentacle. A long sensory structure originating below the eye.
Vent. Posterior opening of the intestine, which may end in a vent tube.
Vent tube. A tube that projects the vent away from the body. It can be in line with the ventral fin (medial), or lie to the right of the fin (dextral).
Ventral. The lower surface of the body.

KEYS TO THE CENTRAL AND SOUTHERN AFRICAN TADPOLES
Tadpoles may change quite markedly during their development. These keys are based on fully grown tadpoles, at the stage where five toes are just visible or older. Many species of frogs are direct developers; the embryos pass through a tadpole stage within the egg and hatch as small frogs. There is thus no free-swimming stage. The keys below cover only free-swimming tadpoles. Keys to the genera will be found in the accounts of each family.

1a. Oral papillae present, and usually also labial tooth rows and keratinized jaw sheaths 3
1b. No papillae, keratinized jaw sheaths, or labial tooth rows 2

2a. Mouth with a fold in the lower lip, and one spiracle opening situated midventrally Microhylidae
2b. Mouth a horizontal slit, tentacles present at oral angle
Pipidae

3a. Upper and lower papillae gaps absent, multiple rows of labial teeth present Heleophrynidae
3b. Upper gap in papillae present 4

4a. A broad lower gap in the oral papillae present, vent median in the fin margin Bufonidae
4b. A lower gap absent, or very narrow if present; the vent is on the right, not on the fin margin 5

5a. A narrow lower gap in the oral papillae present   Rhacophoridae
5b. Lower gap absent   6

6a. Anterior third of the tail muscle obscured by opaque connective tissue, which extends ventrally and dorsally beyond muscles, giving the appearance of a thicker muscle region   Hemisotidae
6b. Tail muscle not obscured anteriorly   7

7a. One anterior row of labial teeth, or anterior tooth rows absent
   Hyperoliidae (part)
7b. Two or more rows of anterior labial teeth   8

8a. Nostrils small and far apart (distance between nostrils greater than 10 times the nostril width), tadpoles typically found in thin mud
   Hyperoliidae
8b. Not as above   Ranidae

Family Bufonidae

The tadpoles are typically small and dark, found in shallow water. Small differences in pigmentation patterns are useful distinguishing characters. A broad gap is present in the lower oral papillae.

KEY TO THE GENERA
1a. Raised flap of skin behind the eyes   *Schismaderma carens*
1b. No raised flap behind eyes   2

2a. Eyes and nostrils surrounded by a doughnut-shaped ring of tissue
   Stephopaedes anotis
2b. Eyes and nostrils not surrounded by a ring of tissue   3

3a. Tail more than twice as long as the body   *Capensibufo*
3b. Tail less than twice as long as body   *Bufo*

Genus *Bufo*

The oral formula is usually 2(2)/3. Tadpoles are bottom dwelling. Not all of the tadpoles are known, and so no key to the species can be

Tadpoles

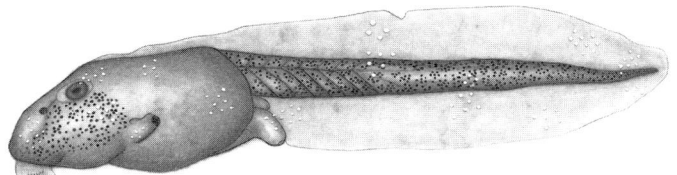

Fig. 307 *Bufo gariepensis*

given. Some details for better-known tadpoles are given below. The tadpole of *B. gariepensis* is illustrated (Fig. 307).

Bufo amatolicus
The tadpole at the earliest five-toed stage is 20 mm long. The tail is more than half the total length with a rounded tip. Eye to nostril distance is greater than eye length. The tadpole remains at the bottom in shallow pools.

Bufo angusticeps
The labial tooth row formula is sometimes 2(2)/3(1). Tail length is 63% of the total length. Nostrils are smaller than the lens of the eye, with a slight median projection. The dorsal and ventral fin margins are nearly parallel. The tadpole at the earliest five-toed stage is about 27 mm long.

Bufo dombensis
The nostrils are large, oval, with a pale raised margin, and situated one nostril length forward of the corner of the eye. The small pineal spot is visible slightly behind a line joining the front of the eyes. The lower gap in the oral papillae is half the oral disc width. The labial tooth row formula is 2(2)/3(1). The tadpole is stippled black dorsally, solidly pigmented over the head and body. The ventral surface is lightly stippled, with a clear midventral band. The tail muscle is lightly pigmented, except for a narrow strip along the ventral margin. The dorsal fin is lightly mottled, while the ventral fin is transparent. They live in rocky pools with gravel substrates.

Bufo fenoulheti
The tadpole is typically black, as are most other toad tadpoles. Its length may reach 23 mm. The dorsal tail fin is mottled, while the

ventral fin is unpigmented. The tadpoles may be found at the bottom of pools in shallow water, often near the edge.

Bufo gariepensis
The tadpole is small and dark. The dorsal and ventral fin margins are nearly parallel, with a rounded tip. The tadpoles are countershaded, dark above and pale on the ventral surface of the fin. The nostrils are larger than the lens of the eye. Metamorphosis can take as little as 20 days.

Bufo garmani
The tadpole has been observed feeding upside down at the surface. It assumes a lighter or darker coloration depending on the background, with lighter tadpoles being found on light backgrounds. Metamorphosis takes 64–91 days.

Bufo gutturalis
The tadpoles are small, up to 25 mm long, black with iridescent spots. There is no pigmentation across the anterior throat region, and the belly midline has little pigmentation. Tadpoles are free swimming within 2–3 days of the eggs being laid. It takes a further 74–75 days to metamorphosis. Tadpoles may be found aggregated on sand at the water's edge.

Bufo hoeschi
The tail possesses a distinct convex curvature of the dorsal and ventral fins. The tail tip is rounded. Pigmentation of the tail muscles covers more than the upper three-fourths, with less dense pigment extending to the ventral margin of the muscles. There is no pigment extending across the throat region. The tadpoles are solitary and bottom dwelling and require less than 24 days to develop from egg to toadlet. They feed by ingesting sand, from which they presumably obtain unicellular algae. No macroscopic algae were present in any of the Namib pools containing tadpoles. These pools were also devoid of dragonfly nymphs, the major tadpole predators. It seems that Hoesch's toad is able to reduce tadpole predation by breeding in ponds that are not selected by dragonflies.

Bufo kisoloensis
Full-grown tadpoles are about 20 mm long. Overall the tadpole is brown, rather than black as is common in many species of *Bufo*.

The upper pigmentation is a uniform dark brown. The lower pigmentation is a uniform lighter brown. The tail is evenly pigmented almost to the lower surface over the front two-thirds. The dorsal fin is completely pigmented, while the ventral fin is only pigmented anteriorly. Some tadpoles have a light mottling on the ventral fin.

Bufo maculatus
The tadpole at the five-toed stage is 14–17 mm long. The tail is 44% of the total length. Pigmentation consists of small dark brown stipples, uniformly covering the back and extending to the sides, with a wide unpigmented belly stripe. The tail muscles are countershaded, with heavy upper pigment, a middle mottled area, and a lower unpigmented region.

Bufo pantherinus
The tadpole possesses distinctly curved margins to the upper and lower fins. Eye to nostril distance is less than eye length. Pigmentation over the tail muscles is confined to the upper two-thirds in front but covers the posterior portion completely. There are no papillae on each side of the mouth within the oral disc.

Bufo pardalis
The tadpole is similar to that of *B. pantherinus*. It possesses distinctly curved margins to the upper and lower fins. Eye to nostril distance is less than eye length. Pigmentation over the tail muscles is confined to the upper two-thirds in front but covers the posterior portion completely. There are no papillae (sometimes one) on each side of the mouth within the oral disc.

Bufo poweri
The tadpole is small and black, found in shallow water at the edges of pools. It possesses a tail with curved upper and lower margins that is less than twice as long as the body. The eye to nostril distance is less than eye length. The tail muscles are well pigmented in front, where more than three-fourths of the upper edge is dark. The throat region is heavily pigmented. The gut cavity is also densely covered with pigment cells. In captivity time to metamorphosis is 73 days.

Bufo rangeri
The tadpole reaches 25 mm in length. It is black and may be distinguished from other toad tadpoles by the curved tail margins, upper and lower. The eye to nostril distance is less than the eye length, and the pigmentation over the caudal muscles is confined to the upper two-thirds along the length of the tail. There are two or more papillae on each side of the mouth within the oral disc.

Bufo robinsoni
The tadpole reaches 28 mm in length. The nostrils are large, about half the width of the eye. The upper surface is solidly pigmented, and the lower surface is very dark. The fins are usually unpigmented.

Bufo vertebralis
The small black tadpole reaches 21 mm in length. Like many other bufonid species, the tadpole has pigment cells called *iridiophores*, which give the surface a golden or silver-flecked appearance. The nostril is longer than half the eye width. They develop rapidly—metamorphosis may occur as soon as 16 days after oviposition.

Genus *Capensibufo*

The tadpoles of the two species are very similar, but as they do not occur in the same areas they can be recognized by the locality where they are found. The tadpole of *C. tradouwi* is illustrated (Fig. 308).

Capensibufo rosei
The tadpole is small and black, with a tail that is more than twice the body length and nearly parallel upper and lower fin margins. The tadpole may reach 21 mm in length. The oral formula may sometimes be 1(1)/3(1). Metamorphosis occurs after 51 days.

Fig. 308 *Capensibufo tradouwi*

Tadpoles

Capensibufo tradouwi

The 18-mm tadpole possesses a long tail with parallel fins. The tadpoles may be found in dense masses, in very shallow water. They gather at the water's edge in full sunlight, presumably to increase the body temperature to speed development.

Genus *Schismaderma*

There is only one species, *Schismaderma carens*. The unusual flap on the head is illustrated (Fig. 309).

Schismaderma carens

The tadpoles are large, up to 35 mm long, and black. The oral formula is 2/3. The tadpole is quite different from other toad tadpoles in this region on two counts: a peculiar flap of skin on the head and its gregarious behavior. The horseshoe-shaped flap of skin extends from the eyes to midway along the top of the body. When the water is very fetid, the tadpoles swim near the surface, with the flap of skin serving as a float. The flap is well supplied with capillaries and functions as a respiratory organ. In an experiment, tadpoles grown in polluted water developed head flaps twice as large as those of tadpoles grown in clean, aerated water. The tadpoles swarm together in a compact ball that appears to roll slowly through the water, with its center below water level, but floating well clear of the bottom. The ball slowly rises and sinks. Small groups of tadpoles are sometimes seen on the bottom of the pond, all facing inward, strongly attracted to each other. The tadpoles are gregarious, forming large swarms. They have been found at False Bay Park (northeastern South Africa) in a mixed swarm with African bullfrog *Pyxicephalus adspersus* tadpoles.

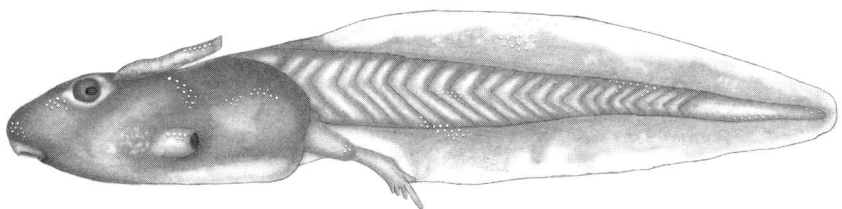

Fig. 309 *Schismaderma carens*

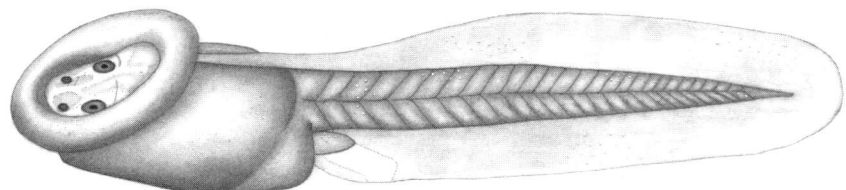

Fig. 310   *Stephopaedes anotis*

Genus *Stephopaedes*

There is only one species in the area covered by this book, *Stephopaedes anotis*. This genus has tadpoles that are specialized to live in small pockets of water trapped in the roots of large forest trees. The tadpole is illustrated (Fig. 310).

Stephopaedes anotis
The tadpole reaches 20 mm in length. It is distinguishable from all other tadpoles in southern Africa by the presence of a "crown." This is a ring of expanded epithelial tissue around the eyes and nostrils. The crown gives the genus its name: *Stephopaedes* means "crown-bearing young." The crown develops after the external gills are lost and remains until metamorphosis. The crown may serve to exclude scum from the surface of the pools where these tadpoles develop, but it is more likely to be an extra respiratory surface, as it is well supplied with capillaries and is in contact with the air. The tadpoles are found in stagnant pools in tree holes, where they cling to the slimy bark of the tree in a tail-down position. They retain external gills that are much longer than those of other toads, and these are lost when they are placed in well-aerated water. The tadpole lacks a gap in the lower papillae. The head and trunk are darkly pigmented, but the crown and fins are not pigmented. The east African forest toad *Mertensophryne* is the only other genus with crowned tadpoles.

Family Heleophrynidae

Genus *Heleophryne*

There are more than 10 posterior labial tooth rows, and typically no upper or lower keratinized jaw sheaths. Tadpoles from the Cape Fold Mountains cannot be identified to species using only morphological characters. Distributional clues can be used, as the species do not occur together. No key to the species is provided. The tadpole of *H. purcelli* is illustrated (Fig. 311).

Heleophryne hewitti
Tadpoles may grow to 62 mm and are indistinguishable from those of Purcell's and the Royal ghost frogs. The tadpoles have large oral discs with multiple rows of labial teeth. No lower keratinized jaw sheath is present. The head is streamlined and wide, and the fins are narrow. The labial tooth row formula is 4/14 to 4/17.

Heleophryne natalensis
The tadpole is large, up to 85 mm long and 20 mm wide at the mouth. Tadpoles of this species differ from the other five species in that they possess a lower keratinized jaw sheath. The labial tooth row formula is 4/12 to 4/17. The tadpole scrapes algae off rocks, leaving distinctive trails. During the day it retires under rocks, and during the night may be found feeding, sometimes even climbing vertical rock faces where water is flowing. If disturbed, it releases its hold and escapes by being washed downstream. Development takes more than a year.

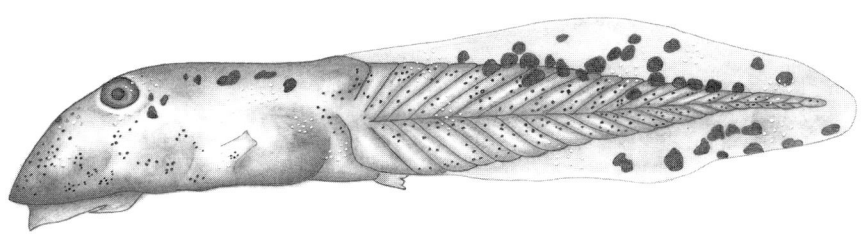

Fig. 311 *Heleophryne purcelli*

Heleophryne orientalis
The tadpole may be up to 60 mm in length. It lacks a lower keratinized jaw sheath, although the early stages possess fanglike teeth, which drop out as the tooth rows begin to appear. The labial tooth row formula is 4/14 to 4/17.

Heleophryne purcelli
The tadpole may be up to 60 mm long, and has many rows of labial teeth, with a labial tooth row formula of 4/14 to 4/17. No lower keratinized jaw sheath is present. The tadpole has been found under stones on a sandy substrate. When disturbed, it attempts to hide by moving under stones and wriggling into the sand. Tadpoles are readily eaten by water snakes *Lycodonomorphus rufulus* in captivity and in the wild. Newly metamorphosed juveniles leave the streams during March and April.

Heleophryne regis
The tadpole may be up to 60 mm long, and has many rows of labial teeth, with a labial tooth row formula of 4/14 to 4/17. No lower keratinized jaw sheath is present. The tadpole is similar to the tadpoles of Hewitt's and Purcell's ghost frogs. Newly metamorphosed tadpoles leave the streams during November to January, after spending about a year in the water.

Heleophryne rosei
It reaches 50 mm in length and has varying amounts of pigmentation. There is no lower keratinized jaw sheath. The labial tooth row formula is 4/14 to 4/16. The tadpole is similar to the other southern species. Larval development takes more than 12 months. Metamorphosing tadpoles have been found leaving seepage areas in late December.

Family Hemisotidae

These large tadpoles are bottom dwellers.

Genus *Hemisus*

The tadpoles of this genus are characterized by a thin membrane over the anterior tail muscle. Not all of the tadpoles are known, and no key to the species is provided. The species for which some detail is known are listed below. The tadpole of *H. marmoratus* is illustrated (Fig. 312).

Hemisus guineensis
The tadpole is pale gray with black spots and a very deep upper fin. The labial tooth row formula is 5(2 – 5)/4(1). The tadpoles are very common in pools.

Hemisus guttatus
The tadpole is large and dark brown. It may reach a length of 65 mm. The posterior part of the tail is pigmented. The labial tooth row formula is 6(3 – 6)/3. There are a few, very long lower papillae. Tadpoles leave the egg chamber when it floods, as tadpoles usually are found in shallow water in flooded grassland.

Hemisus marmoratus
The tadpole reaches 55 mm in length. Like others in this genus, it is characterized by a thickened sheath covering the front of the tail. The mouthparts are characterized by a few long lower papillae. Variation in labial tooth row formula is from 5(2 – 5)/4(1) to 5(3 – 5)/4(1). The eggs hatch into tadpoles after 8 days. The tadpole leaves the burrow by swimming out when it floods, or can be carried by the female to

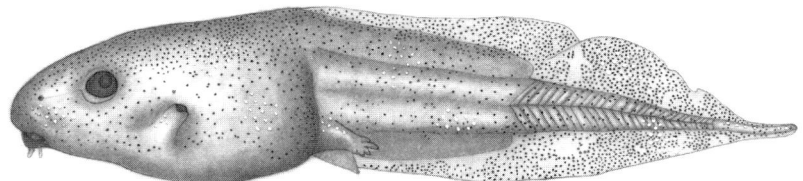

Fig. 312 *Hemisus marmoratus*

a suitable pond. The female also may dig a slide about 1 cm deep in mud, along which the tadpoles follow her to open water. The tadpoles spend the day resting on the bottom of muddy pools. They commonly occur together with sand frog tadpoles. They have been found in flooded grassy depressions or in shallow pans. The tadpoles are slow moving and can be caught by hand.

Family Hyperoliidae

KEY TO THE GENERA
The tadpole of the genus *Kassinula* is unknown.

1a.	Two or more upper rows of labial teeth	*Leptopelis*
1b.	One upper row of labial teeth or none	2

2a. Jaw sheaths heavily developed and keratinized with an additional pair of lateral keratinized plates, dorsal fin originating in a fleshy crest
3
2b. Jaw sheaths not extensively pigmented, dorsal fin not originating in a fleshy crest
4

3a.	Distinct pale stripe along the axis of the tail	*Semnodactylus*
3b.	No distinct stripe along tail axis	*Kassina*

4a.	One upper labial tooth row	*Hyperolius*
4b.	No upper labial tooth rows	*Afrixalus*

Genus *Afrixalus*

The tadpoles in this genus are long and thin, with typically no upper labial tooth rows. The eyes are positioned on the side of the head, with the mouth at the front of the body. No key to the species is provided as not all the species have been described. The tadpole of *A. fornasini* is illustrated (Fig. 313).

Afrixalus dorsalis
The tadpole possesses a longitudinally hatched pattern, brightly colored with spots all over. It is streamlined, without a narrowing at the base of the tail. The tail is twice as long as the body. The throat

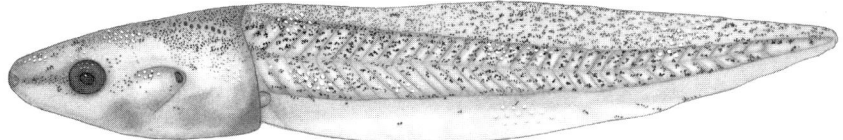

Fig. 313 *Afrixalus fornasini*

of the tadpole has brown spots, some of which are joined. The labial tooth row formula is 0/1. Metamorphosis takes place after 10 weeks.

Afrixalus fornasini
The tadpole reaches a length of 65 mm. It is brown, with darker markings. The tail tip is sharp, and the eyes are on the side of the flattened head. There is a triple row of papillae below the mouth. The labial tooth row formula is 0/1. The tadpole drops into the water after 5–10 days. Metamorphosis takes place after 10–12 weeks.

Afrixalus knysnae
The tadpole may reach 38 mm. The tail is long, twice the length of the body, with a sharp tip. The labial tooth row formula is 0/0. The fins are nearly transparent. The slender tadpoles may grow to 38 mm.

Afrixalus spinifrons
The tadpole reaches 32 mm in length. The labial tooth row formula is 0/0. The tadpole is not well known, except that it has a sharp tail tip.

Genus *Hyperolius*

The tadpoles in this very widespread genus are not well known. The eyes are situated on the side of the head. The labial tooth row formula is 1/3. The details for the better-known species are listed below. No key to the species is provided. The tadpole of *H. marmoratus* is illustrated (Fig. 314).

Hyperolius argus
The tadpole reaches 48 mm in length. It is light brown with a pale underside and mottled fins. The most posterior row of labial teeth

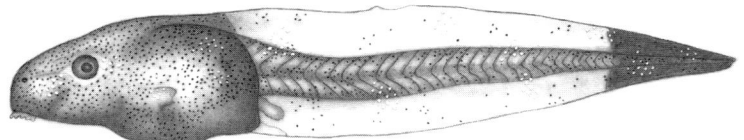

Fig. 314 *Hyperolius marmoratus*

(P3) is short. The papillae are in a double row below the oral disc, with a narrow gap in the middle. The keratinized jaw sheaths are heavy. The tadpoles are known from pools with dense vegetation.

Hyperolius horstockii
The tadpole reaches 40 mm in length. It is brown with longitudinal darker bands on the tail. It has delicate jaw sheaths, with two rows of papillae below the mouth. The tadpole is found in ponds with emergent vegetation, particularly sedges.

Hyperolius marmoratus
The tadpole may grow to 44 mm. Overall it is brown with speckled fins. The tail ends in a sharp point that is tipped with black. The tadpole develops within 5 days. It is a bottom dweller, preferring grassy shallow pools. Metamorphosis occurs after 5 weeks.

Hyperolius mitchelli
The tadpole can be distinguished from other similar reed frog tadpoles by the papillae on the front of the head that are continuous with the oral papillae. Another unusual feature is the complex of papillae that form a dense filter at the front of the mouth. The tadpole was described from specimens collected in the East Usambaras in Tanzania.

Hyperolius nasutus
The tadpole may grow to 33 mm, with a tail more than twice as long as the body. Tadpoles have been found in a small puddle on rock in the Kavango river, which was in the sun and had reached 38 °C.

Hyperolius pickersgilli
The tadpole is similar to that of other reed frogs but has a pair of enlarged papillae in the angle of the mouth.

Hyperolius poweri
The tadpole reaches 33 mm in length. It is brown, with mottled fins. The fins are sharply pointed with a dark tip. The most posterior row of labial teeth (P3) is half the length of the first row (P1). There is a double row of papillae below the mouth. The tadpole is known from deep pools fringed with reeds.

Hyperolius pusillus
The tadpole reaches 35 mm in length. It is brown with a greenish tinge but white below. The fins have a dark edge that fades out rearward. The jaw sheaths are delicate, and a double row of papillae is found below the mouth. Metamorphosis takes place after 5–6 weeks.

Hyperolius semidiscus
The tadpole reaches 48 mm in length. It is a light brown with a pale underside and mottled fins. Row P3 is shorter than row P2. The papillae are in a double row below the mouth, with a narrow gap in the middle. The jaw sheaths are heavy. This relatively large tadpole is similar to others in the genus.

Hyperolius spinigularis
The tadpole has a characteristic black V on the snout tip. The labial tooth row formula is 1/3(1). The tadpole hatches after 5 days and wriggles from the leaf into the water.

Hyperolius tuberilinguis
The tadpole reaches 46 mm in length. It is brown with pale undersides, speckled with golden pigment cells called iridiophores. The jaw sheaths are delicate, and the most posterior tooth row (P3) is much shorter than the other two.

Genus *Kassina*

The tadpoles have very high fins and are found in standing water where there is much vegetation. They feed on plants and have heavy mouthparts with extra accessory plates to enable them to deal with stems and other tough parts. The tadpoles are large and often brightly patterned in stripes or mottles. The eyes are on the side of the head,

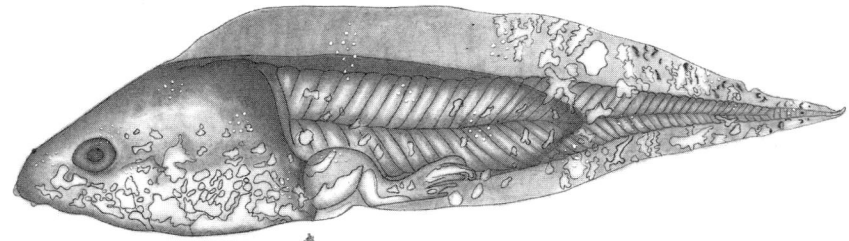

Fig. 315 *Kassina kuvangensis*

and the mouth is at the front. The tadpole of *K. kuvangensis* is illustrated (Fig. 315).

KEY TO THE SPECIES
1a. Three posterior labial tooth rows   *Kassina maculata*
1b. Two posterior labial tooth rows   2

2a. Yellow with dark markings, grows to over 100 mm
                                        Kassina kuvangensis
2b. Red or gold fins with black markings, less than 85 mm
                                        Kassina senegalensis

Kassina kuvangensis
The tadpole is large, up to 102 mm long, with very high fins. The upper fin starts on top of the head. A thin sheath covers the anterior tail muscle, extending onto the inner margins of the fins. The jaw sheaths are heavy, with an accessory grinding plate on each side of the lower jaw sheath. The labial tooth row formula is 1/2(1). The tadpole is bright yellow with darker mottling. It is found beneath water plants, where it is camouflaged in dappled shade.

Kassina maculata
The tadpole is large, up to 130 mm long. The upper fin is high, starting at the back of the head. The tadpole has contrasting markings. The mouthparts are adapted for dealing with tough food: the labial tooth row formula is 1/3, with very heavy jaw sheaths. In addition they have a hardened plate on each side of the jaw sheaths. A gap in the lower papillae is present. The tadpole can consume large amounts

of plant matter, chewing the stems and leaves. Metamorphosis may take 8–10 months.

Kassina senegalensis
The tadpole has very high fins, with the upper fin originating at the level of the eyes, with a thin tail tip. It is large, up to 80 mm long. The tadpole is dark, with red or golden markings on the fins. The labial tooth row formula is 1/2(1), with heavy jaw sheaths and extra hardened plates at the side of the sheaths. The tail tip vibrates, to maintain the position of the tadpole in the pond. The tadpole can bite through stems of waterweeds and is also known to eat mosquito eggs. It tends to be a midwater dweller, often hiding under the leaves of water plants.

Genus *Leptopelis*

The tadpoles have elongated tails with which they wriggle to the water. The labial tooth row formula is 4(2 – 4)/3. No key to the species is provided, as none of the tadpoles have been adequately described. The tadpole of *L. natalensis* is illustrated (Fig. 316).

Genus *Semnodactylus*

There is only one species in this genus. The tadpoles are similar to those of the genus *Kassina*. The tadpole of *S. wealii* is illustrated (Fig. 317).

Semnodactylus wealii
The tadpole reaches 58 mm in length. It has high fins and is brown, with various markings, and a silver stripe along the tail muscles. The oral formula is 1/3, with the most posterior row of labial teeth (P3) being very short. The jaw sheaths are heavy, and there is a hardened

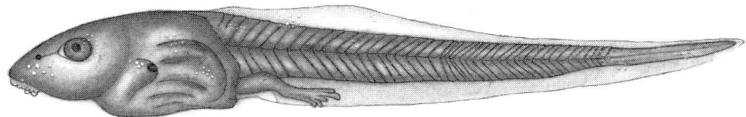

Fig. 316 *Leptopelis natalensis*

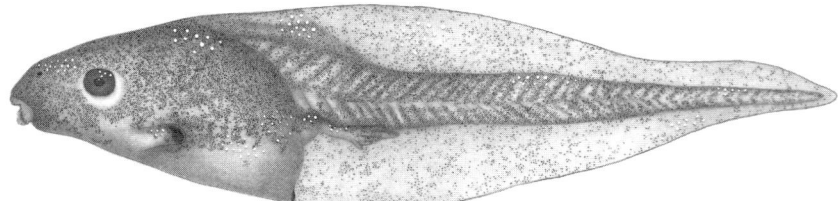

Fig. 317 *Semnodactylus wealii*

plate on each side of the lower sheath. The tadpole is known from permanent ponds with emergent vegetation.

Family Microhylidae

Many of the microhylids in this area have no free-swimming tadpole stage. The genus *Phrynomantis* has tadpoles with high fins and no hard mouthparts. They live in deep water and feed by filtering small particles out of the water.

Genus *Phrynomantis*

The tadpoles form schools and move slowly through the water, feeding. The eyes are situated on the side of the head. The mouth is a wide slit, with a V-shaped lower lip. There are no hard mouthparts. The spiracle is wide, situated on the midline near the posterior end of the body. The tadpole of *P. bifasciatus* is illustrated (Fig. 318).

KEY TO THE SPECIES
1a. Spiracle close to the posterior end of the trunk, back silvery with a black vertebral stripe *Phrynomantis bifasciatus*
1b. Not as above 2

2a. Distance to spiracle forward from the posterior end of the trunk equal to one-fourth the body, back mottled silver and black
  Phrynomantis annectens
2b. Not as above *Phrynomantis affinis*

Tadpoles

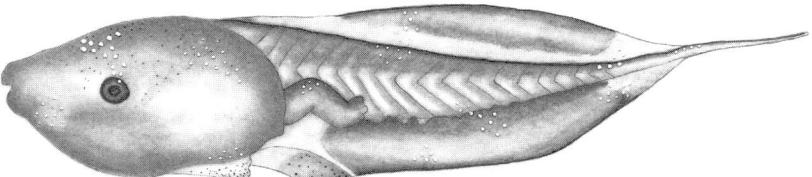

Fig. 318 *Phrynomantis bifasciatus*

Phrynomantis annectens
The tadpoles are transparent, with wide flattened heads and very conspicuous fins. They often exceed 35 mm in length. They are recognizable by the silver and golden flecks against a clear or dark background. The tadpole is a midwater filter feeder, with a remarkable gregarious behavior. They congregate in groups of up to 80, usually three of four tadpoles deep in the center, and up to 50 or more side by side, swimming in the same direction. When disturbed the school breaks up and the tadpoles scatter in all directions, hiding in the smallest crevices and holes. After a few minutes they emerge and the school reforms. The tadpole requires at least eight weeks before metamorphosis.

Phrynomantis bifasciatus
The tadpole has a wide head, which is sharp when viewed from the side. It may reach 37 mm in length. The tadpole is transparent, with darker pigmentation and many iridiophores along the midline. The tail possesses wide black longitudinal bands, sometimes with narrow red bands. The tail tip is thin, extending beyond the pigmented region of the fins. Usually the tadpoles are gregarious, motionless, and remain about one cm below the surface. The tadpole eats mostly floating unicellular algae, along with desmids and diatoms. The tadpoles were found in muddy water pools at 40 °C in Malombe Pan in the Caprivi Strip of Namibia. At this high temperature the tadpoles were not swarming. Metamorphosis takes 90 days in captivity.

Family Pipidae

There is only one genus, *Xenopus*, in this area. A fossil tadpole of the extinct genus *Thoraciliacus* from Botswana is illustrated on Plate 24.

Genus *Xenopus*

The tadpoles of *Xenopus* are transparent, without hard mouthparts. They school in the water column, vibrating the tail tip to remain in position. No key to the species is provided, as many are undescribed, despite the fact that they are routinely bred in many laboratories. The tadpole of *Xenopus muelleri* is illustrated (Fig. 319).

Xenopus fraseri
A grown tadpole is 33 mm long, with tentacles half as long as the body plus the tail. The head of the tadpole is deeply pigmented. In captivity, metamorphosis takes place after 10 weeks.

Xenopus gilli
The tadpole reaches 50 mm in length. It has a longitudinal unpigmented band on each side of the head, running backward from the eye. This band is characteristic and separates this tadpole from the tadpoles of the common platanna *X. laevis*. The tadpole is known to darken at night. It is able to withstand very acid waters, down to pH 3.6 in black water. Development takes 120 days in the field.

Xenopus laevis
The tadpole has a long tail and high fin. The head is flattened and often translucent. The tadpole is transparent with various degrees of pigmentation. It possesses tentacles that may become fairly long, reaching 80 mm. Eggs hatch rapidly into tadpoles, taking only 24 hours in the warmer parts of KwaZulu-Natal. The tail tip vibrates

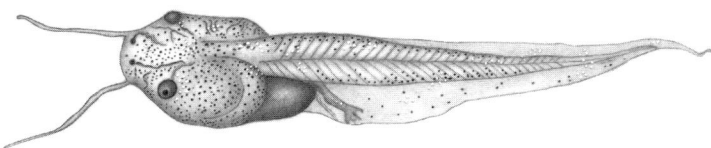

Fig. 319 *Xenopus muelleri*

constantly, maintaining the tadpole in a head-down position. Tadpoles breathe air or water. However, being filter feeders they use the same gill filter surfaces for food trapping and aquatic respiration. When there is a dense food suspension, the tadpoles breathe air more frequently. Tadpoles living in algae-rich ponds may become quite green. The larger tadpoles prefer deeper water, while the smaller tadpoles are often found around vegetation.

The tentacles appear to compensate for poor maneuverability and an anterior blind spot, by preventing the tadpole from becoming trapped in vegetation. The tadpole needs to come to the surface to breathe and does so in unison with other tadpoles, which may offer some advantage against predators. The tadpole maintains its height in the water visually, changing only the amplitude of the tail tip oscillations to adjust position, and schools in parallel with others. It uses the lateral line sensory organs to maintain position in the dark, and eyes to assist during daytime. The gregarious nature of this tadpole is shown by the fact that it tolerates other tadpoles well and will only move if another individual comes within two body lengths during daytime, or within one body length at night. The tadpole is pale in light, becoming more pigmented in the dark. Pale tadpoles choose pale backgrounds, while dark tadpoles choose dark backgrounds. The tadpole is more active at night and prefers a water temperature of 22.4 °C.

Xenopus muelleri
The body is more rounded than the common platanna *X. laevis*. The tentacles are long, more than 25% of the total length. Tadpoles school 50–70 mm apart, with their bodies horizontal in midwater. The tadpole feeds on particles of vegetation and unicellular algae.

Family Ranidae

This large family includes tadpoles found in fast-flowing streams to small ephemeral ponds. They have jaw sheaths and labial tooth rows, and many are a uniform brown.

KEY TO THE GENERA
The tadpole of *Nothophryne* is unknown.

1a. Vent on the right and not continuous with the lower margin of the fin   4
1b. Vent continuous with the lower margin of the fin   2

2a. A small gap present in the row of lower papillae
    Microbatrachella
2b. No gap in the row of lower papillae   3

3a. Distance between outside edges of nostrils less than distance between inner edges of eyes   *Cacosternum*
3b. Distance between outside edges of nostrils more than distance between inner edges of eyes   *Natalobatrachus*

4a. One or more anterior labial tooth rows   5
4b. No anterior labial tooth rows   *Hildebrandtia*

5a. Numerous white-tipped tubercles covering top and sides of body
    Poyntonia
5b. Top and sides of body smooth   6

6a. Three or more posterior rows of labial teeth   7
6b. Less than three posterior rows of teeth   8

7a. Seven posterior rows of labial teeth   *Amietia*
7b. Three posterior rows of labial teeth   *Hoplobatrachus*

8a. Two posterior rows of labial teeth without gaps   *Pyxicephalus*
8b. One posterior row of labial teeth without gap   9

9a. Large dark spots on body and tail, often with distinct skin glands on body   *Amnirana*
9b. No large dark spots or distinct skin glands   10

10a. Two posterior rows of labial teeth   11
10b. Three posterior rows of labial teeth   12

11a. Distance between nostrils greater than six times the nostril width   *Phrynobatrachus*
11b. Distance between nostrils less than six times the nostril width
    Ptychadena

Tadpoles

12a. Lower jaw sheath pigmented to its base — *Strongylopus*
12b. Lower jaw sheath pigmented along its edge only — 13

13a. Tail at least twice as long as head and body — *Afrana*
13b. Tail less than twice as long as head and body — *Tomopterna*

Genus *Afrana*

The tadpoles are large with many labial tooth rows. The tail is at least twice as long as head and body. No key to the species is provided. Many remain undescribed. The tadpole of *A. fuscigula* is illustrated (Fig. 320).

Afrana angolensis
The tadpole grows to a large size, over 80 mm long. Overall the color is brown with flecks. The mouthparts are distinct, with a labial tooth row formula of 4(2 – 4)/3(1 – 2). The tadpole often lies quietly in sunny parts of the water but can move off very smartly when disturbed.

Afrana dracomontana
The tadpoles possess an umbraculum, which is an outgrowth from the top of the pupil that may serve as a sunshade for the eye against UV light. The labial tooth row formula is 4(2 – 3)/3.

Afrana fuscigula
The tadpole may reach 60 mm long in rivers and ponds. The labial tooth row formula is 4(1 – 4)/3(1) to 5(2 – 5)/4(1). The tail is only slightly pigmented, without high fins. The tail tip is pointed. The tadpole can get very large in the permanent ponds at Naukluft in

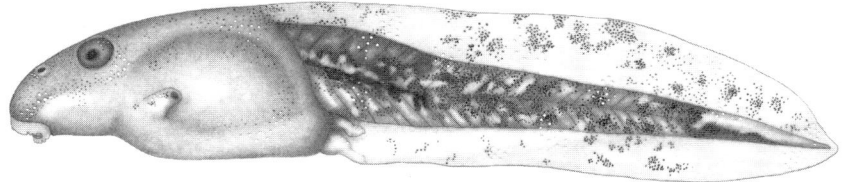

Fig. 320 *Afrana fuscigula*

Namibia, up to 165 mm long and 40 mm high. At this size it already has an adult-like internal anatomy and presumably takes more than a year to metamorphose. Metamorphosis in captivity takes 81 days or more. It is similar to other river frog tadpoles in behavior, resting on the bottom until disturbed, when it conceals itself under vegetation or in holes.

Afrana inyangae
The tadpole is robust with various patterns of speckling. The labial tooth row formula is 6(2 – 6)/4. The tadpoles hatch after 13–15 days, in the cold mountain streams where the water remains below 17 °C. They feed on filamentous algae. Metamorphosis takes 65 days in captivity.

Afrana vandijki
The tadpoles are easy to identify, as they are dark brown or black, with deep fins and a rounded paddle-like tail. Tadpoles grow to 55 mm long. The labial tooth row formula is 7(2 – 7)/7(1).

Genus *Amietia*

There is one species. The tadpoles are similar to those of *Afrana*, but the head is wider and flattened. The tadpole of *A. vertebralis* is illustrated (Fig. 321).

Amietia vertebralis
The body is slightly flattened, and the mouth is large, equipped with many rows of teeth. The oral formula is 7(3 – 7)/4. The tadpole lives in flowing water and shows some adaptations for this lifestyle, like a flattened head. The tadpole is found in water at temperatures below 8 °C.

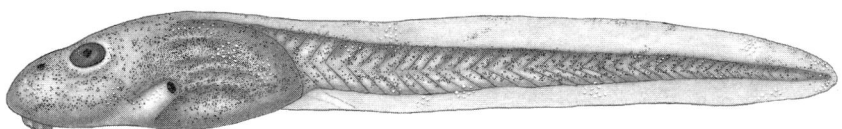

Fig. 321   *Amietia vertebralis*

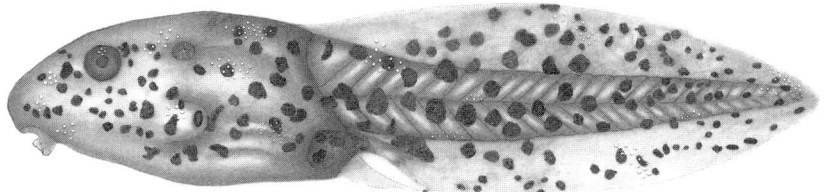

Fig. 322 *Amnirana lemairii*

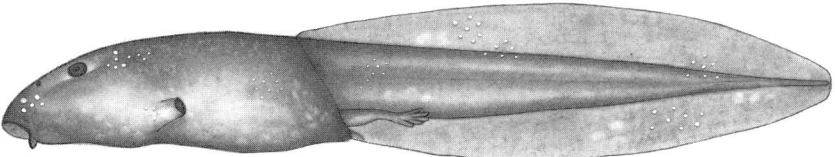

Fig. 323 *Aubria* sp.

Genus *Amnirana*

The tadpoles have very interesting glandular patches arranged in specific patterns on the body. The tadpoles are robust. No key is provided as the tadpoles remain undescribed. The tadpole of *A. lemairii* is illustrated (Fig. 322).

Genus *Aubria*

There is one species in the area covered. The tadpoles form large schools. The eyes are close together on top of the head. The tadpole of a species of *Aubria* is illustrated (Fig. 323).

Aubria masako
The tadpole is about 40 mm long, with eyes close together on top of the head. The labial tooth formula is 5(3 – 5)/3. The tadpoles become progressively darker with age and on the sides and underneath show the adult color pattern of white spots on a dark background. The tadpoles are gregarious, forming large schools in the form of compact balls.

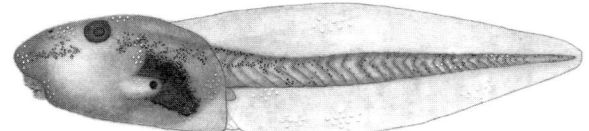

Fig. 324 *Cacosternum boettgeri*

Genus *Cacosternum*

No key is provided, as many species are undescribed. The tadpoles are small, found in shallow vegetated ponds. The distance between the outside edges of nostrils is less than the distance between the inner edges of the eyes. The tadpole of *C. boettgeri* is illustrated (Fig. 324).

Cacosternum boettgeri
The tadpole is small and moderately pigmented. The mouthparts are variable, usually with a labial tooth row formula of 4(2 − 4)/3 or 4(2 − 4)/4, although 3(2 − 3)/3(1) is common. Perhaps different species are confused under this name, as suggested by the variable labial tooth row formula. It takes 37 days to reach metamorphosis in captivity.

Cacosternum namaquense
The tadpole may reach 50 mm in length. It is large bodied, with an overall brown color. The labial tooth row formula is 4(2 − 4)/3. The tadpole has been found in shallow algae-rich pools.

Cacosternum nanum
The tadpole may reach 28 mm in length. It is mostly transparent, with darker stripes and speckles. The labial tooth row formula is 3(2 − 3)/3. Metamorphosis may take as little as 17 days.

Genus *Hildebrandtia*

Only one species occurs in this area. The tadpole is carnivorous, enabling it to grow rapidly. The tadpole of *H. ornata* is illustrated (Fig. 325).

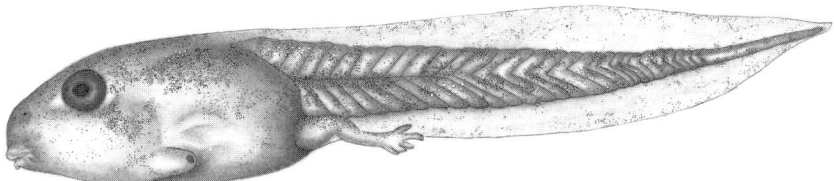

Fig. 325 *Hildebrandtia ornata*

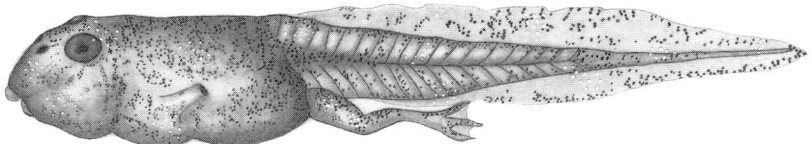

Fig. 326 *Hoplobatrachus occipitalis*

Hildebrandtia ornata
The tadpole is large, up to 95 mm long, and heavily built. The body is dark above and pale below, with a metallic green sheen. The labial tooth formula is 0/2, and the jaw sheaths are massive. The mouth is situated at the front of the head. It hunts tadpoles of other species but will scavenge.

Genus *Hoplobatrachus*

The tadpole is carnivorous, with large keratinized jaw sheaths. One species occurs in the area covered. It feeds on the tadpoles of other species, for example, *Ptychadena*. The tadpole of *H. occipitalis* is illustrated (Fig. 326).

Hoplobatrachus occipitalis
The tadpole is reddish gray with many darker spots but pale gray below. The tail is yellowish with brown marks. The jaw sheaths are well developed with a typical "tooth" on the upper sheath that fits between two "teeth" on the lower sheath. The labial tooth formula is 4(3 – 4)/4(1 – 2). Sometimes only three posterior tooth rows are present.

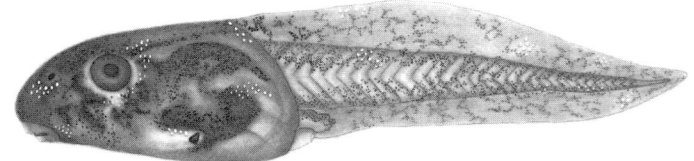

Fig. 327 *Microbatrachella capensis*

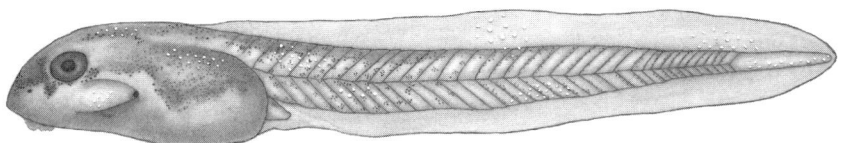

Fig. 328 *Natalobatrachus bonebergi*

Genus *Microbatrachella*

The tadpoles are found in dark-water ponds with a low pH. There is only one species. The tadpole of *M. capensis* is illustrated (Fig. 327).

Microbatrachella capensis
The labial tooth row formula is 3(2 – 3)/3(1).

Genus *Natalobatrachus*

The tadpoles are found in small streams and side pools in forests. The distance between the outside edges of the nostrils is more than the distance between the inner edges of the eyes. Tadpoles are difficult to catch in these sheltered habitats. There is only one species. The tadpole of *N. bonebergi* is illustrated (Fig. 328).

Natalobatrachus bonebergi
The tadpole may reach 41 mm in length. It is gray, and the fins are as high as the body. The oral formula is 5(2 – 5)/3 or 6(2 – 6)/3. The tadpole hatches at 12.5 mm, which is remarkably large, and time to metamorphosis is 60 days.

Genus *Nothophryne*

This genus is restricted to Mount Mulanje in Malawi, where the tadpoles have been seen wriggling across wet rock.

Nothophryne broadleyi
The tadpole is unknown.

Genus *Phrynobatrachus*

The tadpoles are dark and found in almost all slow-flowing stream or pond habitats. The distance between the nostrils is more than six times the nostril width. No key is provided as the tadpoles of many species remain undescribed. The tadpole of *P. natalensis* is illustrated (Fig. 329).

Phrynobatrachus mababiensis
The tadpoles are small, reaching 18 mm in length. They are brown with brown markings on the fins. The labial tooth row formula is 1/2 or 0/1. Metamorphosis takes 5 weeks.

Phrynobatrachus natalensis
The tadpole reaches 35 mm in length. It is brown with clear fins. The labial tooth row formula is 2(2)/2 or 1/2. It is often difficult to find in muddy pools.

Genus *Poyntonia*

The mouth is small, with a single row of lower papillae. Upper papillae are absent, but there are many papillae in the angle of the

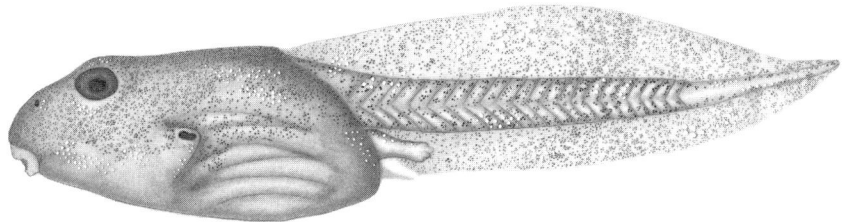

Fig. 329 *Phrynobatrachus natalensis*

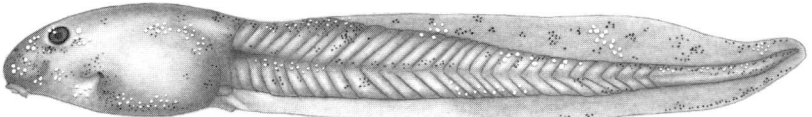

Fig. 330   *Poyntonia paludicola*

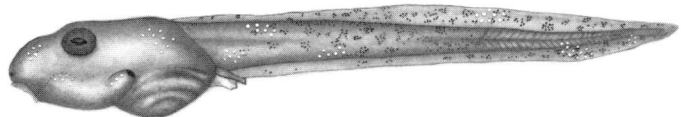

Fig. 331   *Ptychadena broadleyi*

mouth. There is only a single species. The tadpole of *P. paludicola* is illustrated (Fig. 330).

Poyntonia paludicola
The tadpole is quite distinct. It may grow to 32 mm. The tail is long, 72% of the total length. The labial tooth row formula is 1/2 or 2(2)/2. The background is brown with darker speckles, and the fins are lightly pigmented. There are numerous, characteristic, small white-tipped tubercles that cover the top and sides of the body and extend over the front third of the tail. The tubercles are absent below the level of the eyes and nostrils. The tadpoles are found in very shallow water in seepages.

Genus *Ptychadena*

No key is provided as many species remain undescribed. The distance between the nostrils is less than six times the nostril width. The labial tooth row formula is 2(2)/2. The tadpole of *P. broadleyi* is illustrated (Fig. 331).

Ptychadena anchietae
The tadpole reaches 45 mm in length. The upper body is gray to brown, with clear fins, but pale below. The tadpole has been shown to be part of a complex food web involving algae and mineral nutri-

ents in the bottom mud. It takes in bottom mud, grazes on the surface algae, or feeds off the surface film. This promotes the growth of the algae it feeds on by transferring nutrients from the sediment of the pond. In Malawi the tadpole provides food for the midge fly *Chironomus* larva, as this larva eats the feces of the tadpole. Even a dead tadpole in a dry pond serves as a food source for the next batch of tadpoles upon reflooding. The tadpole can withstand temperatures of up to 40 °C in shallow water.

Ptychadena broadleyi
The tadpole develops in a thin film of water. It is long and slender and feeds on algae growing on the rocks. It may do this with part of its body out of the water, exposed to sunlight. The tadpole then wriggles to a new place and then anchors itself with the mouth and the end of the tail, which is twisted to lie flat.

Ptychadena grandisonae
The tadpole has a dark band along the tail, which is relatively long.

Ptychadena mascareniensis
Tadpoles are small, with a spiracle opening against the body. Besides the standard arrangement of labial tooth rows, other labial tooth row formulas are 3(2 – 3)/2 and 4(2 – 4)/2. They are found in temporary pools. Metamorphosis occurs after 9 weeks.

Ptychadena oxyrhynchus
Tadpoles reach 54 mm in length. Besides the standard arrangement of labial tooth rows, other labial tooth row formulas are 1/2 or sometimes 3(2 – 3)/2. Three rows of papillae are present. The tadpole is gray but pale over the head. The throat has no chromatophores, and the fin is clear with spots.

Ptychadena porosissima
The brown tadpoles reach 41 mm in length. The labial tooth row formula is 1/2.

Genus *Pyxicephalus*

The tadpoles form large schools. They are dark, with eyes set close together on top of the head. Two species occur here, but no key is

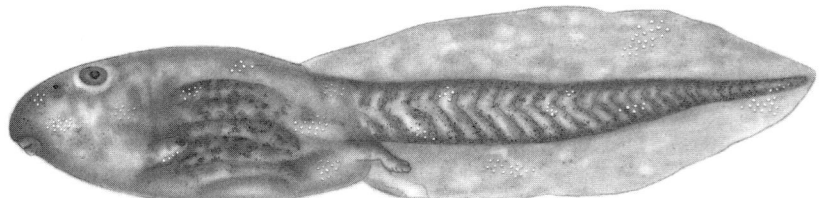

Fig. 332 *Pyxicephalus adspersus*

provided as only one has been described. The tadpole of *P. adspersus* is illustrated (Fig. 332).

Pyxicephalus adspersus
The black tadpoles become large, up to 71 mm long, and robust. They assume a gray color at about 60 mm. The labial tooth row formula is 4(3 – 4)/3. Two posterior rows have no medial gap. The tadpoles are gregarious, and up to 3000 have been estimated to form one school. Large schools like these consist of cohorts of different ages. The tadpoles remain in shallow water, even if deeper water is available. The school may form a ball, raft, or ring. The tadpoles feed on algae, and the schools move to deeper water at night. The individuals in a school dive at 45° to the bottom and return to the surface, while the rest swim over, so that the school appears to roll along. A school can move up to 46 m/h. Sometimes the schools consist of two species: the African bullfrog *Pyxicephalus adspersus* and the red toad *Schismaderma carens* were found schooling together at False Bay Park. Metamorphosis in warm shallow pools may take as little as 18–33 days or up to 47 days in captivity. At Katima Mulilo 60% of the large tadpoles examined had damaged tail tips, probably as a result of the close attention of their siblings.

Many of the shallow pools in which the tadpole develops become very hot during the day. One such pool in southern Zambia was at 40.6 °C in the sun. Observations have led to a theory on how tadpoles survive in such high temperatures. A few loose tadpoles and small schools of less than 50 tadpoles were swimming in the full sunlight. The thousands of other tadpoles in the pool had formed one large school and were swarming in very shallow water in the shade of a tree. The water temperature in the shade near the tadpoles was 38.3 °C. The large school was splashing enough that they could be

Tadpoles

heard from some distance. The splashing results in evaporative cooling, as the water temperature between the writhing tadpoles was 37.3 °C. It would appear from these preliminary observations that the tadpoles are reducing their body temperatures by more than 3° by swimming in the shade and by splashing in very shallow water at the edge of the pool.

Genus *Strongylopus*

The tadpoles are robust, with lower jaw sheaths pigmented to the base. No key is provided as many species remain undescribed. The tadpole of *S. grayii* is illustrated (Fig. 333).

Strongylopus fasciatus
It is an overall brown with darker flecks. The tadpole may reach 70 mm in length. A U-shaped line joins the nostrils to the mouth, and the tail tip is often dark. The labial tooth row formula is 4(2 – 4)/3. Only a single row of papillae is present on the oral disc.

Strongylopus grayii
The labial tooth row formula is 4(2 – 4)/3(1). The jaw sheaths are pigmented to the base. This tadpole might be confused with tadpoles of *Tomopterna*. The tadpoles are large-bodied, dark, and found in standing water.

Strongylopus hymenopus
The tadpole may reach 45 mm in length. It is heavy-bodied and dark, with the tip of the tail pale. An outgrowth from the upper part of the pupil, known as an umbraculum, is present but is lost in adults.

Fig. 333 *Strongylopus grayii*

The umbraculum is believed to serve as a sunshade in high-altitude species, to protect the eyes from UV light. The spiracle is large and round. The labial tooth row formula is 3(2 – 3)/3 or 3(2 – 3)/3(1 – 2). A double row of oral papillae is present.

Strongylopus rhodesianus
The tadpole reaches 36 mm in length. The labial tooth row formula is 3(3)/3(1). A double row of papillae is present below the mouth.

Strongylopus springbokensis
The tadpole grows to 30 mm or more. The labial tooth row formula is 4(2 – 4)/3(1 – 2). There are no papillae above the mouth. The body is uniformly brown, with the lower surface and fins unpigmented. The tadpole hatches from the egg as a free-swimming, well-formed larva.

Strongylopus wageri
The tadpole reaches 55 mm in length. It has a labial tooth row formula of 4(2 – 4)/3, with a characteristic black tip to the tail. The tadpole is often found sunning itself in shallow water.

Genus *Tomopterna*

Tadpoles are heavy-bodied and found in temporary pools. Tail less than twice as long as head and body. No key to the species is provided as some species have not been described. The tadpole of *T. delalandii* is illustrated (Fig. 334).

Tomopterna cryptotis
The tadpole is large-bodied, reaching 39 mm in length. It is brown, sometimes with darker markings. It spends much time resting on the

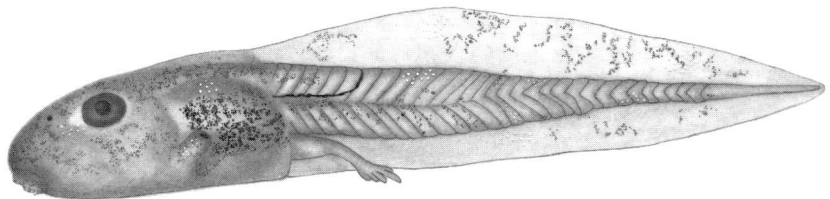

Fig. 334 *Tomopterna delalandii*

Tadpoles

bottom and when disturbed, will dive under the mud or swim to the deeper middle. The tadpole occurs together with terrapins but spends most of the time in the shallow waters, presumably where the terrapins are less likely to be feeding. The tadpole often feeds upside down on the surface film. Metamorphosis may take 5 weeks.

Tomopterna delalandii
The tadpole may reach 44 mm in length. It is bulky, with a brown body and darker speckling. The labial tooth row formula is 2(1 – 2)/3(1). Metamorphosis takes 25–35 days. The tadpole spends most of the time on the muddy bottom of the pool or stream.

Tomopterna natalensis
The tadpole is heavy-bodied and reaches 36 mm in length. The sides and back are covered with pigment cells called iridiophores that impart a golden speckle to the surface. The oral formula is 4(2 – 4)/3 or 5(2 – 5)/3. Like the other species, the tadpole remains on the bottom of the pond for long periods.

Tomopterna tandyi
The labial tooth row formula is 3(2 – 3)/3. The color pattern varies with the turbidity of the pool: the tadpoles are black in a clear pool, mottled in a slightly muddy pool, yet striped in a very turbid pool.

Family Rhacophoridae

Only one genus occurs in Africa. The tadpoles are found in temporary pools in open and wooded savannas.

Genus *Chiromantis*

Three species are found in Africa, of which only one occurs in this area. The mouth is below the front of the head. Upper and lower gaps in the papillae are present. The tadpole of *C. xerampelina* is illustrated (Fig. 335).

Chiromantis xerampelina
The tadpole is small, only 18 mm long, with an oval body. The labial tooth row formula is 3(2 – 3)/3. The lower gap in the papillae is about

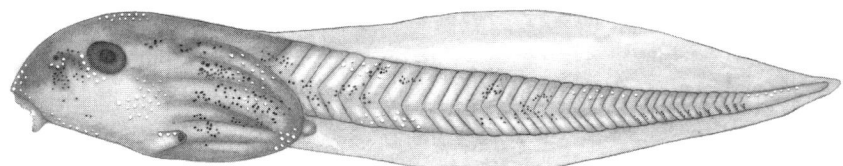

Fig. 335 *Chiromantis xerampelina*

0.6 of the width of the oral disc. They are found in temporary pools in tropical savannas.

KEY REFERENCES: van Dijk 1966, 1971; McDiarmid & Altig 1999.

Bibliography

These sources will serve as an introduction to the literature on frogs from the southern third of Africa. Any library should be able to obtain copies for further reading.

Adler, K. 1989. Herpetologists of the past. In K. Adler (Ed.), *Contributions to the History of Herpetology*, 5–141. St. Louis, Missouri: Society for the Study of Amphibians and Reptiles.
Ahl, E. 1924. Neue afrikanische Frösche. *Zool. Anz.* 61: 99–103.
———. 1926. 12. Anura, Aglossa, Xenopodidae. In E. Kaiser (Ed.), *Die Diamantenwüste Südwest-Afrikas*, 141–2. Berlin: Dietrich Reimer.
———. 1931. Neu oder selten eingeführte Fische, Lurche und Kriechtiere. *Aquarium* (October): 1–4.
Akizawa, T., K. Yamazaki, T. Nakajima, M. Roseghini, G. F. Erspamer, and V. Erspamer. 1982. Trypargine, a new tetrahydro-β-carboline of animal origin: Isolation and chemical characterization from the skin of the African rhacophorid frog, *Kassina senegalensis. Biomed. Res.* 3: 232–4.
Amiet, J.-L. 1973. Notes faunistiques, étholoques amphibiens anoures du Cameroun. *Ann. Fac. Sci. Cameroun* 13: 135–61.
———. 1974. Voix d'amphibiens camerounais. IV—Raninae: Genres *Ptychadena, Hildebrandtia* et *Dicroglossus. Ann. Fac. Sci. Cameroun* 18: 108–28.
———. 1976. Voix d'amphibiens camerounais. V. Bufonidae: Genres *Bufo, Werneria* et *Nectophryne. Ann. Fac. Sci. Cameroun* 21/22: 139–57.
Amiet, J.-L., and A. Schiøtz. 1974. Voix d'Amphibiens camerounais. III. Hyperoliinae: Genres *Leptopelis. Ann. Fac. Sci. Cameroun* 17: 131–63.
Anderson, R.-J., and K. V. Prahlad. 1976. Synergistic effects of herbicide and fungicide on *Xenopus laevis* embryos. *Am. Zool.* 15: 791.
Andrews, P., G. E. Meyer, D. R. Pilbeam, J. A. Van Couvering, and J. A. H. Van Couvering. 1981. The miocene fossil beds of Maboko Island, Kenya: Geology, age, taphonomy and palaeontology. *J. Human Evol.* 10: 35–48.
Araki, K., S. Tachibana, U. Mikio, T. Nakajima, and T. Yasuhara. 1973. Isolation and structure of a new active peptide "Xenopsin" on the smooth muscle, especially on a strip of fundus from a rat stomach, from the skin of *Xenopus laevis. Chem. Pharm. Bull.* 21: 2801–4.

Archbold, M. E. 1974. Letters to the editor. *Bull. E. Afr. Nat. Hist. Soc.* 1974 (April): 60–1.

Arnoult, J., and M. Lamotte. 1968. Les Pipidae de l'Ouest africain et du Cameroun. *Bull. Inst. Fr. Afr. Noire* 30 [Ser. A]: 270–306.

Auerbach, R. D. 1987. *The Amphibians and Reptiles of Botswana*, i–iv, 1–295. Gaberone: Mokwepa Consultants.

———. 1988. First steps in Setswana herpetology. *Botswana Notes Rec.* 18: 71–90.

Baard, E. H. W. 1989. The status of some rare and endangered endemic reptiles and amphibians of the southwestern Cape Province, South Africa. *Biol. Conserv.* 49: 161–8.

Baard, E. H. W., A. L. de Villiers, and M. E. de Villiers. 1988. A contribution to the herpetofaunal distribution of the Verneukpan/Copperton area, north-western Cape Province, South Africa. *J. Herpetol. Assoc. Afr.* 35: 25–32.

Backwell, P. R. Y. 1988. Functional partitioning in the two-part call of the leaf-folding frog, *Afrixalus brachycnemis*. *Herpetologica* 44: 1–7.

Backwell, P. R. Y., and N. I. Passmore. 1990a. Polyandry in the leaf folding frog, *Afrixalus delicatus*. *Herpetologica* 46: 7–10.

———. 1990b. Aggressive interactions and internal spacing in choruses of the leaf-folding frog, *Afrixalus delicatus*. *S. Afr. J. Zool.* 25: 133–7.

———. 1991. Advertisement calls and female phonotaxis in Natal dwarf *Afrixalus* (Anura: Hyperoliidae). *J. Afr. Zool.* 105: 275–80.

Baez, A. M. 1976. El significado paleogeografico y paleoecologico de los pipidos (Amphibia, Anura) fossils de America del sur. *VI Congr. Argeol. Geol. Bahia Blanca* 1975. 1: 333–40.

———. 1981. Redescription and relationships of *Saltenia ibanezi*, a late cretaceous pipid frog from northwestern Argentina. *Ameghiniana* 18: 127–54.

Baird, T. A. 1983. Influence of social and predatory stimuli on the airbreathing behavior of the African clawed frog, *Xenopus laevis*. *Copeia* 1983: 411–20.

Baker, C., and J. White. 1987. Spawning the African clawed frogs. *Freshwater Mar. Aquarium* 10: 84–7.

Balinsky, B. I. 1957. South African amphibia as material for biological research. *S. Afr. J. Sci.* 53: 383–91.

———. 1969. The reproductive ecology of amphibians of the Transvaal highveld. *Zool. Afr.* 4: 37–93.

———. 1985. Observations on the breeding of toads in a restricted habitat. *S. Afr. J. Zool.* 20: 61–4.

Balinsky, B. I., and J. B. Balinsky. 1954. On the breeding habits of the south African bullfrog *Pyxicephalus adspersus*. *S. Afr. J. Sci.* 51: 55–8.

Barbault, R. 1984. Stratégies de reproduction et démographie de quelques amphibiens anoures tropicaux. *Oikos* 43: 77–87.

Barbault, R., and M. T. Rodriques. 1978. Observations sur la reproduction et la dynamique des populations de quelque anoures tropicaux. I. *Ptychadena macarthyensis* et *Ptychadena oxyrhynchus*. *Terre Vie* 32: 441–52.

Barbour, T. 1934. The St. Helena frog. *Copeia* 1934: 183.

Barbour, T., and A. Loveridge. 1928. A comparative study of the herpetological faunae of the Uluguru and Usambara Mountains, Tanganyika Territory with descriptions of new species. *Mem. Mus. Comp. Zool.* 50: 87–265.

Barton, R. A. 1969. The Umtali Museum expedition to Mahenya. 18th November to 29th November, 1968. *J. Herpetol. Assoc. Afr.* 5: 9–13.

Bates, M. F., and D. de Swart. 1990. Life history notes. *Cacosternum boettgeri* and *Xenopus laevis*. *J. Herpetol. Assoc. Afr.* 37: 46.

Beckert, W. H., and W. Doyle. 1968. *Bufo regularis*, a twenty chromosome toad. *Genet. Res.* 11: 209–10.

Biegler, R. 1966. A survey of recent longevity records for reptiles and amphibians in zoos. *Int. Zoo Year Book* 6: 487–93.

Bishop, P. J., and N. I. Passmore. 1993. A new species of *Arthroleptella* Hewitt (Ranidae: Phrynobatrachinae) from the mist belt of the Natal highlands, South Africa. *Ann. Transv. Mus.* 36: 17–20.

Blake, D. K. 1960. Some notes on the feeding habits of the serrated terrapin. *J. Herpetol. Assoc. Rhod.* 9/10: 11.

———. 1963. Umtali Museum expedition to the Chimanimani Mountains—November 1962. *J. Herpetol. Assoc. Rhod.* 21: 6–11.

———. 1965. The fourth Umtali Museum expedition to Mozambique: November–December, 1964. *J. Herpetol. Assoc. Rhod.* 23/24: 31–46.

Bles, E. J. 1907. Notes on Anuran development *Paludicola*, *Hemisus* and *Phyllomedusa*. *Budgett Memorial Volume*, 443–58, pls 22–7. Cambridge: Cambridge University Press.

Bocage, J. V. Barboza du. 1873. Mélanges Erpétolgiques II. Sur quelques Reptiles et Batraciens nouveaux, rares, ou peu connus d'Afrique occidentale. *J. Sci. Math. Phys. Nat.* (Lisboa) 4: 209–27.

———. 1879. Reptiles et batraciens nouveaux d'Angola. *J. Sci. Math. Phys. Nat.* 7: 97–9.

———. 1895. *Herpétologie d'Angola et du Congo*. Lisbonne: Imprimerie Nationale.

Bogart, J. P. 1968. Chromosome number difference in the Amphibian genus *Bufo*: The *Bufo regularis* species group. *Evolution* 22: 42–5.

———. 1972. Karyotypes. In W. F. Blair (Ed.), *Evolution in the Genus Bufo*, 171–95. Austin: University of Texas Press.

———. 1973. Evolution of anuran karyotypes. In J. L. Vial (Ed.), *Evolutionary Biology of the Anurans*, 337–49. St. Louis: University of Missouri Press.

Bogart, J. P., and C. E. Nelson. 1976. Evolutionary implications from karyotypic analysis of frogs of the families Microhylidae and Rhinophrynidae. *Herpetologica* 32: 199–208.

Bogart, J. P., and M. Tandy. 1976. Polyploid amphibians. Three more diploid-tetraploid cryptic species of frogs. *Science* 193: 334–5.

———. 1981. Chromosome lineages in African ranoid frogs. *Monit. Zool. Ital. (N. S.) Suppl.* 15: 55–91.

Bogenschutz, H. 1965. Extraokulare steuerung des farbwechsels bei Kaulquappen. *Experientia* 21: 451.

Bothma, J. du P. 1971a. Food of *Canis mesomelas* in South Africa. *Zool. Afr.* 6: 195–203.

———. 1971b. Reports of some Carnivora (Mammalia) from southern Africa. *Ann. Transv. Mus.* 27: 15–26.

Boulenger, G. A. 1887. A living specimen of a rare African batrachian, *Xenopus laevis*, Daud. exhibited. *Proc. Zool. Soc. Lond.* 1887: 563–4.

———. 1895. An account of the reptiles and batrachians collected by Dr. A. Donaldson Smith in western Somaliland and the Galla country. *Proc. Zool. Soc. Lond.* 1894: 530–40, pls 29, 30.

———. 1907. Description of three new lizards and a new frog, discovered by Dr. W. J. Ansorge in Angola. *Ann. Mag. Nat. Hist.* (7) 19: 212–14.

Bourke, D. O'D. 1968. A toad trap. *Nigerian Field* 33: 143.

Bourlière, F. 1947. Longévité moyenne et longévité maximum chez les vertébrés. *Ann. Biol.* 22: 249–70.

Bourquin, O. 1985. A note on *Hemisus marmoratus*, compiled from the narrative of D. J. Bourquin. *S. Afr. J. Sci.* 81: 210.

Boutilier, R. G. 1986. Respiratory properties of blood from voluntary and forcibly submerged *Xenopus laevis*. *J. Exp. Biol.* 121: 285–300.

Bouwer, S. R. 1952. The skin and the thyroid gland of *Bufo regularis* Reuss in relation to moulting. M.Sc. thesis, University of Natal, Pietermaritzburg.

Bouwer, S. R., D. W. Ewer, and C. Shiff. 1953. Frequency of moulting in Anura. *Nature* 172: 408.

Bowler, J. K. 1977. Longevity of reptiles and amphibians in North American collections. *SSAR Misc. Publ. Herp. Circ.* 6: i–v, 1–32.

Boycott, R. C. 1982a. Green water snake (*Philothamnus hoplogaster*) eating a common river frog (*Rana angolensis*). *Afr. Wild Life* 36(2): cover, 37.

———. 1982b. On the taxonomic status of *Heleophryne regis* Hewitt, 1909 (Anura: Leptodactylidae). *Ann. Cape Prov. Mus. (Nat. Hist.)* 14: 89–108.

———. 1987. Geographical distribution Amphibia. *J. Herpetol. Assoc. Afr.* 33: 30.

———. 1988a. Evidence of tactile communication during courtship in *Heleophryne* (Anura: Heleophrynidae). *J. Herpetol. Assoc. Afr.* 35: 12–14.

———. 1988b. Description of a new species of *Heleophryne* Sclater, 1899 from the Cape Province, South Africa (Anura: Heleophrynidae). *Ann. Cape Prov. Mus. (Nat. Hist.)* 16: 309–19.

———. 1988c. Table Mountain ghost frog. In W. R. Branch (Ed.), South African

Red Data Book—Reptiles and Amphibians. *S. Afr. Nat. Sci. Prog. Rep.* 151: 36–8.

——. 1988d. Amatola toad. In W. R. Branch (Ed.), South African Red Data Book—Reptiles and Amphibians. *S. Afr. Nat. Sci. Prog. Rep.* 151: 111–12.

——. 1988e. Cape mountain toad. In W. R. Branch (Ed.), South African Red Data Book—Reptiles and Amphibians. *S. Afr. Nat. Sci. Prog. Rep.* 151: 113–15.

Boycott, R. C., and W. R. Branch. 1988. Hewitt's ghost frog. In W. R. Branch (Ed.), South African Red Data Book—Reptiles and Amphibians. *S. Afr. Nat. Sci. Prog. Rep.* 151: 33–5.

Boycott, R. C., and A. L. de Villiers. 1986. The status of *Heleophryne rosei* Hewitt (Anura: Leptodactylidae) on Table Mountain and recommendations for its conservation. *S. Afr. J. Wild. Res.* 16: 129–34.

Braack, H. H., I. H. Davidson, J. A. Ledger, and D. J. Lewis. 1981. Records of sandflies (Diptera: Psychodidae: Phlebotominae) feeding on amphibia, with a new record from the Kruger National Park. *Koedoe* 24: 187–8.

Branch, W. R. 1976. Two exceptional food records for the African bullfrog, *Pyxicephalus adspersus* (Amphibia, Anura, Ranidae). *J. Herpetol.* 10: 266–8.

Branch, W. R. (Ed.). 1988a. South African Red Data Book—Reptiles and Amphibians. *S. Afr. Nat. Sci. Prog. Rep.* 151.

——. 1988b. Poynton's caco. In W. R. Branch (Ed.), South African Red Data Book—Reptiles and Amphibians. *S. Afr. Nat. Sci. Prog. Rep.* 151: iv, 205.

——. 1990. The herpetofauna of the Cape Province, South Africa: New distribution records and zoogeography. *J. Herpetol. Assoc. Afr.* 37: 17–44.

——. 1992. Life history notes. *Xenopus laevis laevis* predation. *J. Herpetol. Assoc. Afr.* 41: 40.

Branch, W. R., and H. Braack. 1996 (1995). A new toad from Paradise. *Madoqua* 19: 15–23.

Branch, W. R., and R. W. Patterson. 1975. Notes on the ecology of the giant girdled lizard, *Cordylus giganteus*. *J. Herpetol.* 9: 364–6.

Broadley, D. G. 1963. An expedition to Tete and South Nyasaland. *J. Herpetol. Assoc. Rhod.* 20: 18–26.

——. 1964. The second Umtali Museum expedition to Mozambique 1963–4. *J. Herpetol. Assoc. Rhod.* 22: 13–16.

——. 1974a. Predation by birds on reptiles and amphibians in south-eastern Africa. *Honeyguide* (78): 11–19.

——. 1974b. Vernacular names for Rhodesian reptiles and amphibians. Revised names 1. *J. Herpetol. Assoc. Afr.* 12: 31.

——. 1991. The herpetofauna of northern Mwinilunga district, northwestern Zambia. *Arnoldia Zimbabwe* 9: 519–38.

Burger, M., and A. L. de Villiers. 1993. Life history notes. Amphibia, Pipidae, *Xenopus laevis laevis*, common platanna. Size. *J. Herpetol. Assoc. Afr.* 42: 34.

Cairncross, B. L. 1956. Size of bull frogs. *Afr. Wild Life* 10: 347.

Carlyon, J. 1988. A season at an old tree trunk. *Afr. Wild Life* 42: 28–9.
Carruthers, V. 1973. Froggy went a-wooing. *S. Afr. Panorama* (September): 48–50.
Casalis, A. 1932. *English-Sesuto Vocabulary* (Morija: Sesutu Book Depot).
Casterlin, M. E., and W. W. Reynolds. 1980. Diel activity and thermoregulatory behaviour of a fully aquatic frog: *Xenopus laevis*. *Hydrobiologica* 75: 189–91.
Chabanaud, P. 1921. Contributions á l'étude de la faune herpétologique de l'Afrique occidentale. II Deuxième note. *Bull. Com. Étude Hist. Sci. Afr. Occ. Fr. Paris* 3: 445–72.
Channing, A. 1972a. A description of *Bufo pusillus* tadpoles (Anura: Bufonidae). *Ann. Natal Mus.* 21: 509–11.
——. 1972b. Morphological variation in *Bufo garmani* from South West Africa. *Cimbebasia* (Ser. A) 2: 93–6.
——. 1976a. Life histories of frogs in the Namib Desert. *Zool. Afr.* 11: 299–312.
——. 1976b. Pre-mating isolation in the genus *Kassina* (Amphibia, Anura, Rhacophoridae) in southern Africa. *J. Herpetol.* 10: 19–23.
——. 1978a. A new bufonid genus (Amphibia: Anura) from Rhodesia. *Herpetologica* 34: 394–7.
——. 1978b. A new *Rana* from the Lesotho plateau (Amphibia: Anura). *Ann. Natal Mus.* 23: 361–5.
——. 1979. Ecological and systematic relationships of *Rana* and *Strongylopus* in southern Natal. *Ann. Natal Mus.* 23: 797–831.
——. 1986. A new species of the genus *Strongylopus* Tschudi from Namaqualand, Cape Province, South Africa (Anura: Ranidae). *Ann. Cape Prov. Mus. (Nat. Hist.)* 16: 127–35.
——. 1989a. A re-evaluation of the phylogeny of Old World treefrogs. *S. Afr. J. Zool.* 24: 116–31.
——. 1989b. New frog records from the Eastern Caprivi Strip, South West Africa/Namibia. *Madoqua* 16: 1–4.
——. 1991. The distribution of *Bufo poweri* in southern Africa. *S. Afr. J. Zool.* 26: 81–4.
——. 1993a. Observations on the natural history of *Stephopaedes anotis* (Bufonidae). *J. Herpetol.* 27: 213–14.
——. 1993b. A new grass frog from Namibia. *S. Afr. J. Zool.* 28: 142–5.
Channing, A., and J. P. Bogart. 1996. Description of a tetraploid *Tomopterna* (Anura: Ranidae) from South Africa. *S. Afr. J. Zool.* 31: 80–5.
Channing, A., and R. C. Boycott. 1989. A new frog genus and species from the mountains of the southwestern Cape, South Africa (Anura: Ranidae). *Copeia* 1989: 467–71.
Channing, A., R. C. Boycott, and H. J. van Hensbergen. 1988. Morphological variation of *Heleophryne* tadpoles from the Cape Province, South Africa (Anura: Heleophrynidae). *J. Zool. (Lond.)* 215: 205–16.

Channing, A., and D. G. Broadley. 1992. The tadpole of *Kassina kuvangensis*. *Alytes* 10: 105–12.
Channing, A., and M.-D. Crapon de Crapona. 1987. The tadpole of *Hyperolius mitchelli* (Anura: Hyperoliidae). *S. Afr. J. Zool.* 22: 235–7.
Channing, A., and R. C. Drewes. 1997. Description of the tadpole of *Bufo kisoloensis*. *Alytes* 15: 13–18.
Channing, A., and. M. Griffin. 1993. An annotated checklist of the frogs of Namibia. *Madoqua* 18: 101–16.
Channing, A., D. Hendricks, and A. Dawood. 1994a. Description of a new moss frog from the south-western Cape (Anura: Ranidae: *Arthroleptella*). *S. Afr. J. Zool.* 29: 240–3.
Channing, A., N. I. Passmore, and L. du Preez. 1994b. Status, vocalizations and breeding of two species of African bullfrogs. *J. Zool. (Lond.)* 234: 141–8.
Channing, A., and M. Vences. 1999. The advertisement call, breeding biology, description of the tadpole and taxonomic status of *Bufo dombensis*, a little-known dwarf toad from southern Africa. *S. Afr. J. Zool.* 34: 74–9.
Chapman, J. 1868. *Travels in the Interior of South Africa*, Vol. I, i–xv, 1–454. London: Bell and Daldy.
Charter, R. R., and J. B. C. MacMurray. 1939. On the "frilled" tadpole of *Bufo carens* Smith. *S. Afr. J. Sci.* 36: 386–9.
Chen, K. K., and A. L. Chen. 1933. The physiological action of the principles isolated from the secretion of the South African toad (*Bufo regularis*). *J. Pharmacol. Exp. Ther.* 49: 503–13.
Chinn, M. 1945. Notes pour l'étude de l'alimantation des indigènes de la province de Coquilhatville. *Ann. Soc. Belge Med. Trop.* 25: 57–149.
Clarke, B. T. 1989. Real vs apparent distribution of dwarf amphibians: *Bufo lindneri* Mertens 1955—a case in point. *Amphibia-Reptilia* 10: 297–306.
———. 1997. The natural history of amphibian skin secretions, their normal functioning and potential medical application. *Biol. Rev.* 72: 365–80.
Cochran, D. M. 1972. *Living Amphibians of the World*. New York: Doubleday.
Colley, B. 1987. *Phrynomerus bifasciatus*—An unpleasant experience. *Herptile* 12: 43.
Cott, H. B. 1947. Tree frogs. *Zoo Life Lond.* 2: 55–8.
Cowls, R. B. 1936. Casual notes on the poikilothermous vertebrates of the Umzumbe Valley, Natal, South Africa. *Copeia* 1936: 4–8.
Craig, A. 1974. Whiskered terns feeding on Arum frogs. *Ostrich* 45: 142.
Cruz-Uribe, K., and R. G. Klein. 1982/83. Faunal remains from some Middle and Later Stone Age archeological sites in South West Africa. *J. S. W. Afr. Sci. Soc.* 36/37: 91–114.
Curry-Lindahl, K. 1956. Ecological studies on mammals, birds, reptiles and amphibians in the eastern Belgian Congo. Part I. *Ann. Mus. R. Congo Belge Tervuren 8° Sci. Zool.* 42: 5–78, pls I–VII.

Daly, J. W., and B. Witkop. 1971. Chemistry and pharmacology of frog venoms. In W. Bücherl and E. Buckley (Eds.), *Venomous Animals and Their Venoms*. Vol II. *Venomous Vertebrates*, 497–519. New York: Academic Press.

Damstra, K. St. J. 1983. The anuran skin gland duct—a significant avenue for evaporative water loss. *Proc. Electr. Micro. Soc. S. Afr.* 13: 73–4.

Dawood, A., and A. Channing. 2000. A molecular phylogeny of moss frogs with the description of a new species. *J. Herpetol.* 34: 375–9.

Dawson, P., and P. J. Bishop. 1987. The painted reed-frog (*Hyperolius marmoratus*): Aspects of life history, experimental use and husbandry. *Anim. Techn.* 38: 81–6.

De Fonesca, P. H., and R. Jocque. 1979. A herpetological survey of the Chintheche area in Malawi. *Rev. Zool. Afr.* 93: 797–809.

De Fonesca, P. H., and D. Mertens. 1979. De gouden zeggekikker *Hyperolius puncticulatus* in de natuur en in het terrarium. *Lacerta* 37: 147–51.

Delvinquier, B. L. J., M. B. Markus, and N. I. Passmore. 1993. Opalinidae in African Anura. 3. Genus Cepedea. *Syst. Parasitol.* 24: 53–80.

De Villiers, A. 1988a. Desert rain frog. In W. R. Branch (Ed.), South African Red Data Book—Reptiles and Amphibians. *S. Afr. Nat. Sci. Prog. Rep.* 151: 116–18.

———. 1988b. Micro frog. In W. R. Branch (Ed.), South African Red Data Book—Reptiles and Amphibians. *S. Afr. Nat. Sci. Prog. Rep.* 151: 29–32.

———. 1988c. Cape rain frog. In W. R. Branch (Ed.), South African Red Data Book—Reptiles and Amphibians. *S. Afr. Nat. Sci. Prog. Rep.* 151: 46–8.

———. 1988d. Cape caco. In W. R. Branch (Ed.), South African Red Data Book—Reptiles and Amphibians. *S. Afr. Nat. Sci. Prog. Rep.* 151: 123–5.

De Villiers, C. G. S. 1929a. Some observations on the breeding habits of the Anura of the Stellenbosch flats, in particular of *Cacosternum capense* and *Bufo angusticeps*. *Ann. Transv. Mus.* 13: 123–41.

———. 1929b. Some features of the early development of *Breviceps*. *Ann. Transv. Mus.* 13: 142–51.

De Waal, S. W. P. 1980. The Salientia (Amphibia) of the Orange Free State, South Africa. *Navors. Nas. Mus.* 4: 95–120.

De Witte, G.-F. 1921. Description de batraciens nouveaux du Congo Belge. *Rev. Zool. Afr.* 9: 1–21, pls i–v.

Douglas, R. 1970. Life history notes. *Cacosternum boettgeri*. *J. Herpetol. Assoc. Afr.* 37: 45.

Doyle, W., and W. H. Beckert. 1969. Anuran chromosome variations. *J. Cell Biol.* 43: 32.

Drewes, R. C. 1984. A phylogenetic analysis of the Hyperoliidae (Anura): Treefrogs of Africa, Madagascar, and the Seychelles Islands. *Occ. Pap. Cal. Acad. Sci.* (139): 1–70.

———. 1985. A case of paraphyly in the genus *Kassina* Girard, 1853 (Anura: Hyperoliidae). *S. Afr. J. Sci.* 81: 186–91.

Dubois, A. 1980. Deux noms d'espèces préoccupés dans le genre *Rana* (Amphibiens, Anoures). *Bull. Mus. Nat. Hist. Nat., Paris* 4° sér. 2: 927–31.
———. 1981. Liste des genres et sous-genres nominaux de Ranoidea (Amphibiens Anoures) du monde, avec identification de leurs espèces-types: conséquences nomenclaturales. *Monit. Zool. Ital. (N. S.) Suppl.* 15: 225–84.
———. 1988. Miscellanea nomenclatorica batrachologica (XVII). *Alytes* 7: 1–5.
———. 1992. Notes sur la classification des Ranidae (Amphibiens Anoures). *Bull. Mens. Soc. Linn. Lyon.* 61: 305–52.
Dudley, C. O. 1978. The herpetofauna of the Lake Chilwa basin. *Nyala* 4: 87–99.
Duellman, W. E. 1999. Patterns of Distribution of Amphibians. Baltimore: The John Hopkins University Press.
Du Plessis, S. S. 1966. Stimulation of spawning in *Xenopus laevis* by fowl manure. *Nature* 211: 1092.
Du Preez, L. 1996. Field Guide and Key to the Frogs and Toads of the Free State. Bloemfontein: University of the Orange Free State.
Dyson, M. 1985. Effect of call sound pressure level on the selective phonotaxis of female *Hyperolius marmoratus*. *S. Afr. J. Sci.* 81: 209.
Dyson, M. L., N. I. Passmore, P. J. Bishop, and S. P. Henzi. 1992. Male behavior and correlates of mating success in a natural population of African painted reed frogs (*Hyperolius marmoratus*). *Herpetologica* 48: 236–46.
Eibl-Eibesfeldt, I. 1962. Die Verhaltensentwicklung des Krallenfrosches (*Xenopus laevis*) und des Scheibenzünglers (*Dicroglossus pictus*) unter besonderer Berucksichtigung der Beutelfanghandlungen. *Z. Tierpsychol.* 19: 385–95.
Elepfandt, A. 1982. Accuracy of taxis response to water waves in the clawed toad (*Xenopus laevis* Daudin) with intact or with lesioned lateral line system. *J. Comp. Physiol.* 148: 535–45.
Emara, M., A. A. Gobba, and M. A. Soliman. 1949. A new pregnancy test using the male Egyptian toad. *J. Egypt. Med. Assoc.* 32: 733–6.
Emerson, S. B. 1976. Burrowing in frogs. *J. Morphol.* 149: 437–58.
Estes, R. 1975. Fossil *Xenopus* from the paleocene of south America and the zoogeography of pipid frogs. *Herpetologica* 31: 263–78.
———. 1977. Relationships of the South African fossil frog *Eoxenopoides reuningi* (Anura, Pipidae). *Ann. S. Afr. Mus.* 73: 48–80.
Estes, R., Z. V. Spinar, and E. Nevo. 1978. Early Cretaceous pipid tadpoles from Israel (Amphibia: Anura). *Herpetologica* 34: 374–93.
Estes, R. D. 1982. Systematics and paleogeography of some fossil salamanders and frogs. *Nat. Geog. Soc. Res. Rep.* 14: 191–210.
Feder, M. E., D. B. Seale, M. E. Baraas, R. J. Wassersug, and A. B. Gibbs. 1984. Functional conflicts between feeding and gas exchange in suspension-feeding tadpoles, *Xenopus laevis*. *J. Exp. Biol.* 110: 91–8.

Fenton, M. B., D. H. M. Cumming, J. M. Hutton, and C. M. Swanepoel. 1987. Foraging and habitat use by *Nycteris grandis* (Chiroptera: Nycteridae) in Zimbabwe. *J. Zool. (Lond.)* 211: 709–16.

Fenton, M. B., C. L. Gaudet, and M. L. Leonard. 1983. Feeding behaviour of the bats *Nycteris grandis* and *Nycteris thebaica* (Nycteridae) in captivity. *J. Zool. (Lond.)* 200: 347–54.

Ferreira, J. B. 1906. Algumas especies novas ou pouco conhecidas de amphibios e reptis de Angola. *J. Sci. Math. Phys. Nat.* (Lisboa) [Ser. 2] 7: 159–71.

Fielding, P. 1979. The relative survival abilities of *Xenopus laevis* and *Xenopus gilli* in the low pH blackwater systems of the Cape Point Nature Reserve. Zoology Hons. Project, University of Cape Town. i–ii, 1–37.

FitzSimons, V. 1935. Scientific results of the Vernay-Lang Kalahari expedition, March to September, 1930. Reptilia and Amphibia. *Ann. Transv. Mus.* 16: 295–397, pls vi–viii.

———. 1939. An account of the reptiles and amphibians collected on an expedition to south-eastern Rhodesia during December 1937 and January 1938. *Ann. Transv. Mus.* 20: 17–46.

———. 1946. An account of the reptiles and amphibians collected on an expedition to the Cape Province, October to December,1940. *Ann. Transv. Mus.* 20: 351–377, pls XIV–XVII.

———. 1947. Descriptions of new species and subspecies of reptiles and amphibians from Natal, together with notes on some other little known species. *Ann. Natal Mus.* 11: 111–37, pls I–III.

FitzSimons, V., and G. Van Dam. 1929. Some observations on the breeding habits of *Breviceps*. *Ann. Transv. Mus.* 13: 152–3.

Fleischack, P. C., and C. P. Small. 1979. The vocalizations and breeding behaviour of *Kassina* (Anura; Rhacophoridae) in summer breeding aggregations. *Koedoe* 21: 91–9.

Ford, L. S., and D. C. Cannatella. 1993. The major clades of frogs. *Herpetol. Monogr.* 7: 94–117.

Freeman, S. B. 1968. A study of the jelly envelopes surrounding the eggs of the amphibian *Xenopus laevis*. *Biol. Bull. Woods Hole* 135: 501–13.

Frost, D. R. (Ed.). 1985. *Amphibian Species of the World.* Lawrence, Kansas: Allen Press and Association of Systematics Collections.

Garland, I. 1979. iNtingono notes from Zululand. *Natal Wild Life* 20: 67.

Gasche, P. 1944. Der südafrikanischer Krallenfrosch. *Natur Volk* 74: 1–11.

Gauld, I., and G. Underwood. 1986. Some applications of the Le Quesne compatibility test. *Biol. J. Linn. Soc.* 29: 191–222.

Gilchrist, J. D. F., and C. von Bonde. 1919. *Dissection of the Platanna and the Frog.* Cape Town, South Africa: University of Cape Town.

Gosse, P. 1937. The St. Helena frog, *Rana grayi* Smith. *Copeia* 1937: 229.

Gow, C. E. 1962. Some collecting techniques and general notes. *J. Herpetol. Assoc. Rhod.* 19: 13–14.

———. 1963. Notes on the habitat of *Heleophryne rosei*. *Afr. Wild Life* 17: 113–15.
Gradwell, N. 1974. Descriptions of the tadpole of *Phrynomerus annectens*, and comments on its gill irrigation mechanism. *Herpetologica* 30: 53–62.
Grandison, A. G. C. 1972. The status and relationships of some East African earless toads (Anura, Bufonidae) with a description of a new species. *Zool. Meded.* 47: 30–48, pls 1–4.
———. 1980. A new genus of toad (Anura: Bufonidae) from the Republic of South Africa with remarks on its relationships. *Bull. Br. Mus. Nat. Hist. (Zool.)* 39: 293–8.
———. 1981. Morphology and phylogenetic position of the West African *Didynamipus sjoestedti* Andersson, 1903 (Anura Bufonidae). *Monit. Zool. Ital. (N. S.) Suppl.* 15: 187–215.
Greig, J. C. 1980. Salt tolerance of the common platanna. *Cape Herp News* 3: 13–14.
Greig, J. C., R. C. Boycott, and A. L. de Villiers. 1979. Notes on the elevation of *Rana fasciata montana* FitzSimons, 1946 to specific rank, and on the identity of *Rana fasciata* sensu Burchell, 1824 (Anura: Ranidae). *Ann. Cape Prov. Mus. (Nat. Hist.)* 13: 1–30.
Griffin, C. S., D. Scott, and D. G. Papworth. 1970. The influence of DNA content and nuclear volume on the frequency of radiation-induced chromosome abberations in *Bufo* species. *Chromosoma (Berlin)* 30: 228–49.
Grimm, H. 1952. Beobachtung über bewegungsnormen, Ernährung und Fortpflanzungsverhalten des Krallenfrosches. Ein Beitrag zur vergleichenden Verhaltensforschung bei Anuren. *Z. Tierpsychol.* 9: 230–44.
Grobler, J. H. 1972. Observations on the amphibian *Pyxicephalus adspersus* Tschudi in Rhodesia. *Arnoldia (Rhod.) Misc. Publ.* 6: 1–4.
Guibé, J., and M. Lamotte. 1958. La réserve naturelle intégrale du Mont Nimba. Fasc. IV. XII Batraciens (sauf *Arthroleptis*, *Phrynobatrachus* et *Hyperolius*). *Mem. Inst. Fr. Afr. Noire.* 53: 241–73, pls I–XI.
Gunn, J. W. C. 1921. A note on the use of the South African clawed toad in the biological assay of the digitalis series. *Trans. R. Soc. S. Afr.* 10: 55–6.
Guttman, S. I. 1967. Transferrin and hemoglobin polymorphism, hybridization and introgression in two African toads, *Bufo regularis* and *Bufo rangeri*. *Comp. Biochem. Physiol.* 23: 871–7.
Haacke, W. D. 1982. A cave inhabiting *Xenopus laevis* from the Cango Valley near Oudtshoorn, Cape Province, South Africa. *J. Herpetol. Assoc. Afr.* 28: 26.
Hargreaves, K. C. 1969. The karyotype of *Breviceps adspersus* and *Pyxicephalus natalensis* Zoology Hons. Project, Zoology Department, University of Natal, Pietermaritzburg.
Haughton, S. H. 1931. On a collection of fossil frogs from the clays at Banke. *Trans. R. Soc. S. Afr.* 19: 233–49, pls XXIII–XXIV.

Hewitt, J. 1913. Description *of Heleophryne natalensis*, a new batrachian from Natal and notes on several South African batrachians and reptiles. *Ann. Natal Mus.* 2: 475–84, pl 39.
——. 1919. *Anhydrophryne rattrayi*, a remarkable new frog from Cape Colony. *Rec. Alb. Mus.* 3: 182–9, pl V.
——. 1922. Notes on some South African tadpoles. *S. Afr. J. Nat. Hist.* 3: 60–5.
——. 1925a. Descriptions of three new toads belonging to the genus *Breviceps* Merrem. *Ann. Natal Mus.* 5: 189–94, pl X.
——. 1925b. On some new species of reptiles and amphibians from South Africa. *Rec. Alb. Mus.* 3: 343–69, pls xv–xix.
——. 1926a. Descriptions of new and little-known lizards and batrachians from South Africa. *Ann. S. Afr. Mus.* 20: 413–31, pls 35–7.
——. 1926b. Descriptions of some new species of Batrachians and lizards from S. Africa. *Ann. Natal Mus.* 5: 435–48.
——. 1933. Descriptions of some new reptiles and a frog from Rhodesia. *Occ. Pap. Rhod. Mus.* 1: 45–50, pl 9.
——. 1935. Some new forms of batrachians and reptiles from South Africa. *Rec. Alb. Mus.* 4: 283–357, pls 27–31.
——. 1937. *A Guide to the Vertebrate Fauna of the Eastern Cape Province, South Africa*, Part II. Grahamstown: Albany Museum.
Hey, D. 1986. *Water and Wildlife.* Cape Town: Timmins.
Hobson, B. M. 1958. Polymely in *Xenopus laevis. Nature* 181: 862.
Hoesch, W. 1960a. Beobachtungen am afrikanischen Grabfrosch *Rana adspersa. Natur Volk*: 90: 11–16.
——. 1960b. Über die Tierwelt im Gebiet der südwestafrikanischen Wanderdünen. *Natur Volk* 90: 252–64.
Hogben, L. 1946. History of the Hogben Test. *Br. Med. J.* 2: 554.
Howell, K. M. 1978. Ocular envenomation by a toad in the *Bufo regularis* species group: effects and first aid. *Bull. E. Afr. Nat. Hist. Soc.* 1978 (July/August): 82–7.
——. 1981. The female of *Leptopelis argenteus argenteus. J. Herpetol.* 15: 113–14.
Hughes, B. 1986. Longevity records of African captive amphibians and reptiles: Part 1. Introduction and species list. 1—Amphibians and chelonians. *J. Herpetol. Assoc. Afr.* 32: 1–9.
Huntley, J. 1985. Samango monkeys, tree frogs and Lengwe National Park. *Afr. Wild Life* 39: 43.
Inger, R. F. 1959. Amphibia. *S. Afr. Animal Life* 6: 510–53. Stockholm: Almquist and Wiksell.
——. 1968. Mission H. de Saeger. Amphibia. *Explor. Parc. Nat. Garamba* (Fasc. 52): 1–190.
Inger, R. F., and B. Greenberg. 1956. Morphology and seasonal development of sex characters in two sympatric African toads. *J. Morphol.* 99: 549–74.

Inger, R., and H. Marx. 1961. The food of amphibians. *Explor. Parc Nat. Upemba* 64: 1–86.

Jacobsen, N. H. G. 1982. The ecology of the reptiles and amphibians in the *Burkea africanum—Eragrostis pallens* savanna of the Nylsvley Nature Reserve. M.Sc. thesis, University of Pretoria.

———. 1989. A herpetological survey of the Transvaal. Ph.D. dissertation, University of Natal.

Jaeger, R. G. 1971. Toxic reaction to skin secretions of the frog *Phrynomerus bifasciatus*. *Copeia* 1971: 160–1.

Jennions, M. D., P. R. Y. Backwell, and N. I. Passmore. 1992. Breeding behaviour of the African frog, *Chiromantis xerampelina*: Multiple spawning and polyandry. *Anim. Behav.* 44: 1091–100.

Jennions, M. D., and N. I. Passmore. 1993. Sperm competition in frogs—Testis size and a sterile male experiment on *Chiromantis xerampelina* (Rhacophoridae). *Biol. J. Linn. Soc.* 50: 211–20.

Jenson, H. 1935. Chemical studies on toad poisons. VII. *Bufo arenarum*, *Bufo regularis* and *Xenopus laevis*. *J. Am. Chem. Soc.* 57: 1765–8.

Johansen, K., G. Lykkeboe, S. Kornerup, and G. M. O. Maloiy. 1980. Temperature insensitive O_2 in blood of the tree frog *Chiromantis petersi*. *J. Comp. Physiol.* 136: 71–6.

Kaminsky, S. K., K. E. Linsenmair, and T. U. Grafe. 1999. Reproductive timing, nest construction and tadpole guidance in the African pig-nosed frog, *Hemisus marmoratus*. *J. Herpetol.* 33: 119–23.

Karplus, I., D. Algom, and D. Samuel. 1981. Acquisition and retention of dark avoidance by the toad, *Xenopus laevis* (Daudin). *Anim. Learning Behav.* 9: 45–9.

Katz, L. C., M. J. Potel, and R. J. Wassersug. 1981. Structure and mechanisms of schooling in tadpoles of the clawed toad, *Xenopus laevis*. *Anim. Behav.* 29: 20–33.

Kaul, R., and V. H. Shoemaker. 1989. Control of thermoregulatory evaporation in the waterproof treefrog *Chiromantis xerampelina*. *J. Comp. Physiol.* [B] 158: 643–9.

Kawamura, T. 1984. Polyploidy in amphibians. *Zool. Sci.* 1: 1–15.

Keith, R. 1968. A new species of *Bufo* from Africa, with comments on the toads of the *Bufo regularis* complex. *Am. Mus. Novit.* 2345: 1–22.

Kelly, P. J. 1978. A neuroethological investigation of the paired tentacles of *Xenopus* tadpoles. M.Sc. thesis, University of the Witwatersrand.

———. 1982. A neuroethological investigation of the paired tentacles of *Xenopus* tadpoles. *Zool. Soc. S. Afr. Occ. Bull.* 2: 154.

Knoepffler, L.-P. 1976. Food habits of *Aubria subsigillata* in Gaboon (Anura: Ranidae). *Zool. Afr.* 11: 369–71.

Kobel, H. R., C. Loumont, and R. C. Tinsley. 1996. The extant species. In R. C. Tinsley and H. R. Kobel (Eds.), *The Biology of Xenopus*, 9–33. Zoological Society of London. Oxford: Clarendon Press.

Kobelt, F., and K. E. Linsenmair. 1986. Adaptations of the reed frog *Hyperolius viridiflavus* (Amphibia, Anura, Hyperoliidae) to its arid environment. *Oecologia (Berlin)* 68: 533–41.

Koeman, J. H., A. D. Ryksen, M. Smies, B. K. Na'Isa, and K. J. R. MacLennan. 1971. Faunal changes in a swamp habitat in Nigeria sprayed with insecticide to exterminate *Glossina*. *Neth. J. Zool.* 21: 434–63.

Kok, D., L. H. du Preez, and A. Channing. 1989. Channel construction by the African bullfrog: Another Anuran parental care strategy. *J. Herpetol.* 23: 435–7.

Kok, D. J., and M. T. Seaman. 1988. *Natalobatrachus bonebergi* (Anura: Ranidae) aspects of early development and adult size. *S. Afr. J. Zool.* 23: 238–40.

———. 1989. Aspects of the biology, habitat requirements and conservation status of *Natalobatrachus bonebergi* (Anura: Ranidae). *Lammergeyer* 40: 10–17.

Kokot, M. L. 1973. The bullfrog—A dutiful father. *Afr. Wild Life* 27: 12.

Krüger, J. J. 1942. Die brulpadda. *Huisgenoot* 26: (1056) (June 19): 35, 37.

Kühn, E. R., H. Gevaerts, G. Jacobs, and G. Vandorpe. 1987. Reproductive cycle, thyroxine and cortisone in females of the giant swamp frog *Dicroglossus occipitalis* at the equator. *Gen. Comp. Endocr.* 66: 137–44.

Lambiris, A. J. L. 1971. A note on "parental care" in the bullfrog, *Pyxicephalus a. adspersus*. *J. Herpetol. Assoc. Afr.* 8: 6.

———. 1985a. A description of *Strongylopus grayi rhodesianus* tadpoles (Amphibia: Ranidae). *Arnoldia Zimbabwe* 9: 251–6.

———. 1985b. Oviposition and early development of tadpoles of *Rana johnstoni inyangae* (Anura: Ranidae). *S. Afr. J. Sci.* 81: 203.

———. 1987. Description of the tadpole of *Strongylopus hymenopus* (Boulenger, 1920) (Amphibia: Anura: Ranidae) and a key to described southern African tadpoles of the genus. *Ann. Natal Mus.* 28: 455–62.

———. 1988a. A new species of *Cacosternum* (Amphibia: Anura: Ranidae) from Natal. *S. Afr. J. Zool.* 23: 63–6.

———. 1988b. Golden dwarf reed frog. In W. R. Branch (Ed.), South African Red Data Book—Reptiles and Amphibians. *S. Afr. Nat. Sci. Prog. Rep.* 151: 86–7.

———. 1988c. Pickersgill's reed frog. In W. R. Branch (Ed.), South African Red Data Book—Reptiles and Amphibians. *S. Afr. Nat. Sci. Prog. Rep.* 151: 88–9.

———. 1988d. *Frogs and Toads of the Natal Drakensberg*. Pietermaritzburg: University of Natal Press.

———. 1988e. Hogsback frog. In W. R. Branch (Ed.), South African Red Data Book—Reptiles and Amphibians. *S. Afr. Nat. Sci. Prog. Rep.* 151: 118–9.

———. 1988f. Drakensberg frog. In W. R. Branch (Ed.), South African Red Data Book—Reptiles and Amphibians. *S. Afr. Nat. Sci. Prog. Rep.* 151: 120–1.

———. 1988g. Water frog. In W. R. Branch (Ed.), South African Red Data Book—Reptiles and Amphibians. *S. Afr. Nat. Sci. Prog. Rep.* 151: 122–3.
———. 1988h. Long-toed tree frog. In W. R. Branch (Ed.), South African Red Data Book—Reptiles and Amphibians. *S. Afr. Nat. Sci. Prog. Rep.* 151: 125–6.
———. 1988i. A review of the Amphibians of Natal. *Lammergeyer* 39: 1–210.
———. 1989. The Frogs of Zimbabwe. *Mus. Reg. Sci. Nat. Torino Monogr.* 10: 1–247.
Lamotte, M., and J.-L. Perret. 1961a. Contribution à l'étude des batraciens de l'Ouest africain. XI—Les formes larvaires de trois espèces de *Ptychadena*: *Pt. maccarthyensis* And., *Pt. perreti* G. et L. et *Pt. mascareniensis* D. et B. *Bull. Inst. Fr. Afr. Noire* 23A: 192–210.
———. 1961b. Contribution à l'étude des batraciens de l'Ouest africain. XIII—Les formes larvaires de quelques espèces de *Leptopelis*: *L. aubryi*, *L. viridis*, *L. anchietae*, *L. ocellatus* et *L. calcaratus*. *Bull. Inst. Fr. Afr. Noire* 23A: 855–5.
———. 1963. Contribution à l'étude des Batraciens de l'Ouest Africain. XV—Le développement direct de l'èspece *Arthroleptis poecilonotus* Peters. *Bull. Inst. Fr. Afr. Noire* 25: 277–84.
Lamotte, M., J.-L. Perret, and S. Dzieduszycka. 1959. Contribution à l'étude des batraciens de l'Ouest africain. X—Les formes larvaires de *Cryptothylax greshoffi*, *Leptopelis notatus* et *Ptychadena taeniocelis*. *Bull. Inst. Fr. Afr. Noire* 21A: 1336–50.
Lamotte, M., and F. Xavier. 1980. Amphibiens. In J. R. Durand and C. Lévêque (Eds.), *Flore et faune aquatiques de l'Afrique Sahel-Soudanienne*, 773–816. Paris: Office de la Recherche Scientifique et Technique Outre-Mer.
Lamotte, M., and M. Zuber-Vogeli. 1954. Contribution à l'étude des batraciens de l'Ouest africain. II—Le développement larvaire de *Bufo regularis* Reuss, de *Rana occidentalis* Günther et de *Rana crassipes* (Buch. et Peters). *Bull. Inst. Fr. Afr. Noire* 16A: 940–54.
Laurent, R. 1940a. Description d'un Rhacophoride nouveau du Congo Belge (Batracien). *Rev. Zool. Bot. Afr.* 33: 313–6.
———. 1940b. Contribution à l'osteologie et à la systématique des Ranides africaines. Première Note. *Rev. Zool. Bot. Afr.* 34: 74–97, pls III–V.
———. 1941a. Contribution à l'osteologie et à la systématique des Rhacophorides africaines. Première note. *Rev. Zool. Bot. Afr.* 35: 85–111.
———. 1941b. Les *Megalixalus* (Batraciens) du Musée du Congo. *Rev. Zool. Bot. Afr.* 35: 119–32.
———. 1963. Three new species of the genus *Hemisus*. *Copeia* 1963: 395–9.
———. 1972. Tentative revision of the genus *Hemisus* Günther. *Ann. Mus. R. Afr. Centr. Tervuren Ser. 8° Sci. Zool.* 194: 1–67.
———. 1982. Le genre *Afrixalus* Laurent (Hyperoliidae) en Afrique centrale. *Ann. Mus. R. Afr. Centr. Tervuren Ser. 8° Sci. Zool.* 235: i–v, 1–58.

Laurent, R. F. 1952. Reptiles et batraciens de la région de Dundo (Angola du Nord-Est) (Première note). *Publ. Cult. Comp. Diamant. Angola* 6: 125-36.

———. 1954. Reptiles et batraciens de la région de Dundo (Angola) (Deuxième note). *Publ. Cult. Comp. Diamant. Angola* 23 35: 70-84.

———. 1957. Genres *Afrixalus* et *Hyperolius* (Amphibia Salientia). *Explor. Parc. Nat. Upemba* 42: 1-47.

———. 1964. Reptiles et Amphibiens de l'Angola (Troisième contribution). *Publ. Cult. Comp. Diamant. Angola* 67: 11-165.

———. 1973. The natural classification of the Arthroleptinae. *Rev. Zool. Bot. Afr.* 87: 666-78.

Lescure, J. 1981. L'alimentation du crapaud *Bufo regularis* Reuss et de la grenouille *Dicroglossus occipitalis* (Günther) au Sénégal. *Bull. Inst. Fr. Afr. Noire* 33A: 446-66.

Leslie, J. M. 1890. Notes on the habits and oviposition of *Xenopus laevis*. *Proc. Zool. Soc. Lond.* 1890: 69-71.

Liem, S. S. 1970. The morphology, systematics and evolution of the old world treefrogs (Rhacophoridae and Hyperoliidae). *Fieldiana Zool.* 57: i-vii, 1-145.

Linden, I. 1971. Development of *Leptopelis viridis cinnamomeus* (Bocage) with notes on its systematic position. *Zool. Afr.* 6: 237-42.

Linnaeus, C. 1758. *Systema naturae*, Vol 1, 10th ed. Holmiae, Lauerntii Salvii.

Livingstone, D. 1860. *Missionary Travels and Researches in South Africa Including a Sketch of Sixteen Years Residence in the Interior of Africa*. London: Ward.

Lord, W. B., and T. Baines. 1876. *Shifts and Expedients of Camp Life, Travel and Exploration*. London: Horace Cox.

Loumont, C. 1983. Deux espèces nouvelles de *Xenopus* du Cameroun (Amphibia, Pipidae). *Rev. Suisse Zool.* 90: 169-77.

Loveridge, A. 1928. Field notes on vertebrates collected by the Smithsonian-Chrysler East African expedition of 1926. *Proc. U. S. Nat. Mus.* 73: 1-69.

———. 1932. New frogs of the genera *Arthroleptis* and *Hyperolius* from Tanganyika territory. *Proc. Biol. Soc. Washington* 45: 61-3.

———. 1933. Reports on the scientific results of an expedition to the southwestern highlands of Tanganyika territory. VII. Herpetology. *Bull. Mus. Comp. Zool. Harv.* 74: 197-416, pls 1-3.

———. 1936. Reports on the scientific results of an expedition to rain forest regions in eastern Africa. VII. Amphibians. *Bull. Mus. Comp. Zool. Harv.* 79: 369-430, pls 1-3.

———. 1938. A new frog (*Hyperolius poweri*) from Natal, South Africa. *Proc. Biol. Soc. Washington* 51: 213-4.

———. 1942a. Scientific results of a fourth expedition to forested areas in east and central Africa. IV. Reptiles. *Bull. Mus. Comp. Zool.* 91: 231–373, pls 1–6.

———. 1942b. Scientific results of a fourth expedition to forested areas in east and central Africa. V. Amphibians. *Bull. Mus. Comp. Zool.* 91: 377–436.

———. 1942c. Comments on the reptiles and amphibians of Lindi. *Tanganyika Notes Rec.* 14: 38–51.

———. 1953a. Zoological results of a fifth expedition to East Africa. IV. Amphibians from Nyasaland and Tete. *Bull. Mus. Comp. Zool.* 110: 323–406, pls 1–4.

———. 1953b. Herpetological results of the Berner-Carr entomological survey of the Shire Valley, Nyasaland. *Q. J. Fla. Acad. Sci.* 16: 139–50.

———. 1953c. Zoological results of a fifth expedition to East Africa. VIII. Itinerary and conclusions. *Bull. Mus. Comp. Zool.* 110: 447–87.

———. 1953d. *I drank the Zambezi.* New York: Harpers.

Loveridge, J. P. 1970. Observations on nitrogenous excretion and water relations of *Chiromantis xerampelina* (Amphibia, Anura). *Arnoldia (Rhod.)* 5: 1–6.

———. 1979. Cocoon formation in two species of southern African frogs. *S. Afr. J. Sci.* 75: 18–20.

Low, B. S. 1972. Evidence from parotid-gland secretions. In F. Blair (Ed.), *Evolution in the Genus Bufo*, 244–64. Austin: University of Texas Press.

Lynch, C. D. 1986. The ecology of the lesser dwarf shrew, *Suncus varilla* with reference to the use of termite mounds *of Trinervitermes trinervoides*. *Nov. Nas. Mus. Bloem.* 5: 277–97.

Mahboubi, M., R. Ameur, J. Y. Crochet, and J. J. Jaeger. 1986. El Kohol (Saharan Atlas, Algeria): A new Eocene mammal locality in northwestern Africa. *Palaeontographica (A)* 192: 15–49.

Manaças, S. 1950. Batráquios de Moçambique. *An. Junta Invest. Col. Lisboa* 5: 181–97.

Martin, W. F. 1971. Mechanics of sound production in toads of the genus *Bufo*: Passive elements. *J. Exp. Zool.* 176: 273–94.

Mattison, C. 1986. Repeated spawnings in *Hyperolius marmoratus*. *Bull. Br. Herpetol. Soc.* 5: 6–8.

Maxson, L. R. 1981. Albumin evolution and its phylogenetic implications in African toads of the genus *Bufo*. *Herpetologica.* 37: 96–104.

McAllister, W., and A. Channing. 1983. Comparisons of toe pads of some southern African climbing frogs. *S. Afr. J. Zool.* 18: 110–4.

McCoid, M. J., and T. H. Fritts. 1993. Speculations on colonizing success of the African clawed frog, *Xenopus laevis* (Pipidae), in California. *S. Afr. J. Zool.* 28: 59–61.

McCoid, M. J., G. K. Pregill, and R. M. Sullivan. 1993. Possible decline of *Xenopus* populations in southern California. *Herpetol. Rev.* 24: 29–30.

McDiarmid, R. W., and R. Altig (Eds.). 1999. *Tadpoles. The Biology of Anuran Larvae.* Chicago: University of Chicago Press.

McLachlan, A. 1981. Interaction between insect larvae and tadpoles in tropical rain pools. *Ecol. Entomol.* 6: 175–82.
McLachlan, G. R. 1978. South African Red Data Book—Reptiles and Amphibians. *S. Afr. Nat. Sci. Prog. Rep.* 23.
Mertens, R. 1970. Über den Kapkrallenfrosch, *Xenopus gilli. Aquar. Terrar.* 23: 21–3.
Metcalf, M. M. 1929. An African zoogeographical puzzle. *Collecting Net* 4: 16–17.
Micha, J.-C. 1975. Quelques données ecologiques sur la grenouille Africaine *Dicroglossus occipitalis* (Günther). *Terre Vie* 29: 307–27.
Miller, K. 1982. Effect of termperature on sprint performance in the frog *Xenopus laevis* and the salamander *Necturus maculosus. Copeia* 1982: 695–8.
Milstein, P. le S. 1967. Hibernation of the rain-frog *Breviceps adspersus. Afr. Wild Life* 21: 167–8.
Mitchell, B. L. 1946. A naturalist in Nyasaland. *Nyasaland Agric. Q. J.* 6: 1–47.
Monard, A. 1937. Contribution à la batrachologie d'Angola. *Bull. Soc. Neuchâtel Sci. Nat.* 62: 5–59.
Morescalchi, A. 1967. Note cariologiche su *Phrynomerus* (Amphibia Salientia) *Boll. Zool.* 34: 144.
———. 1968. Initial cytotaxonomic data on certain families of amphibious Anura (Diplasiocoela, after Noble). *Experientia* 24: 280–3.
———. 1973. Amphibia. In A. B. Chiarelli and E. Capanna (Eds.), *Cytotaxonomy and Vertebrate Evolution*, 233–348. London: Academic Press.
Morescalchi, A., G. Gorgiulo, and E. Olmo. 1970. Notes on the chromosomes of some amphibia. *J. Herpetol.* 4: 77–70.
Morgan, B. E., N. I. Passmore, and B. C. Fabian. 1989. Metamorphosis in the frog *Arthroleptella lightfooti* (Anura, Ranidae) with emphasis on neuroendocrine mechanisms. In M. N. Bruton (Ed.), *Alternative Life-History Styles of Animals*, 347–70. Dordrecht: Kluwer.
Müller, R., and U. Scheer. 1970. Klangspektrographische Untersuchung der Lautäusserung beim Krallenfrosch, *Xenopus laevis. Experientia* 26: 435–6.
Munsey, L. D. 1972. Salinity tolerance of the African pipid frog, *Xenopus laevis. Copeia* 1972: 584–6.
Nakajima, T. 1981. Active peptides in amphibian skin. *Trends Pharmacol. Sci.* 2: 202–5.
Nakajima, T., T. Yasuhara, G. F. Erspamer, and J. Visser. 1979. Occurrence of Hyp^3-bradykinin in methanol extracts of the skin of the South African leptodactylid frog *Heleophryne purcelli. Experientia* 35: 1133.
Nevo, E. 1968. Pipid frogs from the early Cretaceous of Israel and pipid evolution. *Bull. Mus. Comp. Zool. Harv.* 136: 225–318.
Newcomer, C. E., M. R. Anver, J. L. Simmons, B. W. Wilcke, and G. W. Nace.

1982. Spontaneous and experimental infections of *Xenopus laevis* with *Chlamydia psittaci. Lab. Anim. Sci.* 32: 680–6.
Newman, A. C. 1963a. Notes on the diet of some snakes at the Umtali Snake Park. *J. Herpetol. Assoc. Rhod.* 20: 10–11.
———. 1963b. Some miscellaneous observations from Umtali Snake Park. *J. Herpetol. Assoc. Rhod.* 21: 12–14.
———. 1964. More observations from Umtali Snake Park. *J. Herpetol. Assoc. Rhod.* 22: 17–19.
Nieden, F. 1910. Verzeichnis der bei Amani in Deutschostafrika vorkommenden Reptilien und Amphibien. *Sitzungsber. Gesellsch. naturf. Freunde Berlin* 10: 441–52.
———. 1926. Amphibia Anura II Engystomatidae. *Tierreich* 49: xv, 1–110.
Nietzke, G. 1969. *Die Terrarientiere*, Vol. 1. Stuttgart: Verlag Eugen Wilmer.
Nieuwkoop, P. D., and J. Faber (Eds.). 1956. *Normal Table of Xenopus laevis (Daudin)*. Amsterdam: North-Holland.
Oatley, T. B. 1970. Observations on the food and feeding habits of some African robins (Aves: Turdidae). *Ann. Natal Mus.* 20: 293–327.
Ohler, A. 1996. Systematics, morphometrics and biogeography of the genus *Aubria* (Ranidae, Pyxicephalinae). *Alytes* 13: 141–66.
Osborne, P. L., and A. J. McLachlan. 1985. The effects of tadpoles on algal growth in temporary rain-filled rock pools. *Freshwater Biol.* 15: 77–87.
Pakenham, R. H. W. 1983. The reptiles and amphibians of Zanzibar and Pemba Islands (with a note on the freshwater fishes). *J. E. Afr. Nat. Hist. Soc. Nat. Mus.* 177: 1–40.
Pahnke, A. 1981. Ein Aqua-Terrarium für *Hyperolius horstockii. Aquarium* 15: 570 + cover.
Pallett, J. R., and N. I. Passmore. 1988. The significance of multi-note advertisement calls in a reed frog. *Hyperolius tuberilinguis. Bioacoustics* 1: 13–23.
Palmer, N. G. 1982. The bushpig and the rain frog. *Afr. Wild Life* 36: 113.
Parker, H. W. 1936. Dr. Karl Jordan's expedition to South-West Africa and Angola: Herpetological collections. *Novit. Zool. Tring* 49: 115–46.
Parry, C. R. 1982. A revision of southern African *Pyxicephalus* Tschudi (Anura: Ranidae). *Ann. Natal Mus.* 25: 281–92.
Passmore, N. I. 1972. Integrading between members of the "*regularis* group" of toads in South Africa. *J. Zool. Lond.* 167: 143–51.
———. 1976. Vocalizations and breeding behaviour *of Ptychadena taenioscelis* (Anura: Ranidae). *Zool. Afr.* 11: 339–47.
———. 1977a. Mating calls and other vocalizations of five species of *Ptychadena* (Anura: Ranidae). *S. Afr. J. Sci.* 73: 212–4.
———. 1977b. *Bufo pardalis* (Anura: Bufonidae): Mating call and calling behaviour. *Zool. Afr.* 12: 234–6.
———. 1985. Sibling species, the acoustic environment and the anuran

specific-mate recognition system. In E. S. Vrba (Ed.), *Species and Speciation*, 125–7. Transvaal Museum Monograph 4. Pretoria: Transvaal Museum.

Passmore, N. I., and V. C. Carruthers. 1975. A new species of *Tomopterna* (Anura: Ranidae) from the Kruger National Park, with notes on related species. *Koedoe* 18: 31–50.

———. 1979. *South African Frogs*. Johannesburg: Witwatersrand University Press.

———. 1995. *South African Frogs*, 2nd ed. Johannesburg: Southern Book Publishers & Witwatersrand University Press.

Patten, G. 1984. Some feeding records. *Witwatersrand Bird Club News* (125): 19.

Paukstis, G. L., and S. L. Reinbold. 1984. Observations of snake-feeding by captive African bullfrogs (*Pyxicephalus adspersus*). *Br. Herpetol. Soc. Bull.* 10: 52–3.

Perret, J.-L. 1958. Observations sur des rainettes africaines du genre *Leptopelis* Günther. *Rev. Suisse Zool.* 65: 259–75.

———. 1966. Les Amphibiens du Cameroun. *Zool. Jahrb. Syst.* 93: 289–464.

———. 1976a. Revision des Amphibiens Africains et principalement des types, conservés au Musée Bocage de Lisbonne. *Arq. Mus. Bocage* (2) 6: 15–34.

———. 1976b. Identité de quelques *Afrixalus* (Amphibia, Salientia, Hyperoliidae). *Bull. Soc. Neuchât. Sci. Nat.* 99: 19–28, pls I–II.

———. 1987. A propos de *Ptychadena schillukorum* (Werner, 1907) (Anura, Ranidae). *Bull. Soc. Neuchât. Sci. Nat.* 110: 63–70.

———. 1988. Sur quelques genres d'Hyperoliidae (Anura) restes en question. *Bull. Soc. Neuchât. Sci. Nat.* 111: 35–48.

Peters, W. 1855. Uebersicht der auf seiner Reise gesammelten Amphibien. *Arch. Naturg.* 21: 43–58.

———. 1882. *Naturwissenschaftliche Reise nach Mossambique*. Anura, 147–81. Berlin: G. Reimer.

Pfeiffer, W. 1966. Die Verbreitung der Schreckreaktion bei Kaulquappen und die Herkunft des Schreckstoffes. *Zeit. Vergl. Physiol.* 52: 79–98.

Picker, M. 1980. *Xenopus laevis* (Anura: Pipidae) mating systems—A preliminary synthesis with some data on the female phonoresponse. *S. Afr. J. Zool.* 15: 150–8.

———. 1983. Territorial behaviour in the bullfrog. *Afr. Wild Life* 37: 238–9.

Picker, M., and A. de Villiers. 1989a. Decline and spread of platannas in South Africa. *Afr. Wild Life* 43: 141, 143, 145.

Picker, M. D. 1985a. Hybridization and habitat selection in *Xenopus gilli* and *Xenopus laevis* in the south-western Cape Province. *Copeia* 1985: 574–80.

———. 1985b. Security fence for *Xenopus gilli* at Cape Point. *Herpetol. Assoc. Afr. Newsletter* 6: 19.

Picker, M. D., and A. L. de Villiers. 1988. Cape platanna. In W. R. Branch

(Ed.), South African Red Data Book—Reptiles and Amphibians. *S. Afr. Nat. Sci. Prog. Rep.* 151: 25–8.

———. 1989b. The distribution and conservation status of *Xenopus gilli* (Anura: Pipidae). *Biol. Conserv.* 49: 169–83.

Picker, M. D., C. J. McKenzie, and P. Fielding. 1993. Embryonic tolerance of *Xenopus* (Anura) to acidic blackwater. *Copeia* 1993: 1072–81.

Pickersgill, M. 1975. Some surprises in the ecology of *Breviceps v. verrucossus* Rapp. *J. Herpetol. Assoc. Afr.* 14: 23–7.

———. 1984. Three new *Afrixalus* (Anura: Hyperoliidae) from south-eastern Africa. *Durban Mus. Novit.* 13: 203–20.

Pienaar, U. de V., N. I. Passmore, and V. C. Carruthers. 1963. *The Frogs of the Kruger National Park*. Pretoria: National Parks Board of South Africa.

Piveteau, J. 1986. Origine et évolution des Amphibiens. In *Traité de Zoologie*, Vol. 14, *Batraciens*, 555–8. Paris: Masson.

Polling, B. 1984. Probleme met platannas. *Visboer* 33: 4.

Pooley, A. C., and J. Visser. 1982. Fanie en Melanie ontdek die klein krokodil: Alles om hom is gevaarlik. *Huisgenoot* (Oct. 14): 102–4.

Power, J. H. 1926. Notes on the habits and life histories of certain little-known Anura, with descriptions of the tadpoles. *Trans. R. Soc. S. Afr.* 13: 107–17, pls VI–IX.

———. 1927a. Notes on the habits and life-histories of South African Anura, with descriptions of the tadpoles. *Trans. R. Soc. S. Afr.* 14: 237–47.

———. 1927b. Some tadpoles from Griqualand West. *Trans. R. Soc. S. Afr.* 14: 249–54, pl XV.

———. 1927c. On the herpetological fauna of the Lobatsi-Linokana area. Part I—Lobatsi, 25° 8′ S 25° 43′ E. *Trans. R. Soc. S. Afr.* 14: 405–21, pls 18–22, map.

———. 1931. The genus *Bufo* as an economic asset. *S. Afr. J. Sci.* 28: 376–7.

———. 1935. A contribution to the herpetology of Pondoland. *Proc. Zool. Soc. Lond.* 1935: 333–46, pl I.

Power, J. H., and W. Rose. 1929. Notes on the habits and life-histories of some Cape Peninsula Anura. *Trans. R. Soc. S. Afr.* 17: 109–15, pl V.

Poynton, J. C. 1963. Descriptions of southern African amphibians. *Ann. Natal Mus.* 15: 319–32.

———. 1964. The Amphibia of southern Africa: A faunal study. *Ann. Natal Mus.* 17: 1–334.

———. 1985. On the *Hyperolius marmoratus* complex (Anura). *S. Afr. J. Sci.* 81: 179–81.

———. 1991. Amphibians of southeastern Tanzania, with special reference to *Stephopaedes* and *Mertensophryne* (Bufonidae). *Bull. Mus. Comp. Zool.* 152: 451–73.

———. 1997. On *Bufo nyikae* Loveridge and the *B. lonnbergi* complex of East African highlands (Anura: Bufonidae). *Afr. J. Herpetol.* 46: 98–102.

———. 1999. Distribution of amphibians in sub-Saharan Africa, Madagascar and Seychelles. In W. E. Duellman (Ed.), *Patterns of Distribution of Amphibians: A Global Perspective*, 483–539. Baltimore: John Hopkins University Press.

Poynton, J. C., and D. G. Broadley. 1967. A new species of *Probreviceps* (Amphibia) from Rhodesia. *Arnoldia Rhod.* 3(14): 1–3.

———. 1985a. Amphibia Zambesiaca 1. Scolecomorphidae, Pipidae, Microhylidae, Hemisidae, Arthroleptidae. *Ann. Natal Mus.* 26: 503–53.

———. 1985b. Amphibia Zambesiaca 2. Ranidae. *Ann. Natal Mus.* 27: 115–81.

———. 1987. Amphibia Zambesiaca 3. Rhacophoridae and Hyperoliidae. *Ann. Natal Mus.* 28: 161–229.

———. 1988. Amphibia Zambesiaca 4. Bufonidae. *Ann. Natal Mus.* 29: 447–90.

———. 1991. Amphibia Zambesiaca 5. Zoogeography. *Ann. Natal Mus.* 32: 221–77.

Poynton, J. C., and W. D. Haacke. 1993. On a collection of amphibians from Angola, including a new species of *Bufo* Laurenti. *Ann. Transv. Mus.* 36: 9–16.

Poynton, J. C., and A. J. L. Lambiris. 1998. On *Bufo pantherinus* A. Smith, 1828 (Anura: Bufonidae), the leopard toad of the southwestern Cape, South Africa, with the designation of a neotype. *Afr. J. Herpetol.* 47: 3–12.

Poynton, J. C., and S. Pritchard. 1976. Notes on the biology of *Breviceps* (Anura: Microhylidae). *Zool. Afr.* 11: 313–8.

Rage, J.-C. 1984. Are the Ranidae (Anura, Amphibia) known prior to the Oligocene? *Amphibia-Reptilia* 5: 281–8.

Rage, J.-C., and Z. Rocek. 1989. Redescription of *Triadobatrachus massinoti* (Piveteau, 1936). *Palaeograph. Abt. A.* 206: 1–16.

Rau, R. E. 1978. The development of *Xenopus gilli* Rose & Hewitt (Anura, Pipidae). *Ann. S. Afr. Mus.* 76: 247–63.

Raw, L. R. G. 1982. A new species of reed frog (Amphibia: Hyperoliidae) from the coastal lowlands of Natal, South Africa. *Durban Mus. Novit.* 13: 117–26.

Reumer, J. W. F. 1985. Some aspects of the cranial osteology and phylogeny of *Xenopus* (Anura, Pipidae). *Rev. Suisse Zool.* 92: 969–80.

Richards, C. M. 1976. The development of color dimorphism in *Hyperolius v. viridiflavus*, a reed frog from Kenya. *Copeia* 1976: 65–70.

———. 1977. Reproductive potential under laboratory conditions of *Hyperolius viridiflavus* (Amphibia, Anura, Hyperoliidae), a Kenyan reed frog. *J. Herpetol.* 11: 426–8.

———. 1982. The alteration of chromatophore expression by sex hormones in the Kenyan reed frog, *Hyperolius viridiflavus*. *Gen. Comp. Endocr.* 46: 59–67.

Rietschel, P., W. Hanke, R. Lotz, F. W. Merkel, and R. Modes. 1957. *Das Tierreich nach Brehms*. Jena: Urania-Verlag.

Rose, W. 1926a. Some field notes on the batrachia of the Cape Peninsula. *Ann. S. Afr. Mus.* 20: 433–50, pl 38.
——. 1926b. The "Plathander." *Nature Notes* 44: 4–5.
——. 1929. *Veld & Vlei.* Cape Town: Specialty Press.
——. 1950. The *Reptiles and Amphibians of Southern Africa.* Cape Town: Maskew Miller.
——. 1956a. Growth of bull frogs. *Afr. Wild Life* 10: 160.
——. 1956b. Parental care in batrachians. *Afr. Wild Life* 10: 257.
——. 1961. *Bushmen, Whale and Dinosaur.* James Drury's forty years at the South African Museum. Cape Town: Howard Timmins.
Roseghini, M., G. F. Erspamer, and C. Severini. 1988. Biogenic amines and active peptides in the skin of fifty-two African amphibian species other than bufonids. *Comp. Biochem. Physiol.* 91C: 281–6.
Rowe-Rowe, D. T. 1977. Variations in the predatory behaviour of the clawless otter. *Lammergeyer* 23: 22–7.
Ruas, C. 1996. Contribuição para o conhecimento da fauna de batráquios de Angola. *Garcia de Orta. Ser. Zool.* (Lisboa) 21: 19–41.
Sanderson, I. T. 1936a. The giant frog problem. *Nigerian Field* 5: 161–70.
——. 1936b. The amphibians of the Mamfe Division, Cameroons. II. Ecology of the frogs. *Proc. Zool. Soc.* 1936: 165–208, pl I.
——. 1937. *Animal Treasure.* London: Macmillan.
Scheel, J. J. 1971. The seven-chromosome karyotype of the African frog *Arthroleptis*, a probable derivative of the thirteen-chromosome karyotype of *Rana* (Ranidae, Anura). *Hereditas* 67: 287–90.
——. 1973. The chromosomes of some African Anuran species. In J. H. Schröder (Ed.), *Genetics and Mutagenesis of Fish*, 113–16. Berlin: Springer-Verlag.
Scherer, J. 1907. Herpetologische Beobachtungen am Kap Verde. *Bl. Aquariumkunde, Magdeburg* 18: 41–5.
Schiøtz, A. 1963. The amphibians of Nigeria. *Vidensk. Medd. Dansk Naturh. Foren.* 125: 1–92.
——. 1964. The voices of some West African amphibians. *Vidensk. Medd. Dansk Naturh. Foren.* 127: 35–83.
——. 1967. The treefrogs (Rhacophoridae) of West Africa. *Spolia Zool. Mus. Haun.* 25: 1–346.
——. 1971. The superspecies *Hyperolius viridiflavus* (Anura). *Vidensk. Medd. Dansk Naturh. Foren.* 134: 21–76.
——. 1974. Revision of the genus *Afrixalus* (Anura) in eastern Africa. *Vidensk. Medd. Dansk Naturh. Foren.* 137: 9–18.
——. 1975. The treefrogs of eastern Africa. Copenhagen: Steenstrupia.
——. 1982. On two *Afrixalus* (Anura) from Central Zaire. *Steenstrupia* 8: 261–5.
——. 1999. *Treefrogs of Africa.* Frankfurt am Main: Edition Chimaira.

Schmid, M., and K. Bachmann. 1981. A frog with highly evolved sex chromosomes. *Experientia* 37: 243–5.

Schmid, M., and C. Steinlein. 1991. Chromosome banding in amphibia XVI. High-resolution replication banding patterns in *Xenopus laevis*. *Chromosoma* (Berl.). 101: 123–32.

Schmidt, K. P., and R. F. Inger. 1959. Amphibians. *Explor. Parc. Nat. Upemba* 56: 1–264.

Schmuck, R., F. Kobelt, and K. E. Linsenmair. 1988. Adaptations of the reed frog *Hyperolius viridiflavus* (Amphibia, Anura, Hyperoliidae) to its arid environment. V. Iridiophores and nitrogen metabolism. *J. Comp. Physiol. [B]* 158: 537–46.

Schmuck, R., and K. E. Linsenmair. 1988. Adaptations of the reed frog *Hyperolius viridiflavus* (Amphibia, Anura, Hyperoliidae) to its arid environment. III. Aspects of nitrogen metabolism and osmoregulation in the reed frog, *Hyperolius viridiflavus taeniatus*, with special reference to the role of iridiophores. *Oecologia* 75: 354–61.

Schneichel, W., and H. Schneider. 1988. Hearing and calls of the banana frog, *Afrixalus fornasinii* (Bianconi) (Anura: Rhacophoridae). *Amphibia-Reptilia* 9: 251–63.

Senfft, W. 1939. Beobachtungen bei der Aufzucht des Krallenfrosches *Xenopus fraseri*. *Blgr. Aquar. Terra-Kunde* 36: 247–9.

Seymour, R. S., and J. P. Loveridge. 1994. Embryonic and larval respiration in the arboreal foam nests of the African frog *Chiromantis xerampelina*. *J. Exp. Biol.* 197: 31–46.

Shaw, J. P. 1985. Tooth replacement in adult *Xenopus laevis* (Amphibia: Anura). *J. Zool. Lond.* 207A: 171–9.

Simbotwe, M. P. 1988. Records of two species of *Hylarana* (Anura: Ranidae). *Herpetol. J.* 1: 312–4.

Simmonds, M. P. 1985. Interactions between *Xenopus* species in the southwestern Cape Province, South Africa. *S. Afr. J. Sci.* 81: 200.

Skelton-Bourgeois, M. 1961. Reptiles et batraciens du Stanley Pool. *Ann. Mus. R. Afr. Centr. Tervuren. Ser. 8° Sci. Zool.* 103: 169–83.

Smith, R. M. A. 1988. Palaeoenvironmental reconstruction of a Cretaceous crater-lake deposit in Bushmanland, South Africa. *S. Afr. Soc. Q. Res.* 19: 27–41.

Spande, T. F., H. M. Gorraffo, M. W. Edwards, H. J. C. Yeh, L. Pannell, and J. W. Daly. 1992. Epibatidine—A novel (Chloropyridyl)azabicyclopentane with potent analgesic activity from an Ecuadorian poison frog. *J. Am. Chem. Soc.* 114: 3475–8.

Spieler, M., and K. E. Linsenmair. 1998. Migration patterns and diurnal use of shelter in a ranid frog of a West African savannah: A telemetric study. *Amphibia-Reptilia* 19: 43–64.

Spinar, Z. V. 1980. The discovery of a new species of pipid frog (Anura, Pipidae) in the Oligocene of central Libya. In M. J. Salem and M. T.

Busrewil (Eds.), *The Geology of Libya*, Vol. 1, 327–48. London: Academic Press.

Stevens, R. A. 1971. A new tree-frog from Malawi (Hyperoliinae, Amphibia) *Zool. Afr.* 6: 313–20.

———. 1972. A new species of *Ptychadena* (Amphibia: Ranidae) from southern Malawi. *Arnoldia (Rhod.)* 5: 1–14.

———. 1974. An annotated check list of the amphibians and reptiles known to occur in south-eastern Malawi. *Arnoldia (Rhod.)* 6: 1–22.

Stewart, M. M. 1967. *Amphibians of Malawi*. Albany: State University of New York Press.

———. 1974. Parallel pattern polymorphism in the genus *Phrynobatrachus* (Amphibia: Ranidae). *Copeia* 1974: 823–32.

Stewart, M. M., and V. J. Wilson. 1966. Herpetofauna of the Nyika Plateau (Malawi and Zambia). *Ann. Natal Mus.* 18: 287–313.

Steyn, H. P. 1984. Southern Kalahari San subsistence ecology: A reconstruction. *S. Afr. Archaeol. Bull.* 39: 117–24.

Steyn, P. 1960. Observations on the African fish eagle. *Bokmakerie* 12: 21–8.

Stjernstedt, R. 1973. Frogs collected in the Northern Province of Zambia. *Puku* 7: 196.

Stone, D. J. M., J. H. Bowie, M. J. Tyler, and J. C. Wallace. 1992. The structure of Caerin-1.1, a novel antibiotic peptide from Australian tree frogs. *J. Chem. Soc. Chem. Commun.* 1992: 1224–5.

Stromer, E. 1926. IX. Reste Land- und Süsswasser-Bewohnender Wirbeltiere aus den Diamantfeldern Deutsch-Südwestafrikas. In E. Kaiser (Ed.), *Die Diamantenwüste Südwest-Afrikas*, 107–53, pls 40–2. Berlin: Dietrich Reimer.

———. 1931. Reste Süsswasser und Land bewohnender Wirbeltiere aus den Diamantfeldern Klein-Namaqualandes (Südwest-Afrika). *S. B. Bayer. Akad. Wiss.* 1931: 17–47.

Stuart, C. T. 1981. Bufotoxins and bufogenins—Their effectivity in protecting their producer and their potential as aversive conditioning agents. *J. Herpetol. Assoc. Afr.* 26: 3–6.

Stuckenberg, B. R. 1959. A *Breviceps* sheds its skin. *Afr. Wild Life* 13: 341.

Sweeney, C. 1959. Notes on *Rhamphiophis oxyrhynchus rostratus* (Peters) in Nyasaland. *J. Herpetol. Assoc. Rhod.* 8: 2–5.

Sweeney, R. C. H. 1971. *Snakes of Nyasaland*. Amsterdam: A. Asher.

Tandy, M., and R. C. Drewes. 1985. Mating calls of the 'kassinoid' genera *Kassina, Kassinula, Phlyctimantis* and *Tornierella* (Anura: Hyperoliidae). *S. Afr. J. Sci.* 81: 191–5.

Tandy, M., and R. Keith. 1972. *Bufo* of Africa. In W. F. Blair (Ed.), *Evolution in the Genus Bufo*, 119–70. Austin: University of Texas Press.

Tandy, R. M. 1972. The evolution of African *Bufo*. Ph.D. dissertation, University of Texas at Austin.

Taylor, P. 1962. Shangaan herpetology. *J. Herpetol. Assoc. Rhod.* 19: 11–2.
———. 1971. Observations on the breeding habits of *Chiromantis xerampelina* Peters. *J. Herpetol. Assoc. Afr.* 8: 7–8.
———. 1973a. A note on colour changes in tadpoles of *Bufo garmani* Meek. *J. Herpetol. Assoc. Afr.* 11: 12–3.
———. 1973b. Notes on the discovery of tadpoles of *Bufo anotis* Boulenger. *J. Herpetol. Assoc. Afr.* 11: 13–4.
———. 1982. Notes on the ecology and life history of the light nosed toad *Bufo garmani* Meek in the lowveld. *Zimb. Sci. News* 16: 60–2.
Taylor, S., and D. W. Ewer. 1956. Moulting in the anura: The normal moulting cycle of *Bufo regularis* Reuss. *Proc. Zool. Soc. Lond.* 127: 461–78.
Telford, S. R. 1985a. Mechanisms and evolution of inter-male spacing in the painted reedfrog (*Hyperolius marmoratus*). *Anim. Behav.* 33: 1353–61.
———. 1985b. Double egg clutch production by female painted reed frogs during a single breeding season. *S. Afr. J. Sci.* 81: 209.
Telford, S. R., M. L. Dyson, and N. I. Passmore. 1989. Mate choice occurs only in small choruses of painted reed frogs *Hyperolius marmoratus*. *Bioacoustics* 2: 47–53.
Telford, S. R., and J. van Sickle. 1989. Sexual selection in an African toad (*Bufo gutturalis*): The roles of morphology, amplexus displacement and chorus participation. *Behaviour* 110: 62–75.
Themido, A. A. 1941. Répteis e batráquios das colónias Portuguesas. *Mem. Mus. Zool. Univ. Coimbra. [Ser. 1]* 119: 1–131.
Thiébaud, C., and M. Fishberg. 1977. DNA content in the genus *Xenopus*. *Chromosoma (Berl.)* 59: 253–7.
Thors, F. 1980. De ontwikkeling van het ruggemerg van de klauwpad, *Xenopus laevis*. [Proefschrift Dr Wis-Nat. Kathol. Univ. Niijmegen.] Doctoral dissertation in Mathematics-Science, Nijmegen Catholic University.
Tihen, J. A. 1972. The fossil record. In W. F. Blair (Ed.), *Evolution in the Genus Bufo*, 8–13. Austin: University of Texas Press.
Tinsley, R. C. 1981a. Interaction between *Xenopus* species (Anura: Pipidae). *Monit. Zool. Ital. (N. S.) Suppl.* 15: 133–50.
———. 1981b. The evidence from parasite relationships for the evolutionary status of *Xenopus* (Anura Pipidae) *Monit. Zool. Ital. (N. S.) Suppl.* 15: 367–85.
———. 1996. Evolutionary inferences from host and parasite co-speciation. In R. C. Tinsley and H. R. Kobel (Eds.), *The Biology of Xenopus*, 403–20. Zoological Society of London. Oxford: Clarendon Press.
Tinsley, R. C., and H. R. Kobel (Eds.). 1996. *The Biology of Xenopus*. Zoological Society of London. Oxford: Clarendon Press.
Tinsley, R. C., and M. J. McCoid. 1996. Feral populations of *Xenopus* outside Africa. In R. C. Tinsley and H. R. Kobel (Eds.), *The Biology of Xenopus*, 81–94. Zoological Society of London. Oxford: Clarendon Press.

Tonge, S., and D. Morgan. 1984. Notes on the herpetofauna of southern Malawi. *Br. Herpetol. Soc. Bull.* 9: 35–42.

Tornier, G. 1898. Die Reptilien und Amphibien Deutsch-Ost-Afrika's. In C. W. Werther (Ed.), *Wissenschaftliche Ergebnisse der Ivangi-Expedition 1896–1897 nebst kurzer Reisebeschreibung*, 281–304. Berlin: Dietrich Reimer.

Trong, Y. le Q. 1976. Étude de la peau et des glandes cutanées de quelques Amphibiens de la famille des Rhacophoridae. *Bull. Inst. Fond. Afr. Noire* 38A: 166–87.

Trueb, L. 1996. Historical constraints and morphological novelties in the evolution of the skeletal system of pipid frogs (Anura: Pipidae). In R. C. Tinsley and H. R. Kobel (Eds.), *The Biology of Xenopus*, 349–77. Zoological Society of London. Oxford: Clarendon Press.

Van Bergeijk, W. 1954. Oscillatory tail movements of *Xenopus larvae* in relation to static pressure reception. *Anat. Rec.* 120: 754.

Van Berkom, W. A. 1975. Die zucht von *Afrixalus dorsalis* im Paludarium. *D. Aquar. Terr. Z. Stuttgart* 28: 282–4.

Van den Berg, M. A., E. Deacon, C. J. Fourie, and S. H. Anderson. 1987. Predators of the citrus psylla, *Trioza erytreae* (Hemiptera: Triozidae), in the lowveld and Rustenberg areas of Transvaal. *Phytophylactica* 19: 285–9.

Van den Elzen, P. 1978. Observation sur l'herpétofaune du Waterberg (Namibie). *Bonn. Zool. Beitr.* 29: 171–82.

———. 1983. Zur herpetofauna des Brandberges, SüdwestAfrika. *Bonn. Zool. Beitr.* 34: 293–309.

Van den Elzen, P., and R. van den Elzen. 1977. Untersuchungen zur Chorstruktur Südwest-Afrikanischer Anuren: Erste Ergebnisse. *Bonn. Zool. Beitr.* 28: 108–16.

Vanderplank, F. L. 1939. *Xenopus Muelleri* (Peters). *Aquarist Pondkeeper* 9: 263–6.

Van Dijk, D. E. 1966. Systematic and field keys to the families, genera and described species of southern African tadpoles. *Ann. Natal Mus.* 18: 231–86.

———. 1971. A further contribution to the systematics of southern African Anuran tadpoles—The genus *Bufo*. *Ann. Natal Mus.* 21: 71–6.

———. 1985a. An addition to the fossil Anura of southern Africa. *S. Afr. J. Sci.* 81: 207–8.

———. 1985b. *Hemisus marmoratum* adults reported to carry tadpoles. *S. Afr. J. Sci.* 81: 209–10.

Van Wyk, J. C. P., and D. J. Kok. 1992. Life history notes. *Pyxicephalus adspersus adspersus* predation on tadpoles. *J. Herpetol. Assoc. Afr.* 41: 40.

Van Wyk, J. C. P., D. J. Kok, and L. H. Du Preez. 1991. Growth and behaviour of *Pyxicephalus adspersus* tadpoles. *Abstr. Herpetol. Assoc. Afr. Symp.* 2: 17–18.

Vawda, A. 1977. A new size record for *Bufo rangeri* (Hewitt). *J. Herpetol. Assoc. Afr.* 16: 5–6.

Vergnaud-Grazzini, C. 1966. Les amphibiens du miocène de Beni-Mellal. *Notes. Serv. Géol. Maroc.* 27: 43–75.

Vigny, C. 1977a. Étude comparée de 12 especes et sous-especes du genre *Xenopus*. D.Sc. thesis, University of Geneva.

——. 1977b. Nouveau critère de détermination dans le genre *Xenopus*: Répartition des bourrelets sensoriels chez 14 espèces et sous-espèces. *Rev. Suisse Zool.* 84: 309–17.

——. 1979a. The mating calls of 12 species and sub-species of the genus *Xenopus* (Amphibia: Anura). *J. Zool. Lond.* 168: 103–22.

——. 1979b. Morphologie larvaire de 12 espèces et sous-espèces du genre *Xenopus*. *Rev. Suisse Zool.* 86: 877–91.

Viljoen, S., and D. H. S. Davis. 1973. Note on stomach contents analyses of various carnivores in southern Africa (Mammalia: Carnivora). *Ann. Transv. Mus.* 28: 353–63.

Visser, J. 1962. Some amphibia of the Cape Peninsula—3. The cricket frog. *Afr. Wild Life* 16: 303–4.

——. 1971. Hunting the eggs of the ghost frog (*Heleophryne purcelli orientalis*, FitzSimons). *Afr. Wild Life* 25: 22–4.

——. 1979. Calling and spawning dates of the south-western Cape frogs. *J. Herpetol. Assoc. Afr.* 21: 21–8.

——. 1985. The fang-like teeth of the early larvae of some *Heleophryne* (Anura: Leptodactylidae). *S. Afr. J. Sci.* 81: 200–2.

Visser, J., and A. Channing. 1997. A new species of river frog from the Swartberg, South Africa (Ranidae: Afrana). *J. Afr. Zool.* 111: 191–8.

Visser, J. D. 1990. The biosystematics of the purcelli group of the frog genus *Heleophryne* (Amphibia: Leptodactylidae). M.Sc. dissertation, University of Natal.

Wager, V. A. 1926. The breeding habits and life-histories of some of the Transvaal Amphibia. *Trans. R. Soc. S. Afr.* 13: 163–74.

——. 1929. The breeding habits and life-histories of some of the Transvaal Amphibians. *Trans. R. Soc. S. Afr.* 17: 125–35, pls VI–X.

——. 1931. The breeding habits and life-histories of two rare South African Amphibia—I. *Hylambates natalensis* A. Smith. II *Natalobatrachus bonebergi* Hewitt and Methuen. *Trans. R. Soc. S. Afr.* 19: 79–91, pls 5–10.

——. 1965. *The Frogs of South Africa*. Cape Town: Purnell & Sons.

——. 1986. *Frogs of South Africa*, 2nd ed. Craighall: Delta Books.

Walker, B. 1967. An elusive frog, *Rana galamensis*. *Nigerian Field* 32: 22–6.

——. 1968. The amphibians of Zaria, in the northern Guinea savannah, Nigeria. *Copeia* 1968: 164–7.

Wassersug, R. J. 1984. The *Pseudohemisus* tadpole: A morphological link between microhylid (Orton type 2) and ranoid (Orton type 4) larvae. *Herpetologica* 40: 138–49.

Werner, F. 1910. Reptilia et Amphibia. Jena Denkschrift 16: 279–370, pls 6–11.
Wheeler, M. R. 1956. Background-selection in tadpoles of *Xenopus laevis*. *Br. J. Anim. Behav.* 4: 77.
Wickbom, T. 1945. Cytological studies on Dipnoi, Urodela, Anura and Emys. *Hereditas* 31: 241–346.
Wickler, W., and U. Seibt. 1974. Rufen und antworten bei *Kassina senegalensis, Bufo regularis* und anderen Anuren. *Z. Tierpsychol.* 34: 524–37.
Withers, P. C., S. S. Hillman, R. C. Drewes, and O. M. Sokol. 1982. Water loss and nitrogen excretion in sharp-nosed frogs (*Hyperolius nasutus*: Anura, Hyperoliidae). *J. Exp. Biol.* 97: 335–43.
Withers, P. C., G. Louw, and S. Nicolson. 1982. Water loss, oxygen consumption and colour change in 'waterproof' reed frogs (*Hyperolius*). *S. Afr. J. Sci.* 78: 30–2.
Yasuhara, T., T. Nakajima, G. F. Erspamer, and V. Erspamer. 1981. New tachykinins, Glu^2, Pro^5-Kassinin (Hylambates-Kassinin) and Hylambatin, in the skin of the African Rhacophorid frog *Hylambates maculatus*. *Biomed. Res.* 2: 613–7.
Zasloff, M. 1987. Magainins, a class of antimicrobial peptides from *Xenopus* skin: Isolation, characterization of two active forms, and partial cDNA sequence of a precursor. *Proc. Nat. Acad. Sci. USA* 84: 5449–53.
Zimmerman, H. 1975. Nachzucht des Marmorriedfrosches *Hyperolius marmoratus marmoratus*. *Aquar. Wupperthal* 9: 261–5.
———. 1979. Durch Nachzucht erhalten: Marmorriedfrosche, *Hyperolius marmoratus*. *Aquarien Mag.* 13: 472–7.

Systematic Index

Order Anura, 39
  Family Arthroleptidae, 41
    Arthroleptis carquejai Ferreira, 1906, 42
    Arthroleptis francei Loveridge, 1953, 43
    Arthroleptis reichei Nieden, 1910, 45
    Arthroleptis stenodactylus Pfeffer, 1893, 46
    Arthroleptis wahlbergii Smith, 1849, 48
    Schoutedenella lameerei (Witte, 1921), 50
    Schoutedenella troglodytes (Poynton, 1963), 51
    Schoutedenella xenochirus (Boulenger, 1905), 52
    Schoutedenella xenodactyloides (Hewitt, 1933), 53
  Family Bufonidae, 56
    Bufo amatolicus Hewitt, 1925, 61
    Bufo angusticeps Smith, 1848, 63
    Bufo beiranus Loveridge, 1932, 64
    Bufo dombensis Bocage, 1895, 65
    Bufo fenoulheti Hewitt & Methuen, 1913, 66
    Bufo fuliginatus Witte, 1932, 68
    Bufo funereus Bocage, 1866, 69
    Bufo gariepensis Smith, 1848, 70
    Bufo garmani Meek, 1897, 72
    Bufo grandisonae Poynton & Haacke, 1993, 73
    Bufo gutturalis Power, 1927, 74
    Bufo hoeschi Ahl, 1934, 77
    Bufo inyangae Poynton, 1963, 78
    Bufo kavangensis Poynton & Broadley, 1988, 80
    Bufo kisoloensis Loveridge, 1932, 81
    Bufo lemairii Boulenger, 1901, 82
    Bufo lindneri Mertens, 1955, 83
    Bufo maculatus Hallowell, 1854, 84
    Bufo melanopleura Schmidt & Inger, 1959, 86
    Bufo nyikae Loveridge, 1953, 87
    Bufo pantherinus Smith, 1828, 89
    Bufo pardalis Hewitt, 1935, 90
    Bufo poweri Hewitt, 1935, 91
    Bufo rangeri Hewitt, 1935, 93
    Bufo robinsoni Branch & Braack, 1996, 95
    Bufo taitanus Peters, 1878, 96
    Bufo urunguensis Loveridge, 1932, 97
    Bufo vertebralis Smith, 1848, 98
    Capensibufo rosei (Hewitt, 1926), 100
    Capensibufo tradouwi (Hewitt, 1926), 102

Order Anura *(continued)*
  Schismaderma carens (Smith, 1848), 103
  Stephopaedes anotis (Boulenger, 1907), 105
  Family Heleophrynidae, 108
    Heleophryne hewitti Boycott, 1988, 109
    Heleophryne natalensis Hewitt, 1913, 111
    Heleophryne orientalis FitzSimons, 1946, 112
    Heleophryne purcelli Sclater, 1898, 113
    Heleophryne regis Hewitt, 1909, 115
    Heleophryne rosei Hewitt, 1925, 117
  Family Hemisotidae, 119
    Hemisus sp., 120
    Hemisus guineensis Cope, 1865, 121
    Hemisus guttatus (Rapp, 1842), 122
    Hemisus marmoratus (Peters, 1854), 124
    Hemisus wittei Laurent, 1963, 125
  Family Hyperoliidae, 127
    Afrixalus aureus Pickersgill, 1984, 130
    Afrixalus brachycnemis (Boulenger, 1896), 132
    Afrixalus crotalus Pickersgill, 1984, 133
    Afrixalus delicatus Pickersgill, 1984, 134
    Afrixalus dorsalis (Peters, 1875), 136
    Afrixalus fornasini (Bianconi, 1849), 137
    Afrixalus knysnae (Loveridge, 1954), 139
    Afrixalus osorioi (Ferreira, 1906), 140
    Afrixalus spinifrons (Cope, 1862), 141
    Afrixalus wittei (Laurent, 1941), 143

Hyperolius angolensis Steindachner, 1867, 148
Hyperolius argus Peters, 1854, 149
Hyperolius bocagei Steindachner, 1867, 151
Hyperolius cinereus Monard, 1937, 152
Hyperolius cinnamomeoventris Bocage, 1866, 153
Hyperolius horstockii (Schlegel, 1837), 154
Hyperolius kachalolae Schiøtz, 1975, 156
Hyperolius kivuensis Ahl, 1931, 157
Hyperolius major Laurent, 1957, 158
Hyperolius marmoratus Rapp, 1842, 159
Hyperolius mitchelli Loveridge, 1953, 165
Hyperolius nasutus Günther, 1864, 166
Hyperolius ocellatus Günther, 1859, 168
Hyperolius parkeri Loveridge, 1933, 169
Hyperolius pickersgilli Raw, 1982, 171
Hyperolius pictus Ahl, 1931, 172
Hyperolius poweri Loveridge, 1938, 173
Hyperolius puncticulatus (Pfeffer, 1893), 175
Hyperolius pusillus (Cope, 1862), 176
Hyperolius quinquevittatus Bocage, 1866, 178
Hyperolius semidiscus Hewitt, 1927, 179
Hyperolius spinigularis Stevens, 1971, 180
Hyperolius steindachneri Bocage, 1866, 182
Hyperolius tuberilinguis Smith, 1849, 183

Order Anura *(continued)*
　　Hyperolius vilhenai Laurent, 1964, 184
　　Kassinula wittei Laurent, 1940, 185
　　Kassina kuvangensis (Monard, 1937), 187
　　Kassina maculata (Duméril, 1853), 189
　　Kassina senegalensis (Duméril & Bibron, 1841), 191
　　Semnodactylus wealii (Boulenger, 1882), 193
　　Leptopelis anchietae (Bocage, 1873), 196
　　Leptopelis argenteus (Pfeffer, 1893), 197
　　Leptopelis bocagii (Günther, 1864), 198
　　Leptopelis cynnamomeus (Bocage, 1893), 200
　　Leptopelis flavomaculatus (Günther, 1864), 201
　　Leptopelis mossambicus Poynton, 1985, 203
　　Leptopelis natalensis (Smith, 1849), 204
　　Leptopelis parbocagii Poynton & Broadley, 1987, 206
　　Leptopelis xenodactylus Poynton, 1963, 207
　Family Microhylidae, 209
　　Breviceps acutirostris Poynton, 1963, 212
　　Breviceps adspersus Peters, 1882, 213
　　Breviceps fuscus Hewitt, 1925, 215
　　Breviceps gibbosus (Linnaeus, 1758), 216
　　Breviceps macrops Boulenger, 1907, 218
　　Breviceps montanus Power, 1926, 219
　　Breviceps mossambicus Peters, 1854, 220
　　Breviceps namaquensis Power, 1926, 222

　　Breviceps poweri Parker, 1934, 223
　　Breviceps rosei Power, 1926, 224
　　Breviceps sylvestris FitzSimons, 1930, 226
　　Breviceps verrucosus Rapp, 1842, 227
　　Breviceps sp., 228
　　Probreviceps rhodesianus Poynton & Broadley, 1967, 229
　　Phrynomantis affinis (Boulenger, 1901), 231
　　Phrynomantis annectens (Werner, 1910), 232
　　Phrynomantis bifasciatus (Smith, 1847), 234
　Family Pipidae, 237
　　Xenopus epitropicalis Fischberg et al., 1982, 239
　　Xenopus fraseri Boulenger, 1905, 240
　　Xenopus gilli Rose & Hewitt, 1927, 241
　　Xenopus laevis (Daudin, 1802), 243
　　Xenopus muelleri (Peters, 1844), 247
　　Xenopus petersii Bocage, 1895, 248
　Family Ranidae, 250
　　Afrana angolensis (Bocage, 1866), 255
　　Afrana dracomontana (Channing, 1978), 257
　　Afrana fuscigula (Duméril & Bibron, 1841), 259
　　Afrana inyangae (Poynton, 1966), 260
　　Afrana johnstoni (Günther, 1893), 262
　　Afrana vandijki Visser & Channing, 1997, 263
　　Amietia vertebralis (Hewitt, 1927), 264
　　Amnirana darlingi (Boulenger, 1902), 266

Order Anura *(continued)*
Amnirana galamensis
(Duméril & Bibron, 1841),
268
Amnirana lemairii (Witte,
1921), 269
Amnirana parkeriana
(Mertens, 1938), 270
Amnirana sp., 271
Anhydrophryne rattrayi
Hewitt, 1919, 272
Arthroleptella bicolor Hewitt,
1926, 275
Arthroleptella drewesii
Channing et al., 1994, 276
Arthroleptella hewitti
FitzSimons, 1947, 277
Arthroleptella landdrosia
Dawood & Channing, 2000,
279
Arthroleptella lightfooti
(Boulenger, 1910), 280
Arthroleptella ngongoniensis
Bishop & Passmore, 1993,
281
Arthroleptella villiersi Hewitt,
1935, 283
Aubria masako Ohler &
Kasadi, 1990, 284
Cacosternum boettgeri
(Boulenger, 1882), 287
Cacosternum capense Hewitt,
1926, 288
Cacosternum namaquense
Werner, 1910, 290
Cacosternum nanum
Boulenger, 1887, 291
Cacosternum platys Rose,
1950, 292
Hildebrandtia ornata (Peters,
1878), 294
Hoplobatrachus occipitalis
(Günther, 1859, '1858'),
295
Microbatrachella capensis
(Boulenger, 1910), 298
Natalobatrachus bonebergi
Hewitt & Methuen, 1913,
299

Nothophryne broadleyi
Poynton, 1963, 301
Phrynobatrachus acridoides
(Cope, 1867), 304
Phrynobatrachus mababiensis
FitzSimons, 1932, 305
Phrynobatrachus natalensis
(Smith, 1849), 307
Phrynobatrachus parvulus
(Boulenger, 1905), 308
Phrynobatrachus perpalmatus
Boulenger, 1898, 310
Phrynobatrachus rungwensis
(Loveridge, 1932), 311
Phrynobatrachus stewartae
Poynton & Broadley, 1985,
312
Poyntonia paludicola
Channing & Boycott, 1989,
313
Ptychadena anchietae (Bocage,
1867), 319
Ptychadena ansorgii
(Boulenger, 1905), 321
Ptychadena broadleyi Stevens,
1972, 322
Ptychadena bunoderma
(Boulenger, 1907), 323
Ptychadena grandisonae
Laurent, 1954, 325
Ptychadena guibei Laurent,
1954, 326
Ptychadena keilingi (Monard,
1937), 327
Ptychadena mapacha
Channing, 1993, 328
Ptychadena mascareniensis
(Duméril & Bibron, 1841),
329
Ptychadena mossambica
(Peters, 1854), 331
Ptychadena obscura (Schmidt
& Inger, 1959), 333
Ptychadena oxyrhynchus
(Smith, 1849), 334
Ptychadena perplicata
Laurent, 1964, 336
Ptychadena porosissima
(Steindachner, 1867), 337

Order Anura *(continued)*
 Ptychadena schillukorum Werner, 1907, 338
 Ptychadena subpunctata (Bocage, 1866), 340
 Ptychadena taenioscelis Laurent, 1954, 341
 Ptychadena upembae (Schmidt & Inger, 1959), 342
 Ptychadena uzungwensis (Loveridge, 1932), 344
 Pyxicephalus adspersus Tschudi, 1838, 346
 Pyxicephalus edulis Peters, 1854, 349
 Strongylopus bonaespei (Dubois, 1980), 352
 Strongylopus fasciatus (Smith, 1849), 353
 Strongylopus fuelleborni (Nieden, 1910), 354
 Strongylopus grayii (Smith, 1849), 356
 Strongylopus hymenopus (Boulenger, 1920), 357
 Strongylopus rhodesianus (Hewitt, 1937), 359
 Strongylopus springbokensis Channing, 1986, 360
 Strongylopus wageri (Wager, 1961), 362
 Tomopterna cryptotis (Boulenger, 1907), 365
 Tomopterna delalandii (Tschudi, 1838), 366
 Tomopterna krugerensis Passmore & Carruthers, 1975, 368
 Tomopterna marmorata (Peters, 1854), 369
 Tomopterna natalensis (Smith, 1849), 370
 Tomopterna tandyi Channing & Bogart, 1996, 372
 Tomopterna tuberculosa (Boulenger, 1882), 373
 Family Rhacophoridae, 375
 Chiromantis xerampelina Peters, 1854, 375
Order Gymnophiona, 379
 Family Scolecomorphidae, 382
 Scolecomorphus kirkii Boulenger, 1883, 382
 Family Caeciliidae, 384
 Boulengerula changamwensis Loveridge, 1932, 384

Alphabetical Index

Afrana, 254
  angolensis, 255; tadpole, 413; Pl 15.7
  dracomontana, 257; tadpole, 413; Pl 15.8
  fuscigula, 259; tadpole, 413; Pl 16.1
  inyangae, 260; tadpole, 414; Pl 16.2
  johnstoni, 262; Pl 16.3
  vandijki, 263; tadpole, 414; Pl 16.4
Afrixalus, 128
  aureus, 130; Pl 6.1
  brachycnemis, 132; Pl 6.2
  crotalus, 133; Pl 6.3
  delicatus, 134; Pl 6.4
  dorsalis, 136; Pl 6.5
  fornasini, 137; egg eating, 139; tadpole, 403; Pl 6.6
  knysnae, 139; tadpole, 403; Pl 6.7
  osorioi, 140; Pl 6.8
  spinifrons, 141; tadpole, 403; Pl 7.1
  wittei, 143; Pl 7.2
Afromontane highland, 8
Amietia vertebralis, 264; tadpole, 414; Pl 16.5
Amnirana, 266
  darlingi, 266; Pl 16.6
  galamensis, 268; Pl 16.7
  lemairii, 269; tadpole, 415; Pl 16.8
  parkeriana, 270
  sp., 271; Pl 17.1
Anhydrophryne rattrayi, 272; Pls 17.2, 17.3

Antibiotics, 20
Antiphony, 76
Arrested development, 357, 361
Arthroleptella, 274
  bicolor, 275; Pl 17.4
  drewesii, 276; Pl 17.5
  hewitti, 277
  landdrosia, 279; Pl 17.6
  lightfooti, 280; Pl 17.7
  ngongoniensis, 281; Pl 17.8
  villiersi, 283; Pl 18.1
Arthroleptis, 41
  carquejai, 42
  francei, 43; Pl 1.1
  reichei, 45; Pl 1.2
  stenodactylus, 46; Pl 1.3
  wahlbergii, 48; Pl 1.4
Aubria masako, 284; tadpole, 415; Pl 18.2

Bat, slit-faced, 321, 377
Boneberg's frog, 299; Pl 19.5
Boulengerula, 384
  changamwensis, 384
Bradykinins, 257, 269, 297, 353, 357
Breviceps, 209
  acutirostris, 212; Pl 12.7
  adspersus, 213; and traditional beliefs, 214; Pl 12.8
  fuscus, 216; Pl 13.1
  gibbosus, 216; Pl 13.2
  macrops, 218; Pl 13.3
  montanus, 219; Pl 13.4
  mossambicus, 220; Pls 13.5, 13.6
  namaquensis, 222; Pl 13.7
  poweri, 223; Pls 13.8, 14.1
  rosei, 224; Pl 14.2

Breviceps (continued)
  sp., 228; Pl 14.5
  sylvestris, 226; Pl 14.3
  verrucosus, 227; Pl 14.4
Bufo, 57
  amatolicus, 61; tadpole, 393; Pl 1.7
  angusticeps, 63; tadpole, 393; Pl 1.8
  beiranus, 64
  dombensis, 65; tadpole, 393; Pl 2.2
  fenoulheti, 66; tadpole, 393; Pl 2.3
  fuliginatus, 68
  funereus, 69
  gariepensis, 70; tadpole, 393, 394; Pl 2.4
  garmani, 72; tadpole, 394; Pl 2.5
  grandisoni, 73
  gutturalis, 74; tadpole, 394; Pl 2.6
  hoeschi, 77; tadpole, 394; Pl 2.7
  inyangae, 78; Pl 2.8
  kavangensis, 80
  kisoloensis, 80; tadpole, 394; Pl 3.1
  lemairii, 82; Pl 3.2
  lindneri, 83
  maculatus, 84; tadpole, 395; Pl 3.3
  melanopleura, 86
  nyikae, 87; Pl 3.4
  pantherinus, 89; tadpole, 395; Pl 3.5
  pardalis, 90; tadpole, 395; Pl 3.6
  poweri, 91; tadpole, 395; Pl 3.7
  rangeri, 93; tadpole, 396; Pl 3.8
  robinsoni, 95; tadpole, 396; Pl 4.1
  sp., 57; Pl 2.1
  taitanus, 96; Pl 4.2
  urunguensis, 97
  vertebralis, 98; tadpole, 396; Pl 4.3
Bullfrogs, 345
  African, 346; as food, 17; parental care of, 348; Pls 22.3, 22.4
  Edible, 349; Pl 22.5

Cacosternum, 286
  boettgeri, 287; tadpole, 416; Pls 18.3–18.5
  capense, 288; Pl 18.6
  namaquense, 290; tadpole, 416; Pl 18.7
  nanum, 291; tadpole, 416; Pl 18.8
  platys, 292; Pl 19.1
Caecilians, 381
Caeciliidae, 384
Capensibufo, 99
  rosei, 100; tadpole, 396; Pl 4.4
  tradouwi, 102; tadpole, 397; Pl 4.5
Cerulein, 19, 190, 194, 243, 246, 248
Chiromantis xerampelina, 375; breeding strategy of, 376; and egg predators, 378; surviving hot and dry, 377; tadpole, 425–26; Pl 24.5
Classification, 36
Clicking frog, 185; Pl 11.2
Cocoon, 200, 225, 377
Collecting amphibians, 15–16
Common frogs, 250
Conservation, 243
Crowned bullfrog, 295; Pl 19.3

Dainty frogs, 286
  Boettger's, 287; Pls 18.3–18.5
  Cape, 288; Pl 18.6
  Dwarf, 291; Pl 18.8
  Flat, 292; Pl 19.1
  Namaqua, 290; Pl 18.7
DDT, 23
Declining populations, 20
Dieldrin, 335
Digital discs, 31
Dorsal, 389

Epinephrine, 76

Fish, exotic, 24
Fishing frog, 284; Pl 18.2
Foam and moan display, 331
Foam nest, 376, 378

Formula, labial tooth row, 390
Fossil frogs, 386
Fossilization, 387

Ghost frogs, 108
  Eastern, 112; Pl 5.2
  Hewitt's, 109; Pl 4.8
  Natal, 111; Pl 5.1
  Purcell's, 113; courtship of, 115; Pl 5.3
  Rose's, 117; Pl 5.5
  Royal, 115; Pl 5.4
Gray tree frog, 375; breeding strategy of, 376; and egg predators, 378; surviving hot and dry, 377; Pl 24.5

Heleophryne, 108
  hewitti, 109; tadpole, 399; Pl 4.8
  natalensis, 111; tadpole, 399; Pl 5.1
  orientalis, 112; tadpole, 400; Pl 5.2
  purcelli, 113; courtship, 115; tadpole, 399, 400; Pl 5.3
  regis, 115; tadpole, 400; Pl 5.4
  rosei, 117; tadpole, 400; Pl 5.5
Hemisus, 119
  guineensis, 121; tadpole, 401
  guttatus, 122; tadpole, 401; Pl 5.7
  marmoratus, 124; tadpole, 401; Pl 5.8
  sp., 120; Pl 5.6
  wittei, 125
Herpetological Association of Africa, 13
Hildebrandtia ornata, 294; tadpole, 416, 417; Pl 19.2
History of Amphibian studies, 9
Hoplobatrachus occipitalis, 295; tadpole, 417; Pl 19.3
Hybrids, 57, 94, 372
Hylambatin, 190
Hyperolius, 144
  argus, 149; tadpole, 403; Pls 7.4, 7.5
  bocagei, 151; Pls 7.6, 7.7
  cinereus, 152

  cinnamomeoventris, 153; Pl 7.8
  horstockii, 154; tadpole, 404; Pl 8.1
  kachalolae, 156; Pl 8.2
  kivuensis, 157; Pl 8.3
  major, 158
  marmoratus, 159–65; and desiccation, 164; and polymorphism, 164; subspecies of, 161; tadpole, 404; Pls 8.4–8.8
  mitchelli, 165; tadpole, 404; Pl 9.1
  nasutus, 166; tadpole, 404; Pls 9.2, 9.3
  ocellatus, 168; Pl 9.4
  parkeri, 169; Pl 9.5
  pickersgilli, 171; tadpole, 404
  pictus, 172; Pls 9.6, 9.7
  poweri, 173; tadpole, 405; Pl 9.8
  punctuculatus, 175; Pls 10.1, 10.2
  pusillus, 176; tadpole, 405; Pl 10.3
  quinquevittatus, 178; Pl 10.4
  semidiscus, 179; tadpole, 405; Pl 10.5
  spinigularis, 180; tadpole, 405; Pls 10.6, 10.7
  steindachneri, 182; Pl 10.8
  tuberilinguis, 183; tadpole, 405; Pl 11.1
  vilhenai, 184

Identification, adults, 29
Internarial distance, 32
Interocular bar, 32
IUCN Red List categories, 25–28

Jaw sheaths, 389

Kassina, 186
  kuvangensis, 187; tadpole, 406; Pl 11.3
  maculata, 189; skin toxins of, 190; tadpole, 406; Pl 11.4
  senegalensis, 191; tadpole, 407; Pl 11.5
Kassinas, 186

Kassinas *(continued)*
  Kuvangu, 187; Pl 11.3
  Red-legged, 189; skin toxins of, 190; Pl 11.4
  Senegal, 191; Pl 11.5
Kassinin, 190
Kassinula wittei, 185; Pl 11.2
Key to families (adults)
  adult anurans, 34
  Gymnophiona, 381
Key to families (tadpoles), 391
Key to genera (adults)
  Arthroleptidae, 41
  Bufonidae, 56
  Hyperoliidae, 127
  Microhylidae, 209
  Ranidae, 250
Key to genera (tadpoles)
  Bufonidae, 392
  Ranidae, 411
Key to species (adults)
  Afrana, 254
  Afrixalus, 128
  Amnirana, 266
  Arthroleptella, 274
  Arthroleptis, 41
  Breviceps, 210
  Bufo, 57
  Cacosternum, 286
  Capensibufo, 100
  Heleophryne, 109
  Hemisus, 119
  Hyperolius, 144
  Kassina, 187
  Leptopelis, 194
  Phrynobatrachus, 302
  Phrynomantis, 231
  Ptychadena, 315
  Pyxicephalus, 345
  Schoutedenella, 49
  Strongylopus, 351
  Tomopterna, 364
  Xenopus, 238
Key to species (tadpoles)
  Kassina, 406
  Phrynomantis, 408
Kimberlite pipes, 386

Labial tooth row, 390
Large-mouthed frog, 264; Pl 16.5

Leptopelis, 194
  anchietae, 196
  argenteus, 197; Pl 11.7
  bocagii, 198; cocoon of, 200; Pl 11.8
  cynnamomeus, 200; Pl 12.1
  flavomaculatus, 201; Pls 12.2, 12.3
  mossambicus, 203; Pl 12.4
  natalensis, 204; tadpole, 407; Pl 12.5
  parbocagii, 206
  xenodactylus, 207; Pl 12.6

Magainins, 245
Male fighting, 233, 348
Marsh frog, 313
  Montane, 313; Pl 20.4
Medial gap, 390
Metatarsus, 31
Micro frog, 297, 298; Pl 19.4
Microbatrachella, 297
  capensis, 298; tadpole, 418; Pl 19.4
Mongrel frog, 301; Pl 19.6
Moss frogs, 274
  Bainskloof, 275; Pl 17.4
  De Villiers', 283; Pl 18.1
  Drewes', 276; Pl 17.5
  Hewitt's, 277
  Landdros, 279; Pl 17.6
  Lightfoot's, 280; Pl 17.7
  Ngongoni, 281; Pl 17.8
Museums
  Bayworld (Port Elizabeth Museum), 15
  Livingstone (National Museum of Zambia), 15
  McGregor, 15
  Museu de Historia Natural, 15
  Natal, 15
  National, 15
  National Flagship Institution (Transvaal Museum), 15
  National, of Malawi, 14
  National, of Zimbabwe, 15
  Natural History, London, 9
  South African, 9, 15
  State, 15

Natalobatrachus boneborgi, 299;
  tadpole, 418; Pl 19.5
Nothophryne broadleyi, 301;
  Pl 19.6
Nycteris grandis, 321, 377

Oral angle, 390
Oral disc, 390
Oral papilla, 390
Ornate frog, 294; Pl 19.2

Parental care, 348
Parotid gland, 32
Phalanges, 32
Phrynobatrachus, 302
  acridoides, 304; Pl 19.7
  mababiensis, 305; tadpole, 419;
    Pl 19.8
  natalensis, 307; tadpole, 419;
    Pls 20.1, 20.2
  parvulus, 308
  perpalmatus, 310
  rungwensis, 311; Pl 20.3
  stewartae, 312
  ukingensis, 307
Phrynomantis, 230
  affinis, 231; Pl 14.6
  annectens, 232; tadpole, 409;
    Pl 14.7
  bifasciatus, 234; skin toxins of,
    235; tadpole, 409; Pl 14.8
Platannas, 237
  Common, 243; feral, 246;
    Pl 15.4
  Fraser's, 240; Pl 15.2
  Gill's, 241; and conservation,
    243; Pl 15.3
  Müller's, 247; Pl 15.5
  Peter's, 248; Pl 15.6
  Southern tropical, 239; Pl 15.1
Potamon, 23
Poyntonia paludicola, 313; tadpole,
  420; Pl 20.4
Pregnancy tests, 18, 237
Probreviceps rhodesianus, 229
Ptychadena, 315
  anchietae, 319; tadpole, 420;
    Pl 20.5
  ansorgii, 321
  broadleyi, 322; tadpole, 421

  bunoderma, 323; Pl 20.6
  grandisonae, 325; tadpole, 421;
    Pl 20.7
  guibei, 326; Pl 20.8
  keilingi, 327
  mapacha, 328; Pl 21.1
  mascareniensis, 329; foam and
    moan display of, 331; tadpole,
    421; Pl 21.2
  mossambica, 331; Pl 21.3
  obscura, 333
  oxyrhynchus, 334; tadpole, 421;
    Pl 21.4
  perplicata, 336
  porosissima, 337; tadpole, 421;
    Pl 21.5
  pumilio, 342
  schillukorum, 338; Pl 21.6
  subpunctata, 340; Pl 21.7
  taenioscelis, 341; Pl 21.8
  upembae, 342; Pl 22.1
  uzungwensis, 344; Pl 22.2
Puddle frogs, 302
  Dwarf, 308
  Eastern, 304; Pl 19.7
  Mababe, 305; Pl 19.8
  Natal, 307; Pls 20.1, 20.2
  Rungwe, 311; Pl 20.3
  Stewart's, 312
  Ukinga, 307
  Webbed, 310
Purines, 165
Pyxicephalus, 345
  adspersus, 346; parental care of,
    348; tadpole, 421–23; Pls 22.3,
    22.4
  edulis, 349; Pl 22.5

Rain frogs, 209
  Black, 215; Pl 13.1
  Common, 213; and traditional
    beliefs, 214; Pl 12.8
  Desert, 218; Pl 13.3
  Forest, 226; Pl 14.3
  Giant, 216; Pl 13.2
  Highland, 229
  Mountain, 219; Pl 13.4
  Mozambique, 220; Pls 13.5,
    13.6
  Namaqua, 222; Pl 13.7

Rain frogs *(continued)*
  Plaintive, 227; Pl 14.4
  Power's, 223; Pls 13.8, 14.1
  Rose's, 224; Pl 14.2
  Strawberry, 212; Pl 12.7
  Whistling, 228; Pl 14.5
Rattray's frog, 272; Pls 17.2, 17.3
Red Data Books, 20
Reed frogs, 144
  Argus, 149; Pls 7.4, 7.5
  Ashy, 152
  Bocage's, 151; Pls 7.6, 7.7
  Cinnamon-bellied, 153; Pl 7.8
  De Vilhena's, 184
  Five-striped, 178; Pl 10.4
  Horstock's, 154; Pl 8.1
  Kachalola, 156; Pl 8.2
  Kivu, 157; Pl 8.3
  Golden-eyed, 168; Pl 9.4
  Greater, 158
  Long, 166; Pls 9.2, 9.3
  Marbled, 159–65; subspecies of, 161; and polymorphism, 164; and desiccation, 164; Pls 8.4–8.8
  Mitchell's, 165; Pl 9.1
  Parker's, 169; Pl 9.5
  Pickersgill's, 171
  Power's, 173; Pl 9.8
  Spiny-throated, 180; Pls 10.6, 10.7
  Spotted, 175; Pls 10.1, 10.2
  Steindachner's, 182; Pl 10.8
  Tinker, 183; Pl 11.1
  Variable, 172; Pls 9.6, 9.7
  Water lily, 176; Pl 10.3
  Yellow-striped, 179; Pl 10.5
Regularobufagin, 19
Ridged frogs, 315
  Anchieta's, 319; Pl 20.5
  Ansorge's, 321
  Broadley's, 322
  Dark, 333
  Grandison's, 325; Pl 20.7
  Grassland, 337; Pl 21.5
  Guibe's, 326; Pl 20.8
  Keiling's, 327
  Many, 336
  Mapacha, 328; Pl 21.1
  Mascarene, 329; foam and moan display of, 331; Pl 21.2
  Mozambique, 331; Pl 21.3
  Rough, 323; Pl 20.6
  Schilluk, 338; Pl 21.6
  Sharp-nosed, 334; Pl 21.4
  Small, 341; Pl 21.8
  Spotted, 340; Pl 21.7
  Udzungwa, 344; Pl 22.2
  Upemba, 342; Pl 22.1
River frogs, 254
  Angola, 255; Pl 15.7
  Cape, 259; Pl 16.1
  Drakensberg, 257; Pl 15.8
  Inyanga, 260; Pl 16.2
  Johnston's, 262; Pl 16.3
  Van Dijk's, 263; Pl 16.4
Rubber frogs, 209, 230
  Banded, 234; skin toxins of, 235; Pl 14.8
  Marbled, 232; Pl 14.7
  Spotted, 231; Pl 14.6
Running frog, 192
  Weale's, 193; Pl 11.6

Sand frogs, 363
  Cryptic, 365; Pl 23.6
  Delalande's, 366; Pl 23.7
  Knocking, 368; Pl 23.8
  Marbled, 369; Pl 24.1
  Natal, 370; Pl 24.2
  Rough, 373; Pl 24.4
  Tandy's, 372; Pl 24.3
Satellite males, 135
Schismaderma carens, 103; tadpole, 397; Pl 4.6
Schooling tadpoles, 397, 408, 409, 411, 415, 421, 422
Schoutedenella, 49
  lameerei, 50
  troglodytes, 51
  xenochirus, 52; Pl 1.5
  xenodactyloides, 53; Pl 1.6
Scolecomorphidae, 382
Scolecomorphus, 382
  kirkii, 382; Pl 24.6
Semnodactylus, 192
  wealii, 193; tadpole, 408; Pl 11.6
Skin glands and toxins, 18

Skin glands and toxins *(continued)*
  Afrana, 257
  Bufo, 19, 76
  Heleophryne, 19, 112
  Hoplobatrachus, 297
  Kassina, 19, 190
  Phrynomantis, 235
  Xenopus, 19
Slit-faced bat, 321, 377
Snout-burrowers, 119
  Barotse, 120; Pl 5.6
  De Witte's, 125
  Guinea, 121
  Marbled, 124; Pl 5.8
  Spotted, 122; Pl 5.7
Snout-vent length, 32
Spiny reed frogs, 128
  Delicate, 134; Pl 6.4
  De Witte's, 143; Pl 7.2
  Fornasini's, 137; and egg eating, 139; Pl 6.6
  Golden, 130; Pl 6.1
  Knysna, 139; Pl 6.7
  Natal, 141; Pl 7.1
  Osorio's, 140; Pl 6.8
  Short-legged, 132; Pl 6.2
  Snoring, 133; Pl 6.3
  Striped, 136; Pl 6.5
Spiracle, 391
Squeakers, 41, 49
  Bush, 48; Pl 1.4
  Carqueja's, 42
  Cave, 51
  Common, 46; Pl 1.3
  Dwarf, 53
  France's, 43; Pl 1.1
  Lameere's, 50
  Plain, 52; Pl 1.5
  Reiche's, 45; Pl 1.2
St. Helena, 356
Stephopaedes anotis, 105; tadpole, 398; Pl 4.7
Stream frogs, 351
  Banded, 352; Pl 22.6
  Chimanimani, 359; Pl 23.2
  Drakensberg, 357; Pl 23.2
  Fülleborn's, 354; Pl 22.8
  Gray's, 356; and arrested development, 357; on
    St. Helena, 356; Pl 23.1
  Namaqua, 360; Pl 23.4
  Striped, 353; Pl 22.7
  Wager's, 362; Pl 23.5
Strongylopus, 351
  bonaespei, 352; Pl 22.6
  fasciatus, 353; tadpole, 423; Pl 22.7
  fuelleborni, 354; Pl 22.8
  grayii, 256; and arrested development, 357; on St. Helena, 356; tadpole, 423; Pl 23.1
  hymenopus, 357; tadpole, 423; Pl 23.2
  rhodesianus, 359; tadpole, 424; Pl 23.2
  springbokensis, 360; tadpole, 424; Pl 23.4
  wageri, 362; tadpole, 424; Pl 23.5

Tachykinin, 19, 139, 190, 194
Tadpole body parts, 390
Tadpole identification, 388
Tadpole mouthparts, 389
Tarsus, 33
Tentacle, 391; subocular, 33
Thoraciliacus, 387; Pls 24.7, 24.8
Tibia, 33
Toads, 57
  Amatola, 61; Pl 1.7
  Beira, 64
  Chirinda, 105; Pl 4.7
  Dark-sided, 86
  Dombe, 65; Pl 2.2
  Fenoulhet's, 66; Pl 2.3
  Flat-backed, 84; Pl 3.3
  Garman's, 72; Pl 2.5
  Grandison's, 73
  Guttural, 74; Pl 2.6
  Hoesch's, 77; Pl 2.7
  Inyanga, 78; Pl 2.8
  Karoo, 70; Pl 2.4
  Kavango, 80
  Kisolo, 81; Pl 3.1
  Lemaire's, 82; Pl 3.2
  Leopard, 90; Pl 3.6
  Lindner's, 83

Toads *(continued)*
  Nyika dwarf, 87; Pl 3.4
  Paradise, 95; Pl 4.1
  Pygmy, 98; Pl 4.3
  Ranger's, 93; Pl 3.8
  Red, 103; Pl 4.6
  Rose's, 100; Pl 4.4
  Sand, 63; Pl 1.8
  Somber, 69
  Sooty, 68
  Taita, 96; Pl 4.2
  Tradouw's, 102; Pl 4.5
  Urungu, 97
  Western leopard, 89; Pl 3.5
Tomopterna, 363
  cryptotis, 365; tadpole, 424; Pl 23.6
  delalandii, 366; tadpole, 424, 425; Pl 23.7
  krugerensis, 368; Pl 23.8
  marmoratus, 369; Pl 24.1
  natalensis, 370; tadpole, 425; Pl 24.2
  tandyi, 372; tadpole, 425; Pl 24.3
  tuberculosa, 373; Pl 24.4
Tree frogs, 194
  Anchieta's, 196
  Bocage's, 198; cocoon of, 200; Pl 11.8
  Cinnamon, 200; Pl 12.1
  Cryptic, 206
  Long-toed, 207; Pl 12.6
  Mozambique, 203; Pl 12.4
  Natal, 204; Pl 12.5
  Silvery, 197; Pl 11.7
  Yellow-spotted, 201; Pls 12.2, 12.3
Trypargine, 189
Tubercle, 33
  metatarsal, 31
  palmar, 32
  proximal subarticular, 32
  subarticular, 33
Tympanum, 33

Umbraculum, pupillary, 32, 264
Urostyle, 33

Vent tube, 391
Ventral, 391
Vomerine teeth, 33

White-lipped frogs, 266
  Darling's, 266; Pl 16.6
  Galam, 268; Pl 16.7
  Hillwood, 271; Pl 17.1
  Lemaire's, 269; Pl 16.8
  Parker's, 270

Xenopsin, 246
Xenopus, 237
  epitropicalis, 239; Pl 15.1
  fraseri, 240; tadpole, 410; Pl 15.2
  gilli, 241; and conservation, 243; tadpole, 410; Pl 15.3
  laevis, 243; feral, 246; tadpole, 410; Pl 15.4
  muelleri, 247; tadpole, 411; Pl 15.5
  petersii, 248; Pl 15.6